GOD *and* WOMEN

GOD *and* WOMEN

WOMAN IN GOD'S IMAGE & LIKENESS

JOHN D. GARR, PH.D.

Published by Golden Key Press
P. O. Box 421218, Atlanta, GA 30342

Copyright © 2011 by John D. Garr

ISBN 978-0-9794514-4-7
Library of Congress Catalog Card Number:
2010914494

All Scripture verses are quoted from the
Authorized King James Version
unless otherwise noted.

Graphic Design by Elizabeth Nason,
Ambassador Productions, Gainesville, FL

*To the three ladies who have had the
greatest impact on my life:*

MY MOTHER, THERESA C. LEONARD GARR,
*whose life of service to the community of faith was
a powerful testimony to God's image and likeness in
women.*

MY WIFE, PAT H. GARR,
*whose dedication to ministry, home, and family has
been a living demonstration of a
true woman of valor fulfilling the
image and likeness of God.*

MY GRANDDAUGHTER, LILLIAN FAITH GARR,
*whose beauty, modesty, and grace
epitomize how a young lady should manifest
the image and likeness of God.*

CONTENTS

Prologue ix

1   Who Is Woman?. 1

2   The Past Reveals the Future 29

3   Recovering God's Self-Image 43

4   Understanding God? 51

5   Imaging God and Humanity: Theology and Anthropology 63

6   Rediscovering the God of Scripture. 73

7   God's Self-Image, Male and Female. 101

8   Feminine Images of God in Scripture 109

9   Feminine Images and the Holy Spirit 121

10   Feminine Images and Divine Wisdom 135

11   The Image and Likeness of God. 149

12   God's Image in Humanity: Spiritual Dimensions. 169

13   God's Image in Humanity: Physical Dimensions. 201

14   The Fullness of God's Image in Humanity:

Relational Dimensions. 223

Epilogue 243

Glossary 249

Bibliography. 257

Index 285

PROLOGUE

When I undertook the task of researching and writing on the subject of biblical womanhood, I planned to write a single book, entitled *Feminine and Free: God's Design for Women*, in which I would return to the beginnings of human existence, the Genesis narratives, to establish the biblical foundations of family and community, particularly as they relate to God's plan for women. I have long been acutely aware that women *per se* have been the most abused people group in human history in continuing and unrelenting maltreatment that has transcended all nationalities, ethnicities, and virtually all religions. I am convinced that it is vitally important to the well-being of family, society, and religious communities that an accurate understanding of the foundations of biblical anthropology, especially as it relates to women, be recovered and restored.

As I delved deeper into Scripture and the massive literature that discusses the lot of women from time immemorial to the present and as I analyzed the dizzying array of concepts, philosophies, and options for the roles of women, I soon realized that I could not possibly address this important subject fairly or adequately in one book. As the research and writing has continued, the *Feminine and Free* project has expanded into five volumes, with a sixth book to serve as a *Readers' Digest* condensed version of the series for those who do not have the time or inclination to study the subject in such depth and detail.

My first premise has been that it is impossible to develop a sound anthropology without first establishing right and proper theology. Inevitably, one's understanding of humanity is profoundly influenced by one's thinking about deity. My writing on the subject of theology became so extensive, however, that I was forced to remove the vast majority of that material from the *Feminine and Free* series and to publish it in a separate book, *Rediscovering the God of Scripture*. Likewise, my comprehensive analysis of the image and likeness of God and its reflection in humanity, male and female, was so extensive that I have had to condense this material drastically for this series. I plan to publish the complete discussion in yet another book, *Imaging the Divine: Mirroring God's Likeness in the Earth*.

God and Women: Woman in God's Image and Likeness is the first of the five volumes of this *Feminine and Free* series. In this book, I undertake to establish a foundation for considering the wide-ranging options that God has provided for women to fulfill the divine call that he has placed upon their lives. That foundation, of necessity, returns to the beginning, to the creation of humanity according to divine design. Following the hermeneutical law of first mention, I maintain that the best place to begin is "in the beginning," or at Genesis 1:1.

Then, I have exercised great care to bypass the Hellenization and Latinization of Christian and Jewish thought by seeking to recover the Hebraic truths that God himself established in Scripture as foundations for successful living in the context of family, society, and community. I am convinced that one of the greatest spiritual aberrations in history occurred when Christianity was wrenched from its moorings in the safe harbor of deep Hebraic faith and was set adrift in a maelstrom of human traditions that were inimical and destructive to the faith and practice of Jesus and the apostles, especially in respect to their teachings concerning human interrelationships and the roles of women and men in the community of faith.

A Voice of Experience

As a young teenager, I was first exposed to what at that time was a radical concept, the idea that earliest Christianity was fundamentally a Jewish religion and that it never should have been detached from its Hebraic foundations. The Christian faith was established on belief in the God of the Jews. It's rule of faith, practice, and discipline was the Hebrew Scriptures, the Bible of the Jews. It was completed and made perfect through the life, death, resurrection, and ascension of Jesus, the Jewish Messiah. And it was extended by him to all human beings in the form of salvation by grace through faith, a salvation that, by Jesus' own confession, is also from the Jews!

As I have searched the Scriptures, history, and extracanonical Jewish and Christian literature, I have become more and more convinced that it is essential to the health of the Christian community around the world that Christianity recover the living Hebrew faith of Jesus and the apostles. I am convinced that the late Edward Flannery was perfectly correct when he said that "an over-Hellenized, over-Latinized Christianity needs a re-Judaization process to restore it to its founding Jewish roots and renew it more in keeping with its own inherent ideals."[1] Incredibly, an international, transdenominational, multiethnic movement of restoration and renewal has emerged in a work that has no single identifiable earthly source but clearly has one heavenly source. In rapidly increasing numbers, people everywhere are catching the spirit of renewal and restoration and are laboring to recover the Jewish roots of their Christian faith.

Many in this movement have been motivated by the opportunity to hear or tell some new thing, while others have been swept up in sentimentality, relishing the novelties and symbols of restoration and reveling in the existential moment. Still, a solid core of this renewal movement has come to understand that the richest legacy that Jews and Judaism have given to Christians is the profound and enduring emphasis on family and community as the locus for social, intellectual, and spiritual development. The very core of the faith of Jesus was the living community of disciples who walked with God in a committed relationship of covenant living that connected them vertically with the God of the universe and laterally with other people of faith. The church of Jesus Christ was and should ever remain a Hebraic community in continuity with the patriarchs, prophets, sages, and apostles of biblical faith.

Impelled by this foundational understanding of God's plan for his people, I have devoted more than forty years to ministry and academia, researching, writing, teaching, and preaching about the Hebraic foundations of the Christian faith. I have been and remain an unabashed Biblicist in that I have total confidence in the divine inspiration and complete trustworthiness of the Hebrew Scriptures—the *Tanakh* (commonly called the "Old Testament") and the Apostolic Scriptures (generally called the "New Testament")—both of which were written by or under the auspices of Jewish spiritual leaders in

---

[1] Edward Flannery, quoted in *Restore!* 1:2.

order to inculcate the Hebraic worldview and the core values of faith in the one God of Scripture. Like the Christian Hebraists of the sixteenth century, who were the progenitors of the Protestant Reformation, I have come to appreciate the mottos *sola scriptura* and *sola fide*. I have come to understand that the most trustworthy path toward establishing the truth that is foundational to faith is the Holy Scriptures that were inspired of God and were conceived, thought, and written by Hebrew prophets, sages, and apostles.

VOLUME 1

In this book, I first offer a general introduction to the overall subject of "God and Women," which I call, "Who is Woman?" So many have written and spoken about "a woman's place," that even the term *a woman's place* has become virtually pejorative, implying that women somehow need to be kept in their "place." This subject has been widely and hotly debated for centuries, even millennia, with profoundly divergent viewpoints.

Second, I offer a discussion on the importance of going back so we can go forward—in this case, going back to the very beginnings of human existence, to the Garden of Eden and the creation, formation, and fashioning of the first human couple.

Third, I discuss the importance of not merely reacting to perceived evils, because such reaction often produces an even greater evil. I suggest, therefore, that it is vital for us to be proactive by going beyond mere perception so that we insist on apperception, a return to original models as a basis for judging current perception.

Fourth, I advance the idea that all good anthropology, including studies of women, has its foundation in good theology; therefore, I discuss a few concepts about the God of Scripture that have been overlooked because of the profound influence of Greek philosophy on historical church theology.

Fifth, I delve into Scripture to establish the fact that neither God nor the biblical authors were hesitant to describe God and his actions in feminine metaphor and that they constantly employed gynomorphic as well as andromorphic imagery to convey insights about God's relationship to humanity.

Sixth, I analyze what it actually means to say that God "created humanity, male and female, in his own image and likeness," wherein every aspect of the human creation, both spiritual and physical, was designed to manifest the *imago Dei.*

Seventh, I discuss the concept of the image of God as it related to the creation of humanity wherein human beings, male and female, were designed by God to be theomorphic—actually revealing the very image and likeness of God. In this way, Scripture clearly demonstrates that both women and men are fully theomorphic.

Finally, I develop the theme that the fullness of God's image is seen in the pure relationality of divine being, and I demonstrate that this relationality was the purpose for the creation of humanity in the beginning and is the fullest manifestation of God's image in humanity.

VOLUME 2

In the second volume in the *Feminine and Free* series, entitled *Feminine by Design: God's Plan for Women,* I analyze the process of humanity's creation. I explore the amazing detail that is found in the Hebrew text of the Genesis narratives, including the manner in which God created humanity by forming a body from the dust of the earth, employing the skills of a potter to mold humanity from the humus. I review what occurred when God created a living being "out of nothing" by breathing his own divine breath into the earthen body that he had formed and then proceeded to create gender-specific beings by fashioning a woman from the side of the already-formed human entity, "building up" the crowning element of his creation.

I develop the biblical ideas that male and female are delicately counterbalanced by divine design so that both are equally essential to the well-being of humanity. Then I discuss the fact that femininity is indispensable for humanity by analyzing the contributions and roles that are unique to the female half of humanity and then encouraging women to feel free to be fully feminine. I analyze the various aspects of femininity that were created by divine design and are essential to women in God's image. Finally, I describe the ideal human experience as God designed it in the beginning: "Heaven on Earth" as it were, God's will accomplished on earth precisely as it is in heaven.

VOLUME 3

The third book in the *Feminine and Free* series is entitled *Free and Equal: The Biblically Hebraic Woman.* In this volume, I chronicle the lives of the many women who are mentioned in the Hebrew Scriptures and demonstrate how they serve as paradigms for the modern woman who is committed to imaging God in the earth by fulfilling his calling and purposes for her life. I compare what the Scriptures say regarding Eve with the erroneous positions that both Jewish and Christian scholars have developed under the influence of Greek and other non-biblical worldviews. Next, I proceed to a discussion of the roles that women chose to fulfill in the Hebraic culture of antiquity within the context of the nomadic and agrarian societies in which they lived. I analyze the lives of women of godly character and divine calling such as Sarah, Rebekah, Rachel, Miriam, Deborah, Ruth, Hulda, Esther, and others, pointing out the high level of spiritual leadership that they demonstrated in their families, society, and religion.

Next, I discuss the changes in Jewish perspectives on women that emerged in late post-exilic times when some of the sages of second-temple Judaism began to be influenced by Hellenism and its dim view of womanhood and departed from biblically Hebraic views of women and the roles available to them.

Then, I analyze the impact that Jesus made upon second-temple Judaism through the reformation of restoration in which he often insisted that his Jewish compatriots abandon Greek-influenced traditions and return to the heart of the Torah on which the faith of God had been established. I demonstrate that Jesus' reforming ideas strongly contrasted with those of some of his contemporaries, particularly in the markedly different attitude and perspective that he demonstrated regarding women.

Finally, I discuss the revolutionary positions on women's rights that Paul, the Jewish rabbi and Christian Apostle, espoused in a gynophobic and misogynistic world. By returning the teachings of this much-misunderstood apostle to their Hebraic matrix, I provide a hermeneutically sound context that aids in a radically different, yet contextually accurate exegesis and exposition of Pauline thought.

VOLUME 4

The fourth book in the *Feminine and Free* series is *Bound and Gagged: Secular and Ecclesiastical Misogyny and Its Impact on Women*. In this volume, I discuss the implications of God's statement to Eve following humanity's fall into sin: "Your turning will be to your husband, and he will rule over you." I confirm that this is one prediction that has been fulfilled across the eons of time and in virtually every human society.

I analyze the impact of sin upon humanity and the malevolent dominance/submission codependency in which sin has universally entrapped both men and women. I detail various worldviews and the cultural implications of those perspectives on women. I focus on the mindset of the Greek world and the perspectives on women that it produced, detailing the impact of those perverse viewpoints on all of the West and much of the rest of the world as well.

I also evaluate the impact of Hellenism on Judaism and Christianity, detailing the Hellenization (and Latinization) of original Hebraic Christian views on the nature and roles of women. I expose the degree to which this toxic influence transformed Christian women from highly active leaders and teachers in a domestic-based, congregational faith into bound-and-gagged victims of male bureaucracies, a condition that began in ante-Nicene times and persists in varying degrees even to the present day.

VOLUME 5

The fifth volume in the *Feminine and Free* series is entitled *Free Indeed: Releasing Women for Divine Destiny*. In this book, I first chronicle the lives and works of the many women who, in the nearly two millennia since the time of Jesus and the apostles, refused to be silenced by the androcentric bureaucracies which demanded that all women be at least figuratively bound and gagged.

I also discuss the way in which church leaders used Hellenic and Latin philosophies and sociological perspectives to enforce their general gynophobia and their frequent misogyny. I demonstrate how, from the time of the first Greek influence in the church near the end of the first century until the present day, women have either been silenced and cloistered or openly abused, tortured, and even murdered simply because they tried to follow the divine call on their lives to proclaim God's Word.

Next, I discuss the intention of Jesus and the apostles to restore womanhood to its high status of freedom and equality with men so that the prophecy of Joel could be fulfilled: "Your daughters will prophesy." Then, I analyze what it means to be feminine and free.

Finally, I challenge women of God to discern by the Holy Spirit the calling that God has placed on their lives and to free themselves from the shackles of the secular and ecclesiastical past to enter into the fulfillment of their own divine destinies, whatever they may be.

CLIFFSNOTES

All of the extensive material in these five volumes is then condensed into a *Readers' Digest* version in *Feminine and Free: God's Design for Women* with references to detailed analysis of each point in the other volumes of the *Feminine and Free* series. This book is greatly simplified but still contains basic ideas from the research and argumentation that I have advanced in this entire series.

WOMEN AND ACADEMIC STUDIES

Some of my colleagues and advisers have encouraged me to take a less academic approach to this subject, adopting what I suppose is the much-celebrated K.I.S.S. methodology: "Keep It Simple, Stupid!" I realize, and I agree with them, that so many in today's world, both men and women, live at such a frenetic pace that they often have neither the interest nor the time for details. Because of the pressures of life, so many of us simply do not have time for in-depth study.

On the other hand, I simply refuse to believe the pernicious viewpoint that has been maintained for centuries by philosophers, poets, playwrights, politicians, and preachers that women are not as intelligent as men and that they do not have the capacity for logical thought. I do not believe that women are the irrational, emotionally consumed creatures that men have portrayed them to be (and in some cases that they have even come to think themselves to be!). I do not share the idea that women who are academically inclined are deficient in their womanhood, as some scholars in history have boldly proclaimed.[2] Women are as capable of critical thought and exhaustive study as men are, and they may even have a greater capacity than men for intuitive thought.

I think that it is about time for women to have access to biblical and historical facts about womanhood and to critical analysis directed toward establishing a biblical anthropology that is solidly grounded

---

[2] See Anita Bernstein, quoted in Caroline A. Forell and Donna M. Matthews, *A Law of Her Own: The Reasonable Woman as a Measure of Man* (New York: New York University Press, 2000), p. 16.

on scriptural theology. Too much is at stake to resort to platitudes and emotional fluff. It is time to return to that most Hebraic of concepts, the challenge to think. Thinking may be the most painful process known to humanity, but it is essential in today's ignorant and apathetic world where too often the answer to even the most important questions is, "I don't know, and I don't care." It is time to do more than a casual, cursory review of surface thought in history, Scripture, theology, and anthropology. It is time for women and men to make in-depth, critical analysis of every aspect of human relations—particularly those of female-male interrelationships and male and female roles and responsibilities—and to find foundations on which clearly biblical and godly perspectives can be lived out in the context of families, communities, and congregations throughout the world.

A wonderful Hebraic maxim says, "Life is for learning, and learning is for life." Regardless as to how much erudition we may have or how great we may become as teachers, we all are still only learners. Indeed, submission to the discipline of learning is the essence of biblical discipleship. As Jesus said, "Take my yoke upon you and *learn* of me."[3] The easy yoke of discipleship is learning, submitting oneself to the rigors of "searching the Scriptures" and acquiring the information on which accurate understanding can be established.

The preeminence of learning in the biblically Hebraic world was underscored by the fact that the Hebrew word for learning, *lamad*, is also a Hebrew character, the letter ל (*lamed*), which is positioned at the middle of the Hebrew *aleph-bet* and is its tallest and largest letter. It is also no coincidence that the word *lamad* means both "to learn" and "to teach," which confirms the fact both the inculcation of knowledge and the reception of knowledge form a contimuum that, when properly employed, never ends. Before *lamed* was a letter, it was a pictograph representing an ox goad. This confirms that teaching and learning are the means of discipline by which God goads human beings toward achieving success in life as well as right relationship with their creator.

The sages of Israel also found great importance in the fact that the two words at the very center of the Torah text are *derosh derash* ("search diligently"),[4] from which they concluded that the purpose of

---

[3] Matthew 11:29.
[4] Leviticus 10:16.

life was to devote oneself to a careful analysis of God's Word. Indeed, the righteous person whose life flourishes like a tree planted by rivers of water is one who "meditates" in God's Word "day and night."[5] When we seek God, we have his promise that we will find.[6] When we ask, we will receive. If we lack wisdom, we need only ask God, and he will give it.[7] When we knock, the door of understanding will be opened to us.[8] Never underestimate your capacity for knowing God in the intimacy of true relationship as you delight in his Word.[9]

If, as you read this volume and other books in the *Feminine and Free* series, you find language and concepts that are challenging, I encourage you to take the time to educate yourself by mastering the vocabulary and evaluating the thought for yourself. I have offered a Glossary at the end of this volume. Another quick and easy-to-use tool can be found on the Internet at www.Dictionary.com, which, along with its related site, www.Thesaurus.com, will rapidly expand your vocabulary and your knowledge base. Another invaluable tool for in-depth study of the Scriptures and other resources is BibleWorks by Hermeneutica (see www.BibleWorks.com). You may prefer another of the many Bible programs that are available for your computer or smart phone. For an online library resource, I also recommend www.Questia.com.

Follow the Word and Spirit

Please do not accept anything that I have written without evaluating it for yourself. You have the liberty—and the responsibility—to "be fully persuaded in your own mind," which is the conclusion of Paul's wonderful argument for pluriformity.[10] Rely, therefore, on the Holy Spirit to "guide you into all truth."[11] I have attempted to fulfill my responsibility by sharing my insights on these subjects as I believe I have received them from God. I do not claim to have the imperial word of the Lord. In the spirit of 1 Corinthians 14:29, I gladly submit myself to the discernment of the greater community of faith, for I believe and practice the idea that peer review is a significant part of the

---

[5] Psalm 1:3.
[6] Matthew 7:8.
[7] James 1:5.
[8] Luke 11:10.
[9] Psalm 37:4; Psalm 1:2.
[10] Romans 14:5.
[11] John 16:13.

Hebraic mindset exemplified in Scripture. It is the responsibility of all believers to discern or judge for themselves whether what anyone says is the truth.[12] We are encouraged in Scripture to walk "circumspectly" in wisdom.[13] We do so when we are "diligent to present ourselves approved unto God" by accurately explaining the word of truth.[14]

It is time that all believers in the God of Israel recover for themselves another important principle of Hebraic understanding which affirms that study is a high form of worship because it intrinsically involves engaging our hearts so that we "wholly follow the Lord," as Caleb of old said.[15] Ezra taught us that the exercise of study is for the purpose of doing God's will and then for teaching those precepts which we have learned to God's people wherever they may be.[16] Indeed, our doing in itself becomes teaching through a dynamic modeling of the Word of God in our own lives. When we study God's Word with a view toward doing God's Word, we do, indeed, engage in worship, for thereby we demonstrate our submission to God's will or, as the Hebrew and Greek words that are translated "worship" indicate,[17] we figuratively prostrate ourselves before the Eternal.

There is no excuse for continuing the historical Christian practice of luxuriating in nescience and naiveté, thinking that ignorance is bliss. It is time to "gird up the loins of our minds,"[18] to use Peter's metaphor, and commit ourselves to the rigors of study, critical analysis, and careful application of divine truth as it is revealed in the Holy Scriptures. We must be diligent to search the Scriptures[19] so that we can be mature and equipped unto every good work[20] that causes others to glorify our Father in heaven.[21] If we search diligently, we will find.[22] If we lack wisdom or erudition, we can enlist the active participation of the Holy Spirit in our lives by asking God for his assistance. James assures us that God will generously give us wisdom without condemning us.[23]

---

[12] 1 Corinthians 14:29.
[13] Ephesians 5:14.
[14] 2 Timothy 2:15.
[15] Deuteronomy 1:36.
[16] Ezra 7:10.
[17] The Hebrew word for "worship" is *shachah*, which means "to prostrate onself." The Greek word is *proskuneo*, which has an even moe graphic meaning of "a dog licking its master's hand."
[18] 1 Peter 1:13.
[19] John 5:39.
[20] 2 Timothy 2:21; 3:16-17.
[21] Matthew 5:16.
[22] Matthew 7:7.
[23] James 1:5.

The subject *Who Is Woman* is too important for both men and women in today's world for us to be nonchalant and apathetic toward it. We must diligently search for solid answers that will make a dramatic impact on our own lives and on the lives of those around us by liberating us in the way that only the truth of Scripture can do. "You shall know the truth, and the truth will make you free,"[24] Jesus assured us. In the words of John, "If we walk in the light as God is in the light, we have fellowship one with another."[25] As its etymology clearly confirms, education will lead us out of ignorance and superstition. Truth will liberate us from the shackles of prejudice and perversion.

APPRECIATION

I would like to express my thanks to a number of my personal friends and colleagues who have contributed their insight and gifts to the creation of this series. Drs. Marvin Wilson and Robert Bleakney have made copious notes, corrections, and recommendations in careful critiques of the manuscript. Drs. Jennifer Scrivner and Victoria Sarvadi have also studied the manuscript and have made excellent suggestions. Judy Grehan has contributed her usual expertise and tireless labor in copyediting my works. Elizabeth Nason has added her genius to this project by patiently creating the graphic designs, the covers, and the layouts for these books.

CHALLENGE AND BLESSING

As you read this and the other volumes in this series, I pray that you will be enlightened and inspired with an even greater passion for biblically Hebraic truth. May you use the golden key of Hebraic insight to unlock for yourself the treasures of Holy Scripture that will enrich your life. May you recover the Hebraic foundations of your Christian faith that will illuminate your understanding and invigorate your walk with God in Spirit and in truth. May you be blessed with all spiritual blessings in heavenly places in the Messiah.[26]

Shalom & Blessings!
John D. Garr, Ph.D.
Succot, 2010

[24] John 8:32.
[25] 1 John 1:7.
[26] Ephesians 1:3.

CHAPTER I

WHO IS WOMAN?

The role of women in family, society, and church has been one of the most hotly debated issues in the history of the Christian church. Across the annals of time, it has remained among the most volatile and emotionally charged subjects of discussion that have engaged the community of believers. Presently, from the one extreme of chauvinism and even misogyny to the other extreme of militant feminism—and everywhere else between—strident voices continue to clamor for a bully pulpit from which they can pontificate and speak for God, giving everyone *the* answer to the question of a "woman's place."[1] Unfortunately, like so many other controversial issues in Christian doctrine and polity, this subject has generated far more heat than light.

Perhaps more important than the issue of a woman's place is the foundational question underlying the issue: "Who is woman?" or "What does it mean to be a woman?" Even though there have been rare occasions in history when women were considered paragons of virtue in an evil male world,[2] the predominant answer that has transcended cultural, geographical, and generational lines has been the charge that woman is inherently evil. "For millennia, the 'feminine' has been deeply associated with the body, flesh, sensuality, earth, and nature, while the 'masculine' has been associated with spirit, heaven,

---

[1] The very term *woman's place* is in itself essentially pejorative, suggesting that there is a place where women must be segregated in order to keep them under control.
[2] In mid-nineteenth century America, women were celebrated for "natural piety and morality" while maleness "seemed to carry a certain odor of contamination." See John Demos, *Past, Present, and Personal: The Family and the Life Course in American History* (New York: Oxford University Press, 1986), p. 55.

and transcendence over nature."[3] In the sixth century B.C., Confucius, China's greatest philosopher, boldly declared that "women are a necessary evil" only because "men must have mothers."[4] Also in the sixth century, B.C., Pythagoras, one of the earliest of the Greek philosophers, postulated, "There is a good principle which created order, light, and man, and an evil principle which created chaos, darkness, and woman."[5] In the fifth century B.C., Buddha argued that "the female's defects . . . are greater than the male's," and he urged women to seek to be "freed from the impurities of the woman's body" by acquiring "the beautiful and fresh body of a man."[6] Also in the fifth century B.C., Socrates, the founding father of Western rationalism, called females the "weaker sex" and argued that being born a woman was a divine punishment, because, in his words, woman is "halfway between a man and an animal."[7] In the fourth century B.C., Socrates' disciple, Plato, argued that women resulted from the reincarnation of the most evil men, and his disciple, Aristotle, asserted that woman was a "monstrosity,"[8] a "deformed male."[9] During this same time, Euripides purported that one man is better than ten thousand women.[10]

In the second century A.D., Tertullian argued that woman "destroyed so easily God's image, man" and that because of woman "the Son of God had to die."[11] In the early third century A.D., Clement of Alexandria said that a woman "must become a man" so that she can become "manly and perfect."[12] Shortly thereafter, Origen declared, "What is seen with the eyes of the creator is masculine, and not feminine, for God does not stoop to look upon what is feminine and of

---

[3] Sue Monk Kidd, *The Dance of the Dissident Daughter: A Woman's Journey from Christian Tradition to the Sacred Feminine* (San Francisco: HarperCollins, 1996), p. 84.

[4] Confucius, quoted in W. Dallmann, *The Battle of the Bible with the "Bibles"* (St. Louis: Concordia Publishing House, 1926), p. 36.

[5] Pythagoras, quoted in *Sisterhood Is Powerful: An Anthology of Writings from the Women's Liberation Movement,* ed. Robin Morgan (Random House, 1970), p. 31. Pythagoras first propounded the idea that God is the principle of good while matter is the groundwork of evil. While he allowed women to become members of his society (which was radical for the time), he still viewed them in the dualism of spirit vs. matter that became foundational for much of Greek philosophy.

[6] Buddha, quoted in Diana Y. Paul and Frances Wilson, *Women in Buddhism: Images of the Feminine in Mahayana Tradition* (Berkeley, CA: University of California Press, 1979), p. 308.

[7] Socrates, quoted in Plato, *Timaeus,* tr. H.D.P. Lee (Baltimore, MD: Penguin Press, 1965), 42A-C, 90C, 91A.

[8] Aristotle, quoted in *Aristotle, Volume XIII: The Generation of Animals,* tr. A. L. Peck (Cambridge: Harvard University Press, 1963), 4.3: 767.b.8-9.

[9] Aristotle, in *Aristotle,* 2.3; 737.a.25-30.

[10] Euripides, *Iphigeneia at Aulis,* 1376-1394.

[11] Tertullian, *On the Apparel of Women,* I.1.1.

[12] Clement, *Paedagogus* I.6.31.

the flesh."[13] In the fifth century A.D., Augustine taught that marriage is the "union of the one ruling and the other obeying."[14] Around the same time, Cyril of Alexandria concluded that "the female sex as a whole . . . is slow in comprehension."[15] In the seventh century A.D., Mohammed declared, "We have not been left any calamity more detrimental to mankind than woman."[16]

In the twelfth century A.D., French monk Roger de Caen expressed the horrific views of many religions on womanhood in this diatribe: "If her bowels and flesh were cut open, you would see what filth is covered by her white skin. . . . There is no plague which monks should dread more than women: the soul's death."[17] In the thirteenth century A.D., Thomas Aquinas, considered by many to be "the most influential thinker in Christian history,"[18] maintained that woman "is defective and misbegotten."[19] At the same time, Bonaventure was arguing that "woman is an embarrassment to man, a beast in his quarters . . . the undoing of a virtuous man, an oppressive burden."[20] In the fourteenth century A.D., the English poet Geoffrey Chaucer said, "Women are born to thralldom and to penance, and to be under man's governance."[21] In the sixteenth century A.D., Martin Luther made this broadside attack against women: "God created Adam master and lord of living creations, but Eve spoilt all. . . . 'Tis you women, with your tricks and artifices, that lead men into error."[22] Then, he callously concluded that in the event that women "become tired or even die, that does not matter. Let them die in childbirth, that's why they are

[13] Origen, *Selecta in Exodus* XVIII.177.

[14] Augustine, *The Good of Marriage*, I.

[15] Cyril of Alexandria, quoted in Janice Nunnally-Cox, *Foremothers: Women of the Bible* (New York: Seabury, 1981), p. 152. Cyril's observation about women in general was extrapolated from his wonderment of how Mary Magdalene could not have recognized Jesus immediately when he appeared to her following his resurrection!

[16] Mohammed, quoted in Thomas Patrick Hughes, *A Dictionary of Islam* (London: W. H. Allen & Co., 1896), p. 678.

[17] Roger de Caen, *Carmen de Mundi Contemptu*, quoted in Liz Wilson, *Charming Cadavers: Horrific Figurations of the Feminine in Indian Buddhist Hagiographic Literature* (Chicago: University of Chicago Press, 1996), p. 77.

[18] Richard M. Pope, *The Church and Its Culture: A History of the Church in Changing Cultures* (St. Louis: Bethany Press, 1965), p. 276.

[19] Thomas Aquinas, *Summa Theologica*, Q 92.I

[20] Bonaventure, quoted in Emma T. Healy, *Women According to Saint Bonaventure* (New York: Georgian Press, 1956), p. 46. Also quoted in Ruth A. Tucker, *Women in the Maze: Questions and Answers on Biblical Equality* (Downers Grove, IL: InterVarsity Press, 1992), p. 156.

[21] Geoffrey Chaucer, *Canterbury Tales* II, B, [1], quoted in Margaret Hallissy, *A Companion to Chaucer's Canterbury Tales* (Westport, CT: Greenwood Press, 1995), p. 95.

[22] Martin Luther, "The Bondage of the Will" (1527), quoted in George Seldes, *The Great Thoughts* (New York: Random House, 1985), pp. 280-281.

there."[23] During this time, Valens Acidalius argued that women were not human, even linking them "with dogs and demons."[24]

In the Age of Reason of the seventeenth century A.D., Immanuel Kant declared that "woman is intolerant of all commands and all morose constraint. . . . I hardly believe that the fair sex is capable of principles."[25] In the eighteenth century, A.D., Enlightenment philosophers very clearly remained in the dark in their views of women, as evidenced by Rousseau's stereotypes and prejudices,[26] Montesquieu's contention that women's "weak state" did not "permit them to be preeminent,"[27] and Voltaire's portrayals of women as weak and ineffectual creatures who served as vessels of disease and used sexual favors to obtain their desires.[28] In mid-eighteenth century Europe, deranged secular and clerical misogynists escalated the witch hunts that had begun in the fifteenth century based on the view that women were "by nature instruments of Satan."[29] The result was a virtual gynocide in which it is likely that over a million women were tortured and burned to death on suspicion of congress with the devil, when, in fact, most were expressing spirituality in a world of cold and clinical male rationalism.

In the nineteenth century, A.D., Napoleon Bonaparte declared, "Nature intended women to be our slaves. They are our property. . . . Women are nothing but machines for producing children."[30] Also in the nineteenth century, Paul Broca concluded from his pioneering research on the anatomy of the human brain that "the relatively small

[23] Martin Luther, *D. Martin, Luthers Werke, Kritische Gesamtausgabe Tischreden* (Weimar: Verlag Hermann Böhlaus Nachfolger, 1912), p. 25.
[24] Manfred P. Fleischer, "'Are Women Human?'—The Debate of 1595 between Valens Acidalius and Simon Gediccus," *Sixteenth Century Journal* (1981), vol. 12, p. 108.
[25] Immanuel Kant, "Of the Distinction of the Beautiful and Sublime in the Interrelations of the Two Sexes," in *Philosophy of Woman: An Anthology of Classic to Current Concepts*, ed. Mary Briody Mahowald (Indianapolis, IN: Hackett Publishers, 1983), p. 196.
[26] See Jean-Jacques Rousseau in *Rousseau on Women, Love, and Family*, ed. Christopher Kelly, Eve Grace (Hannover, NH: Dartmouth College Press, 2009). Rousseau said, "Women, in general, are not attracted to art at all, nor knowledge, and not at all to genius."
[27] See Charles de Secondat, Baron de la Brede et de Montesquieu, *Spirit of the Laws* (New York: D. Appleton and Company, 1900).
[28] See Voltaire, *Candide: Or Optimism*, tr. John Butt (London: Penguin Books, 1947). See also Roland Stromberg, "The Philosophes and the French Revolution: Reflections on Some Recent Research," Eighteenth-Century Studies, vol. 21, pp. 321-339.
[29] Heinrich Kramer, *Malleus Maleficarum*, published in Germany in 1487. The book, the title of which is Latin for "The Hammer of Witches," served as the default handbook for inquisitors during the Inquisitions. Noted in Tirzah Firestone, *The Receiving: Reclaiming Jewish Women's Wisdom* (San Francisco: HarperSanFrancisco, 2003), p. 217. See also Stephen Katz, *The Holocaust in Historical Context* (New York: Oxford University Press, 1993), vol. 1, pp. 438-439.
[30] Napoleon Bonaparte, quoted in *Sisterhood Is Powerful*, ed. Robin Morgan (New York: Vintage Press, 1970), p. 2.

size of the female brain depends in part upon her physical inferiority and in part upon her intellectual inferiority."[31] Likewise, Friedrich Nietzsche boldly declared, "Woman, at bottom, is a serpent . . . from woman comes every evil in the world."[32] Even at the beginning of the twentieth century, French social psychologist and sociologist Gustave Le Bon concluded that because some women's brains "are closer in size to those of gorillas," female inferiority "was so obvious that no one can contest it for a minute."[33] Based on history's unrelenting parade of such misogynistic statements, Claus Westermann remarked that "for two millennia now the Judeo-Christian tradition has placed man a little lower than the angels and woman a little higher than the demons."[34] History's unrelenting gynophobia and misogyny have led many to conclude that "differential treatment of men and women according to their sex appears to be endemic to the human condition."[35]

As a reaction to this almost universal perception of the "dangerous feminine," a wide array of spiritual leaders and theologians through church history and into the present have sought to control what has been viewed as the inherent evil in women by constructing "an entire hierarchy, made up of 'submission' and 'authority,'" and to engage in what Paul Evdokimov described as an endless exercise of "horribly cerebral, dry discussions which include, implicitly, an ominous call for silence addressed to every woman."[36] The tragedy is that these hierarchies have been profoundly harmful to both men and women because they have strengthened and further concretized the male-female domination/submission codependencies that have proven spiritually and psychologically debilitating to both genders.

On the other side of the coin, many avowed feminists—especially militant secular feminists—engage in the same kind of rhetoric, stereotyping, and caricature that they decry in male-dominated society and church. What they vociferously condemn in the patriarchialists

---

[31] Paul Broca, quoted in Stephen Gould, *The Mismeasure of Man* (New York: Norton Publishing, 1981), pp. 136-137.
[32] Friedrich Nietzsche, *The Antichrist* (New York: Alfred A. Knopf, 1920), pp. 137-138.
[33] Gustave Le Bon, in Alice Widener, *Gustav Le Bon: The Man and His Work,* (Indianapolis, IN: Liberty Fund, Inc., 1979), p. 271.
[34] Claus Westermann, *Genesis 1-11: A Commentary* (Minneapolis: Augsburg Press, 1984), pp. 148-155.
[35] Joseph Martos and Pierre Hégy, *Equal at Creation: Sexism, Society, and Christian Thought* (Toronto: University of Toronto Press, 1998), p. 3.
[36] Paul Evdokimov, *Woman and the Salvation of the World,* tr. Anthony P. Gythiel (Crestwood, NY: St. Vladimir's Seminary Press, 1994), p. 20.

whom they vilify, they practice when they identify men as inherently evil, emotionally and hormonally inclined to violence, hopelessly narcissistic, and violators of the earth. Valerie Solanas typifies these extreme stereotypes when she characterizes men as "biological accident[s] . . . incomplete female[s]" and declares that maleness is "a deficiency disease."[37] Such feminists make caricatures of men while projecting women as innately peace loving, warm and nurturing, filled with equanimity, and protectors of "mother" earth. Indeed, when they charaterize the earth as "mother earth," they engage in the same egregious mistake employed by those who style the God of Scripture as being male! Arguments such as this do little to establish a common ground on which agreement can be found in the quest to answer the questions *Who is woman?* and *What does it mean to be a woman?*

Militant secular feminists have transformed the terms *wife, mother,* and *homemaker* into virtual expletives and in the process have ripped from women's innermost beings the rights, responsibilities, and roles that provide emotionally stable women with their greatest sense of satisfaction and personal accomplishment. Any woman who would chose to be a wife, mother, and homemaker must be out of her mind, they say, or else she is still bound in the chains of the patriarchialist past. Because of such feminist deprecations, such women are often shackled with the shame of describing themselves as being "just a homemaker."

In principle, militant feminism maintains that only masculinized women can have true self-actualization and freedom. They argue that as long as women maintain femininity, they can never be free, when the truth is that *only* when women are fully feminine can they ever be truly free. While feminism purports to promote egalitarianism, more often than not it actually produces masculinized women and requires love to be "rational" and "hygienic" to such a degree that it "degrades human beings into males and females, and robs them of their mystery."[38] In this system, the feminine mystique is often lost in brazen, shameless vulgarity or in an utter lack of social grace and dignity. Tragically, most of those who fall victim to such humanist propaganda are burdened with the heavy guilt of never having time

---

[37] Valerie Solanas, *SCUM Manifesto* (San Francisco: AK Press, 1996), quoted in Dawn Keetley, *Public Women, Public Words: A Documentary History of American Feminism* (Lanham, MD: Rowman & Littlefield Publishers, 2002), vol. 3, p. 172.
[38] Evdokimov, p. 26.

for their families or for the individuals who bring true satisfaction to their lives.

Feminist agendas, along with those fabricated by other social engineers, have also succeeded in emasculating entire generations of males to such a degree that men no longer have any idea what it means to be a man. Gender identity drift has become an increasingly difficult problem that affects both males and females. Feminism and feminist agendas have wreaked havoc upon boys in the classroom who are no longer allowed to be boys but are forcibly subjected to psychobabble that confuses them and *pharmacia* that subdues them, both of which open doors to the kingdom of darkness.[39] Basing the fight to change the evils of a patriarchialist past on the arrogance and intellectual imperialism of postmodernist relativism's grand vision of the future rather than on the bedrock of biblical revelation has proven to be a disaster of mammoth proportions that has only driven women on forced marches from one gulag to another.

On another front, many women have been required to abandon their spirituality and their femininity by unrelenting societal and ecclesiastical restrictions and abuse and by pressures from postmodern nihilism. Most women have retreated into a self-protective shell, a compliant posture that provides some relief but does not remove the pain of humiliation. Others have abandoned their own inclination toward modesty and have become brash, lubricious, and manipulative, using their "feminine wiles" to advance themselves while all the time feeling hollow and full of bitterness. The danger in this glorification of the dark side of femininity is what Alice von Hildebrand described in this way: "When piety dies out in women, society is threatened in its very fabric; for a woman's relationship to the sacred keeps the Church and society on an even keel, and when this link is severed, both are threatened by total moral chaos."[40] It can rightly be said that the way in which women view and treat themselves is a barometer that confirms either the health or sickness that is manifest in both society and the church.

---

[39] See Christina Hoff Sommers, *The War Against Boys: How Misguided Feminism Is Harming Our Young Men* (New York: Touchstone, 2000). See also Sommers, *Who Stole Feminism? How Women Have Betrayed Women* (New York: Touchstone, 1994). Sommers maintains that older forms of feminism have been co-opted by newer varieties that are advancing agendas not espoused by older feminism and which are doing great harm to both male and female.

[40] Jennifer Ferrara and Sarah Hinlicky Wilson, "Ordaining Women: Two Views," *First Things* (April 2003), p. 33ff.

The truth is that the position of the woman is also "a yardstick by which the culture of a people may be measured."[41] The degree to which any individual, social group, society, or nation is controlled by evil can be accurately measured by the manner in which women are treated, for the original and continuing sin of humanity is rebellion against divinely established parameters for healthy, happy living, driven by an uncontrollable lust for exploitation and domination of what is not rightfully given. Who is woman? A clear indicator of where a family, a society, a religion, or a culture can be found on a scale between the zenith of health and the nadir of infirmity!

It is unfortunately true that in virtually every society in the world and for virtually all of human history, women have been "denied political, economic, legal, and educational rights" and that even today in "no country in the world are these yet equal to men in practice."[42] As Elizabeth Johnson observes, this is only the tip of the iceberg, for "to make a dark picture even bleaker, women are bodily and sexually exploited, physically abused, raped, battered, and murdered," and it is an "indisputable fact that men do this to women in a way that women do not do to men."[43] These terrible truths have led to the conclusion that "sexism is rampant on a global scale."[44] One can only deduce from this that the human family is dysfunctional and desperately needs proactive intervention to restore God's design for women.

WHERE DOES TODAY'S CHURCH STAND?

For centuries, far too many ecclesiastical leaders have answered the question *Who is woman?* with the same conclusion that Tertullian reached: woman is "the devil's gateway."[45] One can only stand in utter disbelief that the religion founded on the faith that Jesus and Paul anchored in woman-honoring biblical Judaism could have degenerated to the point that such a synopsis by one of its greatest theologians would

---

[41] Menachem M. Brayer, *The Jewish Woman in Rabbinic Literature: A Psychosocial Perspective* (Hoboken, NJ: KTAV Publishing House, 1986), p. 14.
[42] Elizabeth A. Johnson, *She Who Is: The Mystery of God in Feminist Theological Discourse* (New York: The Crossroad Publishing Company, 1998), p. 25.
[43] Johnson, p. 25.
[44] Johnson, p. 25. For clear documentation of the universal abuse of women, see Mary Daly, *Gyn/Ecology: The Metaethics of Radical Feminism* (Minneapolis: Winston, 1985), pp. 33-50.
[45] Tertullian, *On the Apparel of Women*, I.1.1. Tertullian was particularly perplexed by the immorality of women outside the church and their potential impact on both women and men within the church; a strong series of epithets against such women in his sermons contributed profoundly to the church's official position that women in general were inherently evil solely because of their gender and their potential to inflame the passions of "rational" men.

not only have been tolerated but also adopted as proper teaching by a significant portion of the historical leaders of the church. Ironically, at the same time that the church was disparaging women in general, it was also praising Mary, the mother of Jesus, calling her the "Queen of Heaven."[46] Essentially, however, the church's veneration of Mary was made possible in the profoundly gynophobic world of early Greek and Latin Christianity only by transforming her into "a third being, outside the common human essence" so that she came to be viewed as "Virgin and Mother, but . . . not a woman."[47] This became tacitly true because "there seems to be no possible middle ground between the Virgin and the diabolical creature that tempted the hermits."[48] Noting the supreme irony of the profound contradiction of terms between women as "the devil's gateway," and Mary as the "Queen of Heaven," Paul Jewett sardonically drew this particularly apropos conclusion: "One cannot but pause in astonishment over such a paradox. How could the same creature be loaded with such opprobrium and yet exalted to such honor?"[49] In reality, Mary has been so exalted because in church lore, she became the perpetual virgin who never experienced the "degrading" physical aspects of normal feminine embodiment and sexuality.[50]

On the one hand, much of today's church continues to stumble about in the obscurity spread across the face of Christianity before and during the Dark Ages.[51] On the other hand, a significant portion of the church has launched itself into the utter darkness of humanism, fatalism, nihilism, New Age philosophies, and neo-paganism.

[46] For many centuries, the title *Queen of Heaven* has been applied to Mary, the mother of Jesus, by Roman Catholic sources, particularly in the recitation of the Litany of Loreto, which was approved in 1587. While not embracing the Catholic dogma of the assumption of Mary (body and soul) into heaven, Orthodox churches have also called Mary Theotokos (God-bearer) since the fourth century.

[47] Evdokimov, pp. 23-24.

[48] Evdokimov, pp. 23-24.

[49] Paul K. Jewett, *The Ordination of Women: An Essay on the Office of Christian Ministry* (Grand Rapids, MI: William B. Eerdmans Publishing Company, 1980), pp. 4-5.

[50] Some have even suggested that when Jesus was born to Mary he miraculously passed through the side of her uterus in something akin to a supernatural caesarian section, and since he did not pass through her cervix and vagina, her hymen—and, therefore, her virginity—was preserved. Hints of this teaching are found in Ambrose of Milan's *The Consecration of a Virgin and the Perpetual Virginity of Mary,* 8:52 (c. 391 A.D.) and in Augustine's Tractate 91:3. John Damascene is even more specific in *On the Orthodox Faith* IV.14.

[51] The term *Dark Ages* describes the period of cultural deterioration following the decline of the Roman Empire. The Latin term *saeculum obscurum* was first used in 1602. See John C. Dwyer, *Church History: Twenty Centuries of Catholic Christianity* (Mahwah, NJ: Paulist Press, 1985), p. 155. Generally speaking, the Dark Ages are considered to have extended from 400 A.D. until 1000 A.D.

Morbidly afraid of the pure light of biblical truth that would liberate and bless, blind leaders from both extremes lead immature, myopic disciples on mad dashes into one ditch or another,[52] ruining lives and destroying the witness that the church should have in the world. All the while, millions of women have been and continue to be victimized, condemned to live second-class lives in male-dominated ecclesiastical and political systems or expected to divest themselves of all vestiges of femininity and essentially become male clones. The androcentricity of official Christianity has succeeded in "making women mostly invisible, inaudible, and marginal, except for the supportive services they provide."[53]

For centuries, the entire focus of the church has been on the masculine. Despite official pronouncements to the contrary, for all intents and purposes, it has imaged God as a male being.[54] Masculinity has been said to represent perfection in rationality, strength, and self-control. Femininity has been considered to be an imperfection focused in emotion and susceptibility to evil. Some theologians have taught that only males reflect the "image of God" and that females can only manifest the "image of man."[55] Others have even wondered if women have souls![56] Still others have argued that since Jesus was a man, women, because of their gender alone, can never hope to be christomorphic, bearing Christ's image, and that they, therefore, can never be teachers, leaders, or priests in the church.[57] Such teaching prompted Karen Jo Torjesen's observation that "women's physical embodiment becomes a prison that shuts them off from God, except as mediated through the christic male"[58] because women's bodies are "capable of representing only their sexuality, not God."[59] These and other ecclesiastical positions have often been established and

---

[52] Matthew 15:14.

[53] Johnson, p. 24.

[54] See John Zizioulas, *Being as Communion* (Crestwood, NY: St. Vladimir's Seminary Press, 1985), pp. 110-142.

[55] Peter Abelard, *Introductio ad Theologiam*, vol. 1, p. 991.

[56] John Donne, *To the Countesse of Huntingdon*, I.1.2, 177. Donne, poet and chaplain to King James I declared in this poem: "Man to God's image, Eve to man's was made. Nor finde wee that God breath'd a soule in her."

[57] See "Declaration on the Question of the Admission of Women to the Ministerial Priesthood," in *Women Priests: A Catholic Commentary on the Vatican Declaration,* ed. Leonard Swidler and Arlene Swidler (New York: Paulist Press, 1977).

[58] Johnson, p. 153.

[59] Karen Jo Torjesen, *When Women Were Priests: Women's Leadership in the Early Church and the Scandal of Their Subordination in the Rise of Christianity* (San Francisco: HarperCollins, 1995), p. 223.

reinforced in the self-serving prejudice, ignorance, and arrogance of male leaders, then confirmed and "substantiated" by misinterpreted and misapplied Holy Scripture, and finally implemented in polities that have marginalized and restricted women in virtually every aspect of their lives.

In recent times, however, a church that has been increasingly held in the grip of postmodernity has witnessed an impassioned and often vituperative reaction to historical ecclesiastical restrictions on women. Forms of militant secular and religious feminism have goaded many women into jettisoning all reason and biblical context in favor of a headlong pursuit of everything in the man's world. Militant feminism has succeeded in thrusting many women into brash, aggressive roles that have left them as both haters of manhood and despisers of womanhood. For a growing number of religious feminists, the church's intransigence in its stances toward women—virtually all of which are restrictive to some degree—has produced a reactive move away from the church and its perceived patriarchal theology and into the world of the "sacred feminine"[60] where they achieve emotional release in the delusion of a fantasy world that never existed except in the vivid imagination of feminist wishful thinking.

WOMEN'S PAINFUL DILEMMA

Women of varied backgrounds experience the pain and emotional struggle associated with confronting these issues in society and in the church. Many are caught in a dull, lifeless world of ambiguity and ambivalence somewhere between the extremes, where they often find themselves being dragged toward one or the other extremity and often toward both at the same time. Personal ambivalence and the pressures of expectations for feminine quiescence and conformity leave many in a spiritual limbo, not really knowing which way to turn or which choices to make. The one thing that is certain for growing numbers of women is that things cannot remain as they have been. In their heart of hearts, they know that they must do something, no matter how small, to confront the prejudices and pressures of a male-dominated

---

[60] See Anne Baring and Andrew Harvey, *The Divine Feminine: Exploring the Feminine Face of God Throughout the World* (Berkeley, CA: Conari Press, 1996); Rosemary Radford Ruether, *Goddesses and the Divine Feminine: A Western Religious History* (Berkeley, CA: University of California Press, 2005); and Franceska Perot, *The Re-Emergence of the Divine Feminine and its Significance for Spiritual, Psychological and Evolutionary Growth* (Boca Raton, FL: www.dissertation.com, 2008).

society and church. Unfortunately, this deep-seated frustration has often produced very questionable results.

One such example is Sue Monk Kidd, a woman who has chronicled her personal journey from being a "Church Handmaiden" and, therefore, a "Silent Woman" (an essentially invisible pastor's wife in an ultraconservative Christian denomination), to her embrace of the "goddess within." She describes her experience thus: "[I] sensed rebirth as my heart opened wider toward the Divine Feminine presence."[61] Ultimately Kidd confessed, "I came to know myself as the embodiment of Goddess."[62] A pivotal moment that propelled her along the road of her personal journey from fundamentalist Christianity to goddess worship occurred in a touching and outrageous incident involving her 14-year-old daughter. As Kidd proudly observed her industrious daughter kneeling on the floor, intently engaged in straightening rows of toothpaste in her after-school drug store job, she was shocked when a well-dressed, middle-aged man passed by, nudged his male companion, and condescendingly remarked, "Now that's how I like to see a woman: on her knees."[63] Was this just an isolated incident? Hardly! Most men of the past have held similar opinions, and far too many still do.

Anne Schaef describes the almost universal feminine frustration that Kidd confessed. She sees women as being victimized and in "hidden despair" by the generationally recurring "original sin of being born female."[64] She observes that "to be born female . . . means that you are born 'tainted' . . . that your birthright is one of innate inferiority."[65] Rebecca Groothuis concludes that "it is no wonder that women—especially Christian women—have, in general, lower self-esteem than men."[66] During virtually all of ecclesiastical history since the end of the first century, the "inferiority" of woman has been internalized by women, "even by those who were not ordinary women."[67] And herein the tragedy lies, for in countless situations, even the most

---

[61] Kidd, pp. 125-127.

[62] Kidd, p. 160.

[63] Kidd, p. 7.

[64] Anne Wilson Schaef, *Women's Reality: An Emerging Female System in a White Male Society* (San Francisco: Harper & Row, 1981), p. 278.

[65] Schaef, p. 278

[66] Rebecca Merrill Groothuis, *Good News for Women: A Biblical Picture of Gender Equality* (Grand Rapids, MI: Baker Books, 1997), p. 67. Also David Neff, "Women in the Confidence Gap," *Christianity Today*, 22 July 1991, p. 13.

[67] Alvin John Schmidt, *Veiled and Silenced: How Culture Shaped Sexist Theology* (Macon, GA: Mercer University Press, 1989), p. 95.

gifted women have resigned themselves to inferiority and, as a result, to mediocrity. Indeed, the brightest and best feminine minds have often been cloistered in church-erected emotional and spiritual prisons, stripped of their feminine essence and gifting, and consigned to silence.

Emil Brunner has argued that "man, as the actually dominating shaper of history, culture, [and] the conditions of the law and of public education . . . has artificially riveted woman to her natural destiny."[68] In so doing, male-dominated power structures have "hindered the free development of [woman's] mind and spirit, to which she, as well as the man, as one who has been made in the image of God, has been called."[69] The impact of these historical conditions is more far reaching than many—even most—women recognize: "Even at the present day, and to a far greater degree than we usually realize, woman is still the slave of man, even the woman in the higher classes, even the educated woman."[70] This sad truth has led some women to conclude that "a woman may see herself as like God . . . but she can never have the experience that is freely available to every man and boy in her culture, of having her full sexual identity affirmed as being in the image and likeness of God."[71] It is no wonder then that many women have wryly observed that "women do most of the work at church, but men do most of the leading. So there you have it: fatherless homes and motherless churches—and a whole lot of Christians who wonder why we aren't a healthy family."[72] The true "Mothers in Zion" who have been anointed by God for leadership and service in family, society, and church have been largely restricted to subservient roles. Likewise, unless men have been a part of the clergy, they have often not been viewed—or have not viewed themselves—as having significant spiritual value to the community of faith.[73]

Many Christian feminist theologians consider what they view as the historical powerlessness of women to be an aberration focused on

---

[68] Emil Brunner, *Man in Revolt: A Christian Anthropology*, tr. Olive Wyon (Philadelphia, The Westminster Press, 1947), pp. 352-353.

[69] Brunner, pp. 352-353.

[70] Brunner, pp. 352-353.

[71] Johnson, p. 38.

[72] Sarah Sumner, *Men and Women in the Church* (Downers Grove, IL: InterVarsity Press, 2003), p. 322.

[73] Because of the influence of Platonic dualism in historical Christianity, men who were not elevated to the clergy were seen as doing only "secular" work while priests did "God's" work. The ecclesiastically imposed clergy-laity gap denied non-clergy men and women their rightful roles as spiritual leaders in their families, roles that were ceded to or arrogated by the clergy.

inherent masculine evil that has been supported and substantiated by patriarchalist Scripture. Many of these have essentially given up on the church and the Bible as hopelessly androcentric and misogynistic, and, with the historical record of the ecclesiastical world, who could blame them? Elizabeth Fiorenza[74] and Rosemary Radford Ruether[75] both agree that attempts to teach feminism from the Bible are hopeless. Fiorenza argues for a "hermeneutic of suspicion"[76] and has taken her point of departure in modern feminism, maintaining that one must begin from a commitment to feminism and then proceed from there to put the Bible in order[77] in what she describes as an imaginative reconstruction of historical reality.[78] She maintains that the "main task of a critical feminist hermeneutic is not to defend biblical authority but to articulate the theological authority of women."[79] Esther Fuchs goes further in viewing the Bible only as a "cultural-literary text" rather than a "religious or historical" one.[80] Letty Russell argues that "it has become abundantly clear that the scriptures need liberation, not only from existing interpretations but also from the patriarchal bias of the texts themselves,"[81] while Susan Brooks Thistlethwaite even makes the preposterous contention that Scripture is actually the basis for the rape and battering of women.[82] Daphne Hampson simply concludes that Holy Scripture and feminism are incompatible.[83] Ruether has advocated "ecofeminist spirituality" in which the God of Scripture is related to or perhaps is even replaced by *Gaia*.[84] Barbara Brown Zikmund even argues that "for those who want to stay within the Jewish and Christian legacy, the work of neo-pagan or non-biblical feminist spirituality is important" because "goddess religions have powerful

---

[74] See Elisabeth Schüssler Fiorenza, *In Memory of Her: A Feminist Theological Reconstruction of Christian Origins* (New York: The Crossroad Publishing Company, 1983).
[75] See Rosemary Radford Ruether, *Sexism and God-Talk* (Boston: Beacon Press, 1983).
[76] Fiorenza, p. 68.
[77] Fiorenza, referenced in Clark Pinnock, "Biblical Authority and the Issues in Question," in Alvera Mickelsen, *Women, Authority, and the Bible* (Downers Grove, IL: InterVarsity Press, 1986), p. 52.
[78] Fiorenza, pp. 167-168.
[79] *Anchor Bible Dictionary*, ed. Noel Freedman (New Haven, CT: Yale University Press), vol. 2, p. 785.
[80] Esther Fuchs, *Sexual Politics in the Biblical Narrative* (London: Sheffield Academic Press, 2000), p. 11.
[81] Letty Russell, ed., *Feminist Interpretation of the Bible* (Philadelphia: Westminster Press, 1985), p. 11.
[82] Susan Brooks Thistlethwaite, "Every Two Minutes: Battered Women and Feminist Interpretation," in Letty Russell, ed., *Feminist Interpretation*, pp. 96, 104-106.
[83] See Daphne Hampson, *Theology and Feminism* (Oxford: Basil Blackwell, 1990).
[84] See Rosemary Radford Ruether, *Gaia and God: An Ecofeminist Theology of Earth Healing* (London: HarperCollins, 2002).

symbols that stretch our understanding of religious practice and human experience."[85] These and other feminists, both secular and religious, agree that virtually nothing can be salvaged from the past and that only the future has hope for resolving the condition of woman.

WOMEN OF FAITH: CAUGHT IN THE MIDDLE

The majority of church women, however, are caught in the middle between the restrictive requirements of the past that continue to be staunchly defended in the present and the demands of women's liberationists that have echoed across society for over a century and have created clouds of dust in the pristine sanctuaries of the church. Godly women have an unwavering commitment to godliness, to adhering to the principles of conduct that they know instinctively must be taught by Holy Scripture. They cannot bring themselves to jettison the Bible as a relic of an antiquated patriarchal male God in order to accommodate the demands of some feminists. They know intuitively, however, that something is wrong with the historical church's positions on women that still carry over into the present to one degree or another. Surely these positions do not reflect God's eternal will for women.

At the same time, women are often bidden by an inner calling of the Holy Spirit to roles that have been traditionally forbidden to women. Divine *charismata*[86] create open doors for Spirit-directed action: "A person's gift makes room for him [or her]."[87] When those to whom these gifts have been given by the Spirit are feminine in gender, however, inhibitions cloud the issue, imposing spiritual and psychological constraints. No godly woman wants to be a "Jezebel," nor does she even want to be viewed as one; therefore, most who receive *charismata* become shrinking violets, adorned with the beauty of divine calling but afraid to stand out in the light of day.

This leaves so many women observing a human need, sensing a divine call on their lives, and then praying with all their might that God will send a man to do the work. In doing so, they are precisely like the nineteenth-century pioneer missionary Gladys Aylward, who confessed: "I wasn't God's first choice for what I've done for China. There was somebody else. . . . It must have been a man—a wonderful

---

[85] Barbara Brown Zikmund, "Feminist Consciousness in Historical Perspective," in Russell, ed., *Feminist Interpretation*, p. 29.
[86] *Charismata* are the gifts of the Spirit that are spoken of in 1 Corinthians 12 and Romans 12.
[87] Proverbs 18:16.

man. A well-educated man. I don't know what happened. Perhaps he died. Perhaps he wasn't willing . . . and God looked down . . . and saw Gladys Aylward."[88]

Many, if not most, of the extraordinary women in the history of Christianity have suffered from feelings of inferiority, which they have internalized after being force-fed the prejudices of arrogant and dominant males. Countless numbers have been unable to overcome the disparagement and deprecation that Letty Russell experienced when she graduated from Harvard Divinity School in the 1950s. "The faculty was reluctant to grant top honors to the only two women in the class because it might reflect poorly on the qualifications of the men,"[89] she reported. If this was not enough, her subsequent teaching experience as a professor at Princeton was commonly met with the reaction of one male pastor who, in Russell's words, "was sure that everything I said about the meaning of vocation was radical and heretical because I was a woman." Then, when she assured him that what she was teaching was affirmed by outstanding male theologians of history, he summarily declared her classes to be worthless "because they offered nothing new!"[90]

What is a woman to do? Ingrained into the very fiber of her being are the historical church's demands for female submission and silence. And, more often than not, standing ready to wield the broadaxe of ecclesiastical judgment is a male bureaucrat, who has wrapped himself in the vestments of divine authority. The resultant suffering of the female heart is inexorable and excruciating. Is she to obey God or man? And, the answer more often than not is "man," for a man is immediately at hand to shush her, summarily dismiss her, and insist that she return to her "woman's place!" Consequently, women have suffered rejection and restriction, disparagement and derogation. In effect, they have been bound and gagged. They have been psychologically and spiritually abused just as much as if they had been physically beaten, and the hurt has been much greater. Most have retreated into a shell and slumped into the codependency of abuse-victimization. Some have refused to be bound and gagged and have suffered deprecation, recrimination, excommunication, incarceration, corporal pun-

---

[88] Gladys Aylward, quoted in Phyllis Thompson, *A Transparent Woman: The Compelling Story of Gladys Aylward* (Grand Rapids: Zondervan Publishing Company, 1971), pp. 182-183.
[89] Letty M. Russell, *Household of Freedom: Authority in Feminist Theology* (Philadelphia: The Westminster Press, 1987), p. 12.
[90] Russell, p. 12.

ishment, and even death—all for being called of God.

But, the story does not end with the emotional and spiritual duress of church women themselves. The female that has suffered the most is the church herself. The passion and vitality, the commitment and sensitivity of women have been restricted, as women have been denied the opportunity to contribute to the church the gifts which are inherent and dominant in womanhood and which are often limited in manhood. This is particularly ludicrous in light of the fact that women represent far more than half of the church's constituency and, therefore, its witnessing force. The gospel that is best communicated out of love and in the context of relationship is often off limits to women, the very individuals who have the greatest capacity for both. The community of faith is the greatest loser when the women in the church are so restricted. Theologians and church leaders who disregard this fundamental truth do so at their own peril and at the peril of the church itself. Those "who transfer the conditions of a hierarchically organized church to marriage in particular, and to the position of women in relation to men in general" cause not only women, but also the church, to endure great suffering and shame. When "their monotheism knows only monarchy . . . and [when] the man is accordingly the monarch in marriage . . . with a God-given leadership role, and [when] the woman is destined to serve, in subordination to him,"[91] the androcentric, self-serving bureaucracies that have historically robbed the church of the depth and experience of the Spirit are perpetuated.

Once and for all, contemporary Christianity must come to the realization that the faith of God was never intended to be androcentric and that the church was never designed to be dominated by a male bureaucracy. "Hierarchic patriarchy is not intrinsic to Christianity, to its message, to its eschatological vision of the social order, or to its countercultural origins," observes Karen Jo Torjesen, and "neither are gender hierarchy and the denigration of sexuality necessary components of authentic Western religion."[92]

How to Know What God Thinks

When will the cycle of abuse end? Has the time come for a reexamination of traditional positions on this vital issue? Surely it is time

[91] Jürgen Moltmann, *The Spirit of Life: A Universal Affirmation* (Minneapolis: Fortress Press, 1992), p. 240.
[92] Torjesen, p. 268.

17

for biblical scholars, male and female, to take the time to study these complicated issues exhaustively, committing themselves to the process of rediscovering the original design of the Maker for both men and women. If such an examination is to be effective, however, it must not proceed out of emotion or only as a reaction to a perceived evil. While it is important to observe and recognize when something is not right, simple reaction to evil can more often than not produce an equal or greater evil, as the pendulum swings from one extreme to the other. Sometimes, reaction can cause one to fly off on a tangent and be forever lost in space.

Mary Evans is right when she suggests that "we need drastic reappraisal of our whole outlook" so that men and women can "live out their diversity, unity, and complementarity."[93] It is time that Christian theologians, leaders, and laity lay aside emotions and make a concerted effort to find the answers to the dilemma that faces the church in its perspectives on women and its relationships with them. It is time to be proactive by returning to the only source of information that can be trusted, the Holy Writ. As Phyllis Trible has suggested, the "Bible is a pilgrim wandering through history to merge past and present on its way to the future."[94] While Christians can draw "courage and strength from the memory of the future,"[95] visions of brighter days filled with the glory of the Lord must be grounded in the revealed knowledge and wisdom of God. In this way, believers in the God of the Bible become "pilgrims of the future," in the words of paleontologist Pierre Teilhard de Chardin, by following in the footsteps of "nomads of faith" like Sarah and Abraham.[96] Without reference to the words of divine revelation, discerning lasting answers to present dilemmas is impossible. When confronting perceived evils in today's world, it is wise to remember the immortal declaration of Jesus in similar circumstances: "From the beginning it was not so."[97] Recognizing that humans alter God's design to conform to their own machinations, Jesus appealed to the original order of creation to identify the ideal for human conduct. Returning to the beginning of creation, then, can reveal amazing truths

---

[93] Mary Evans, *Woman in the Bible: An Overview of All the Crucial Passages on Women's Roles* (Downers Grove, IL: InterVarsity Press, 1983), pp. 109, 132.
[94] Phyllis Trible, *God and the Rhetoric of Sexuality* (Philadelphia: Fortress Press, 1978), pp. 1, 202.
[95] Russell, p. 73.
[96] Isaac C. Rottenberg, "The Reign of God," *Restore!* vol. 10:2, p. 21.
[97] Matthew 19:8.

that stratified layers of generational human tradition have obscured to the point of rendering them virtually unrecognizable.

Rightly dividing the Word of truth will always provide a solid foundation for equipping humanity unto every good work.[98] In doing so, however, careful detail must be given to engaging the text with biblical hermeneutics, interpreting Scripture in the way in which Jesus and the apostles did—with an apostolic hermeneutic, as it were. Somehow, somewhere, honest study must be made on the important issues of life. A diligent search of the Scriptures must be based on the presupposition that they represent the very Word of God that is profitable for teaching, for instruction in righteousness, for maturing every believer, and for equipping the people of God for every good work.[99] This presupposition is the only one that cannot be ignored in an effort toward objectivity in confronting the vital issues of family and community. Old prejudices must be laid aside as believers come before God and his holy Word with humble hearts to hear what he has said and not what they wish he had said. And, when the Word of truth is rightly divided by cutting a straight line[100] that does not waver or flex like a polygraph needle, clearly established truth will be discovered, a foundation on which all believers can build sound and productive lives.

Fundamentally, Scripture must interpret Scripture in the hermeneutical circle in which individual passages are interpreted in the light of the whole of Scripture and the whole of Scripture is interpreted in the light of individual passages. Texts must never be set in opposition to other texts and then weighted according to the predispositions of the interpreter so that parts of Scripture are deemed more inspired than other parts. This is nothing more than what has been called a "cafeteria theology" where interpreters "choose only the biblical passages that suit their taste and pretend that other texts are simply not there or are no longer relevant."[101] With the hermeneutical circle, obscure, isolated, or topical texts can be rightly interpreted in light of and in conformity with the overall message of the Bible. At the same time the whole of Scripture can be clarified and nuanced by the in-

---

[98] 2 Timothy 2:15; 3:17.

[99] 2 Timothy 3:17.

[100] The word translated "rightly dividing" in the KJV rendering of 2 Timothy 2:15 is *orthotoméo* which literally means "to cut a straight line" or "to proceed on a straight path." As a consequence, "rightly dividing the word of truth" can only be accomplished when one "cuts a straight line" of interpretation through each text of Scripture.

[101] Alvin J. Schmidt, "Fundamentalism and Sexist Theology," in Marla J. Selvidge, ed., *Fundamentalism: What Makes It So Attractive?* (Elgin, IL: Brethren Press, 1984), p. 104.

dividual passages. Scripture must never be interpreted in the light of popular culture or the psychobabble of postmodernism.

Likewise, a second fundamental principle of biblical hermeneutics must be carefully and diligently applied by insisting that context interpret text. Any text that is lifted out of its context, either grammatically or historically, becomes a pretext that is then advanced as a proof text designed to add support to preconceived notions. This is a sound principle of what has been termed the grammatico-historical hermeneutic,[102] often called the Reformation hermeneutic, in which Scripture is interpreted within the constraints of the grammar of the texts themselves and within the history and culture of the people to whom and through whom Scripture was originally given.[103] The grammatico-historical hermeneutic is firmly established on the time-honored *peshat* principle of the Hebraic hermeneutics which Jesus and the apostles generally employed, in which the plain and simple meaning of Scripture is established and becomes the basis for all other interpretative possibilities. This method of interpretation was the focus of the third-century Antiochan School that followed the principles laid down earlier by Lucian of Samosata.[104] It was dedicated to the integrity of history and to the natural sense of the text itself in contradistinction to the Alexandrian School which insisted that the texts of Scripture must be interpreted allegorically and reached its zenith in Origen, the allegorist *par excellence*.[105] The Carthaginian School that was founded by Tertullian in the third century attempted to bring about a synthesis between these two contradictory methods, thereby providing some balance for later interpreters.[106]

Similarly, proper biblical interpretation must flow from true ex-

---

[102] Walter C. Kaiser and Moses Silva, *An Introduction to Biblical Hermeneutics* (Grand Rapids, MI: Zondervan Publishing House, 1994), p. 221. Also Keith Augustus Burton, *The Blessing of Africa* (Downers Grove, IL: InterVarsity Press, 2007), p. 131.

[103] This means that every text must be interpreted in its Jewish context, for the Jews simply are the people to whom, through whom, and for whom Scripture was given. The texts that were either thought or written in Hebrew must be interpreted in the context of the Hebrew language, and they must also be interpreted in the light of Jewish history and culture.

[104] James Hastings and John A. Selbie, eds., *Encyclopedia of Religion and Ethics* (Edinburgh: T. & T. Clark, 1927), part 2, p. 593. Also, Hubert Jedin and John Patrick Dolan, eds., *Handbook of Church History* (New York: Herder and Herder, 1965), vol. 1, p. 242.

[105] John Whitman, *Interpretation and Allegory: Antiquity to the Modern Period* (Leiden: Brill, 2000), p. 10. Also, David S. Dockery, *Biblical Interpretation Then and Now: Contemporary Hermeneutics in the Light of the Early Church* (Grand Rapids, MI: Baker Book House, 1992), pp. 101ff.

[106] Duncan Sheldon Ferguson, *Biblical Hermeneutics: An Introduction* (Atlanta, GA: John Knox Press, 1986), p. 151. Also, Milton Spenser Terry, *Biblical Hermeneutics: A Treatise on the Interpretation of the Old and New Testaments* (New York: Phillips & Hunt, 1883), p. 654.

egesis in which the meaning of each text is "drawn out"[107] of the text rather than allowing eisegesis to become the interpretive standard. When both scholars and laity prefer to engage in eisegesis by reading *into* Holy Scripture what they want it to say[108] rather than maintaining exegesis by drawing *out of* Scripture what it actually does say, they cannot hope to uphold a standard for "rightly dividing the Word of truth."[109] Those who attempt to read into Scripture what is not there are guilty of "hermeneutical gerrymandering,"[110] and exegetical gymnastics.[111] Scripture must also be respected in its own context as divine revelation that is not subject to "improvement" by the "enlightened" understanding of spiritual evolution in the mindset of the traditional modernist or enlightenment view that human understanding is always progressing and improving. Humans are no more intelligent now than they were thousands of years ago. Only knowledge—not intelligence—has increased.[112] Human intellect, in any case, is not the arbiter of divine truth. Scripture itself is the final answer, for it represents divine revelation, not human musing. The principal understanding that was given in Scripture is proper for all people for all time and can never be superseded by so-called advancements in human knowledge. The answers to truth are not in the present or in the future: they are in the past—in God's revealed Word. While God is constantly revealing what he has concealed by illuminating the hearts of both men and women,[113] all that unfolds in the realm of divine revelation must be firmly grounded in the written Word. No other foundation is ever acceptable.

Finally, careful attention must be given to the details of the all-important interpretive devices that make application of the texts possible. In this case, the principles of the ancient texts of Scripture must be contextualized for application in the present world, in the every-

---

[107] The Greek word *exegesis* is from *ex* (out) + *(h)ege* (of *hegeisthai* (to lead) + *sis*, *exegesis* means "drawing out."

[108] The Greek word *eisegesis* is from *eis* (into) + *(h)ege* (of *hegeisthai* (to lead) + *sis*, *eisegesis* means "leading into."

[109] 2 Timothy 2:15.

[110] David M. Scholar, "1 Timothy 2:9-15 and the Place of Women in the Church's Ministry," in Alvera Mickelsen, ed., *Women, Authority and the Bible* (Downers Grove, IL: InterVarsity Press, 1986), p. 206, note 38.

[111] This is clearly the case when interpreters read Scripture with Greek, Latin, German, or American eyes rather than with Jewish eyes. Failure to interpret Scripture from its Jewish matrix leads to pure eisegesis and to the neglect of foundational Hebraic truths that are essential to the spiritual health of believers.

[112] Daniel 12:4.

[113] Amos 3:7.

day lives of believers.[114] Any interpretation that cannot be indigenized and made applicable in the lives of all human beings is not an accurate one. Concepts that can be lived out only in small circles or in isolated ethnicities are not manifestations of divine scriptural principles, for God's Word is a universal declaration that can be effectively worked out in the lives of all human beings regardless of their gender, ethnicity, or socio-economic status.

Attention to well-established hermeneutical principles, to careful exegesis, and to practical application forms a solid foundation for healthy, holistic understanding of a biblically based life for today's—and tomorrow's—world. Only when care is taken not to handle the Word of God deceitfully[115] or to use it for the advantage of individual presuppositions and personal benefit will solid answers be discovered on which the community of faith can build mature lives that bring honor to God and respect to the church both within and without.

It is humanly impossible, however, for anyone to study a subject with total objectivity. Everyone approaches each issue with many filters of subjectivity, based on worldview, tradition, environment, and a thousand other factors. As James Packer said, "We may be sure . . . that any version of Christianity produced anywhere at any time will bear marks of one-sidedness or myopia, not only because of imperfect exegesis and theologizing but also for reasons of cultural limitation."[116] Secular science's boasts of objective research are just that: boasts, often inflated by ego and reckless abandon. Presuppositions are a part of every investigative endeavor, for one establishes a hypothesis and then works to prove or disprove it based on the evidence gathered; however, often the only evidence that is gathered is that which supports the hypothesis. And, as Benjamin Rush wryly observed, there is no idea so absurd that it cannot be supported by some biblical passage.[117]

A FRESH START

One thing is certain: things will not continue as they are. Too much is at stake. Women who, in general, have tasted a newfound level

---

[114] Krister Stendahl, *The Bible and the Role of Women: A Case Study in Hermeneutics,* tr. Emilie T. Sander (Philadelphia: Fortress Press, 1966), p. 9.
[115] 2 Corinthians 4:2.
[116] James I. Packer, "The Gospel—Its Content and Communication: A Theological Perspective," *Gospel and Culture,* ed. John Stott and Robert T. Coote (Pasadena: William Care Library, 1979), p. 140.
[117] Benjamin Rush referenced in Schmidt, p. 29.

of freedom and have gained new opportunities for fulfillment will not allow themselves to continue to be shackled in male-designed prisons. They will insist on breaking free from chains of restriction and on removing the gags of imposed silence. If the church does not return to the Bible and find there the answers to this dilemma, it will be the greatest victim of its own excesses either in the form of entrenched androlatrous bureaucracies intent upon maintaining the demands of the past or in the form of rabid feminism focused on the destruction of Judeo-Christian values. Unfortunately, the church's reactionary posturing on women's rights and roles has kept it from leading the way toward a new day of freedom. Evdokimov has underscored the tragedy that has resulted from the lack of a proactive position in Christian bureaucracies: "Christianity is behind the times. The Church has the message of liberation, but it is others who 'liberate.' . . . In the East, woman emerges from slavery, and her lips pronounce other names than that of Christ. The world is outdistancing Christianity."[118]

Ruether has argued for the emergence of a middle ground between androcentric patriarchy and postmodern individuality: "Feminist anthropology must thus reject both the patriarchal family, where only the patriarch is fully a person, and liberal individualism, where all are assumed to be autonomous persons but isolated from relationships."[119] Such a balance, she has suggested, must be achieved "in order to envision new families in a new society where individuation and community can be interrelated."[120] Is it possible to have the best of both worlds? Indeed, it is, but only when one returns to the firm foundation that God established in the beginning and has continually reformed and renewed, despite long periods of neglect and abuse.

First, the history of official Christianity's abuse toward women must be recognized, confessed, and corrected. Torjesen suggests how this can occur: "Contemporary Christian theologians need to undertake the same task of extricating the essential teachings of the Christian gospel from the patriarchal gender system in which it is embedded," and she urges Christian churches to begin by rejecting "the patriarchal norms of the Greco-Roman gender system."[121] Rob Palkovitz

---

[118] Evdokimov, p. 19.
[119] Rosemary Radford Ruether, "Christian Understandings of Human Nature and Gender," in *Religion, Feminism, and the Family,* ed. Anne Carr and Mary Steward Van Leeuwen (Louisville, KY: Westminster John Knox Press, 1996), p. 108.
[120] Ruether, p. 108.
[121] Torjesen, pp. 268-269.

sums it up well by noting that ultimately "commitment to Christian principles based on biblical literacy [will] require less focus on gender and role dichotomies and greater emphasis on living out kingdom principles in a manner that affirms the value of others, be they wives, husbands, men, women, or children."[122] He concludes that "change of a truly significant magnitude [will occur] when individual men and women come to an understanding of who they are before God, and in relating to God . . . find all other relationships transformed."[123]

Second, it is time to stop the blame game. For centuries, men have blamed women for all the ills of society and have made every effort to control them in order to make the world a better place (for themselves!). Now, women increasingly blame men for their long-term experiences of being constrained and silenced and for having their gender deprecated as an inherent evil. If blame is to be affixed, it must be nailed to the door on which it belongs: sin. The sin of the male and the sin of the female are equally responsible for the aberrations in interpersonal human behavior. God predicted that because both Adam and Eve had chosen to disobey his directive and had sinned in the beginning, a terrible codependency of submission and abuse would result.[124] And so it has. Now, the answer is not in affixing blame: it is in discovering the original design and intent for proper human interaction before sin changed everything and then finding ways in which God's original design can be restored. Androcentric domination and gynocentric submission are consequences of the primeval fall into sin that can be fully resolved only by truly living the life of a new creation in the Messiah.[125] Male and female can be liberated into a whole new world of biblical relationship when both recognize sin as the cause of aberrant behavior and repent of sin by turning from it and resolving never to repeat it.[126] Indeed, the level of success in biblical discipleship that one has achieved can be accurately measured by the degree to which self, with its propensity for seeking domination over others, has been mastered by the Spirit-directed life.

Third, a fresh look at the Scriptures must be undertaken in which everything that is written is evaluated both on the basis of the grammar

---

[122] Rob Palkovitz, "The 'Recovery' of Fatherhood?" in Carr and Van Leeuwen, p. 322.
[123] Palkovitz, p. 322.
[124] Genesis 3:16-17.
[125] 2 Corinthians 5:17.
[126] The Hebraic understanding of repentance is recognition of sin, remorse for sin, turning away from sin, restitution for sin, and resolution not to repeat the sin.

of the Hebrew texts themselves[127] and on the history and culture of the Hebrew peoples through whom Scripture was given. A radically new examination of the Scriptures from this perspective will take the most foundational and trustworthy principles of biblical hermeneutics to their logical and proper conclusion. Scripture must also be read from a relational perspective beginning with the relational, personal God of divine self-disclosure and extending and replicating that relationship to and through the human race. A balanced review of Scripture will also underscore the often misunderstood and underappreciated relational power and opportunities that Hebraic women shared with men. This will help to ameliorate the feeling of universal powerlessness and victimization which so many women have experienced when the pendulum has swung from one extreme to the other and interpreters have chosen to read the dynamics of other cultures, including their own, into Scripture rather than recognizing what is clearly recorded there. As the true equality of women and men is recognized by both male and female, women can challenge "theories restricting [their] service" and "take the Scriptures and reclaim [their] borders."[128]

Finding real answers to today's problems will occur only when Scripture itself is recognized as originating in the personal initiative of divine self-disclosure and when the divine revelation of Scripture is accepted as the final arbiter of truth.[129] Scripture is God's Word. It must be contextualized, but it must never be rewritten, redacted, or revised. A strong curse still remains on those who either add to or take from God's Word.[130] Indeed, all of the ills of the world, including history's dreadful record relating to women, can be traced to those who have dared to do so! In order to find the answers for the perplexing questions of human relationships, the Hellenized and Latinized church of today must return to the Hebraic foundations of the Christian faith. The Scriptures must be viewed through the same lenses through which they were recorded in the first place. Anything

---

[127] Both the Hebrew Scriptures and the Apostolic Scriptures are Hebrew texts. Some of the Apostolic Scriptures were first written in Hebrew and later translated into Greek (particularly the Gospels, all of which are filled with Hebraicisms that were essentially nonsensical to the Greek mind), and the remaining texts were *thought* in Hebrew by Jewish apostles or their disciples and then translated into Greek.

[128] Faith Martin, *Call Me Blessed: The Emerging Christian Woman* (Grand Rapids, MI: Wm. B. Eerdmans Publishing Co., 1988), p. 27.

[129] The truth people discover in science, philosophy, math, etc., is also God's truth because it conforms to reality even though it is not mentioned in Scripture. Truth can be found outside Scripture; however, the final arbiter of truth is Scripture.

[130] Revelation 22:18-19.

less than a full restoration of the church's Jewish roots will only per-petuate—and perhaps even worsen—the aberrant perspectives with which non-Jewish philosophies and mythologies have perverted the faith of Jesus and the apostles.

There can be no doubt that "the solution to contemporary social dilemmas is at least 2,000 years old."[131] Indeed, the answers are even four millennia older than the teachings of Jesus: they can be discov-ered in the book of Genesis, which documents God's original design for humanity—male and female—and answers the question *Who is woman?* The solid answers that, in reality, all women and men seek are found in the profound declaration of the Almighty when he cre-ated humanity: "Let us make humanity *in our image, after our like-ness.*" Only when womanhood is understood to be a full reflection of the image and likeness of God will a foundation be laid for right relationships between women and men. Only when men and women recognize that the image of God is manifest equally in each other will a face-to-face relationship of true equality be established and main-tained as a buttress that can withstand the unrelenting assault of the sins of discrimination and injustice and their insidious, debilitating effects upon both female and male.

Springboard for Discussion

1. Evaluate the universal mistreatment of women as second-class citizens. Why do you think that women have been viewed as infe-rior, misbegotten, and even second-class citizens in almost every cul-ture and at almost every time in history? How was it possible that for nearly twenty centuries the church upheld this view? What legacy has this historical thinking bequeathed to you, and how does it affect you today?

2. Analyze secular feminism's proposition that women can have value only when they are engaged in what have been historically viewed as male roles. How has this impacted the average woman to-day? How important are the roles of wife and mother to you and your spouse? Is the feminine capacity for motherhood merely biological, or does it extend into other areas of life?

---

[131] Palkovitz, pp. 324-325.

3. What has been the impact of feminist agendas on children in the past several generations? Is there any correlation between the increasing lack of civility and morality among children and Western societies' feminist agendas?

4. Evaluate the impact of media and entertainment on women today. To what degree have women abandoned biblical modesty and morality? How has this impacted society in general and you in particular? How might women's self-image affect the health or illness of society?

5. Discuss the ways in which male domination in home, society, and church has restricted the development of spirit and mind in women. How have women reacted to the dilemma of being gifted for service in family, society, and church and yet finding themselves restricted? Have you or a loved one experienced such restrictions? What do you think you can do to help solve the problem?

6. Discuss the importance of "rightly dividing" Scripture in order to establish a foundation for God's perspectives on men and women. How important are objectivity and integrity to the task of interpreting Scripture? How important is it to understand the biblical principles for interpreting Scripture?

7. How have Christian feminists approached the problem of historical inequality between the sexes? Are they right to challenge the integrity of the Scriptures themselves?

8. Discuss the way in which the gospel is most effectively communicated through relationship and empathy. Are women more effective in these areas than men? How has church restrictions on women through the centuries negatively impacted the church's growth and maturity?

CHAPTER 2

THE PAST REVEALS
THE FUTURE

Clear answers to difficult questions are found most often when the accretions of human traditions that have been layered upon the Word of God by interpretations or explications of the past are peeled away. Some of the traditions that bias many readings of Scripture are culturally based and well intended. Some, however, are sinister, birthed in compromise with concepts that are at bottom inimical to the very foundations of the Holy Scriptures. Conceived, verbalized, and written in the Hebrew language in order to distill the Hebraic worldview and mindset, the Bible is a Hebrew book, written about the Hebrew people by Hebrew people as they were inspired by the God who identified himself as the God of the Hebrews.[1] If biblical truth is to be determined, layers of Americanism, Europeanism, Latinism, Hellenism, and even paganism must be stripped away. Seekers of truth must return to the Jewish roots of the Christian faith, the foundation of the life and religion of Jesus and the apostles.

Yet another round of perception and reaction is not what is needed. History is littered with just such emotional responses to the questions that face humanity, especially the question *Who is woman?* Mere perception of perceived evils (on both sides of the spectrum) must be transcended. More than simple reaction is needed, because reaction often creates more confusion and consternation and, potentially, something even more perverse than the perceived evil against which reaction is directed. Instead of perception and reaction, apperception

[1] Hebrews 11:16.

and proaction are needed today, especially in determining the proper answer to the question of God's design for women.

THE ARROGANCE OF THE PRESENT

One of the problems with finding solutions to current problems is the fact that most of the postmodern world has determined the past to be passé and of little or no value. Whereas modernity, which began in the Enlightenment, taught that knowledge is both certain and attainable[2] and that "all-inclusive" definitions can be established,[3] postmodernity posits that there is no such thing as absolute truth. As a matter of fact, for the proponents of postmodern philosophy the only absolute of which they are absolutely certain is that there are absolutely no absolutes! The corollary to this idea is that no objective meaning can be established, especially from interpretations of Scripture. As Thomas Howe has demonstrated, however, those who posit these postmodern theories violate the fundamental law of non-contradiction.[4]

Postmodernism has been described as a view of the world "which doubts that reality has an absolute order which man's understanding can comprehend."[5] Everything is based in the existential moment, and everything is subject to moral relativism. This postmodern philosophy was introduced in incipient form by Friedrich Nietzsche, who attacked history's "myopic view" of truth, morality, and language and declared that "the essential fabrication permeating culture is that there should be 'obedience ... in a single direction' that leads to 'unfreedom of the spirit.'"[6] Holding the view that the notion of "right and wrong" is nonsensical,[7] Nietzsche attacked truth and morality as a "mendacious fabrication," declaring that truth is "a sum of human relations, which have been enhanced, transposed, and embellished poetically

---

[2] Max Horkheimer and Theodor W. Adorno, *Dialectic of Enlightenment*, tr. John Cumming (New York: Continuum Press, 1999), pp. 6-9.

[3] Jean-François Lyotard, *The Inhuman: Reflections on Time*, tr. Geoffrey Bennington and Rachel Bowlby (Stanford, CA: Stanford University Press, 1991), pp. 65-69.

[4] Thomas Howe, *Objectivity in Biblical Interpretation* (Longwood, FL: Advantage Books, 2004), p. 465. The law of non-contradiction maintains that it is not possible for something to be both true and not true at the same time and in the same context. The law of contradiction posits the idea that two contradictory statements cannot both be true. Because postmodernism is self-contradictory, it violates both principles.

[5] Huston Smith, *Beyond the Post-Modern Mind: The Place of Meaning in a Global Civilization* (Wheaton, IL: Quest Books, 1989), p. 10.

[6] Friedrich Nietzsche, *Beyond Good and Evil: Prelude to a Philosophy of the Future*, tr. Walter Kaufmann (New York: Random House, 1966), p. 101.

[7] Friedrich Nietzsche, "The Genealogy of Morals: An Attack," in *The Birth of Tragedy and The Genealogy of Morals*, tr. F. Golffing (New York: Doubleday, 1956), p. 208.

and rhetorically, and which after long use seem firm, canonical, and obligatory."[8] Calling morality a "dying tree" that cannot possibly be saved, Nietzsche called for a "free spirit," liberated from the constraints of the external moral law. As a result of this philosophy, moral values for Nietzsche were simply a matter of taste, "created rather than discovered."[9] Ultimately, as Isaac Rottenberg observed, this "reasoning" came to be manifest in *"Blut und Boden"*[10] that focused on "the superhumanity of the German soul *(Übermensch)* and the sacredness of the Fatherland soil"—the Nazi version of nature worship and neo-paganism that prompted the "wild forces of the pagan heart" to burst forth and to permit what Elie Wiesel called the "Kingdom of Night" to take over, producing the Holocaust.[11] The result is history, but even that history is meaningless to the neo-pagan, postmodern heart!

Indeed, postmodernity decries history itself, maintaining, in the words of Nietzsche, that "there are no facts, only interpretations."[12] Leszek Kolakowski, however, argued that Nietzsche's idea has "a dangerous meaning," for it "abolishes the idea of human responsibility and moral judgments" because it "considers any myth, legend, or fable just as valid, in terms of knowledge, as any fact that we have verified as such according to our standards of historical inquiry."[13] In the Nietzschean postmodern view, "there are no valid rules for establishing truth; consequently, there is no such thing as truth."[14] Kolakowski is perfectly right in concluding that "there is no need to elaborate on the disastrous cultural effects"[15] of such theories.

For those who are subscribers to the postmodern concept of relativity, the idea of absolutes that are established on historically revealed and demonstrated truth is untenable and, indeed, anathema. Anyone who would dare to suggest that lessons for successful living in the present world can be found in the metanarrative of Scripture is at best

---

[8] Friedrich Nietzsche, "On Truth and Lie in an Extra-Moral Sense," in *The Portable Nietzsche,* ed. and tr. Walter Kaufmann (New York: Penguin Books, 1954), pp. 46-47.

[9] John T. Wilcox, *Truth and Value in Nietzsche: A Study of His Metaethics and Epistemology* (Ann Arbor, MI: University of Michigan Press, 1974), p. 11.

[10] *Blut und Boden* means "Blood and soil [land]."

[11] Isaac C. Rottenberg, *Judaism, Christianity, Paganism: A Judeo-Christian Worldview and Its Cultural Implications* (Atlanta: Hebraic Heritage Press, 2007), pp. 34-35. For Wiesel's comments see Elie Wiesel, *Night,* tr. François Mauriac (New York: Penguin Books, 1981), p. 23.

[12] Friedrich Nietzsche, *Notebooks* (Summer, 1886-Fall, 1887).

[13] Leszek Kolakowski, speech given on November 5, 2003, upon being awarded the first Kluge Prize for lifetime achievement in the Humanities and Social Sciences. See http://www.loc.gov/loc/kluge/news/kolakowski.html.

[14] Kolakowski, speech.

[15] Kolakowski, speech.

naïve and foolish and at worst fascist. Today's Golden Rule says, "Do unto others before they do unto you," or "The one who has the gold makes the rules." Hedonism is more and more the order of the day. As Ernest Hemmingway said, "What is moral is what you feel good after, and what is immoral is what you feel bad after."[16] Catholic Sister Joanne Gallagher says, "God is where my deep center is."[17] This is all part of what Rottenberg described as a "heavy and linguistic fog emanating from various New Age circles" which is welcomed by many Christians and Jews who have become "tired of struggling with the idea of authoritative truth revealed to humanity by a transcendent Deity."[18] More and more such people are happy to be told that "God is to be found in the inner depth of human existence . . . a notion that is part and parcel of the pagan impulse."[19]

As Luke Timothy Johnson has noted, "For our present age, in which the 'wisdom of the world' is expressed in individualism, narcissism, preoccupation with private rights, and competition, the 'wisdom of the cross' is the most profoundly countercultural message of all."[20] Gary Macy agrees, arguing that in much of the church today, a kind of "ecclesial Darwinism" is operative "in which the present is seen as an advancement over the past inasmuch as the present is better able to judge what from the past must be normative." This evolutionary concept of an ever-improving faith, he affirms, "results in the viewpoint that what counts is the present, since the past depends on the present for its authorization and authentication."[21] This idea is untenable, however, because it makes the present existential moment the standard for judging the truth or the right application of Holy Scripture. As Gustavo Gutiérrez has correctly observed, "The bourgeois unbeliever, atheist, and skeptic have become the principal interpreters of modern history,"[22] and the ideas of postmodernity have so infiltrated the church that Christian interpreters make parallel arguments in con-

---

[16] Ernest Hemmingway, quoted in Alexander Lowen, *Love and Orgasm* (New York: Macmillan Publishing Company, 1975), pp. 317-318.

[17] Joanne Gallagher, quoted in Jack Miles, "Faith Is an Option; Religion Makes a Comeback. (Belief to Follow.)" in the *New York Times Magazine,* December 7, 1997.

[18] Rottenberg, p. 32.

[19] Rottenberg, p. 32.

[20] Luke Timothy Johnson, *The Real Jesus: The Misguided Quest for the Historical Jesus and the Truth of the Traditional Gospels* (San Francisco: HarperSanFrancisco, 1996), p. 166.

[21] Gary Macy, "The Ordination of Women in the Early Middle Ages," *Journal of Theological Studies* 61:3 (2000), p. 481.

[22] Gustavo Gutiérrez, *The Power of the Poor in History: Selected Writings*, tr. Robert R. Barr (Maryknoll, NY: Orbis Books, 1983), p. 178.

tradistinction to revealed truth. If the present is the only important thing in current theological trends, how much more is the present the driving force in secular life? And so it is.

Perhaps the only characteristic of the classical world that has been tenaciously maintained in the current world is its narcissism. The focus of today is on the almighty "I." What is best for me? How can I best achieve self-actualization? If it feels good, do it. Madison Avenue advertising reverberates with narcissism: "Have it your way."[23] "Go for the gusto!"[24] "The question is, when you turn your car on, does it return the favor?"[25] Popular music echoes the same theme: "I did it my way!"[26] "It can't be wrong if it feels so right!"[27] All of this narcissistic hedonism eventuates in a Shirley MacLaine standing by the ocean and screaming: "I am God!"[28] Or it results in a Cybill Shepherd boastfully announcing, "I'm a Christian Pagan Buddhist Goddess worshipper, but I'm also a feminist," and claiming, "I really think that probably God is a woman, [and] that helped me to break through that celestial glass ceiling."[29]

In this world, everything revolves around the existential moment, the quest for pleasure that fulfills the apostolic prediction about "dangerous times" when people would be utterly narcissistic,[30] avaricious,[31] boasters, haughty,[32] blasphemers, disobedient to parents,[33] ungrateful, impious, inhuman, implacable, malicious slanderers, profligate, brutal, haters of good, traitors, reckless, hedonistic,[34] more than lovers of God.[35] The apostle accurately predicted that even with all of these vile traits the generation of which he spoke would still "retain the outer form of religion" but that they would "deny its power."[36] He also

---

[23] Advertising slogan for Burger King.

[24] Advertising slogan for Schlitz Brewing Company.

[25] Advertising slogan for Cadillac division of General Motors.

[26] From the Paul Anka song based on a 1967 French pop song, later popularized in 1969 by Frank Sinatra.

[27] From the Joe Brooks ballad popularized in the 1970s by Debby Boone.

[28] Shirley MacLaine, quoted in LaGard Smith, *Crystal Lies* (Ann Arbor, MI: Servant Publications, 1998), pp. 16-17. MacLaine's statements in her book, *Out on a Limb* (New York: Bantam Books, 1983) were dramatized in a television adaptation in which she faced the Pacific Ocean and shouted, "I am God!"

[29] Cybill Shepherd, quoted in Hollie McKay, "Cybill Shepherd Blames the Mormons and Catholics for Passing of Proposition 8," FoxNews, May 11, 2009.

[30] *Phílautos*, literally "self-lovers."

[31] *Philárguros*, literally "money lovers."

[32] *Huperephanos*, literally "showing above" or "treating others with contempt."

[33] *Apeitheis*, literally "inveterately disobedient."

[34] *Philédonos*, literally "lovers of pleasure."

[35] 2 Timothy 3:2-4, NASB.

[36] 2 Timothy 3:4-5, COMPLETE JEWISH BIBLE.

concluded that Christians should "keep away from people like that."[37] Could anyone two millennia ago have more accurately predicted the hubris of existential narcissism that dominates the present era?

When the entire focus of life is in the arrogance of the present, there is no concern to learn from the past. As a matter of fact, the past serves only to be rewritten by revisionist "historians" in order to make it conform with the present or with one's grand design for the future. Learning from the past is only carried out in the context of learning what not to do. The ancients were savages at best. Thankfully, profound improvement has been made on the path of evolution. What good, then, could possibly be learned for today's sophisticated society by observing the past, particularly the biblical past? Humanity needs only to trust its current, momentary perceptions of reality—and using the plural word *perceptions* is precisely correct, for there are as many perceptions as there are people, and everyone is right!

WITNESSING THE PAST

Trying to navigate in the present without reference to the past is much like trying to pilot an airplane in a fogbank without any instruments. Sure, an arrogant, self-confident, narcissistic pilot thinks that he can trust his perceptions and have total confidence in his feelings. After all, he *knows* what he is doing! The awful truth, however, is that what one perceives can be completely different from reality: in such circumstances, up can be down, and down can be up. Human sensory perception will very often confirm the opposite of the truth. The inner ear that is designed to provide equilibrium in normal earth-bound gravitational existence just cannot be trusted in the very different environment found miles above the earth. Sometimes, even when a pilot has instruments, perceptions dictated by the inner ear can drown out logical interpretations of those instruments. The result is the downward and unalterable death spiral which has left countless know-it-all pilots horrified in disbelief as they see the earth rushing upward for a head-on, terminal-velocity crash. The lesson here is twofold: 1) if one has no instruments, he should not attempt to navigate in uncertain circumstances, and 2) if one does have instruments, he must trust instruments over feelings.

Humanity is not traveling on a clear day of perfect insight. At best, life is confusing, emotions are unstable, and feelings are untrust-

[37] 2 Timothy 3:4-5.

worthy. This is all the more true when one lives in an era such as this when the question is "How do you feel . . . ?" rather than "What do you think . . . ?" or "What do you know . . . ?" Following feelings in a quest for the existential moment is less trustworthy than odds in a gambling casino. The earth is hurtling through space in a fogbank. It's not quite day, and it's not quite night. Perception, therefore, cannot be trusted, and feelings cannot be relied upon. Humanity needs points of reference, established facts on which present and future actions can be predicated. As American revolutionary patriot Patrick Henry affirmed, "I have but one lamp by which my feet are guided; and that is the lamp of experience. I know no way of judging the future but by the past."[38]

This is why both the God of revelation and the revelation of God are essential to humans. Without God and divine revelation, as Rottenberg observed, "One may find divine power in the spirits that inhabit the universe . . . one may believe in a nameless numinous power, a nebulous *mysterium tremendum* . . . or . . . find God in one's own ego as part of the divine 'All.'" The God of Scripture, however, "does not invite us to . . . philosophize about divine being, but rather to recognize God as *being there*, present as the Holy One in our midst, involved in historical existence."[39] Jürgen Moltmann wisely observed that "the more the covenant is taken seriously as the revelation of God, the more profoundly one can understand the historicity of God and the history in God."[40]

Finding points of reference from the past in order to navigate through the present and into the future is increasingly difficult in the present age, for the arrogance of the present does not permit reference to the past—or hope for the future, for that matter. The fixation on present existentialist "feelings" in which everything is relative and nothing is absolute and in which the past, especially the biblical past, cannot be trusted is diametrically opposed to the Hebraic connection between past and future. As a matter of fact, the Hebrew word עוֹלָם (*olam*), which is frequently translated "forever," literally means "in the far distance" and can refer to the distant past as well as to the distant future. Since the Hebrew Scriptures use the same word to refer to the

---

[38] Patrick Henry, Speech at the Virginia Convention, March 1775.
[39] Rottenberg, p. 160.
[40] Jürgen Moltmann, *The Crucified God,* tr. R. A. Wilson and John Bowden (New York: Harper & Row, 1974), p. 271.

past and the future, there must be a connection between the future (as well as the present) and the past. In Hebrew thought, both time and space are always oriented toward the east, "where God is."[41] The Hebrew word קֶדֶם (*kedem*) means both "east" and "the past." While most cultures occupied their time with trying to discern the future, the Hebraic culture was content to observe the past for lessons about how to live in the present while trusting the future to the God who "will be there."[42] In the Hebrew mindset, the past is in front of one, while the future is behind one.[43] One can only observe the past as one moves through the present into the future. Indeed, without the past, there is no future. This understanding is confirmed by Solomon's dictum, "There is nothing new under the sun,"[44] which was based on his observation that "whatever is has already been, and what will be has been done before; for God will seek to do again what has occurred in the past."[45]

MORE THAN MERE PERCEPTION

In observing the present, what is needed is not mere perception but apperception, a term coined by Gottfried Liebnitz[46] to describe the process whereby the mind transforms sensory perceptions into conscious knowledge by connecting them with known or established truth. Johann Herbart, the founder of scientific pedagogy, asserted that apperception is the basis of all learning activity.[47] To find answers for today and for the future, it is necessary to look back to the past. Perception allows for observation of what the senses indicate in the present, and it allows for looking into what is seen and even for seeing beyond what is seen. Perception, however, does not provide understanding or wisdom, for perception does not bring with it context. As a matter of fact, perception can, and often does, lead to deception.

---

[41] The origin of the word *oriented* is from this concept. In ancient Near-Eastern thought (or on an ancient map of the Near-East), east is up (where the sun comes up), south is to the right, north is to the left, and west is down (where the sun goes down). Hence, the word for south תֵּימָן (*teyman*) is from the word יָמָן (*yaman*) which means "to the right." In Jewish tradition, the Messiah comes from the east.

[42] "I will be there" is one of the possible translations of *"ehyeh asher ehyeh,"* though it is usually rendered in most translations of Exodus 3:14 as "I AM THAT I AM" or "I AM WHO I AM."

[43] The image is that of a person in a rowboat, facing the known past and rowing into the unknown future.

[44] Ecclesiastes 1:9.

[45] Ecclesiastes 3:15, NET.

[46] See Karl Lange, *Apperception* (Boston: D. C. Heath & Co., 1903).

[47] See George Frederick Stout, *Analytic Psychology* (New York: Macmillan & Co., 1896).

It can also lead to self-deception, which is the most insidious form of decption. What is perceived must be connected with what is known to be real and true from the past in order to place it in a context that allows the perception to be interpreted rightly. One must go back in order to go forward. One must look back to see where one came from in order to know where one is in order to chart a course that will take one to the future that one desires.

What is perceived must be compared with the norms of what is known to be absolute truth. There is no other source except the written Word of God, which is alive and powerful[48] because it is God-breathed and is, therefore, profitable for making believers complete and equipping them to every good work.[49] In the case of Christians, the answers to troubling questions can be found in the most remote past, in the venerable Hebraic heritage of the Christian faith.

There is something terribly wrong about reacting to perceptions obtained by observing today's world. Without apperception for bringing what is perceived into a context of truth, reaction can be an exercise in futility. Like the apostles of Jesus, everyone must value perceptions and observations that are of profound importance; however, there is something that is more certain and dependable than all of human experience or existential moments, and that is God's Word. "We have a more sure word of prophecy,"[50] Peter declared as he recounted his own personal encounters with the living Jesus. As Walter Kaiser has observed, "the way out of the relativist or perspectivalist conundrum is to identify the presence of those aspects of thought that are self-evident first principles of thought that transcend every perspective, and act the same way for all people, all times, and all cultures."[51]

A key passage in the song that Moses sang in the presence of all of Israel as he neared the conclusion of his life featured these words: "Remember the days of old; consider the generations long past. Ask your father and he will tell you, your elders, and they will explain to you."[52] Jeremiah later encouraged Israel to "ask for the ancient paths, where the good way is, and walk in it; and you will find rest for your

---

[48] Hebrews 4:12.
[49] 2 Timothy 3:16.
[50] 2 Peter 1:19.
[51] Walter C. Kaiser, Jr., "Correcting Caricatures: The Biblical Teaching on Women," *Priscilla Papers*, 19:2, Spring 2005, p. 5. Also Thomas Howe, *Objectivity in Biblical Interpretation* (Longwood, FL: Advantage Books, 2004), p. 463.
[52] Deuteronomy 32:7, NIV.

souls."[53] Remembering God's majestic works in salvation history is vital to the experience of every believer, whether Jewish or Christian. It is central to faith and to human destiny to have clear self-identity and to have some idea where one is going; therefore, it is vital to know the past and what has brought humanity to its present state. Jesus underscored the truth of this matter when he observed, "Therefore every teacher of the Torah who has been instructed about the kingdom of heaven is like the owner of a house who brings out of his storeroom new treasures as well as old."[54] It is the connection with God's past that gives humans perspective for the present and points the way to the future. It is for this reason that one-tenth of the Decalogue is given to instructions that the human family "remember."[55]

The wise learn from history; fools repeat it. This is why Bildad the Shuhite offered this advice to Job: "Please inquire of past generations, and consider the things searched out by their fathers. . . . Will they not teach you and tell you, and bring forth words from their minds?"[56] In good times and in bad, success is determined first by whether or not one remembers God and seeks his wisdom and then by whether or not one inquires of the past to discover the principles of success that can be applied to the present circumstances to ensure success in the future. Analyzing the present with no frame of reference in God or the past is only a stab in the dark and an invitation to total disaster. As George Santayana observed in the oft-misquoted aphorism, "Those who cannot remember the past are condemned to repeat it."[57] And, indeed, history does repeat itself in a never-ending cycle of action and reaction because the principles that govern human actions never change, and people keep making the same mistakes.[58] The importance, therefore, of searching history in order to arrive at apperceptive understanding for the present is readily apparent. In the words of Leszek Kolakowski, "We must absorb history as our own, with all its horrors and monstrosities, as well as its beauty and splendor, its cruelties and persecutions as well as all the magnificent works of the human mind

---

[53] Jeremiah 6:16.
[54] Matthew 13:52, author's translation.
[55] Exodus 20:8.
[56] Job 8:8, 10, 11, 13, NASB.
[57] George Santayana, "Reason in Common Sense," in *Life of Reason* (New York: Charles Scribner's Sons, 1905), p. 284.
[58] One need only observe the rise and fall of empires around the world and throughout history to confirm the fact that humans have continued unrelentingly to make the same mistakes with the same results.

and hand; we must do this if we are to know our proper place in the universe, to know who we are and how we should act."[59]

FROM REACTIVE TO PROACTIVE

When perception is placed in perspective by apperception, a context is established for moving from the reactive to the proactive. Guided by the wisdom of rock-solid truth principles, observations can be contextualized and proactive moves can be made to go from where one is to where one knows he should be. And, such action can be taken with full confidence when proaction is founded on the infallible precepts of the words that God spoke through the prophets and sages of Israel and through Jesus and his disciples.

Proactive men and women have the capacity for transforming the church and the world by restoring and reforming. Restoring reconnects the church's disconnect from the past, renewing the foundations of the Christian faith. Reforming assumes the monumental task of keeping everything that is good while pruning away what has sapped the vitality of the community of faith. The dictum of the Reformers formulated it well: *Ecclesia reformata et semper reformanda est* ("the church is reformed and always reforming"). Proactive reformation works from the proposition that much, if not most, is good and that only what is diseased, counterproductive, or parasitic must be removed. In this way, the whole is simply re-formed. Reactive thinking, on the other hand, produces the inevitable "throwing-the-baby-out-with-the-bathwater" syndrome that subsequently leaves individuals and communities with a profound disconnect and sense of inexplicable loss. Proactive believers refuse to wallow in the status quo, which only reacts to the next perceived evil. They plan and act, rather than wait and react. The proactive "take the bull by the horns," foresee the problems, and take action to remedy the situation.

Nothing could be more obvious than the need to address the deplorable condition of women in the world—and in the church, for that matter. How can a real difference be made in this generation and in the next so that the freedom that God instituted and Christ reinforced can be extended to the whole human race, not just to half of it? This is clearly the case in the quest to answer the question *Who is woman?* Apperception and proaction will take the seeker back to the

[59] Kolakowski, speech.

archetypes, back to the Owner's Manual, the Sacred Scriptures them-selves. They will escort the inquirers back to the beginning where they will discover answers for today's questions, a solid foundation for re-alizing objective meaning and "deciding between various truth claims and even between differing perspectives and different worldviews."[60] As Evdokimov has noted, "Without a return to the beginning, the human being can never be grasped; there will always remain a residue that is irreducible to history and pure phenomenology."[61] True bibli-cal anthropology "has its origin in paradise," and from that origin—and only in the context of that origin—"flows into the fullness of the *plêrôma* of the Kingdom, into the mystery of the final *apocatastasis*, the recapitulation of all things in heaven and earth in Christ."[62] With-out a clear and accurate perception of the past, understanding proper human relations is utterly impossible in the present, and much more so in the future. The very foundation of a right anthropology can be found in the account of the most ancient event of human history, that of creation itself.

As Winston Churchill aptly said, "The further backward you can look, the further forward you can see." And there, concealed in the creation narratives of the Bible's first book are clear answers to the ontology of the human creation and to the roles and relationships of male and female, for there are recorded these foundational words:

וַיִּבְרָא אֱלֹהִים אֶת־הָאָדָם בְּצַלְמוֹ בְּצֶלֶם אֱלֹהִים בָּרָא אֹתוֹ זָכָר וּנְקֵבָה בָּרָא אֹתָם

("So God created humanity in his own image, in the image of
God created he him: male and female created he them.")[63]

These twelve simple Hebrew words contain a profound wealth of God-given information about the creation of humanity, a virtual gold mine of understanding that provides answers to the continuing questions of woman's identity, women in God's image, and God's design for women.

---

[60] Kaiser, p. 465.
[61] Paul Evdokimov, *Woman and the Salvation of the World*, tr. Anthony P. Gythiel (Crestwood, NY: St. Vladimir's Seminary Press, 1994), p. 16.
[62] Evdokimov, p. 38.
[63] Genesis 1:27.

SPRINGBOARD FOR DISCUSSION

1. Discuss the impact of postmodernism, situational ethics, and lack of absolutes on society in general and on the church in particular. How have these viewpoints affected you and your family?

2. Consider the impact of narcissism upon the ancient Greek world. Analyze narcissism in the present world. Since increasing love of self is becoming the distinguishing mark of Western societies today, how can God's people resist the temptation to live only for self? What does Scripture say about responsibility before God to sacrifice your own personal interests for the well being of your family, your community, and your church?

3. Evaluate ways in which feelings and assumption can cause significant trouble in your life. What is the difference between what you *think* and what you *feel*? Consider the importance of rightly interpreting your feelings in the light of what Scripture says.

4. Evaluate the importance of knowing about the past. How can the patriarchs and matriarchs of biblical faith provide models that can make your life successful and your relationships with family, community, and church happy and rewarding? What lessons have you learned from the Bible and its people? How important is it that you to fine-tune your feelings and your reactions to the established laws and principles in the Scriptures?

5. Consider the difference between reactive and proactive approaches to problems. In what ways can mere reaction to perceived evils be counterproductive and wrong? Discuss the importance of being proactive rather than reactive. What kind of proactive measures can you take to the problems that you perceive in male/female relationships in society, in the workplace, in home, and in church?

6. What answers for today's question about "Who is woman?" can be found in the pages of Holy Scripture in records of events that are as much as 6,000 years old? Are answers to your questions yet to be discovered in the future, or are they in the past, in Scripture itself? Consider how you can find answers to life's issues in the Bible. What lessons have you learned from the Bible and its people?

CHAPTER 3

RECOVERING GOD'S SELF-IMAGE

In order to ascertain God's purposes for women, it is essential to understand the implications of the biblical declaration that God created humanity—male and female—in his own image and likeness. It is impossible, however, to comprehend what is meant by the "image of God" unless fundamental understanding about God's being and nature is first established (to the degree that it is possible for humans to "understand" God). Misconceptions about God will inevitably result in flawed understanding of the "image of God" and in perverted perspectives on humans. In order to have an accurate perception of God, however, an image of God that conforms to the terms in which he chose to reveal himself to humanity must be affirmed; therefore, restoring God's own self-image—not merely one of the millions of human images of deity—is essential. God must be understood in the context of the divine revelation of the Hebrew Scriptures. Anything less is simply futile human speculation.

Restoring the divine image will inevitably involve reimaging the Divine. When one speaks of such reimaging, however, red flags fly, and sirens blare stern warnings of impending disaster. For those who have grown comfortable with their own image of God, the thought of reimaging the Divine is highly intimidating. "You're just trying to create a God in your own image," the alarmed theological and ecclesiological establishment will charge. And, if one were simply trying to accommodate the God of the Bible to the politically correct pluralism and syncretism of postmodern society—as is generally the case when theologians do attempt to reimage God—then the outcries should rightly be loud and unrelenting.

Abraham Joshua Heschel stated very succinctly the difficulties involved in imaging God when he said, "An idea or a theory of God can easily become a substitute for God, impressive to the mind when God as a living reality is absent from the soul."[1] The problem with God-imaging is that the God of Scripture has already been reimaged and reimaged again and again throughout history. As John Calvin noted, "The mind of man is . . . a perpetual factory of idols," that dares "to conceive of God according to its own standard and, being sunk in stupidity and immersed in profound ignorance, imagines a vain and ridiculous phantom instead of God. . . . Therefore the mind begets an idol."[2] Calvin also observed that because the "individual mind [is] a kind of labyrinth," not only has "each nation adopted a variety of fictions," but "almost every man has had his own god." He further expanded this thought by saying, "To the darkness of ignorance have been added presumption and wantonness, and hence there is scarcely an individual to be found without some idol or phantom as a substitute for Deity." He concluded that "like water gushing forth from a large and copious spring, immense crowds of gods have issued from the human mind, every man giving himself full license, and devising some peculiar form of divinity, to meet his own view."[3] Unfortunately, as William Phipps has noted, these "mental idol factories" throughout Christian history "have produced more patriarchal deities than anything else."[4] Nicolas Berdyaev lamented the fact that as "people . . . stamped upon the image of God their own desires," more often than not they fabricated exclusively male images of Deity in which they ascribed to God "traits of inhumanity, cruelty, and love of power" rather than those of "humanity or sympathy."[5]

On the one hand, much of postmodern Christianity's increasing irrelevance results from the fact that it has insisted on maintaining long-antiquated images of God that were developed in post-Nicene

---

[1] Abraham Joshua Heschel, *The Prophets* (New York: Harper and Row, 1962; reprint New York: HarperCollins, 2001), p. 285.

[2] John Calvin, *The Institutes of the Christian Religion,* ed. John McNeill (Philadelphia: Westminster Press, 1960), vol. 1, chap. 11, par. 8.

[3] John Calvin, *The Institutes of the Christian Religion,* vol. 1, chap. 5, sec. 12, quoted in Eliott M. Simon, The Myth of Sisyphus (Cranbury, NJ: Associated University Press, 2007), p. 317.

[4] William E. Phipps, *Genesis and Gender: Biblical Myths of Sexuality and Their Cultural Impact* (New York: Praeger Publishers, 1989), p. 6.

[5] Nicolas Berdyaev, *The Divine and the Human* (London: Geoffrey Bles, 1949), p. 3.

and Medieval Christianity as a means of supporting the imperial church's androcentric, hierarchical bureaucracy. Official Christianity's imaging of God as distant, aloof, irrelational, and vindictive has made it vulnerable to seemingly unanswerable questions of theodicy and to absurd and vicious mischaracterizations of God by atheistic and agnostic scholars. One of the most vituperative of these atheistic diatribes was advanced by Richard Dawkins who boldly denounced the God of the Bible as "arguably the most unpleasant character in all fiction . . . jealous and proud of it, a petty, unjust, unforgiving control freak, a vindictive, blood-thirsty ethnic cleanser, a misogynistic, homophobic, racist, infanticidal, genocidal, filicidal, pestilential, megalomaniacal, sado-masochistic, capriciously malevolent bully."[6] As Dawkins and his adoring audiences revel in such rancorous excoriations, he also arrogantly asserts that belief in a supernatural God is a "pernicious delusion,"[7] and he maintains that "the idea of a personal God is quite alien . . . and seems even naïve."[8] While not as vitriolic as Dawkins, Karen Armstrong points out what she considers to be utter inconsistencies in views on the God of Scripture: "[God] is omnipotent but powerless to control humanity; omniscient but ignorant of human yearning; creative but a destroyer; benevolent but a killer; wise but arbitrary; just but partial and unfair."[9] While most Christians and Jews would never countenance such caricatures of God, the increasing numbers of people drawn to the world of the increasingly secularist, agnostic, and atheistic West not only agree with them but also gleefully enjoy their pronouncements.[10]

On the other hand, significant parts of Christianity have made the mistake of attempting to reimage God in terms of the philosophies of the Enlightenment and of modernity and in more recent times in accord with the New Age philosophies and neo-pagan concepts of postmodernity. The problem with both of these approaches to the study of God and the communication of such ideas to the larger Christian community and the world at large is that neither works. Clinging tenaciously to the Hellenized, Latinized Christianity of the

---

[6] Richard Dawkins, *The God Delusion* (New York: Houghton Mifflin Co., 2006), p. 51.
[7] Dawkins, p. 31.
[8] Dawkins, p. 15.
[9] Karen Armstrong, *In the Beginning: A New Interpretation of Genesis* (New York: Alfred Knopf Publishers, 1996), p. 117.
[10] For example, see Christopher Hitchens, *God Is Not Great: How Religion Poisons Everything* (New York: Hachette Book Group, 2009) and Victor J. Stenger, *God: The Failed Hypothesis: How Science Shows That God Does Not Exist* (New York: Prometheus Books, 2007).

past perpetuates a distorted image that is a sad misrepresentation of the Eternal God of the Hebrews. Compromising with the syncretism of postmodernism's purposeful destruction of everything absolute has produced a willy-nilly God of "love" who gushes cheap grace,[11] luxuriates in sloppy *agape*, has no absolute standards, and, therefore, means essentially nothing. Indeed, this God is no God at all!

Perhaps one of the worst examples of taking the reimaging of the Divine to the absurd occurred in 1994 when the World Council of Churches sponsored a "Decade of Churches in Solidarity" conference. Many of the 2,000 women in attendance hailed this event as "The Second Reformation" because its ceremony featured a "reimaging" event to introduce the new female version of God and to reveal a new road to salvation. First, participants rejected both the incarnation and the atonement of Jesus as "patriarchal constructs." Then, they "blessed, thanked, and praised Sophia [divine wisdom] as a deity." Instead of the elements of communion, they substituted their own "banquet table of Creation," and boldly offered this collect: "Sophia, we celebrate the nourishment of your milk and honey." Finally, these avant-garde Christian women collectively made the following "liturgical" proclamation: "Our Maker, Sophia, we are women in your image, with the hot blood of our wombs we give form to new life . . . with nectar between our thighs we invite a lover . . . with our warm body fluids we remind the world of its pleasures and sensations."[12] This is only one example of Christian feminism's reaction to historical androcentric patriarchy's projection of God in male imagery. Indeed, there are many reactions that are far more radical, including women who have abandoned Christianity altogether in favor of worship of the purported Divine Feminine, the "goddess within."[13]

The most obvious evil that has resulted from historical Christendom's reimaging of the God of Scripture to accommodate its ever-shifting philosophies and worldviews has been its continuing deprecation of women and womanhood. The projection of God as a male autocrat has left generations of women with deficient views of their

---

[11] "Cheap grace" is a term coined by Dietrich Bonhoeffer to describe Christian experience that is devoid of the discipline of discipleship. Dietrich Bonhoeffer, *The Cost of Discipleship*, tr. R. H. Fuller (New York: SCM Press, 1959), pp. 43, 54, 68, 70, 83.

[12] Susan Crye, "Fallout Escalates Over 'Goddess' Sophia Worship," *Christianity Today* (4 April 1994), p. 74.

[13] Sue Monk Kidd, *Dance of the Dissident Daughter* (San Francisco: HarperCollins, 2002), pp. 125-127.

own womanhood and with limited potential for seeing themselves as being theomorphic or as having divine worth in the world. Women, however, have escaped historical educational limitations imposed upon them by male-dominated political and ecclesiastical systems, becoming more and more erudite. Now, historical androcentric imagery for God that women of previous generations were forced to accept has become increasingly irrelevant to many women, leaving them with no choice but to look elsewhere for their models and their faith.

The core of this problem fits the conclusion that Wolfhart Pannenberg reached from his own study of religious history when he observed that most of the religions that have faded from existence became extinct when they were unable to relate their ideas about God to the world within the context of then-current experience.[14] Abraham Joshua Heschel similarly concluded that "religion declined not because it was refuted, but because it became irrelevant, dull, oppressive, insipid." He further maintained that "when the crisis of today is ignored because of the splendor of the past; when faith becomes an heirloom rather than a living fountain; when religion speaks only in the name of authority rather than with the voice of compassion—its message becomes meaningless."[15] When philosophers, theologians, and politicians have changed the biblical image of God into something that does not resemble divine self-disclosure, the God of Christianity has become increasingly remote and irrelevant to the lives of many individuals. As a result, significant numbers have become disillusioned at best, feeling distant and alienated from "God."

RESTORING GOD'S SELF-IMAGE

The question that begs to be asked is this: How can Christianity be made relevant to current experience without perverting the principles and intent of the originators of the faith? First, if there are no theological nonnegotiables, then there is no true faith. Then, on the other hand, if the biblical God and the religions derived from the understanding of that God have become irrelevant in the minds of increasing numbers of people, is the problem entirely with the people,

---

[14] Wolfhart Pannenberg, "Toward a Theology of the History of Religions," in *Basic Questions in Theology: Collected Essays*, tr. George Kehm (Louisville, KY: Westminster John Knox Press, 1983), vol. 2, pp. 65-118.
[15] Abraham Joshua Heschel, *God in Search of Man: A Philosophy of Judaism* (New York: Farrar, Straus and Giroux, 1955), p. 3.

or is it with the image of God? Has the God of the Bible been misrepresented? Is there a clear disconnect between how God imaged himself in revelatory moments to prophets, sages, and apostles in the past and how he has been interpreted in subsequent generations, including in the present?

The problem for most of Christianity is that God has already been reimaged by the nearly twenty centuries of Hellenization and Latinization of the Christian faith. Categories of Greek philosophy have been imposed upon the God of the Hebrew Scriptures, transforming him into something different from the Being whom the Hebrew prophets, sages, and apostles experienced and described. Indeed, the introduction of metaphysical terms into theology was "the imposition of a static Greek way of thinking upon the dynamic semitic [*sic*] worldview."[16]

What is now desperately needed in both theology and anthropology is a re-reimaging of the Divine, a restoration of the biblical understanding of the essence and nature of the God of the Bible. The church must recover the Hebraic foundations of its theology before it can arrive at a biblical anthropology, particularly a biblical understanding of God and women. When a pure, biblical image of God is recovered from the encrusted layers of Hellenization and Latinization that have so obscured him from view, a new level of freedom and blessing will come to all human beings, male and female. Fortunately, as Elizabeth Johnson has observed, "in the circle of life where Christ's way is followed, a new possibility of shalom, of redemptive wholeness, is made experientially available and can be tasted in anticipation, even now, as the struggle of history goes on."[17] As Krister Stendahl opined, true theology is "worrying about what God is worrying about when God gets up in the morning: the mending of creation."[18] Letty Russell reckoned that "the mending of creation begins with the jubilee image of liberation for the oppressed, [and] women are the 'oppressed of the oppressed' in every land."[19] Clearly, God is worried about the plight of his female children and their unmitigated suffering and oppression,

---

[16] Alister E. McGrath, *Christian Theology: An Introduction* (Malden, MA: Wiley-Blackwell Publishing, 1993), p. 210.

[17] Elizabeth A. Johnson, *She Who Is: The Mystery of God in Feminist Theological Discourse* (New York: The Crossroad Publishing Co., 1998), p. 151.

[18] Krister Stendahl, "God Worries About Every Ounce of Creation," *Harvard Divinity Bulletin* 9 (5):5 (June/July 1979).

[19] Letty M. Russell, *Household of Freedom: Authority in Feminist Theology* (Philadelphia: The Westminster Press, 1987), p. 71.

and a jubilee of freedom is on the horizon as God universally issues to the world and to the church the same mandate that he gave to Pharaoh: "Let my people go that they may serve me."[20]

SPRINGBOARD FOR DISCUSSION

1. Compare some of the ways in which God has been imaged in history to the ways God is imaged in today's world. How do they compare with the image of the God of Scripture?

2. Is humanity created in God's image or have human beings created gods in their own image? Discuss some misconceptions about God that you have had in the past. How have they impacted your own life and the lives of those around you?

3. Have you ever envisioned God as a man? If so, why? If not, why not? How has the way some have imaged God in masculine terms impacted the world and the church? What impact, if any, has it made on your life?

4. Do you think that God needs to be visualized or considered in terms that are different from the ways in which he has been viewed in the past? Does God need to be reimaged, or does the original image of God in Scripture need to be restored?

5. Consider the impact of Greek philosophy on the image of God in Christianity. How does the God that is generally worshipped in the church differ from the God of Scripture?

---

[20] Exodus 5:1.

CHAPTER 4

UNDERSTANDING GOD?

It must be admitted—and, indeed, it is specifically stated in Scripture[1]—that God is utterly transcendent, wholly other, and, as such, utterly incomprehensible. In perhaps the Bible's most ancient book, Job was confronted by Zophar's rhetorical question: "Can you fathom the mysteries of God? Can you probe the limits of the Almighty?"[2] The answer to this question will always be a resounding "Never!" God is not even minimally understood by human investigation or by human exercise of the empirical or scientific method. His judgments are "inscrutable"[3] and his ways "unfathomable."[4] The teaching of divine incomprehensibility "is a corollary of . . . divine transcendence,"[5] for "even and especially in revelation God remains the wholly other, blessedly present but conceptually inapprehensible, and so God."[6]

At the same time, however, the author of Hebrews made the reassuring declaration that "in the past God spoke to our forefathers through the prophets at many times and in various ways, but in these last days has spoken to us by his Son."[7] The Holy Scriptures are "the inspired literary precipitate of communities" that worshipped the one true God.[8] The mystery of the divine–human equation is that the

---

[1] 1 Timothy 6:15-16.
[2] Job 11:7.
[3] Romans 11:33, CJB.
[4] Romans 11:33, NASB.
[5] Elizabeth A. Johnson, *She Who Is: The Mystery of God in Feminist Theological Discourse* (New York: The Crossroad Publishing Co., 1998), pp. 104-105.
[6] Johnson, pp. 104-105.
[7] Hebrews 1:1-2, NIV, NASB.
[8] Elizabeth A. Johnson, "The Incomprehensibility of God and the Image of God Male and Female," in *Theological Studies,* 45:3 (1984), p. 443.

unknowable God has chosen to reveal himself. If he had not elected to do so, he would have forever remained unknown and unrevealed. What humans understand about God, therefore, is solely the product of divine self-disclosure arising from God's own initiative. As Paul Ricoeur claims, the naming of God is always dependent upon God's own prior "summons" to propositions of meaning issuing from the Bible.[9] Humans can understand only what God has chosen to reveal and nothing more, and, even then, they only "know in part."[10] Even the single declaration, "God is," remains "an understatement."[11] As Augustine said, "If you have understood, then what you have understood is not God."[12]

The Christian thinkers of the fourth and fifth centuries, who took the fundamental theological and Christological statements in Apostolic Scripture and formulated from them the foundations of the Christian creed, unanimously and consistently confessed that their statements were inadequate to define the essence of God.[13] In the final analysis, all human understanding of the Divine is totally faith-based: "Through faith we understand that the worlds were framed by the word of God."[14] Revelation, therefore, is not merely a "making known of facts about God, but a self-revelation of God."[15] This divine revelation has been accomplished solely by God's determination in "his pre-eternal counsel" to convey to humanity enough information about himself that they could consider the myustery of theology. In Scripture, God utterly and consistently forbade the construction of any image of the Divine, and he resisted those who sought to discover his transcendent nature. He did so, however, "because the initiative of revelation belongs to Him alone" and because he had determined to recapitulate the history of his chosen people in one unique event that would sum up "the whole of history and of the whole nature of the universe."[16] It was for this reason, therefore, that God hid "the depths

---

[9] Paul Ricoeur, quoted in John Wall, *Moral Creativity* (New York: Oxford University Press, 2005), p. 51.
[10] 1 Corinthians 13:9.
[11] Abraham Joshua Heschel, *God in Search of Man* (New York: Harper & Row, 1965), p. 121.
[12] Augustine, *Sermo* 52, 6.16.
[13] Athanasius, Basil, and the Cappadocian fathers, Gregory of Nyssa and Gregory of Nazianzus made this acknowledgement.
[14] Hebrews 11:3, KJV.
[15] Alister E. McGrath, *Christian Theology: An Introduction* (Malden, MA: Wiley-Blackwell Publishing, 1993), p. 209.
[16] Vladimir Lossky, *In the Image and Likeness of God*, ed. John H. Erickson and Thomas E. Bird (Crestwood, NY: St. Vladimir's Seminary Press, 1974), pp. 132-133.

of His Being until the decisive moment, only making Himself known to His elect by His authority."[17]

The finite cannot even begin to investigate and circumscribe the Infinite; however, the Infinite can disclose a block of information (be it ever so infinitesimal) to the finite. God's revelation is, therefore, at the same time both a "revealing and a concealing."[18] Finite creatures can receive authentic knowledge of God; however, that knowledge can be only partial and inadequate,[19] for "no human concept, word, or image, all of which originate in experience of created reality, can circumscribe divine reality, nor can any human construct express with any measure of adequacy the mystery of God who is ineffable."[20] Ultimately, most things about God are, indeed, ineffable, in that they are beyond human language and comprehension.

The essential and ultimate incomprehensibility of God has led many philosophers and theologians to resort to an apophatic theology, in which they have concluded that humans may know only what God is not, because it is impossible for humans to know what God is. Much of this thinking has been advanced by Greek philosophy, by Hinduism, Buddhism, and Islam, and by Jews and Christians influenced by these philosophies. This concept does not, however, conform to the image of the Holy Scriptures themselves, for they deliver an entirely different message. Scripture does confirm that "God is not a human being,"[21] but this in no way implies that God is utterly unknowable.

GOD'S SELF-DISCLOSURE

The good news is that God has chosen to reveal himself. He has done so by three means: his spoken Word (which became the written Word), his incarnate Word (the person of Jesus), and his creation, the things that he has made. As John Sanders has noted, "we have no knowledge of God apart from the way he has created us and revealed himself to us."[22] The spoken Word was first issued at the beginning

---

[17] Lossky, pp. 132-133.

[18] William Hill, *Knowing the Unknown God* (New York: Philosophical Library, 1971), p. 138.

[19] Hill, p. 138.

[20] Johnson, pp. 104-105. See also Abraham Joshua Heschel and Morton M. Leifman, *The Ineffable Name of God—Man: Poems* (New York: The Continuum International Publishing Group Inc., 2005).

[21] Numbers 23:19.

[22] John Ernest Sanders, *The God Who Risks: A Theology of Divine Providence* (Downers Grove, IL: InterVarsity Press, 2007), p. 29.

of creation when "God said. . . ." Subsequently, the spoken Word was conveyed to humans who repeated and recorded that Word, "not by their own will" but as they were "carried along by the Holy Spirit."[23] The ultimate truth about this divine impartation was that what these human mouthpieces expressed was not weighted, clouded, or influenced by their own "personal interpretation."[24] Because the one quality that they all shared was that they were "holy,"[25] they reported God's revelatory expressions just as they received them.

Ultimately—and with finality—God chose to make the fullest possible disclosure of himself in the person of his only-begotten Son, Jesus, who was the Word (*Logos, D'var,* or *Memra*) incarnate. The writer of Hebrews spoke in absolute terms about this personal revelation of God: "God . . . in these last days has spoken to us in his Son . . . who is the radiance of God's glory and the exact representation of his being."[26] The apostle John confirmed the revelatory function of the Son: "No one has seen God at any time; the only begotten God who is in the bosom of the Father, he has made him known."[27] Paul further explained "God . . . has shone in our hearts to give the light of the knowledge of the glory of God in the face of Christ."[28] This is why Jesus did not hesitate to declare, "He who has seen me has seen the Father,"[29] for it was in Jesus, the Word of God made flesh, that the divine nature of God was once and for all disclosed to the greatest degree possible. Finally, "from beginning to end Scripture testifies a condescending approach of God to man. The entire revelation of God becomes concentrated in the Logos, who became 'flesh.' It is as it were *one* humanization, one incarnation of God."[30]

The fact that God also chose to manifest a revelation of himself in his creation was confirmed by Paul, the Jewish rabbi who became the Christian apostle to the nations, when he declared unequivocally that even God's eternal power and deity can be understood "by the things that are made."[31] J. Philip Newell has pointed out a Celtic tradition

---

[23] 2 Peter 1:21.
[24] 2 Peter 1:20, NASB.
[25] 2 Peter 1:21.
[26] Hebrews 1:1, 3.
[27] John 1:18, NASB.
[28] 2 Corinthians 4:6, NASB.
[29] John 14:9.
[30] Herman Bavinck, *The Doctrine of God* (Grand Rapids, MI: Wm. B. Eerdmans Publishing Co., 1951), pp. 85-86.
[31] Romans 1:20.

that expands on this Pauline concept by suggesting that the mystery of God is revealed through two "texts": a "little" book, Holy Scripture, and a "great" book, the Creation.[32] The agent of creation was and is the person of the Word (*Logos, D'var*) of God.[33] The agent of the revelatory Word was and is the person of the Spirit (*Ruach*) of God.[34] These two persons within the Godhead are the agents of divine disclosure who revealed all that humanity can comprehend about the transcendent Father. In this manner the one God opened up the mystery of deity through self-limitation of the unfathomable, condescending love that is the very essence of Deity[35] though even that love can never be fully comprehended by human beings.[36]

Central to the imaging of God is what Karl Barth termed, "event-conceptuality,"[37] which represents the only way in which God can be known. "All we can know of God according to the witness of Scripture are His acts. All we can say of God, all the attributes we can assign to God, relate to these acts of His; not, then, to His essence as such."[38] As Abraham Joshua Heschel wisely observed, "The prophets had no theory or 'idea' of God. What they had was an *understanding*. Their God-understanding was not the result of a theoretical inquiry, of a groping in the midst of alternatives about the being and attributes of God. To the prophets, God was overwhelmingly real and shatteringly present."[39]

The acts of divine self-disclosure contain within themselves the compounding and extension of the mystery of divine incomprehensibility. Consistently from Genesis to Revelation, the Scriptures maintain the constant teaching that God can never be exhaustively known even in his own self-disclosure, for even divine revelation is still enshrouded in divine mystery. Hans von Balthasar has suggested that the act of divine disclosure does not cause God to cease from being transcen-

---

[32] J. Philip Newell, *The Book of Creation* (Norwich, UK: Canterbury Press, 1999), p. 26.

[33] John 1:3; 2 Peter 3:5.

[34] 1 Corinthians 2:11-12; 2 Peter 1:21.

[35] 1 John 4:7-8.

[36] 1 John 4:9-12.

[37] Colin E. Gunton, *Becoming and Being: The Doctrine of God in Charles Hartshorne and Karl Barth* (Oxford: Oxford University Press, 1978), p. 142. Also Eberhard Jüngel, *The Doctrine of the Trinity: God's Being Is in Becoming* (Edinburgh: Scottish Academic Press, 1976), pp. 62f; and Jürgen Moltmann, *The Crucified God: The Cross of Christ as the Foundation and Criticism of Christian Theology* (London: SCM Press, 1974), p. 247.

[38] Karl Barth, *Church Dogmatics I/1: The Word of God* (London: T & T Clark International, 1936), p. 260.

[39] Abraham Joshua Heschel, *The Prophets* (New York: HarperCollins Publishers, 1962), p. 285.

dent and incomprehensible. Instead, it profoundly confirms a "powerful incomprehensibility" by taking the mystery of divine love even beyond incomprehensibility.[40] The lack of complete understanding on the part of the prophets who were the vehicles of divine self-disclosure does not, however, imply that their revelation was somehow defective. The fact remains that God chose to disclose truth about himself—not *all* truth, but truth nonetheless—through the prophets and more fully and finally in Jesus, the "exact representation" of God's being and person.[41]

IMAGES AND DIVINE REVELATION

Sensory perception was created by God himself. Human beings are affected by what they see, what they hear, what they smell, what they touch, what they taste. Faith, therefore, is not some sublime mental exercise or even an attempt to detach oneself from both mind and body in some effort to contact the "god within," as monists do. When people interact with God, therefore, it is not just through subliminal meditation. They see God, they hear God, they taste God, they smell God, they touch God—not literally, but through the things that he has commanded or that they have devised to literalize their interaction with him. God is seen in visible symbols. He is heard in music and the spoken Word. God is tasted in the table fellowship of the Christian meal that is shared among believers in any setting. Humans can smell God in the rich aromas of fragrant incense, pungent anointing oil, and smoldering candles, as well as in the flowers in Spring. They can touch God when they hold his Word in their hands and when they embrace "the least of his brethren."[42]

Paul Tillich has noted that "symbols point beyond themselves to something else, something moreover in which they participate. They open up levels of reality, which otherwise are closed, for us, and concomitantly open up depths of our own being, which otherwise would remain untouched."[43] Symbols, then, make possible insight that would otherwise not be recognized or experienced. Symbol and

---

[40] Hans Urs von Balthasar, "The Unknown God," in *The Von Balthasar Reader*, ed. Meard Kehl and Werner Löser, tr. Robert Daly and Fred Lawrence (New York: Crossroad Publishers, 1982), p. 186.

[41] Hebrews 1:1-3.

[42] Matthew 25:40.

[43] Paul Tillich, *Dynamics of Faith* (New York: Harper & Row, 1957), pp. 41-48. Also quoted in Johnson, p. 46.

meaning, therefore, establish man's world and create emotional safety in that world.[44] This is why Terrence Fretheim argued repeatedly that "metaphors matter," for "the kind of God one believes [in] is not only important, it is crucial."[45] Mental images that "construct a false image of God and have the power of wreaking havoc in people's faith and life"[46] are just as vile as the images of stone that the Scriptures decry. It is through symbols, however, that God chose to manifest himself in divine self-disclosure, for it is through such imagery that the finite human mind is able to comprehend something of the Infinite, that which he has chosen to reveal.

Symbols imply more than their mere appearance indicates. They have the capacity for generating emotional response in those who see them, thereby manifesting much more than their physical forms indicate. Two millennia ago, Ovid observed that a symbol is "a form which means more than what is actually seen, an image of design with a significance ... beyond its manifest content ... an object or pattern which ... causes effect in [people] beyond recognition of what is literally presented in the given form."[47] Paul Ricoeur demonstrated that the dynamism inherent in a true symbol is that it participates in the reality that it signifies.[48] In this context, religious symbols would be of no intrinsic value if they did not generate emotions in the hearts of those who use them.[49] It is this emotional response to the image that gives longevity and enduring significance to the symbol itself. The "perennity of symbols, which survive their various and passing explanations, is conditioned by the perennity of man's condition."[50]

Without doubt, the reality of God's salvation has become substantive and understandable to humanity through the symbolism that God has employed. It was God who chose to use such symbols and images to make it possible for humans to "understand" him. Clearly, "the idea of God to which Christian orthodoxy binds us is itself a practical idea. The stories of exodus, of conversion, of resistance and suffer-

---

[44] Suzanne Langer, *Philosophy in a New Key* (Cambridge, MA: Harvard University Press, 1957), pp. 6-20.
[45] Terrence Fretheim, *The Suffering of God: An Old Testament Perspective* (Philadelphia: Fortress Press, 1984), pp. 1-2.
[46] Fretheim, p. 2.
[47] Ovid, *Heroides*, Epistle XIII, 155.
[48] Paul Ricoeur, *Symbolism of Evil*, tr. Emerson Buchanan (New York: Harper & Row, 1967), pp. 347-355.
[49] R. M. MacIver, "Signs and Symbols," *Journal of Religious Thought*, X (1953), p. 103.
[50] Elias Bickerman, quoted in Paul Friedman, "On the Universality of Symbols," *Religions in Antiquity*, ed. Jacob Neusner (Leiden: E. J. Brill, 1968), p. 610.

ing belong to its doctrinal expression."[51] Consequently, "the pure idea of God is, in reality, an abbreviation, a shorthand for stories without which there is no Christian truth in this idea of God."[52] This is why the Hebrew Scriptures—including the apostolic writings that also were either penned by Jewish authors or written under the auspices of Jewish spiritual leaders—have continued to transform the lives of people over passing millennia. These sacred writings have done so because they have succeeded in representing the transcendent God in immanent expressions that humans can understand and in which they can participate. It was the wisdom of God to reveal himself in relational terms that humans can comprehend.

Ricoeur detailed diverse semantic genres of discourse through which the Israelite community interpreted its experience of God: "The naming of God, in the originary expressions of faith, is not simple but multiple . . . complex forms of discourse as diverse as narratives, prophecies, laws, proverbs, prayers, hymns, liturgical formulas, and wisdom writings."[53] A profusion of images for God and his interaction with his people is manifest within the matrix of these forms, including models of the family: "father, mother, spouse, brother," while also manifesting the models of "the monarch, the judge . . . the rabbi, the servant."[54] Still other images of God in Scripture are those of friend, shepherd, farmer, potter, nurse, midwife, laundress, merchant, physician, teacher, homemaker, baker, builder, general, counselor.[55] While scriptural imagery is weighted toward male images, profoundly significant female images are also manifest in the Bible, even though seminaries and pulpits have tended to ignore them.

Images and visualizations help humans understand things about God in his relationship with them. What they understand from these images, however, is not necessarily the reflection of a dimension of God. Hence, "speech about God in female metaphors does not mean that God has a feminine dimension . . . nor does the use of male metaphors mean that God has a masculine dimension" any more than metaphors of God as a rock give God a mineral dimension or being named

---

[51] Johannes B. Metz, "Theology Today: New Crises and New Visions," *Catholic Theological Society of America Proceedings* 40 (1985), p. 7.

[52] Metz, p. 7.

[53] Paul Ricoeur, "Naming God," in *Figuring the Sacred: Religion, Narrative, and Imagination*, tr. David Pellauer (Minneapolis: Fortress Press, 1995), p. 26. Also in *Union Seminary Quarterly Review* 34 (1978-1979), p. 222.

[54] Ricoeur, "Naming God," Union, p. 233.

[55] Ricoeur, "Naming God," Union, p. 233.

as a lion gives God an animal dimension.[56] The importance of images is their ability to convey meaning about God to human beings even when they clearly do not define or characterize God by their imagery.

The predominant way in which Scripture relates God to humanity is by employing images and symbols, particularly anthropomorphisms that apply human characteristics and features to God[57] and theriomorphisms that attribute animal qualities to him.[58] These images help humans understand what God has chosen to reveal about himself. While prominent Jewish and Christian theologians[59] have followed the thinking of Xenophanes, who in the sixth century B.C. was perhaps the first to rail against all anthropomorphic imaging of deity,[60] Herman Bavinck has argued with good reason that "Scripture does not merely contain a few anthropomorphisms; on the contrary, *all* Scripture is anthropomorphic." He demonstrated that "whereas God's revelation in nature and Scripture is definitely directed to man, God uses language to reveal himself and manifests himself in human forms."[61] Humans have experienced reality in God because God has revealed himself in images that they can understand. "God disclosed his truths in language taken from the life experiences of the Hebrews and the early Christians to describe for them that which far transcended all that they ever knew."[62]

As Bavinck explained, "if God were to speak to us in divine language, no one would be able to understand him; but ever since creation, he, in condescending grace, speaks to us and manifests himself to us in human fashion."[63] God's self-revelation, then, does much more than merely convey ideas about himself. It is "a presence as much as a content," and "knowing God is not simply a collection of data about God, but a personal relationship" with the Divine.[64] It is no wonder, then, that "from beginning to end Scripture testifies a condescending

[56] Johnson, p. 54.
[57] See Exodus 9:3; Genesis 6:8.
[58] See Hosea 5:14 and Amos 1:2.
[59] See Gordon Kaufman, *In the Face of Mystery: A Constructive Theology* (Cambridge, MA: Harvard University Press, 1993), and John Hick, *An Interpretation of Religion: Human Responses to the Transcendent* (New Haven, CT: Yale University Press, 1989), cited in Sanders, p. 27. (See n. 18, p. 294).
[60] Xenophanes, quoted in W. T. Jones, *A History of Western Philosophy: The Classical Mind* (New York: Harcourt, Brace, and Jovanovich, 1970), p. 19.
[61] Herman Bavinck, *The Doctrine of God*, tr. William Hendriksen (Grand Rapids, MI: Wm. B. Eerdmans, 1951), pp. 85-86.
[62] A. Berkeley Mickelsen, *Interpreting the Bible* (Grand Rapids, MI: Wm. B. Eerdmans Publishing Co., 1963), pp. 307-308.
[63] Bavinck, pp. 85-86.
[64] McGrath, p. 209.

approach of God to man."[65] At the end of the process "the mystery of the living God is evoked while the human thinker ends up, intellectually and existentially, in religious awe and adoration."[66]

While it is "constitutive of the human mind to employ anthropomorphic analogy" when considering God's relationship with humanity,[67] it must be understood that biblical use of such imagery is based not in regarding God anthropomorphically as bearing the image of humans, but in recognizing humanity as being theomorphic, bearing the image of God.[68] This distinction grounds biblical anthropomorphisms in God's declaration that humans are theomorphic: God is not created in man's image; humans are created in God's image. There is correspondence, therefore, between God and humans; however, it is generated from the divine and not from the human perspective. Men cannot rightfully impose anthropomorphisms on God, forcing God to conform to human imagery; however, God can—and does—reveal his own image and likeness in humanity.

An integral part of the divine design in creating humanity was so that human beings, male and female, would image God. Humankind was to be a theomorphic manifestation of otherwise incomprehensible understanding about God. They became the most dynamic of all of God's self-revelational efforts, for they revealed the very image and likeness of the Divine. Imagery and symbols, then, are alive and powerful, for through them God and his Word are materialized, taken from the abstraction of faith and manifest in the reality of good works that glorify the Father in heaven.[69] Just as love is not love unless it proceeds from abstraction to action, so faith is not faith until its seed is brought to full flower in good works.[70] The invisible things of God are understood by a wide range of symbols but most completely in the reality of human existence in which both female and male are essential for the "image and likeness" of God to be fully manifest.[71] Both female and male equally and fully image God in the material creation. The absence of either renders God's image incomplete, for

---

[65] Bavinck, p. 86.
[66] Elizabeth Johnson, quoted in Catherine Vincle, *Celebrating Divine Mystery: A Primer in Liturgical Theology* (Collegeville, MN: Liturgical Press, 2009), p. 89.
[67] Gerald O'Collins in *The Incarnation: An Interdisciplinary Symposium on the Incarnation of the Son of God,* Gerald O'Collins ed. (Oxford: Oxford University Press, 2002), p. 41.
[68] Gerhard von Rad, *Old Testament Theology* (Edinburgh: Oliver & Boyd, 1962), p. 145.
[69] Matthew 5:16.
[70] James 2:20-26.
[71] Romans 1:20.

God clearly said, "Let us make humanity in our image, according to our likeness," and when he proceeded to accomplish his intention, he created them in his image, "male and female."

SPRINGBOARD FOR DISCUSSION

1. Discuss divine transcendence and the idea of the incomprehensibility of God. Is it really possible to understand anything about God? Can humans only speculate about God, or are there things that we can know for sure?

2. How can God be revealed through creation itself? Is there anything that we can understand about God by analyzing what God has created? On what basis is this possible? Can we find God through science?

3. Consider the idea that God has chosen to make himself known through the act of self-disclosure that Scripture calls revelation. How, and to what degree, does God still remain shrouded in mystery even in the very act of self-disclosure through revelation? How can God be incomprehensible and be understood at the same time?

4. Did the prophets and apostles of Scripture really experience God or did they merely philosophize about God and invent stories to illustrate their thinking?

5. Discuss the images that God has given and those that men have created in order to relate to God. Why are images important? How do images impact your life? How do metaphors help you relate to God?

6. Analyze the importance of anthropomorphisms to our understanding of God. Is it idolatrous to think of God in human terms?

7. Discuss the nature of biblical anthropomorphisms as actually being human understanding of theomorphisms. Why would it matter if people envision God in anthropomorphic terms when God made humans in his image specifically to reveal something about himself?

8. Evaluate the statement of Scripture that male and female are both made in God's image and likeness. How does this statement impact your thinking about men and women?

CHAPTER 5

IMAGING GOD AND HUMANITY
THEOLOGY AND ANTHROPOLOGY

Anthropology, the study of humanity, is profoundly affected by theology, the study of God. How one views and values humanity, male and female, is largely determined by one's understanding of the nature and qualities of God. At the same time the converse is also true: how one views Deity is influenced by how one views the world and particularly humanity in the world, for theology is also affected by anthropology. There is, therefore, considerable interplay between theology and anthropology, with both influencing the other in many ways. Moses Jung has rightly observed that more than a few "maladjustments and neuroses in adult life are traceable to faulty training, or lack of training in religion."[1]

This is the thrust of Paul's observations to the Romans about Hellenism, the philosophy, culture, and religion that formed the foundation of ancient Greek society and profoundly influenced the Roman world as well: "Since the creation of the world God's invisible qualities—his eternal power and divine nature—have been clearly seen, being understood from what has been made, so that men are without excuse."[2] The apostle attested that this culture "knew God" but made the mistake of failing to glorify him as God. Though the Greek poets, playwrights, philosophers, and politicians professed themselves

---

[1] Moses Jung, "Religion in the Home," in *Marriage and the Jewish Tradition: Toward a Modern Philosophy of Family Living* (New York: Philosophical Library, 1951), p. 183.
[2] Romans 1:20, NIV.

to be wise, their thinking became "futile."[3] They became "fools" by changing the glory of the incorruptible God into images resembling men and animals, choosing to worship the creature rather than the creator. Because they adopted a worldview rooted in polytheism and humanism, God gave them over to the depravity of narcissism and sexual perversion that became the downfall of both the Greek and the Roman civilizations.[4]

Because these and other ancient societies had improper views about deity, they deprecated womanhood and concluded that only men mattered, and they wrapped their male leaders in increasingly glorified mantles of divinity that led to extreme narcissism, megalomania, and sociopathic behavior. The "honor" of the leaders of Greek society was so important to them that they often risked the very annhilation of their people in order to protect it. Their theology allowed—and even encouraged—them to maintain unacceptable and perverse perspectives on humanity, especially on women. The patrician/plebian class distinctions could be justified and perpetuated because only the aristocracy mattered; the remainder of society existed only for exploitation. Because of perverse philosophical and religious beliefs and practices, women could be routinely used and abused in these societies.

In similar fashion, much, if not most, of the ancient world tolerated or encouraged polygamy. Interestingly enough, polygamy (multiple marriages) has almost never taken the form of polyandry (multiple husbands): it has always been polygyny (multiple wives)! With the unity and sanctity of marriage destroyed, it was openly proclaimed that a woman "was not the partner of man's life, but the instrument of his selfish pleasure; that if made from him at all, she was made not from the region of his heart, but from his feet."[5] Unfortunately, when a woman in the ancient world was not respected as a wife or as a mother, she had no honor at all as a human being because, apart from her reproductive functions, woman was essentially a nonentity.

Emma Thérèse Healy rightly observed that "retrogression goes hand in hand with false religions. Lacking the power to raise man out of the mire, sooner or later the gratification of lust with the resulting debasement of woman becomes the central feature of their pagan

---

[3] Romans 1:22.
[4] Romans 1:24-25.
[5] Emma Thérèse Healy, *Woman According to Saint Bonaventure* (Erie, PA: Villa Maria College, 1956), p. 44.

worship."[6] This is why in ancient Babylon, women were sold in slave markets, and parents considered it a great honor to give their daughters to be temple prostitutes. Indeed, every Babylonian woman was required to prostitute herself at the altars of the principal deities. In the Persian Empire that succeeded Babylon, women were considered at best to be "the maid of man."[7] This unrelenting parade of perversion continued in succeeding empires.

Greek mythology projected all women as descendants of Pandora,[8] who was designed by Zeus, head of the Greek pantheon of gods, as the ultimate punishment for mortal violation of the Olympian fire. Pandora, the "beautiful evil,"[9] produced the "deadly race" of women to live "amongst mortal men to their great trouble"[10] as the "specious curse of man."[11] At the same time, dominant philosophical and political thought considered women to be nothing more than "monstrosities,"[12] "deformed males,"[13] or a result of the corruption of original and perfect hermaphroditism.[14] Just such theological, philosophical, and political concepts as these prompted Arthur Verral to conclude that the Greek attitude toward females was the "radical disease, of which, more than anything else, ancient civilization perished."[15]

One's image of the Divine, therefore, is very important. Unclear or aberrant views of God result in perverse views of humanity and of the world. This is true of virtually all worldviews that are not aligned with Hebraic thought. In each of these, God is imagined by humans and not from the perspective of divine self-disclosure as in the biblical understanding of God. Among the most perverse of these has been the imaging of God as the ultimate expression of absolute power. As Nicolas Berdyaev has observed, "the social categories of dominance

---

[6] Healy, p. 43.
[7] Healy, p. 43.
[8] Hesiod, *The Theogony in Hesiod, the Homeric Hymns and Homerica*, tr. Hugh H. Evelyn-White (Cambridge: Harvard University Press, 1936), pp. 502-620.
[9] Hesiod, p. 14.
[10] Hesiod, p. 14.
[11] Euripides, *Hippolytus*, pp. 616-617.
[12] Aristotle, *Aristotle, Volume XIII: The Generation of Animals*, tr. A. L. Peck (Cambridge: Harvard University Press, 1963), 4.3: 767.b.8-9.
[13] Aristotle, 2.3: 737.a.25-30.
[14] In his *Symposium* 189-190, Plato argued that human beings were hermaphrodites in their original, perfect form and that in order to control the pride and strength of these dual-sexed beings, Zeus split humanity into male and female parts.
[15] Arthur Verral, *Euripides the Rationalist* (New York: Russell & Russell, 1967), quoted in T. R. Glover, *The Conflict of Religions in the Early Roman Empire* (Boston: Beacon Press, 1960), p. 163.

and power have been transferred to God in an "evil sociomorphism." He concluded that God is not "a wielder of power" and that "the worship of God as power is still idolatry."[16] While it is manifestly true from the 39 references to divine power in the Apostolic Scriptures alone that God is an all-powerful God, it is also very clear from Scripture that God's power is something that is wielded sparingly in tender loving care and tempered with profound mercy. Tragically, the most consistent manifestation of power in human history has been abusive domination of other human beings and the very earth itself. The most perpetual example of such perverted application of power has been male dominance over women.

FAULTY DIVINE IMAGING AND HUMAN CONSEQUENCES

If one believes God is merely part of—or the sum total of—nature, such a pantheistic view of God produces a perception that humans are only one among the millions of species of animal life. It also elevates the religion of humanism which teaches a "terrestrial gospel" that makes the earth "our own flesh and blood."[17] In the context of this worldview, anthropology—including the interaction of the sexes—is largely a study of the human genome and its relationship with the rest of the animal kingdom, with the vegetation, and with the inanimate elements of planet earth. Human actions, including interaction between the genders, are governed by chemical reactions and are the products of evolution, heredity, and environment. Since humans are merely another member of the animal kingdom—indeed, evolved from lower species—they can be expected to act like animals, driven by the instinct for survival and the unending quest for pleasure—ultimately, in a lifestyle of hedonism. The "survival of the fittest" is not only expected but is desirable as weaknesses are continually bred out of the species by the eugenics of evolution. In reality, though, "survival of the fittest" is merely "survival of the survivor," for even the strongest and most intelligent are often victimized by their own arrogance and recklessness or by blind chance!

In India, the Hindu brand of monism encourages neglect for humanitarianism since those who suffer are merely working out their

---

[16] Nicolas Berdyaev, *The Divine and the Human*, tr. R. M. French (London: Geoffrey Bles, 1949), p. 4.
[17] Nikos Kazantzakis, *The Saviors of God: Spiritual Exercises* (New York: Simon & Schuster, 1960), pp. 121-122.

bad karma and any attempt to relieve such suffering could merely prolong the agonizing transmigration of their souls on the wheel of reincarnation, preventing their escape into the highest Hindu ideal: nonexistence. This worldview has also permitted—even promoted— systematic and unrelenting abuse of women, including extraction of exorbitant dowries from hapless parents of female children, murder of wives so that men can collect yet another dowry, insistence that widows immolate themselves on their husbands' funeral pyres, and a horrendous tradition of female infanticide (which, with the advent of sonogram technology, has produced the wholesale abortion of female fetuses).

In Islam (the religion so named because Allah, Islam's distant, austere god, demands "submission"), theology is mirrored in an anthropology that has little value for human life, as is clearly evidenced by the senseless terrorist activities in nations around the world where the radical Islamist target of choice for murder and mayhem is more often than not innocent women and children. Over 90% of the current military conflicts on this planet have been initiated and are perpetuated by Islamic extremists and fundamentalists. In a religion that was founded in and is often fixated on violence, it should come as no surprise that Islam also promotes and institutionalizes the abuse of women.

Some Islamic religious leaders have even argued that Muslim men should not be emotionally attached to their wives and that love between husband and wife should not be encouraged or tolerated. Some of these have even suggested that such love is a deadly enemy of Islamic civilization.[18] Not surprisingly, therefore, the Qur'an, Islam's holy book, has been used to establish, justify, and institutionalize polygamy—but only in the form of polygyny (never polyandry!) wherein a man can have up to four legal wives at a time.[19] In effect, however, Muslim men can legally engage in unlimited serial polygyny through a divorce policy that often leaves women and their children victims of male lust and abuse. According to most scholars, any Muslim marriage can be summarily terminated if a husband declares to his wife three times, "I divorce you." Upon this pronouncement, he is

---

[18] Fatima Mernissi, *Beyond the Veil: Male-Female Dynamics in Modern Muslim Society* (Bloomington, IN: Indiana University Press, 1987), p. 107. Though Mernissi's contentions are much debated by those who contend that the Qur'an encourages marital love, others indicate that love should be exclusively devoted to Allah.

[19] Islam allows a Muslim man to have four wives at a time; however, if he marries a fifth, the marriage is not void but merely irregular.

free to contract another marriage. Likewise, in many Muslim nations, where adultery—particularly that of the offending woman—is often punished by death, marriages of convenience can be legally arranged with predetermined durations of an hour, a day, a week, a month, or a year. These fixed-term "marriages" are called in Arabic *Nikah Mut'ah*, meaning literally "marriage of pleasure" or "marriage of use."[20] While all of these "marriages" terminate automatically upon the passing of the agreed time and the man's payment of the established price to the woman, everyone is assured that this practice is not a form of prostitution, for it fits within the parameters of some Islamic views of marriage.

Another example of the low regard for female life that some adherents of Islam can be seen in a Muslim practice in which women have often been murdered by their own parents and siblings in so-called "honor killings" based on their view that somehow these females have disgraced the family's honor either by attitudes or actions. Even in the United States and Europe, such honor killings have become increasingly common. A particularly egregious example was the recent "honor killing" of a young girl in which a she was physically restrained by her own mother while her Muslim father plunged a kitchen knife into her heart. Could any theology possibly foster a more horrific anthropology when male "honor"—or so-called "family honor"—is valued above the life of a young girl?[21]

Further disregard for half of the human race is also manifest in the practice of some Islamic nations where child brides (with no minimum legal age of consent) are routinely "married" to older men, often in their 60's and 70's in what appears to most of the non-Islamic world as little more than legalized pedophilia.[22] Then, in an appalling

---

[20] The *"Nikah Mut'ah"* is a time-delimited marriage contract and requires a certain reward paid by the man to the woman. It can be arranged by a woman only every two months. Presumably a man can arrange one as often as he wishes. Though some have argued that *Nikah Mut'ah* is an un-Islamic concept and a circumvention of adultery laws, the practice is established and supported by the Usuli Shia schools of Shari'a (Islamic law). Cf. Shahla Haeri, *Law of Desire: Temporary Marriage in Shi'l Iran* (Syracuse, NY: Syracuse University Press, 1989).

[21] See Ellen Francis Harris, *Guarding the Secrets: Palestinian Terrorism and a Father's Murder of His Too-American Daughter* (New York: Charles Scribner's Sons, 2005). Zein Isa, a Palestinian terrorist who lived in St. Louis, was convicted of killing his daughter Palestina in 1989. Investigators say he was furious she had a black boyfriend, went to a school dance and got a job at Wendy's. Palestina's mother held her down as Isa plunged a 9-inch knife into his daughter's chest, actions the FBI observed live via wiretap as they investigated Isa for his terrorist ties and exposed the level of his religiouisly inspired treachery.

[22] Technically, a girl is not to be handed over to her husband and sexual intercourse is not to be forced upon her until "she is fit for marital congress." See Reuben Levy, "The Social Structure of Islam," in *Orientalism: Early Sources*, vol. XII (London: Routledge, 1957), p. 106.

outworking of systematized androcentric abuse of women that some Islamists religiously justify, barely pubescent Christian girls are routinely kidnapped by Muslims in the Darfur region of Sudan to be sold into slavery as sex toys for wealthy and self-avowed "devout" Muslim men, subsequently to be discarded like so much expendable refuse when the newness wears off.[23] Amazingly, the Western media—as well as most leaders of the African-American community—choose to ignore this form of enslavement of African children by Arab Muslims.

In China, Confucianism also presented a worldview that encouraged and institutionalized the abuse of women. Confucius considered women a necessary evil, and as necessary evils, they were easy targets for abuse. A "woman's way" (dao) was to be wife and mother, and her chief virtue was obedience, first to father, then to husband, and finally to a grown son. Asian women were looked upon as fragile, exotic, sexual flowers, whose primary function is for men to use in whatever way they wish. Such religious views became the basis for the gruesome practice of foot-binding.[24] Based on a male fetish that considered small feet to be extremely erotic in women, the so-called "Lotus Feet" tradition began in the tenth century with young girls having their feet wrapped so tightly in bandages that they could not develop normally. The ideal was the perfect three-inch "Grand Lotus" foot.[25] Simply because the dominant male found a deformed female foot sexually stimulating, millions of Chinese women were rendered horribly handicapped in a practice that lasted for more than a thousand years. Amazingly, there are elderly women living today in China who are still suffering from the effects of foot-binding. To this day, religious traditions of the Far East continue to foster a climate that makes much of the area a haven for the perversion of human trafficking and child prostitution.[26]

It is easy to see, then, that theology and philosophy seriously influence anthropology. What one thinks about deity creates a climate

[23] See Damien Lewis and Halima Bashir, *Tears of the Desert: A Memoir of Survival in Darfur* (New York: Random House, 2009). See Alfred Taban, "Activist Says Child Slavery Exists in Sudan," report by Reuters, July 19, 1997.

[24] See Wang Ping, *Aching for Beauty: Footbinding in China* (Minneapolis: University of Minnesota Press, 2000). See also Dorothy Ko, *Every Step a Lotus: Shoes for Bound Feet* (Berkeley, CA: University of California Press, 2001).

[25] Jicai Feng, David Wakefield, and Howard Boldblatt, eds., *The Three-Inch Golden Lotus* (Honolulu, HI: University of Hawaii Press, 1986), p. 81.

[26] Louise Shelley, *Human Trafficking: A Global Perspective* (Cambridge: Cambridge University Press, 2010), p. 183. Also, Sally W. Stoecker and Louise I. Shelley, *Human Traffic and Transnational Crime: Eurasian and American* (Oxford: Rowman & Littlefield Publishers, 2005), p. 79.

that either protects the weaker in society or leaves them vulnerable to exploitation. Women have been victimized since time immemorial and almost universally throughout the world because of perverse perspectives on God or religion. And, unfortunately, this condition has also been manifest in historical Christianity where aberrant views of God have often created a climate for widespread, unrelenting, and systematic abuse of women. If proper perspectives on God's design for women are to be established, therefore, it is essential that a proper understanding of God be affirmed. If correct theology is not established, wrong treatment of women will inevitably be perpetuated, with no real end in sight. It is time, then, to get theology right by rediscovering the God of Scripture.

Springboard for Discussion

1. Analyze the concept that theology makes a profound impact upon anthropology. Cite examples of ways in which faulty perspectives on God create and reinforce faulty perspectives on human beings. How have women been impacted through the centuries by perverted views of deity?

2. Consider the Greek understanding of their pantheon of gods and the resultant view of both manhood and womanhood that was produced from that worldview. How did narcissism impact the Greek culture? Why were the ancient Greeks gynophobic? How strong was misogyny in the Greek world? How are narcissism and misogyny interconnected?

3. Evaluate the Pandora myth. How does this understanding of woman compare with the biblical view of woman? Do you believe that women are the reason for evil in the world? Why or why not?

4. Explore the implications of evolution theory upon anthropology, including its impact upon thinking about both men and women. Is there any reason for humans to act differently from animals if they are nothing more than another step on the ladder of evolution from lower forms of animal life? How does atheism impact thinking about human beings and their value?

5. Discuss the monistic perspective on theology and the implica-

tions of this worldview on anthropology. How are women generally treated under the auspices of religions like Hinduism and under philosophies like Buddhism? How does monistic religion and philosophy impact the value of human life, particularly that of women, in these cultures?

6. Analyze the teachings of Islam regarding God and consider how they impact the Muslim view of human life and its value for womanhood. How are women generally treated in the Islamic world?

7. Consider the teachings of Confucianism. How does this philosophy impact women in China?

8. Discuss reasons why you believe it is important for everyone to have a proper view of Deity so that they can arrive at a proper view of humanity and then of human relationships. How has your own view of manhood and womanhood been shaped or impacted by your viewpoints on God? What is the basis for your understanding of God? Is there a proper way in which one can understand who God is and what he actually thinks about humanity, male and female?

CHAPTER 6

REDISCOVERING THE GOD OF SCRIPTURE

The God of the Bible is not a capricious Jovian despot sitting in regal splendor on an Olympian throne hurling thunderbolts earthward in fits of rage against anyone suspected of daring to disrespect him. God is not a reclusive, irascible curmudgeon, scowling over a flowing white beard with darting eyes, hoping to catch some poor, hapless soul in violation of one of his many overbearing demands for punctilious performance. God is not a craftsman who impulsively decided to construct a universe that he could observe from a distance to prove to himself his own genius. God is not a spoiled child who is insanely jealous over the toys that he has created to while away his time, nor is he a mad scientist who tinkers with humanity and the rest of creation, ever experimenting to see just what might happen.

The Hebrew God is not cold, aloof, and utterly and forever hidden. He is not the *deus otiosus* that Deism claims created the universe only to retire and remain essentially idle or unemployed thereafer. He is not the *deus absconditus* of Thomistic theology who has consciously left the universe to hide somewhere "out there." True, God dwells in light to which no human can approach, and he has never been seen, nor can be seen, by human eyes.[1] From the human perspective, he is utterly transcendent, unknown, and inscrutable. At the same time, though, he has chosen to reveal himself through his Word and his Spirit. The very fact that God has elected to disclose himself proves that he is a relational being who manifests true personhood.

---

[1] 1 Timothy 6:16.

The God of Scripture is not an isolated, static, emotionless tyrant but the engaged, dynamic, sentient epitome of relational love.

The problem with any attempt to understand God is that he has been so reimaged through the centuries that for most people he is no longer the one who revealed himself successively to the prophets of old and finally in the person of Jesus. The God of Scripture has been reimaged in the likeness of the politico-religious potentates who have used him to consolidate and validate their power and privilege. This God has even been portrayed as capricious and Machiavellian. He has been transformed into a model for empire builders and sadistic controllers, both civil and ecclesiastical. The fact that God has been so often mischaracterized in Christian churches is confirmed by Thomas Matthews' conclusion that his training as a preacher's kid made him think, even in adulthood, that God was "a watchful, vengeful, enormous, omniscient policeman, instantly aware of the slightest tinge of irreverence in my innermost thought, always ready to pounce."[2]

Part of the reason for the historical imagery of God as an ominous judge has been the mischaracterization of the God of the Hebrew Scriptures by Christian thinkers. Despite the fact that the Hebrew people always viewed their God as a father exercising perfect *chesed* (tender mercy) toward his creation in general and toward his chosen people in particular, much of Christianity has failed to grasp that imagery, often preferring to conceive of God as a distant, detached, vengeful despot. Unfortunately, this has also contributed to a sad Christian misrepresentation of the Father as an austere judge whose verdict was always the death penalty. This God has been viewed very unfavorably when compared with Jesus, the loving Savior of grace who interposes himself between an angry God and a weak and unfortunate humanity.

Interestingly enough, the first heresy that challenged the earliest Christian church focused on just such mischaracterization and reimaging of the God of the Hebrews when a theology adapted from Greek Gnosticism infected a significant part of the second-century church. In this reimaging of God, Marcion of Sinope (in modern Turkey) asserted that the God of the Hebrews was not the God of the church. For him, the God of the Jews was a vicious and vengeful character whom he identified as the Demiurge of Platonism, the craftsman who

---

[2] Thomas Matthews, quoted in Terrence Fretheim, *The Suffering God: An Old Testament Perspective* (Philadelphia: Fortress Press, 1984), pp. 4-5.

had created the universe and in so doing had entrapped higher spiritual realities in evil matter. Jesus was the good God whose task it was to destroy the evil Hebrew God and cast him into Hades. Even though Marcion was excommunicated from the church by his own father and branded a heretic for his radical Gnostic ideas, his theology, which distorted Christianity in his generation, has continued to influence Christian thought to one degree or another ever since that time. Even in the present day, a virtual neo-Marcionism continues to manifest itself in the form of antinomianism, supersessionism, Judaeophobia, anti-Judaism, and anti-Semitism, not to speak of various ongoing mischaracterizations of the God of Scripture, both subtle and overt.

As a consequence, the God who revealed his ineffable name as Yahweh and thereby defined himself as "I will be [there]" has been reimaged by philosopher-theologians as a withdrawn, distant, or absent emotional iceberg. The Marcionic caricature of God that sets Jesus in opposition to the Hebrew God has made God appear to be schizophrenic at best. The "Old Testament" God has been viewed by Christians as a judge: angry, vengeful, and obsessed with obsequious obeisance. It was necessary for Jesus to be manifest in the "New Testament" in order to reveal the other, hidden side of God, the love dimension. Then, in spite of its creedal statements that emphasized the absolute humanity of Jesus as being consubstantial with his absolute deity, the church increasingly detached itself in practice from the humanity of Jesus the Jew and eventually lost sight of the manifestation of God in the human Jesus to the point that the Jewish Jesus came to be imaged as the transcendent—and, therefore, distant—cosmic Christ.[3] This cosmic Christ was totally "stripped of the inconveniences of his tribal Jewish heritage . . . equipped with the standardized toneless gestures . . . and refined in the astringent essence of rational formalism."[4] In the cosmic Christ, rationalist philosopher-theologians discovered, in effect, a Jesus who was different from the Jesus whom the apostles described and in whom they placed their

---

[3] The concept of the "cosmic Christ" originated in patristic literature to identify the Christ as utterly transcending the humanness of Jesus. In more recent times, however, the term has come to identify those who, following the traditions of the Gnostics, consider Jesus to have become the "cosmic energy" that permeates the universe and is thought to unify all religions in a syncretism that ultimately Christ as being the "Christ within," a postmodernist version of classical monism. See Joerg Rieger, *Christ and Empire: From Paul to Postcolonial Times* (Minneapolis, MN: Fortress Press, 2007), pp. 269-270.

[4] Robert C. Neville, *A Theology Primer* (New York: State University of New York Press, 1991), pp. 148-150.

unreserved faith. Indeed, their Jesus is no Jesus at all. Paul was very emphatic in his argument that anyone who came preaching "another Jesus" should be rejected.[5] Any theology or Christology that does not clearly affirm that Jesus is both God and Messiah—as both the divine *Logos* and the human Jewish Jesus—is clearly heretical from all biblical perspectives and must not be entertained by anyone who believes in the authority of Holy Scripture.

DIVINE RELATIONALITY

Despite Christian theology's dominant tradition that has stressed metaphysical concepts of God—the God of transcendence and independence from the world—in more recent times, some theologians who have worked at recovering biblical emphases about God have advanced the view that the concept of divine relationality solves many of the problems current in Christian faith and practice by restoring God's self-image, the image that he chose to reveal for himself in the Hebrew Scriptures. H. Richard Niebuhr has argued that truth about God is manifest in "certainties about fundamental, indestructible relations between persons."[6] The God of Scripture is Spirit,[7] but a real person, not an "it" or a "force." The personhood of God may not equate with personality as it is understood in today's world; however, in Hebraic thought, it confirms God's actions in history in the context of relationality both within himself and with his people. The distinct difference between Judaism (and Christianity which emerged from its matrix) and other religions is a clear focus on the personhood of God, a personhood that requires and is worked out in relationship.

God's personhood demands interrelationship and mutuality within his own being. It also made the creation an inescapable eventuality for the full demonstration and manifestation of divine relationality through God's voluntary self-limitation of divine power and prerogatives in order to create relational beings. Though the interrelationality of the persons within God's being did not demand or require creation, that interrelationality prompted the creation. God formed humanity in his own image and likeness to demonstrate the divine relationality between human beings as well as the relationship between God

[5] 2 Corinthians 11:4.
[6] H. Richard Niebuhr, *The Meaning of Revelation* (Louisville, KY: Westminster John Knox Press, 1941), p. 76.
[7] John 4:24.

and humanity. It is clear that God created humanity for the "I-Thou" relationship that Martin Buber described,[8] a relationship that would be "mutual, reciprocal, symmetrical, and contentless," one in which "both partners retain their own subjectivity in the encounter, in which they become aware of the other person as a subject, rather than an object."[9] By his own initiative, God is the source of the "I-Thou" relationship with humanity. As a personal God, he cannot remain detached from humanity in an "I-It" relationship.[10]

Rabbi Allan Lazaroff described the relational and interpersonal nature of the Hebrew Scriptures: "The concern [of Scripture] is not conceptual knowledge but rather relations between people and between them and God, the latter relationships forming a model for the former."[11] It should come as no surprise, therefore, that the God of Scripture is preeminently a tender lover, not a despotic judge. This God says, "You are precious in my eyes, and I love you."[12] Everything about the divine being exudes love, for love is God's very essence,[13] and it demands expression and action, not static being. This is why the Hebrew language always focuses on verbs, not nouns. "Of all the languages, Hebrew conveys most faithfully the dynamism of the word of God, and always shows us an action in it."[14] This is why "the authority of faith is more dependent upon orthopraxy than upon orthodoxy."[15] Believing is demonstrated by doing.

As Abraham Joshua Heschel argued, nouns do not adequately describe God: adverbs modify and indicate the verbal nature of God in his relationship with humanity.[16] Gerhard von Rad agreed that Israel's starting point has always been "event over *logos*"[17] that has grounded Hebrew thinking in "historical traditions," a concept that is foreign to

---

[8] Martin Buber, *I and Thou*, tr. Ronald Gregor Smith (New York: Charles Scribner's Sons, 1958), pp. 20-30.
[9] Alister E. McGrath, *Christian Theology: An Introduction* (Malden, MA: Wiley-Blackwell Publishing, 1993), p. 208.
[10] Buber, pp. 20-30.
[11] Allan Lazaroff, quoted in Jerald M. Stinson, "A Love Story" in a sermon at First Congregational Church, Long Beach, CA.
[12] Isaiah 43:4.
[13] 1 John 4:8, 16.
[14] Paul Evdokimov, *Woman and the Salvation of the World*, tr. Anthony P. Gythiel (Crestwood, NY: St. Vladimir's Seminary Press, 1994), p. 140.
[15] Letty M. Russell, *Household of Freedom: Authority in Feminist Theology* (Philadelphia: The Westminster Press, 1987), p. 24.
[16] Abraham Joshua Heschel, *God in Search of Man* (New York: Harper & Row, 1965), pp. 160-161.
[17] Gerhard von Rad, *Old Testament Theology: The Theology of Israel's Prophetic Traditions*, vol. I (Louisville, KY: Westminster John Knox Press, 1962), p. 116.

the Greek "urge towards a universal understanding of the world" by seeking a "uniform natural principle" of the cosmos.[18] This idea underscores the historical emphasis of Hebrew thinking, in which function is preferred over form and deed is preferred over creed. Henry Jansen concludes, therefore, that the Old Testament does not "speak abstractly about God but only about God in relation."[19] The God of Scripture is not the abstract God of creation. He identified himself as the God of Abraham, the God of Isaac, and the God of Jacob.[20]

This is why neither the Hebrew Scriptures nor the Jewish people describe God as the "God of creation." As a matter of fact, only a miniscule portion of the Hebrew Scriptures is devoted to creation narratives. The preponderance of information contained therein deals with God in the context of his relationship with humanity. Only three chapters of *B'reshit*—"In Beginnings" (Genesis)—deal with creation; 12 chapters tell the story of God's covenantal relationship with Abraham, and the remaining 24 chapters rehearse God's faithfulness to maintain that relationship with Abraham's son, grandson, and great-grandson. Indeed, God described himself not as "the God of Creation" or "the God of the Universe," but as "the God of Abraham, the God of Isaac, and the God of Jacob."[21] It is clear, therefore, that God is not merely a self-contained, all-pervasive force, Aristotle's "Unmoved Mover," but is a purely relational being. Even in the most ancient of Hebraic prayer formulae, the *Berachot*, God is consistently addressed with the benediction, "Blessed are you, O Lord our God, sovereign of the universe." Significantly, God is perceived as "our God," before he is praised as "sovereign of the universe."

"It is perhaps easy," says Karen Armstrong, "to imagine [a] lofty deity as long as we place him in heaven."[22] In the Hebrew Bible, however, "God does not remain wholly transcendent, locked into the celestial sphere" but "enters human history and becomes inextricably involved with humanity."[23] Hebraic thinking, then, speaks of God not from philosophical categories but from the perspective of relationship. This model, based on the Hebrew Scriptures themselves, reveals

[18] von Rad, p. 116.
[19] Henry Jansen, *Relationality and the Concept of God* (Amsterdam-Atlanta, GA: Rodopi B.V., 1994), p. 86.
[20] Genesis 28:13; Exodus 4:5; Matthew 22:32.
[21] Exodus 3:6.
[22] Karen Armstrong, *In the Beginning: A New Interpretation of Genesis* (New York: The Ballantine Publishing Group, 1996), p. 13.
[23] Armstrong, p. 13.

a "better way" that Christian theologians should adopt—a way in which theological discussions about God have their beginning point in experience, not in theory. This represents what Elizabeth Johnson calls a theology of God "from below" that does not "seek to prove the existence of such a God by reasoning," but instead begins from the point of experience and then engages "in the hermeneutical task of interpreting the meaning . . . that far transcends any esoteric puzzles of one or three in a literal mathematical sense."[24] In maintaining continuity with the Hebraic approach to God as being God in relationship with his people, understanding about God is not based on rationalism, philosophical categories, or metaphysics, but on history and experience. And the only history that is meaningful in the Hebraic culture is that of family relationship. This is confirmed by the fact that the only Hebrew word that suggests a concept of history is *toledot*, which means genealogy (literally "generations").

PERSONHOOD AND DIVINE RELATIONALITY

It should be noted that the use of the generic term *he* in reference to God in Scripture serves the function of connoting personhood, not gender. Since the God of the Bible is genderless, "when Scripture speaks of God as 'he,' the pronoun is primarily personal (generic) rather than masculine (specific); it emphasizes God's personality . . . in contrast to impersonal entities."[25] If God were only a force, a neuter reference ("it") would be proper; however, in Hebrew there is no neuter, and in any group of people in which both genders are represented, reference to the group as a whole is always masculine. This is the nature of the language. It is not, however, an attempt to ascribe masculine gender to God, for God is genderless despite having characteristics and qualities common to and more predominant in both genders. In similar fashion, the human gender of Jesus was a part of his own experience of humanity as he was enfleshed and tabernacled among the human family. While it was essential to his humanity—like all the other anthropological constraints that he assumed—Jesus' gender was in no way reflective of the divine Logos that became incarnate in his human body. Neither the Father nor the Son (the eternally

---

[24] Elizabeth Johnson, *She Who Is: The Mystery of God in Feminist Theological Discourse* (New York: Crossroad Publishing Company, 1998), p. 123.
[25] Carl F. H. Henry, *God, Revelation and Authority* (Wheaton, IL: Crossway Books, 1999), p. 159.

prexistent *Logos*) is masculine: both are genderless.

Yet another factor that contributed to masculine references to Deity in Hebrew Scripture was its strong "polemic against goddess worship," because of which the writers of Scripture favored "the use of the masculine singular pronoun to refer to Yahweh, God of Israel."[26] Since it was characteristic of pagan worship to focus on sexual activity between a male god and his female consort(s), both divine and human, God considered it important to insulate the chosen people from such idolatry. This is why God commanded that no image should be made, whether male or female, and it is, no doubt, the predominant reason why male identifiers were used to describe the Divine. Jacques Doukhan has argued convincingly that this was also the primary reason why women were not included in the priesthood of Israelite worship though they did have functions in both tabernacle and temple.[27]

God is also identified as Father only for the purpose revealing his personhood and of underscoring his relationship to the creation and to his chosen people in terms of blessing and keeping, the unique roles of fatherhood.[28] The term *Father*, then, is a relational term, not an ontological statement. As J. Philip Newell observes, "Fatherhood imagery [points] to the One from whom we have come, to God as our seed or origin of life."[29] Since Hebraic fatherhood was the most visible theme in the biblical society where men assumed responsibility for the protection of and provision for the family, it was virtually unavoidable that God, the all-sufficient provider and the all-powerful protector would have been imaged as Father. While this anthropomorphic metaphor may account for the fact that God is universally referred to in Scripture as "Father," it is not, however, an indication of any masculinity in God. The God of Scripture is Father only to define the nature of his relationship with his children. "To say that God's behavior toward us can be characterized as fatherly (or motherly) is a

---

[26] Kristen E. Kvam, Linda S. Schearing, and Valarie H. Ziegler, eds., *Eve and Adam: Jewish, Christian, and Muslim Readings on Genesis and Gender* (Bloomington, IN: Indiana University Press, 1999), p. 25.

[27] Jacques B. Doukhan, "Women Priests in Israel: A Case for Their Absence," in *Women in Ministry: Biblical & Historical Perspectives* (Berrien Springs, MI: Andrews University Press, 1998), p. 38.

[28] The blessing and keeping functions of fatherhood are seen in the first of the three blessings included in the three-in-one Aaronic Benediction: "The Lord bless you and keep you." This first blessing is from God as Father and reveals the qualities that are unique to fatherhood both in the realm of deity and in the realm of humanity.

[29] J. Philip Newell, *Echo of the Soul: The Sacredness of the Human Body* (Norwich, UK: Canterbury Press Norwich, 2000), p. 3.

statement about how God exercises divinity *with us.* It is a functional assertion, not an ontological claim."[30] As Gregory Nazianzus said, the word *Father* is not the name of a nature or essence but of a relation.[31] God is not ontologically Father; he is relationally Father.

THE GOD "WHO IS" IS "GOD WITH US"

In the Hebrew Scriptures, then, one discovers the God who is engaged with his people. Indeed, the name by which he revealed himself confirms this truth. While the many names that men have given to God underscore their attempt to define him in terms of power, majesty, dominion, judgment, and the like, the sacred name by which God revealed himself is Yahweh, the condensate of God's self-revelational statement about himself, "I am that I am," or "I will be what I will be," or "I will be [there]."[32] Implied in God's self-designated personal name and in his own definition of his name are 1) an affirmation of his aseity, for "I am because I am" is an indication that God is the source of his own existence, 2) a declaration of his eternity, for "I will be what I will be" is a declaration that God is the one who exists in the eternal present, the one who is both within and outside of time, and 3) a proclamation of his immutability, for "I will be there" indicates that God's covenantal faithfulness never changes. Each of these categories, however, is secondary to the name's declaration of God's constancy, his faithfulness to his relationships. "I am that I am" is not a Greek metaphysical or philosophical statement. It is a declaration of the constancy of divine relationality.[33]

When God is understood in terms of his own self-disclosure, a foundation is established for recognizing that true being is relational. Because of the influence of Greek thought, however, most of the Western world today considers being as abstract, static, and imper-

[30] Catherine LaCugna, "Problems with Trinitarian Reformulation," *Louvain Studies* 10 (1985), pp. 337-338.

[31] Gregory Nazianzus, "The Third Theological Oration," *Nicene and Post-Nicene Fathers,* tr. Philip Schaff and Henry Wace (Grand Rapids, MI: Wm. B. Eerdmans Publishing Co., 1974), pp. 301-309.

[32] When Moses inquired about God's name, the Almighty replied in Exodus 3:14, "אֶהְיֶה אֲשֶׁר אֶהְיֶה" ("Ehyeh-Asher-Ehyeh," "I am that I am"). This is the meaning of the name with which God subsequently commissioned Moses: יהוה (YHWH), which is commonly represented as *Yahweh* and universally translated "Lord." It is clear this God-revealed name is a statement of God's relationality, not his dominion or dominance over creation. It is a statement that God will always be God in utter faithfulness to his covenantal relationship with all his creation, with humanity, and with his uniquely chosen people.

[33] See John D. Garr, *Rediscovering the God of Scripture* (Atlanta, GA: Golden Key Press).

sonal rather than dynamic, concrete, and personal. All being, however, is relational. In relationship to God, being should be understood not as a substantive but as a verb and as an intransitive verb, connoting continual dynamic action unlimited by any predicate. It is in this context that God's being not only created the universe but also sustains it moment by moment with the same continually spoken word: "Let there be." This is why John Macquarrie has spoken of God's being as a "letting-be," a being that enables and empowers his creation.[34]

The God who facilitates relationality between humans does so because he himself is pure relationality, the God of love and pathos. Relationality was not, therefore, an acquired trait for God; it was an ontological fact of the very essence of divine being. Relationality was not a quality that was manifest in time; it was a characteristic that was present in the very nature of God from before all time. As John Zizioulas has said, "The substance of God, 'God,' has no ontological content, no true being, apart from communion."[35] Without relationality there is no God, for "nothing in existence is conceivable in itself, as an individual, such as the τοδε τι [*tode ti*] of Aristotle, since even God exists thanks to an event of communion." In reality, it was from the revelation of God in Scripture that the "ancient world heard for the first time that it is communion which makes being 'be': nothing exists without it, not even God."[36]

In similar manner, God's very being could be revealed "only through personal relationships and personal love. Being means life, and life means *communion*."[37] This understanding affects even the very essence of God: "The being of God is a relational being: without the concept of communion it would not be possible to speak of the being of God."[38] Indeed, "while the solitary God of classical theism is associated with a bare, static, monolithic kind of unity, a unity of divine nature, the triune symbol calls for a differentiated unity of variety or manifoldness in which there is distinction, inner richness, and complexity."[39] Because the one God who is tripersonal exists eternally as the loving communion of Father, Son, and Holy Spirit, "there is no

---

[34] John Macquarie, *Principles of Christian Theology* (London: SCM, 1977), p. 179-182.
[35] John D. Zizioulas, *Being as Communion* (Crestwood, NY: St. Vladimir's Seminary Press, 1985), p. 16.
[36] Zizioulas, p. 17.
[37] Zizioulas, p. 16.
[38] Zizioulas, p. 16.
[39] Johnson, p. 220.

problem of the lonely God" in the God of Scripture. The triune God did not have to create "in order to experience love,"[40] for that love was and is eternally manifest within the very being of God in the mutual divine interpenetration and the interchange of infinite love within and among the persons of God. This understanding affirms the truth that "God did not need the creation in order to be God."[41] God's creation of humanity resulted not from a lack in God but from the divine desire to lavish the love experienced within God intratrinitarily upon a creation formed in the divine image and likeness.[42] God's choice to create involved his determination to produce beings in his image who would mirror the divine love and the relationality that it produces and requires as its dynamic expression. The God of Scripture is Immanuel, "God with us."[43] This was the reason that God chose to make his fullest self-disclosure in the person of his only begotten Son, Jesus. God became human in order to participate fully in humanness so that he could profoundly and in all actuality be "God with us." The prophet Isaiah accurately predicted the manner in which God would become truly immanent: "For unto us a child is born, unto us a son is given, and his name shall be called . . . Immanuel."

GOD AS FAMILY AND COMMUNITY

The unity and uniqueness of divine being form the cornerstone of monotheism that is foundational to all biblical religion; however, in order to understand God as a relational being, one must first comprehend the full biblical meaning of monotheism from both the Hebrew Scriptures and the Apostolic Scriptures. Biblical monotheism is not a rigid insistence upon absolute singularity and utter transcendence in God. It is rather the insistence on the absolute unity and uniqueness of God.

The most basic statement in all of Scripture is this: "Hear, O Israel, the Lord our God, the Lord is one."[44] Jesus himself affirmed this declaration as being the first and greatest commandment or word of instruction from God.[45] Millions of Jewish people through the centuries

---

[40] John Ernest Sanders, *The God Who Risks: A Theology of Divine Providence* (Downers Grove, IL: InterVarsity Press, 2007), p. 184.
[41] Sanders, p. 185.
[42] See David Burrell, *Freedom and Creation in Three Traditions* (South Bend, IN: University of Notre Dame Press, 1993).
[43] Isaiah 7:14.
[44] Deuteronomy 6:4.
[45] Matthew 22:37-38.

have described this statement simply as the *Shema*, the Hebrew word for "hear (and obey)," "listen," or "understand." Three times daily in synagogal prayers, they have faithfully recited the *Shema* as a declaration of their faith, and countless numbers have whispered these words as they took their last breath, sanctifying God's name in martyrdom.[46] The *Shema* is, however, more than a statement about the singularity of God: it is a declaration of God's utter uniqueness. The Hebrew of this text can also be translated, "Understand this, Israel, the Lord is our God, the Lord alone." YHWH is *sui generis*, uniquely God. All other gods are not gods at all.[47] The God who maintains convenantal relationship with the universe, with the earth, with humanity, and with his chosen people is the only God. There is no God except the God of love and relationality, the God who stands in relationship within his own being and in relationship with his creation.

Within this most ancient and most powerful of human declarations of faith, however, is a key to understanding the God who in his own being is relational and who extends that relationality to the universe, to his chosen people Israel, and to all humanity. The Hebrew word אֶחָד (*echad*), which is usually rendered "one," does not exclusively connote absolute singularity. The Hebrew word for absolute numeric singularity is יָחִיד (*yachid*). *Yachid*, not *echad*, is used in the Hebrew Scriptures when "one and only" is intended as in God's instruction to Abraham, "Take your one and only [*yachid*] son, Isaac."[48] While *echad* is used as the numeral "one," it denotes not singularity but uniqueness: "the only one, the incomparable."[49] At its foundation, *echad* means "to unite, to join together, to be in unity" and, therefore, implies a com-

[46] From the slaughter of the Jews in the Rhineland in the first crusade of 1096 until the Holocaust, the death of Jewish martyrs was seen in the context of "sanctifying the name of God." See Jeremy Cohen, *Sanctifying the Name of God: Jewish Martyrs and Jewish Memories of the First Crusade* (Philadelphia: University of Pennsylvania Press, 2004). This was an extension of the Jewish understanding that a Jew should conduct his life in such a way that non-Jews would recognize Judaism as a good religion and would be brought nearer to God (in much the same way that Jesus said, "Let your light so shine before men that they may see your good works and glorify your Father who is in heaven" (Matthew 5:16). See Joseph Telushkin, *The Code of Jewish Ethics: You Shall Be Holy* (New York: Random House, 2006), p. 456.

[47] Isaiah 44:6, 8.

[48] See Genesis 22:2: "Take your only (יָחִיד—*yachid*) son"; Judges 11:34: "She was Jephthah's one and only (*yachid*) child"; and Amos 8:10: "I will make it like a time of mourning for an only (יָחִיד—*yachid*) son."

[49] This concept is preserved in the Greek of the Apostolic Scriptures where εἷς (*heis*) means "one" in the same sense as *echad* while μόνος (*monos*) means "one and only" or "only" in the same sense as יָחִיד—*yachid* (e.g., εἷς—*heis* is used in 1 Corinthians 8:6: ". . . there is but one [εἷς—*heis*)] God, the Father . . . " while μόνος is used in 1 Timothy 1:17: "Now to the King eternal, the immortal, invisible, the only [μόνος—*monos*] wise God."

pound cohesion in the midst of diversity. The truth of this definition is seen in God's pronouncement that the "glued-together"[50] Adam and Eve would be one (*echad*) flesh—in this case two distinct persons united to form one superentity, the human family.

When the Jewish followers of Jesus observed his life, his actions, his death, and his resurrection, they recognized that he was more than a mere human being: they concluded that he was God. Because their strict Jewish upbringing was grounded in the Hebrew Scriptures, however, they could never have conceived of Jesus as a man who became God. He could only have been the one God who had become human—the same God who had manifest himself in the theophanies of biblical history.[51] They came to understand that the person who indwelt the human body of Jesus of Nazareth preexisted his incarnation, for Jesus had truthfully said of himself, "Before Abraham was, I am,"[52] clearly associating himself with the language of God's self-disclosure to Moses, "I am that I am."[53] Indeed, they saw in Jesus the Messiah of whom the prophet Micah had ascribed existence prior to his birth: he was the one whose "goings forth" were "from everlasting,"[54] a phrase that David had defined as being "before the earth was formed."[55] The one whom the disciples recognized to be the Messiah was also the one who had existed before the earth was formed. Indeed, they came to understand by faith that Jesus had been the one who had formed the heavens and the earth in the beginning, and they described him as the divine *Logos*, the incarnation of God.[56]

These Jews faced the challenge of describing and defining what they as "eyewitnesses" had observed.[57] As typical Jews, they moved from experience to concept, from the concrete verbal reality of action to the conceptual understanding of the substantive. Christian faith came to be grounded in the revelatory declaration that erupted from the lips of two of Jesus' Jewish disciples, one female, the other male.

---

[50] The Hebrew word דָּבַק (*dabak*), which is translated "cleave," "cling," or "united" in Genesis 2:24 literally means to "be glued together."

[51] Examples of theophanies (appearances of Deity to humans) include Genesis 18:1ff, Genesis 32:24-30, Exodus 3:16, Exodus 24:8-11, Exodus 33:19-21, 1 Kings 11:9, and Isaiah 6:1. The theophanies were actually Christophanies, with the pre-incarnational Jesus (the person of the Word) appearing to Abraham, Jacob, Moses, Isaiah, and others in the form of a man or an angel.

[52] John 8:58.

[53] Exodus 3:14.

[54] Micah 5:2, KVJ.

[55] Psalm 90:2.

[56] Colossians 1:16; Hebrews 11:3.

[57] Luke 1:2; 2 Peter 1:16.

Both Martha and Peter exclaimed to Jesus, "You are the Messiah, the Son of God."[58] The high Christology of the earliest disciples of Jesus, like the God-consciousness of their ancestors, was based in what they knew they had experienced: ". . . what we have heard, what we have seen with our eyes, and what we have looked at and touched with our hands, concerning the Word of life."[59] They understood by experience that Jesus' high self-awareness was more than delusion, egocentricity, or megalomania. He was who he said he was, the Son of God. The disciples moved, therefore, from experience to concept, attempting to verbalize and explain what they had personally witnessed.

The apostle John set forth the prologue of his Gospel with these words: "In the beginning was the Word, and the Word was with God, and the Word was God. . . . And the Word became flesh and tabernacled among us."[60] In doing so, he unmistakably paralleled the structure and language of the introductory words to the Genesis account of creation: "In the beginning God created the heavens and the earth."[61] This Jewish apostle understood that the creation narrative in which the one God referred to himself as "us" and created one human being whom he called "them"[62] actually chronicled and demonstrated the emergence of the person of the Word of God from the bosom of the divine Father[63] following the brooding of the Holy Spirit over the waters of the primordial chaotic creation.[64] In the light of the first three verses of Holy Scripture, "where God is described as Father-Designer of the cosmos (v.1), as nurturing, protecting Spirit (v.2), and as creative Word (v.3)," the plural pronouns used for God could well introduce God in terms of "the multipersonality existing within the Triune God."[65] While in and of themselves these pronouns do not prove that the nature of God is that of a tripersonal unity, they do establish a striking parallel between the Eternal and the first human entity created in God's image, which was divinely described both as

---

[58] Matthew 16:16; John 11:27.

[59] 1 John 1:1-3.

[60] John 1:1, 14.

[61] Genesis 1:1.

[62] Genesis 1:26. Interestingly enough, God who is "he" and "us" also speaks of man as "him" and "them" (male and female): "Let us make humanity [singular] in our [plural] likeness . . . in the image of God created he [singular] him [singular]; male and female he created them [plural]." This interchange of the singular and the plural is reflected both in the One(s) having the image and the one(s) bearing the image.

[63] John 1:18.

[64] Genesis 1:2, NIV.

[65] Gilbert Bilezikian, *Beyond Sex Roles: What the Bible Says About a Woman's Place in Church and Family* (Grand Rapids, MI: Baker Book House, 1985), p. 23.

"him" and as "them." As such, they suggest that when God said, "Let us," he could well have been representing an act of discourse among the three persons in the one Deity. Whatever the case may have been, it is clear that before the creation of the universe, God was a community of three persons—Father, Son, and Spirit—in one divine being of spirit substance. In bringing forth creation, God the Spirit and God the Word emerged to reveal, to move, and to create.

As a Jewish rabbi, Paul expanded on this concept from his rock-solid grounding on the foundation of Israel's faith and experience, the *Shema*. Taking the words *God (Elohim)* and *Lord (YHWH)* in the *Shema*, he extrapolated and explicated the *Shema* as an affirmation of Christian faith in this manner: "For us, there is but one God [*Elohim*], the Father, from whom are all things . . . and one Lord [*YHWH*], Jesus Christ, by whom are all things."[66] The Father, then, is not self-contained God, all of God that exists. The Father and the Son are required together with the Spirit to reveal the one divine being of substance. The apostles took the statements in Hebrew Scripture that virtually personified divine Wisdom[67] and combined them with the tradition of using the term *Word of God* as a substitute for *God* in the *Targumim* (Aramaic translations of the Hebrew Scriptures)[68] and used these facts to confirm the truths that they had heard from the lips of Jesus: Yeshua was both Lord and Christ, Yahweh and Messiah.

As the earliest Christians recognized that the localized manifestation of God in the form of *Shekhinah*[69] and other material objectifications (such as the bodily form of a dove that appeared upon Jesus on the occasion of his baptism[70]) attributed personhood to the Spirit, the Holy Spirit then came to be understood as the third person in the trinity of the one God. Indeed, many ante-Nicene fathers even posited the idea that in some way the Spirit manifest feminine imagery in the one God. These considerations that became foundations for most of the creedal formulae of later Christianity were not, however, based on concepts or ideas that were borrowed from eastern mystery religions, as many scholars from both Jewish and Christian communities have

---

[66] 1 Corinthians 8:6, NASB.
[67] Proverbs 3:19; Psalm 104:24; 136:5.
[68] *Targumim* were compiled during the time between the second-temple period until the Middle Ages as Aramaic translations of the Hebrew Scriptures. Their purpose was to make the Hebrew Scritpures more understandable to Jews who were no longer conversant with Hebrew.
[69] The Hebrew word *shekhinah* means "dwelling," "inhabiting," or "settling." It indicated the presence or the glory of God.
[70] Luke 3:22.

suggested.[71] They were founded in pre-Christian speculation about God by Jewish sages whose ideas were later developed in the writings of Jewish philosophers who viewed the Divine in terms of three emanations — King, Word, and Spirit[72] — an idea that was later expanded to include ten divine emanations called *sefirot*.[73]

Far from being the solitary, self-contained, and self-sufficient individual envisioned by many, the God of the Bible has always been, is, and will ever be a divine relational community of three-in-one. God is one divine being of spirit substance manifest in three divine persons who are coequal, consubstantial, and coeternal, dwelling together in perfect mutuality, encircling and interpenetrating one another in infinite coinherence. The interrelationality of the divine persons in the one being of substance has ever been a part of the essence of divine being, not merely an added dimension or temporal manifestation. There was never a time when there was not the One, and there was never a time when the One was not three. Zizioulas confirms this truth: "It would be unthinkable to speak of the 'one God' before speaking of the God who is 'communion.'" He rightly notes that God as three-in-one "is a primordial ontological concept and not a notion which is added to the divine substance or rather which follows it."[74] God, then, must first be seen as a community of three and then as one wholly unique, single being.

GOD REVEALED IN CREATION

Efforts to understand the three-in-one nature of God are enhanced by utilizing a principle that Paul established when he unequivocally declared that even God's "eternal power and deity" are "understood" by the things that God has created.[75] Many basic structures that are fundamental to creation itself reveal principles about the interrelational community of the tripersonal one God. Among these are the elements of the universe itself, the dimensions of space, and the composition of light.

---

[71] See Samuel Angus, *The Mystery-Religions and Christianity: A Study in the Religious Background of Early Christianity* (New York: Dover Publications, 1966).

[72] See Rabbi Tzvi Nassi (Hirsch Prinz), *The Great Mystery or How Can Three Be One?* (London: William Macintosh, 1863).

[73] Ultimately the teaching about *sefirot* was expanded and became central to Jewish mysticism. See Howard Schwartz, *Tree of Souls: The Mythology of Judaism* (Oxford: Oxford University Press, 2004), pp. 7-19.

[74] Zizioulas, p. 16.

[75] Romans 1:20.

The universe is actually a triuniverse, a continuum comprised entirely of space, time, and energy/matter. Space is everywhere in the universe, with even the atomic and subatomic structure of matter composed of space. Similarly, time is also everywhere in the universe such that nothing could exist without time. Likewise, energy, which is interchangeable with matter (as confirmed by Einstein's formula: $E=mc^2$), is everywhere in the universe.[76] In reality, the universe is not part space, part time, and part energy/matter. It is all space, all time, and all energy/matter—and all at the same time. God, like the universe he created, is Father, Son, and Holy Spirit, a community of three in one, a community that is all Father, all Son, and all Spirit because of their mutual interpenetration of each other in which the Father is in the Son, the Son is in the Father, and the Spirit is in both Father and Son and vice versa.[77]

Similarly, the one predominant metaphor that is used to describe God throughout the Scriptures is light.[78] God is light, a pristine light that pervades the universe and beyond. God clothes himself in a garment of light,[79] dwelling in light so intense that no human can approach his dwelling place.[80] The first thing that God did to initiate the process for bringing order out of chaos in the creation was to say "Let light be."[81] Though to the naked eye light appears to be absolutely uniform and completely one in essence, it is demonstrably a three-in-one phenomenon. When subjected to prismatic refraction, pure white light is divided into three colors and three spectra equal length: red, blue, and yellow. When sunlight is refracted by water droplets in the atmosphere, a rainbow often appears featuring seven colors that are formed by the overlapping of these three primary colors of light. Without each of the three colors, light is not light at all. In similar manner, the three persons in the community of the one Deity make the one clear, pristine God who is Light personified.

Likewise, three spatial dimensions—length, width, and depth—define all perceivable reality. The dimension of length is unknown, unrevealed, and incomprehensible without the addition of the dimension of width. The only way a line (representing length) can be seen is

---

[76] Matter is essentially energy in a different form.
[77] John 17:21; Luke 4:1; Isaiah 48:16.
[78] John 1:8-9; 1 John 1:5.
[79] Psalm 104:2.
[80] 1 Timothy 6:16.
[81] Genesis 1:3.

if the line has width. Likewise the Father is unknown and unrevealed without the Son, the person of the Word. It is the unique function of the Son to reveal the Father by making him visible, in effect, putting a face on the Father.[82] Furthermore, though concepts can be *seen* and *understood* in two dimensions (e.g., a blueprint of a building or a photograph), they can never be *experienced* without the third dimension of depth. Through the person of the Word, humans can understand God; however, they cannot experience God except through the person of the Spirit. The Holy Spirit is the dimension of God who brings into the reality of human experience the understanding of God that the Word reveals to the human mind. This is why Jesus taught his disciples that it was better for them that he return to heaven and send the Spirit to lead them into truth and empower them for divine service.[83] Just as in the creation, when three spatial dimensions together produce reality that can be experienced, so it is in God: a three-dimensional, tripersonal community of three-in-one makes it possible for humans both to understand and to experience God.

In efforts to explain the mystery of God as three-in-one, great theologians have used various other images from the material world, particularly from geometry. Eastern trinitarian theology is often conceived as a straight line from Father, to Son, to Holy Spirit, to the world while Western trinitarian theology is described as a triangle or circle.[84] Instead of using either of these geometric symbols, however, Elizabeth Johnson has suggested an image drawn from the biology of human DNA that is perhaps much more apropos to the task of understanding God. Since human being was designed by God to image divine being, the chromosome of DNA is composed of a double helix that encodes the genomes of all human life and as such is one of the most mysterious and powerful images in creation. Both of the helices are congruent along a singular axis, and they interact with each other while remaining distinct from each other. "The strands of the helix do not originate from each other but are simply there together, not statically but moving in a dance of separation and recombination."[85] They are not clones of each other, nor do they exist independently of each other. Human life is incomplete with just one of the helices: both

---

[82] John 1:18; 2 Corinthians 4:6.
[83] John 14:16; 16:13; Acts 1:8.
[84] Walter Kasper, *The God of Jesus Christ,* tr. Matthew O'Connell (New York: The Crossroad Publishing Co., 1984), p. 306.
[85] Johnson, p. 221.

are required—a two-in-one as it were. By adding a third dimension to the double helix, Johnson envisions a "triple helix" representing God's tripersonal communion. Because it images the coinherence of the three persons of God, "the image of a triple helix intensifies this life-giving movement. It connotes the unfathomable richness of holy triune mystery, inwardly related as a unity of equal movements, each of whom is distinct and all of whom together are one source of life."[86] The three-in-one divine person is manifest in three persons who coinhere and mutually interpenetrate one another without replicating and rendering one another superfluous.

Each of these images from the material creation reveals something about the true nature of God, even his power and deity, for each demonstrates the absolute relational nature of God. Since God is tripersonal, the very essence of Deity is established in divine relationality, not in solitary isolation and egocentricity. The divine persons are not even persons except in their mutual relationship one with the other. While each of the three persons can be characterized individually, the unity of God as the three-in-one must be seen to consist in the divine community. Relationality, therefore, is at the very core of all existence, divine and human. Simply stated, God exists in the community and communion of Father, Son, and Spirit, a "perfect sociality" which "embodies those qualities of mutuality, reciprocity, cooperation, unity, peace in genuine diversity,"[87] a community in which total and absolute equality provides for mutuality and diversity of manifestation.

DYNAMICS OF DIVINE INTERRELATIONALITY

This imagery also confirms that the tripersonal interrelationship in deity is one of absolute equality and mutuality with respect for distinctives, not one of hierarchical domination and subordination. The understanding of God as being an entirely relational, personal being, a community of three persons in one divine being of substance, promotes an anthropology that encourages diversity, promotes mutuality, and builds community. The foundational understanding of God as pure relationality that is manifest in a community of equality and mutuality provides the model for humanity to relate as a community of equals. Through mutual submission, all humans receive complete

---

[86] Johnson, p. 221.
[87] Anne E. Carr, *Transforming Grace: Christian Tradition and Women's Experience* (San Francisco: Harper & Row, 1988), pp. 156-157.

liberty to manifest and express their own individuality without imposing such on others and to benefit from the otherness of others. This is true of society, church, and family.

Most attempts to explain the manner in which three divine persons can interrelate in equality and mutuality leave unresolved the problem of subordination, which implies that both the Son and the Spirit are ontologically inferior to the Father. As an answer to this problem, the Cappadocian fathers[88] of the Eastern church conceived the interrelationship of Father, Son, and Spirit as a perichoresis[89]—an encircling and interpenetration each of the other[90]—by which they function as a real community or family. The etymology of the Greek word *perichōrēsis* indicates a cyclical movement or revolving action. Perichoresis implies both a static "dwelling or resting within another" and a dynamic "interweaving of things with each other" so that the "divine life circulates without any anteriority or posteriority, without any superiority or inferiority of one to the other."[91] It is a mutual indwelling or coinherence of the three persons of Deity in which every action of the Divine is accomplished "cooperatively and conjointly."[92] As understood in terms of perichoresis, the triunity of God is a "non-hierarchical community. . . . It is not a single subject in the Trinity which constitutes the unity; it is that triadic inter-subjectivity which we call perichoresis."[93] The unity of God is, therefore, not "the monarchy of the Father," nor is it the Spirit who constitutes "the bond of unity" (the Augustinian view).[94] It is in the perichoresis of relationality and mutuality that the unity of God is manifest in terms of Karl Barth's description of God as "being in becoming," a concept which Eberhard Jüngel expands.[95]

In the human family, individuality and freedom are fully manifest only when husband and wife (in the family) and all members of the

---

[88] Basil, Gregory of Nyssa, and Gregory Nazianzus.

[89] In the Western Church, the Latin-based term *circumincession* is used for the Eastern Church's Greek-based term *perichoresis*.

[90] This understanding was based on John 17:21: "Thou Father, art in me, and I in thee," which was taken to mean that the Father and the Son indwell each other. In similar manner, the Holy Spirit indwells both the Father and the Son.

[91] Johnson, p. 220.

[92] Kevin Giles, "The Subordination of Christ and the Subordination of Women," in Ronald W. Pierce, Rebecca Merrill Groothuis, and Gordon D. Fee, eds., *Discovering Biblical Equality: Complementarity without Hierarchy* (Downers Grove, IL: InterVarsity Press, 2004), p. 340.

[93] Jürgen Moltmann, *Experiences in Theology* (Minneapolis, MN: Fortress Press, 2000), p. 317.

[94] Moltmann, p. 317.

[95] Eberhard Jüngel, *God's Being in Becoming: The Trinitarian Being of God in the Theology of Karl Barth* (Edinburgh: T & T Clark, Ltd., 2001), pp.77-78.

community (in the church) are mutually submitted to one another[96] and function together in mutuality and true fellowship. Each must make room for the other,[97] for fullest expression of the gifts and callings of one another just as Father, Son, and Holy Spirit do. Anything less than the ideal imaged from and patterned after the Divine results in ontological subordination and consequent idolatry of the exalted ego. God is a family, marriage constitutes a family, the church is a family, and in some way, all humanity is a family, the children of God.[98] In each level of human relationship, God can be imaged on earth solely in the context of pure relationality.

THE DYNAMICS OF THE DIVINE FAMILY

In the understanding of God reflected in both the Hebrew Scriptures and the Apostolic Writings, it is clear that God is a family, a community of three persons in one divine being of substance. As such, the persons are coequal, consubstantial, and coeternal, as the earliest Christian creeds affirmed.[99] There is absolutely no inequality or subordination in the God family. This truth is established by the apostle who asserted that Jesus "existed [and continued to exist] in the form of God," and as such he did not consider being "equal with God" something to which he should grasp.[100] Though he voluntarily surrendered his equality with God in order to become human, Jesus never had to grasp at or desperately hold on to that equality. One can voluntarily subject himself to another only when both are equal. Any other subjection is based in ontological inferiority. The voluntary choice of Jesus to become less than equal with God made it possible for him to accomplish the divine mission of human redemption. Because of this condescension, Jesus has been highly exalted to sit on God's throne.[101] That Jesus is seated "at the Father's right hand" means that Jesus is seated on God's throne, not on a separate throne beside him. God and

---

[96] Ephesians 5:23.
[97] 1 Corinthians 13:5.
[98] Acts 17:24-29.
[99] The term *coequal* originated in the discourse of the Nicene era. The concept of consubstantiality was enunciated in the Nicene Creed in the phrase "very God of very God." The concept of coeternity was established in both the Nicene Creed and the Creed of Chalcedon, which also established the consubstantiality of Jesus with all humanity in the incarnation. The Eastern and Western churches developed their own forms of the creeds. The Eastern creeds tended to be more metaphysical while the Western creeds were inclined to be more practical.
[100] Philippians 2:6; John 5:18.
[101] Philippians 2:9.

the Lamb have only "one throne."[102] They are seated together as One, for "the Son of Man has . . . taken His seat on the Father's throne."[103]

It should come as no surprise, then, that even prior to the time of Jesus, the sages of Israel often used the terms *God* and *Word of God* interchangeably, usually with the term *Word of God* serving as a substitute for the word *God.* Since they were so supersensitive about protecting the honor and name of God, they eventually adopted the tradition of not attempting to pronounce the ineffable name YHWH,[104] and they also began to use other terms as substitutes for the word *Elohim* (God).[105] This tradition became very evident in the translations of the Hebrew Scriptures into Aramaic, the *Targumim*[106] that were produced in order to make the Scriptures more understandable among the Semitic peoples who were not conversant in Hebrew.[107] In these texts, the term *Word of God* was substituted hundreds of times where the word *God* or the word *Lord* (YHWH) actually appeared in the Hebrew text of Scripture.[108] In order to preserve and revere the transcendence of God, the rabbis also posited the existence of a divine mediator between God and humanity whom they personified as the *Memra* (Aramaic for "word" or "spoken word"). They chose the Aramaic word *memra* over the Hebrew word *d'var* because *memra* came etymologically from the Hebrew/Aramaic verbal root *'mr*, which actually means "to say." This nuance was in context with the

---

[102] Jack Cottrell, *What the Bible Says About God the Redeemer* (Joplin, MO: College Press, 1987), p. 126.

[103] Henry Barclay Swete, *The Ascended Christ* (London: Macmillan, 1916), p. 12.

[104] The enunciation of the name YHWH was suspended in an effort to ensure that one did not violate the third commandment of the Decalogue: "You shall not take the name of the Lord your God in vain."

[105] A good example of this is seen in the use of the word *heaven* in Matthew's Gospel as a substitute or euphemism for *God*, as in "kingdom of heaven." This is likely also the underlying reason for the statement, "Heaven help us," rather than "God help us."

[106] There were two official *Targumim: Targum Onkelos* and *Targum Jonathan* which followed the midrashic interpretations of the *Tanakh* at the time. The *Targumim* were read in the ancient synagogue services after the reading of the same texts in the Hebrew. This was done to help explicate the Hebrew texts. When Aramaic was no longer a predominant language of commerce, this exercise was abandoned.

[107] Interestingly enough, the ancient Christian Syriac Church used the *Targumim* as their version of the Hebrew Scriptures.

[108] In both of the *Targumim*, the tradition of substituting *Word* for *God* was maintained. For example, *Targum Onkelos* of Genesis 28:20-21 makes the same substitution: "So that I come again to my father's house in peace; then shall the *Word of the Lord* be my God" (emphasis added). Likewise, *Targum Jonathan* of Deuteronomy 4:7 substitutes the phrase the *Word of the Lord* for the phrase the *word of YHWH* ("the Lord") in the statement: "The *Word of the Lord* sits upon His throne high and lifted up, and hears our prayer what time we pray before Him and make our petitions" (emphasis added). Numerous other examples could be cited from the texts of the *Targumim* wherein the word *memra* is used as a substitute for the words *Elohim* and YHWH.

Genesis narratives of creation which declare that it was only when God "said" (or issued the spoken Word) that the universe and all living beings came into existence (e.g., "God *said*, Let there be light, and there was light.").[109] The *Memra*, therefore, was a virtual hypostasis of the Word of God—written, spoken, and living. John the apostle used this same line of reasoning when he declared that "in the beginning . . . the Word was with God and the Word was God."[110] Rather than borrowing concepts from Eastern mystery religions, as many scholars, both Christian and Jewish, have asserted, John was simply explaining the rabbinic concept of the *Memra* in context with the apostolic understanding that God had become human in the person of Jesus.

Likewise, the term *Spirit of God* is also used interchangeably with the word *God*[111] to the extent that many scholars in history have mistakenly suggested the idea that the Holy Spirit is merely the emanation or force of God or that the Holy Spirit is another term for the Father who alone is God while the Son is a being that God created to be his representative.[112] It is clear, however, that the Holy Spirit also has personhood.[113] The three persons of God are interrelated and interactive. Accordingly, the terms *Spirit* and *Word* are also used interchangeably.[114] Jesus could rightly say, "the *words* that I speak unto you are *spirit* and life."[115] It is a simple fact, therefore, that Father, Son, and Holy Spirit are ontologically coequal.

The coequality of Father, Son, and Holy Spirit in the one God of Scripture is mirrored in humanity, the creation in the image and likeness of God. Adam and Eve were first one human entity called *ha-adam* (the-adam). Everything necessary for gender-specific human existence was present in original undifferentiated humanity. The male and female were surgically separated as God removed what pertained to the feminine from the side of *ha-adam* and constructed woman. Im-

---

[109] Some scientists have suggested that the universe may have been created out of sound waves. See Gabriel A. Oyibo, *Highlights of the Grand Unified Theorem: Formulation of the Unified Field Theory or the Theory of Everything* (Hauppauge, NY: Nova Science Publishers, 2001), p. 13.
[110] John 1:1.
[111] 1 Corinthians 3:16; 1 John 4:2.
[112] These concepts are fundamental to Unitarianism, which is based in the heresy propounded by Arius in the early fourth century that was rejected by the church because it did not recognize the absolute deity of Jesus.
[113] Jürgen Moltmann, *The Spirit of Life: A Universal Affirmation* (Minneapolis, MN: Augsburg Fortress Publishers, 2001), pp. 268-309. Also Floyd H. Barackman, *Practical Christian Theology: Examining the Great Doctrines of the Faith* (Grand Rapids, MI: Kregel Publications, 1981), pp. 195-229.
[114] Ephesians 6:17; cf. Galatians 4:6.
[115] John 6:63, emphasis added.

mediately thereafter, the male and female were then reunited in "one flesh." Of necessity, the two were coequal in order to image the coequality of the persons in God. This is why the superentity *ha-adam* is referred to as both "him" and "them." The equality of the Adamic creation was also manifest in the fact that God said, "Let them [not him] have dominion," so that authority over the rest of the terrestrial creation was shared between the two persons in the superentity of humanity such that neither was subordinate to the other.

The coequality of the three persons of God is fundamentally based on their consubstantiality, the fact that they are of one and the same substance or being.[116] The persons of the Word and Spirit are not of a different substance from that of the Father. In the words of the creeds they are "God of God."[117] Father, Son, and Holy Spirit are one in profound unity: they are of one essence. If they were not consubstantial, the three could not be ontologically equal: one would of necessity be inferior to the other(s) and, if so, would not be God. Son and Spirit would be created beings if they were not of the same substance as the Father. If Word or Spirit were created beings, they could not be God. Indeed, if the Word were a created being, he created himself (which is impossible), for Scripture unequivocally declares that all things in heaven and earth were created by the Word.[118] It is essential to the understanding of God, then, that one recognize fully that all that God is—Father, Son, and Holy Spirit—is of one and the same substance. The foundation of divine being (as well as of human being made in the divine image) is, therefore, the consubstantiality of the three persons in the one God.

The understanding of God as three divine persons existing in one divine being of substance with complete consubstantiality is clearly mirrored in the first human entity (or superentity) in the Genesis account of creation. Within the first body and living being that God created, the essence of both male and female were present in one, later to be surgically separated into two and then rejoined into one. These two were one, and, like their Creator, were coequal and consubstantial.

---

[116] The Greek description of the oneness of Father, Son, and Spirit declared that they were *homoousios* ("of the same being"), from the Greek word *ousia* ("being"). Since Latin lacks a present active participle for the verb "to be," Western authors translated the Greek *ousia* as *substantia* ("substance") and *homoousios* as *consubstantialis* ("of the same substance"). This translation was not intended, however, to imply materiality or physicality in God, for the Latin fathers recognized the substance and the very being of the tripersonal one God as spirit.
[117] The Nicene Creed introduced the formula "God of God" to describe Jesus.
[118] Colossians 1:16.

Because of their consubstantiality, both male and female humanity were coequal from the moment of their creation, and they continued to function together as one in complete mutuality with no hint of subordination either ontological or economic.

Finally, Father, Son, and Spirit are coeternal. There was never a time when either of the three did not exist, and there will never be a time when either will not exist. Charles Hodge correctly noted that "according to the Scriptures, the Father created the world, the Son created the world, and the Spirit created the world."[119] When, in the beginning, God created, it was a work of three who took counsel together and acted in concert. They did so as consubstantial persons who were coequal. There is absolutely no hint, therefore, of ontological subordination in the three persons of the one God from eternity past to eternity future. The concept of subordination in Deity has been and continues to be completely heretical.[120] "If Christ's subordination is not limited to a specific project or function but characterizes his eternal relationship with God, then Christ in not merely functionally subordinate; he is by nature subordinate,"[121] which is impossible if he is truly divine. "Jointly, inseparably, mutually," then, "the three persons dwell within each other" such that "sequence . . . does not necessitate subordination."[122] Historical attempts to establish a creedal understanding of God were and remain efforts to describe the perfect relationality that is manifest in the divine community. No one of the three persons in God was ever subordinate to the other (except when the Son became incarnate and as such became less than Father, Word, and Spirit), and they never will experience either ontological or economic subordination even when the Son delivers everything up to the Father, for then, the Godhead, not the Father, will be supreme ("all in all").[123]

The coeternity of the three persons in God is also mirrored in the human creation in that humanity, male and female, were created simultaneously, that they were comortal, and that they had the equal oppor-

---

[119] Charles Hodge, *Systematic Theology* (Grand Rapids, MI: Baker Book House, 1988), pp. 167-168. See Malachi 2:10; Colossians 1:16; Job 26:13; Psalm 104:30.

[120] Harold O. J. Brown, *Heresies* (New York: Doubleday, 1984), pp. 91-92.

[121] Rebecca Merrill Groothuis, *Good News for Women: A Biblical Picture of Gender Equality* (Grand Rapids, MI: Baker Book House, 1997), p. 57.

[122] Johnson, p. 196.

[123] The state in which the three persons of God dwelled together in undifferentiated oneness before the initiation of creation (wherein Father, Word, and Spirit were personified in assuming separate roles) will be restored when the purpose of all creation is fulfilled. The fact that then the "Godhead" will be all in all is confirmed by the use of the Greek ὁ θεός (o theos), literally "the God" or "the Godhead" to describe the God who is "all in all" in 1 Corinthians 15:28.

tunity to partake of the tree of life and become coimmortal. Likewise, there was no priority of creation for the male or the female. As God is coeternal, so humanity—male and female—was contemporaneous in creation: male and female were created simultaneously in one living being: *ha-adam*.[124] The lack of temporal differentiation in the being of God is mirrored in the same lack of temporal differentiation in the being of humanity. This, too, contributes to the understanding of the absolute equality of humanity, for there is no priority of existence to indicate—or even imply—either ontological or functional subordination. They were created simultaneously, and they were separated simultaneously; therefore, neither had precedence or priority over the other.[125]

RENEWING ANCIENT TRUTH

Instead of trying to establish an exaggerated spectacle of divine aloofness from the world, a Hebraic approach to theology underscores the relationality of divine being in creating and sustaining the universe and in maintaining interaction with the human creation. As a result, the mystery of God is even more glorious and incomprehensible. In the final analysis, God is inscrutable, and his ways are beyond discovery. At the same time, however, believers can find a means of considering the Divine in a way that respects both the transcendence of God and accepts the fact that God chose to become immanent—first by creating the universe, then by revealing himself to prophets and wise men, and finally by becoming incarnate in the person of his Son, Jesus the Messiah. This understanding frees God to maintain his own self-image, the one that he has chosen to reveal, and not be straightjacketed into a human image that limits him to human expectations and thereby does not allow him to be God. The God of Scripture is entirely relational, both within his own being and in his actions toward his creation: God is a tripersonal community, and he is "God with us." This is the God who created humanity to represent "in his own image and likeness." So it is that human beings, male and female—coequal, consubstantial, and comortal—are the image and likeness of God, Father, Son and

---

[124] *Ha-adam* (humanity) was undifferentiated as to gender until the divine surgery separated what pertained to the feminine, leaving what then was masculine.

[125] The argument that Adam was superior to or had the divine right of authority over Eve because he was created first lacks support both in Scripture and logic. If priority of creation indicated superiority, then the animals are superior to human beings. The fact was that both male and female were present in undifferentiated humanity from the moment of human creation.

Spirit—coequal, consubstantial, and coeternal. The God of pure intra-deity relationality is most perfectly imaged by the inter-human inter-relationality that mirrors the infinite love of divine being.

Springboard for Discussion

1. Discuss the historical imaging of God as a vengeful judge. Why do you think God has been viewed in this manner? How has this image impacted your own life?

2. Study the impact of Marcion on the Christian church during the second century A.D. How was his thinking rooted in Gnosticism? Why did he arrive at such a perverted and perverse view of the God of the Hebrew Scriptures? See if you can identify practices in the Christian church today that are rooted in ideas similar to those of Marcion.

3. Evaluate the personhood of the God of the Bible. What is there about God that reveals personhood?

4. Consider the nature of relationality that exists in God. How is God relational within his own being? How is the relationality of God's own being the foundation for his relationship with creation and humanity?

5. Discuss the fact that Hebraic tradition does not focus on God as "creator" but on God in relationship with his people. How does this tradition reflect God's own self-identity? What does it mean that God insists on having an "I-Thou" relationship with human beings?

6. Evaluate the Hebraic concept of history as being revealed in the birth of children. How important do you think it is to understand God in the context of his interaction with succeeding generations of people in covenant with him? How does this affect your own image of who God is, how he relates to human beings, and why he does the things that he does?

7. Consider the references in Scripture to God as "Father." Why do you think that this term was used to describe God? Does the use of this term indicate that God is masculine?

8. Discuss the concept that all beings—including God—are in relationship. What does Scripture mean when it says that God is love?

What is love (in Hebraic thinking)? How does God manifest love as a reflection of his own being?

9. Consider how God, within his own being, is the pattern for relationships of family and community. How do Father, Son, and Spirit interrelate to one another? How can the pure interrelationality within God be reflected in the human family and community?

10. Evaluate the declaration of the *Shema*, the most fundamental Jewish prayer, that God is one. Is this a statement of singularity, uniqueness, or unity? How are Father, Son, and Spirit one (as Jesus said, "I and my Father are one.")? How should the oneness of God be imaged in humanity and in the church? How is the oneness of husband and wife a part of the image and likeness of God?

11. Discuss the various images of three-in-one from the created universe with a view toward the truth that "the invisible things of God, even his power and Godhead, are understood by things that are made." How do these material manifestations help you understand more about the personhood of God and the interrelationality of three persons within the one God?

12. How did the disciples of Jesus come to the conclusion that he was more than man and that, indeed, he was God manifest in the flesh? Did they begin with a theory and then add documentation and argumentation to that theory, or did they begin with experience and then seek to explain it in the light of Scripture and their own tradition?

13. Consider whether subordination is possible among the persons of God. Can equal persons be ontologically subordinate and still be equal? Since male and female are equal, is ontological subordination possible in marriage? Is it possible for equal individuals to subject themselves one to another in an act of their own will? How is this different from ontological subordination?

14. Analyze the idea that the interrelationship within God is dependent upon the coequality and the consubstantiality of the persons in God, Father, Son, and Spirit. How was the equality of female and male in original humanity connected with the consubstantiality of the first human couple? Discuss the reasons for God's constructing the woman from the substance of humanity such that male and female were of the same substance and, indeed, of the same being.

CHAPTER 7

GOD'S SELF-IMAGE, MALE AND FEMALE

The God of Scripture is not the product of anthropomorphic imaginations of human beings who were attempting to create a god in their own image. Instead, God took the initiative to reveal himself in a form of divine self-disclosure by creating human beings so that they would be theomorphic, literally imaging the Divine. God simply decided to have personal representatives in the earth who would manifest his own image and likeness, and to that end he created humanity.

As Abraham Joshua Heschel has noted, instead of contending that God is like humans, it is more proper to say that humans are like God and to say that human qualities like concern for love and justice mirror God's concern for love and justice—not merely as anthropomorphisms applied by humans to God, but as theomorphisms applied by God to humanity. Humans are in the image of God, not vice versa.[1] David Blumenthal maintains that "it is not we [humans] who project ourselves onto God, but God Who projects Godself onto humanity."[2] Carl Henry agrees, noting that "Scripture declares not that God properly or actually exists in man's image, but that man was specially made in God's image."[3] He further observes that it would be a "colossal projection" for human beings to conceive that "the one God [is] a human

[1] Abraham Joshua Heschel, *The Prophets* (New York: Harper & Row, 1962), vol. 2, pp. 51-52.
[2] David R. Blumenthal, "Tselem: Toward an Anthropopathic Theology of Image" in Tikva Frymer-Kensky, David Novak, Peter Ochs, Michael Singer, and David Fox Sandmel, *Christianity in Jewish Terms* (Boulder CO: Westview Press, 2002), p. 338.
[3] Carl F. H. Henry, *God, Revelation, and Authority,* Vol. 5 (Wheaton, IL: Crossway Books, 1999), pp. 166-167.

personality inflated to infinity."[4] Instead humans are finite depictions of the infinite Personality. The creation of humanity in God's image and likeness should, therefore, be viewed more in terms of human theomorphism rather than in terms of divine anthropomorphism.[5]

Humankind was carefully created, formed, and constructed with only one purpose in mind: to serve as a theomorphic representation of the creator himself, not to inspire an image of God as a superhuman being but to image infinite Being in finite existence. Then, so that humans could comprehend God's self-disclosure, he employed understandable symbols, including anthropomorphisms that apply human characteristics and features to him[6] and theriomorphisms that ascribe animal qualities to him.[7] Whatever imagery is employed in Scripture serves to elucidate human knowledge of God's qualities and character with the clear understanding that God alone is to be worshipped and not human beings, animals, the earth, the stars, or the universe.

God chose to image himself in humanity, both male and female, equally and indiscriminately: "In the image of God created he him, male and female created he them." In order to confirm this foundational truth, it is essential to acknowledge that God has imaged himself in both male and female metaphor. The God of Scripture is no more reluctant to be viewed in feminine terms than he is to be seen in masculine terms. This truth is essential to the understanding that all of humanity, both male and female, is truly theomorphic—that both male and female equally manifest the image of God.

In any attempt to recover the biblically Hebraic self-image of God as he has chosen to reveal himself in Scripture, it is important that the various feminine images that are applied to God be affirmed and understood alongside those that are clearly masculine. Recognizing feminine images in God is essential in order to establish the truth that God is absolutely genderless and is not a masculine God. Scripture is clear: God describes himself and is described by the biblical writers in both feminine and masculine terms. Both women and men are, therefore, equally theomorphic: the feminine reveals something about God that the masculine does not, and the masculine reveals something about God that the feminine does not.

[4] Henry, pp. 166-167.
[5] Blumenthal, pp. 337-339.
[6] Isaiah 52:10.
[7] Psalm 91:4.

Willem Visser't Hooft was correct in pointing out that "we cannot eliminate fatherhood from the gospel without destroying its very meaning."[8] In the Hebrew Scriptures, God is clearly and unequivocally identified as Father.[9] In the incarnation, Jesus—even to the consternation of his fellow countrymen—regularly referred to God as "my Father,"[10] prayed to God as "Father,"[11] and instructed his disciples to pray, "Our Father."[12] At the same time, however, Visser't Hooft wisely concluded that while the fatherhood of God should remain the dominant Christian symbol, it should not be an exclusive symbol but should be open to the inclusion of other symbols "such as mother."[13]

References to motherly qualities of God exist in Scripture; however, they are not nearly as prevalent and, in some cases, they are rather oblique. At no time in Scripture is God specifically referred to as "Mother." Donald Bloesch concedes that "it might . . . be permissible on occasion to address the deity in terms such as 'Holy Mother, Wisdom of God' or "Wisdom of God, our Mother,' since such usage has some biblical support." He also suggests that the Holy Spirit could be portrayed in feminine terms "as the indwelling presence of God within the church, nurturing and bringing to birth souls for the kingdom," even though he asserts that the Spirit who acts on humanity with transforming power "is properly designated as masculine."[14] Still, he wisely argues that functional terms such as "Primal Matrix" or "Womb of Being" cannot be substituted for ontological symbols like Father and Son without bordering on the heresy of modalism.[15] Such imagery makes a mockery of Holy Scripture by introducing terminol-

---

[8] Willem Adolph Visser't Hooft, *The Fatherhood of God in an Age of Emancipation* (Geneva: World Council of Churches, 1982), p. 133.

[9] God is referred to as "Father" in twenty-two passages in the Hebrew Scriptures, including Psalm 89:26; Isaiah 9:6; 63:16; 64:8.

[10] Matthew 11:27; Luke 22:29; John 5:17.

[11] Matthew 26:39, 42; Luke 22:42; John 17:24.

[12] Matthew 6:9.

[13] Visser't Hooft, p. 133.

[14] Donald G. Bloesch, *Is the Bible Sexist? Beyond Feminism and Patriarchialism* (Westchester, IL: Crossway Publishing Co., 1982), pp. 25, 72-73.

[15] Donald G. Bloesch, *The Battle for the Trinity: The Debate over Inclusive God-Language* (Ann Arbor, MI: Servant Press, 1985), p. 31. There are two kinds of modalism: Modalistic Monarchianism and Dynamistic Monarchianism. Modalistic Monarchianism teaches that one God has been manifest in three different modes or aspects at different times: the modalistic monarchian God is a monopersonal being who changes modes, manifesting himself in the role of Father in the Hebrew Scriptures, then as Son in the person of Jesus, and finally as Spirit after the death, burial, and resurrection of Jesus. Dynamistic Monarchianism posits the idea that the man Jesus ultimately became the Son of God by adoption: the dynamist monarchian divine element was an impersonal power that was sent from God into the man Jesus, thereby elevating him to the status of Deity.

ogy and imagery that are simply not supported by the sacred texts.

Feminists Mary Daly and Ruth Duck, on the other hand, assert that reference to God as "Our Father" originates "in human imagination" and "castrates women"[16] and that no parental metaphors for God should be used at all, since gender connotations are so "ambiguous"[17]—a contention that is patently absurd, for if anything is clearly unambiguous, it is gender. Thankfully, some scholars, like Ted Peters, offer a middle ground by urging the exploration of "the biblical texts themselves" for drawing out "the many positive stories and symbols of women and divine feminine imagery already present in the Bible."[18] Neill Hamilton suggests that when Christians recognize the implications of biblical depictions of the Spirit in feminine terms they will discover that God "begins to parent us in father and mother modes."[19] Jürgen Moltmann has taken the idea of male/female imagery further, suggesting that God should be imaged as both a "motherly father" and a "fatherly mother."[20]

William Phelps offers an appropriate caveat for discussing female imagery in God by underscoring the fact that the "andromorphic and gynomorphic images . . . intended to convey something about the divine nature" must be recognized only as "pointing signs."[21] God strongly declared, "You did not see any form on the day the LORD spoke to you at Horeb from the midst of the fire,"[22] and he commanded: "For your own sake, therefore, be most careful . . . not to act wickedly and make for yourselves a sculptured image in any likeness whatever: the form of a man or a woman."[23] Indeed, as Phelps has noted, when Isaiah, speaking on behalf of God, frequently used extended metaphors that ascribed feminine qualities to the Divine, he

---

[16] Mary Daly, *Beyond God the Father: Toward a Philosophy of Women's Liberation* (Boston: Unitarian Universalist Association of Congregations in North America, 1973), p. 19. Daly takes this imagery to another level, declaring that "the divine patriarch castrates women as long as he is allowed to live on in the human imagination. The process of cutting away the Supreme Phallus can hardly be a merely 'rational' affair. The problem is one of transforming the collective imagination so that this distortion of the human aspiration to transcendence loses its credibility." While this assertion may resonate with some feminists, it is far too strident to warrant consideration.

[17] Ruth C. Duck, *Gender and the Name of God* (New York: Pilgrim Press, 1991), pp. 126-127.

[18] Ted Peters, *God—The World's Future* (Minneapolis: Augsburg Fortress Press, 2000), p. 47.

[19] Neill Hamilton, quoted in John Dart, "Balancing Out the Trinity: The Genders of the Godhead," *Christian Century*, February 16-23, 1983, pp. 147-150.

[20] Elisabeth Moltmann-Wendel and Jürgen Moltmann, *Humanity in God* (New York: Pilgrim Press, 1983), p. 89.

[21] William E. Phipps, *Genesis and Gender: Biblical Myths of Sexuality and Their Cultural Impact* (New York: Praeger Publishers, 1989), p. 6.

[22] Deuteronomy 4:15, NASB.

[23] Deuteronomy 4:15-16, TNK.

still consistently quoted God as asking the rhetorical question, "To whom will you liken me?" The implied answer was "that God is beyond exact comparison."[24] Likewise, the prophet consistently "satirized idol-makers who presumed that the transcendent God could be identified with objects of human experience."[25]

James Muilenberg has observed that "Yahweh has no mother goddess at his side; he includes within his nature both husband and wife, both father and mother. The feminine attributes as well as the masculine are absorbed into his holy being."[26] The truth is, therefore, that "neither man nor woman provides a completely adequate similarity or dissimilarity to the genderless deity,"[27] for "God stands quite outside human sexual differentiation as masculine or feminine."[28] Any attribution of sexuality to God, therefore, is a reversion to paganism, and any imagery that would gravitate in that direction, no matter how well-intended, is dangerous. Moving from a perverse historical andromorphic view of God to an equally perverse gynomorphic view of goddess merely exchanges one pagan deception for another.

Much caution is needed, therefore, even in the exploration of scriptural imagery. As Mary Hayter has noted, "Many people harbor illusory views about the importance of recovering and appreciating feminine theological vocabulary in the Old Testament."[29] This is especially true for many extremists who begin their expositions not from respect for the authority and trustworthiness of Scripture itself but from preconceived philosophical notions. In such cases, "not only is the methodology . . . often semantically confusing and exegetically unsound," but in many, if not most cases, their "approaches to feminine imagery exaggerate the significance of their subject matter."[30]

In reviewing the Scriptures for feminine imagery, therefore, care must be exercised not to extrapolate from either the grammar of the texts or from their historical/cultural context what is not clearly present in the texts themselves. Ignorance or violation of this principle has been the fundamental mistake of so many attempts that have been

[24] Isaiah 40:18-26; 44:7-20.
[25] Phipps, pp. 5-6.
[26] James Muilenburg in *The Interpreter's Bible,* ed. George Buttrick (Nashville; Abingdon-Cokesbury, 1952), vol. 1, p. 301.
[27] Phipps, p. 7.
[28] Mary Hayter, *The New Eve in Christ: The Use and Abuse of the Bible in the Debate about Women in the Church* (Grand Rapids, MI: William B. Eerdmans Publishing Co., 1987), p. 41.
[29] Hayter, p. 41.
[30] Hayter, p. 41.

made to read masculine imagery into biblical texts. One reason for acting with such circumspect exegesis and exposition is that "biblical symbols modulate with amazing versatility."[31] It is also abusive to the text and even problematic to the interpretation of the text when exegetes "try to insist that the grammatical gender of the image is indicative of the essential maleness or femaleness of the referent."[32] For example, the Hebrew word for house (בַּיִת —*bayit*) is masculine in gender while the word for door (דֶּלֶת —*delet*) is feminine in gender. This does not mean, however, that the essence of all houses is masculine and the essence of all doors is feminine.

Working to uncover the feminine imagery of God from Scripture and history can easily leave one vulnerable to the insidious dangers of Gnosticism, one of the first and most specious heresies to attack the nascent church. Gnosticism insisted that humans are saved, not by grace through faith, but by knowledge, specifically esoteric self-knowledge (*gnosis*). In the earliest centuries of Christian faith, Gnosticism infected Christian groups with its heretical ideas, and some of those ideas have survived in dualistic concepts that are still being taught in many Christian communions today. Some of these groups have extolled the virtues of the Gnostic documents discovered at Nag Hammadi in Egypt in 1945. Many feminist theologians have been particularly attracted to these documents because they contain much more feminine imagery of God than the canonical literature.[33] Some scholars argue that the Nag Hammadi corpus represents explanatory amendments that supply information either missing or expunged from Apostolic Scripture by gynophobic and misogynistic male church leaders. In truth, however, these documents were actually attempts to hijack the teachings of Jesus from their proper Hebraic matrix and to conform them to an extreme Hellenistic worldview. The Nag Hammadi documents reveal that the adherents to this "Christianized" Gnosticism worshipped a dyadic god, consisting of both male and female elements. One of the prayers of this community made this absurd and heretical affirmation: "From thee, Father, and through thee, Mother, the two immortal names, Parents of the divine being."[34]

Despite the musings of the Gnostics and countless other pagans,

---

[31] Hayter, p. 41.
[32] Hayter, p. 33.
[33] See Elaine Pagels, *The Gnostic Gospels* (New York: Vintage, 1981).
[34] Elaine Pagels, "What Became of God the Mother?" in *Womanspirit Rising: A Feminist Reader in Religion*, ed. Carol P. Christ and Judith Plaskow (San Francisco: Harper & Row, 1979), p. 109.

God still is neither male nor female nor a mixture of the two. Any compromise, therefore, with imagery arising from Greek philosophy or religion or from Eastern mystery religions contains grave danger for the faith of the believer and should be avoided at all cost. The risks posed by Gnosticism and its attendant heresies and revisionist history again point out the importance of returning to the original "faith once delivered to the saints"[35] so that today's faith is anchored—as was the faith of Jesus and the apostles—on the solid rock of divine revelation established in the *Tanakh*,[36] the Hebrew Scriptures. Grasping at straws from pseudepigraphical and heretical texts in order to affirm feminine imagery in God is perverse and unacceptable.

At the same time, however, continuing to ignore the feminine imagery that the Scriptures themselves attribute to God in an effort to preserve the androcentric *status quo* of historical theology, ecclesiology, and anthropology is perhaps even more perverse and unacceptable. The Scriptures must be released from incarceration in androcentric exegeses and exposition so that they can speak for themselves and bring the liberty that they contain for all believers, male and female. Those who are working in the mode of the prophets of old will always urge the people to turn from idolatry and serve only the living God, breaking the images of androcentric deity in a work of prophetic iconoclasm. The light of truth always dispels the darkness of error, and the Word of God smashes the images of false religion. This prophetic iconoclasm often features a struggle between bureaucrats and prophets in which the former create idols while the latter expose and demolish them. In some cases, the former construct idols to yesterday's fire and the latter seek to replace the idols with fresh fire.[37] In any case, the battle continues. In the final analysis, however, as Jesus declared, "You will know the truth, and the truth will make you free."[38]

SPRINGBOARD FOR DISCUSSION

1. Discuss the reasons why we should describe humans as theomorphic rather than view God in anthropomorphic terms. How does

---

[35] Jude 1:3.
[36] The word *TaNaKh* is an acronym for *Torah* (Law), *Nevi'im* (Prophets), and *Ketuvim* (Writings), the three divisions of the Hebrew Scriptures commonly called the "Old Testament."
[37] This is the lesson of Leviticus 6:11, where the priests were commanded to remove and bury the ashes of the previous day's fire while maintaining the fresh fire on the altar of sacrifice.
[38] John 8:32, NASB.

this viewpoint align more accurately with the biblical description of humanity's creation?

2. Evaluate anthropomorphisms in Scripture. How do anthropomorphisms help us as human beings understand truths about God? Is the use of such images proper? How do theriomorphisms help us comprehend things about God? Review some of the anthropomorphisms and theriomorphisms that are applied to God in Scripture. Do these mean that God is actually a human being or an animal?

3. Confirm the truth that the God of Scripture is neither male nor female. How does attribution of either femininity or masculinity to God become essentially a reversion to paganism? Discuss the historical religions that promoted male and female deities and why such imagery inappropriate to the biblical God.

4. Analyze the ways in which God manifest himself in terms that reflected both feminine and masculine images. Why is it important that God be understood in both masculine and feminine terms even though he is clearly genderless?

5. Discuss the care which one must exercise in discussing either masculine or feminine images in God. How important is it that believers in the God of Scripture eschew efforts that make God either feminine or masculine or both? Can the genderless nature of God be understood while at the same time attributing masculine and feminine qualities to God in the form of anthropomorphisms? How is this possible in the context of humanity's being theomorphic with male and female reflecting the image of God?

6. Evaluate Gnosticism and the dangers it poses to Christian and Jewish faith. Why is it important that scholars today avoid the pitfalls of Gnostic thought regarding God and gender? Should the care exercised in avoiding Gnosticism forbid interpreters and believers in general from exploring scriptural images of God as they relate to male and female humanity?

7. In what ways do the words of Jesus, "You shall know the truth, and the truth shall make you free," resound in importance to your life? How can you be sure you know the truth? Can you build on any other foundation than the Word of God?

CHAPTER 8

FEMININE IMAGES OF GOD IN SCRIPTURE

There is ample evidence directly from the Hebrew Scriptures that God chose to reveal himself to humanity by means of both male and female images—and often both at the same time. Neither God nor the prophets, sages, or apostles suffered from gynophobia or misogyny. Since the God of Scripture was neither male nor female, he could cause himself to be understood by using metaphor and imagery taken from both his female and his male creations. God demonstrated to humanity intrinsic facts about himself by using imagery that could be readily understood by both genders of humanity and to which both could relate either from experience or from observation. Since both male and female were made in the image and likeness of God, both were equally theomorphic and could, therefore, legitimately consider the mystery of the Deity in anthropomorphic terms that were both andromorphic and gynomorphic. More than incidentally, then, the God of the Bible clearly chose to image himself in gynomorphic terms.

EL SHADDAI: THE BREASTED GOD

Feminine imagery applied to God would have come as no surprise to the Hebrews themselves, for the ancient name for God that was revealed to Abraham contained vivid feminine imagery. *El Shaddai,* which is generally translated "The Almighty,"[1] was likely derived from the Hebrew word *shad*, which means "breast." Indeed, the first mention of *Shaddai* in Scripture confirms this truth: "The arms of his hands were made strong by . . . *El Shaddai* (שַׁדַּי) who blesses you with . . . blessings of the breasts (שָׁדַיִם—*shaddim*) and of the womb (רְחַם—*rechem*)."[2] Some scholars have asserted that the ultimate diphthong *ai* in the word *Shaddai* may have been an ancient feminine ending, making it possible to render the name or title as "The Breasted One." Larry Edwards, however, suggests that the suffix is the possessive personal pronoun, which, if true, would cause *Shaddai* to mean "my breast."[3] The accuracy of translating *El Shaddai* as "The Breasted God" or as "the God (*El*) of my breast (*Shaddai*)" is confirmed by the immediate textual relationship between the name *Shaddai* and the subsequent metaphors: blessings of the "breasts" (שָׁדַיִם—*shaddim*) and the "womb" (רְחַם—*rechem*). What would be more natural as a benefit from "The Breasted God" than blessings of "the breasts" and of "the womb"?

G. Campbell Morgan says that "the name or title *El Shaddai* is peculiarly suggestive [but] we miss much of the beauty by our rendering 'God Almighty.'"[4] While the idea of almightiness is, indeed, present in the text, it is better expressed as "The Pourer or Shedder-forth" or "The Breasted One."[5] Andrew Jukes says, "His Almightiness is of the breast, that is, of bountiful, self-sacrificing love, giving and pouring itself out for others."[6] Lewis Sperry Chafer notes that the title *El Shaddai* "conveys the truth that God sustains His people. The term indicates more than that God is a God of strength . . . [it] includes the impartation of His strength as a child draws succor from the mother's

---

[1] The preferred translation of *Shaddai* as "Almighty" has been based on the argument that the word *Shaddai* is from the Akkadian word *Shadu*, which means "mountain" since mountains are mentioned in the next verse (Genesis 49:26). See David Biale, "The God with Breasts: *El Shaddai* in the Bible" in David Biale, *History of Religions*, 21:3 (Feb., 1982), pp. 240-256. Others suggest that *El Shaddai* is from the root *shadad*, which means "to overpower" or "to destroy." Still others argue that *El Shaddai* is derived from the Aramaic word *shda*, which means "hurler of lightning and thunder," or from the Arabic term *sadda*, which means "heaper of benefits." See Daniel Hillel, *The Natural History of the Bible* (New York: Columbia University Press, 2006), p. 208. So *El Shaddai* can be either "The Overpowerer" or "the God of the mountains," or "the hurler of lightning and thunder," or "the heaper of benefits." It would appear, however, that each of these translation alternatives represents an attempt to evade the obvious, which is clear not only from etymology but also from the context of the text itself.

[2] Genesis 49:24-25.

[3] Larry D. Edwards, *The Twelve Generations of the Creation!* (Longwood, FL: Xulon Press, 2006), p. 52.

[4] G. Campbell Morgan, quoted in Herbert Lockyer, *All the Divine Names and Titles in the Bible* (Grand Rapids, MI: Zondervan Publishing House, 1988), p. 14

[5] Morgan, p. 14.

[6] Andrew Jukes, quoted in Lockyer, p. 14.

breast."[7] The God of Scripture, then, chose to image himself to his people not just as a military conqueror ("The Almighty") but as a gentle All-Sufficient One, the provider of everything that they needed. While there were occasions in their lives that called for the intervention of a delivering military conqueror, more often than not, they needed the simple gift of daily sustenance and provision. This was a metaphor that nomadic shepherds could easily understand by simply observing the way in which the ewes of their flocks were "more than enough" for their lambs. In like manner, they could powerfully consider *El Shaddai* in those same feminine terms by envisioning their God as the all-sufficient provider of sustenance—indeed, of life itself—for his children. They readily understood that their very existence depended upon the provision of grace from the breasts of their God. God's grace was always "more than enough" for their needs.

In conjunction with the imagery of God as the "breasted one," the Hebrew word most commonly associated with divine grace also manifests distinctively beautiful and graphic feminine imagery. The word חֶסֶד (*chesed*) means "goodness," "lovingkindness," or "faithfulness" and is often translated "grace," "favor," or "mercy."[8] Like so many of the words that describe attributes of the divine, *chesed* is also feminine in gender. Tirzah Firestone observes that *chesed* in Hebrew thought is "likened to the surge that a nursing mother feels when her milk lets down."[9] Somehow, when a hungry baby cries, "as any lactating mother knows, the milk lets down" regardless as to how occupied the mother is "or how beautiful the chiffon evening dress she is wearing is when the call comes."[10] This is a powerful image of the divine feminine quality in God that reacts immediately to the needs of his children and does so with a super-abundance of kindness and faithfulness that is always *Shaddai*, more than enough. *Chesed* "is the unmethodical profusion of nourishment that seems to be quite beyond our control," Firestone observes. Asking rhetorically, "Is there any surprise that Chesed is often seen as a natural strong suit for many women?" she gives the obvious answer: "One might say that nature

---

[7] Lewis Sperry Chafer, *Systematic Theology* (Grand Rapids, MI: Kregel Publications, 1948, 1976), p. 56.

[8] The Hebrew word *chanan* is another word that is commonly translated "mercy" or "grace" though it actually means "graciousness," "beauty," or "favor." The word *chesed* is more generally applied to God to denote his favor in the sense of lovingkindness.

[9] Tirzah Firestone, *The Receiving: Reclaiming Jewish Women's Wisdom* (San Francisco: HarperCollins Publishers, 2003), p.167.

[10] Firestone, p. 167.

has built the nurturing quality of Chesed into [women's] very molecules to make for successful childbearing and the continuation of the species."[11]

THE WOMB OF GOD

Divine mercy, one of the most profound and enduring qualities of God, was also imaged throughout the Hebrew Scriptures as being clearly related to the female anatomy. Yahweh is consistently portrayed as being merciful—indeed, full of mercy.[12] Even divine justice is measured and balanced with mercy in a theme that was repeatedly affirmed by kings, prophets, and sages in Israel with the declaration: "his mercy endures forever."[13] In Exodus 33:19, God introduced a term for mercy that contains powerful feminine imagery when he said, "I will show mercy [רָחַם—racham)] on whom I will show mercy [רָחַם—racham)]." Since *racham*, meaning "mercy," is from the same root as *rechem*, meaning "womb," in Hebrew thought divine mercy has remained a consistent and clear application of feminine imagery to God. Tragically, this and other depictions of God in graphic feminine terms have often been obscured in most translations of Scripture.

Phylis Trible expands this understanding further when she maintains that the concrete anatomical meaning of *rechem* (womb) "expands to the abstractions of compassion, mercy, and love," letting the metaphor develop in "the semantic movement from a physical organ of the female body to a psychic mode of being."[14] She suggests that *rachamim* (mercies) literally means "movements of the womb."[15] In the language that God uses, it is clear that divine mercy is portrayed as parallel with the safety of the womb. Indeed, as Elizabeth Johnson observes, "when God is spoken of as merciful, the semantic tenor of the word indicates that the womb is trembling, yearning for the child, grieved at the pain" so that "what is being showered upon the wayward is God's womb-love."[16]

In describing divine mercy in terms of the womb, the Scriptures

---

[11] Firestone, p. 167. It is a baby's cry—a specific one—that triggers the lettting down of a mother's milk. This is a graphic image that speaks of the response of God to the cries of his children in distress.

[12] Psalm 86:15; 119:64; 145:8.

[13] Psalm 136 is a chapter of 26 verses, all of which end with the phrase *"for his mercy endures forever."*

[14] Phyllis Trible, *God and the Rhetoric of Sexuality* (Philadelphia: Fortress Press, 1978), p. 33.

[15] Trible, p. 33.

[16] Johnson, p. 101.

have attached solid feminine imagery to the understanding of God that cannot be obviated or circumvented. The uterus is the only part of human anatomy that has absolutely no corollary in the male body; therefore, reference to God's womb cannot be extrapolated to have some metaphorical masculine application.[17] The Hebrew language itself, therefore, strongly maintains that God has maternal qualities.[18] Contrary to the God imaged in Greco-Roman Christian thought, the God of Israel did not shy away from describing himself or being described by others in feminine terms or from manifesting qualities that were directly associated with the female anatomy. In Hebrew thought, femininity *per se* was not considered evil or degrading as it was in Greek thought.

Perhaps Clement of Alexandria was right when he said, "For what is more essential to God than the mystery of love? Look then into the womb (*kolpon*) of the Father, Which alone has brought forth the only begotten Son of God."[19] Clement's discourse became even more poignant when he continued: "God is love, and for love of us has become woman (*ethēlynthē*). The ineffable being of the Father has out of compassion with us become mother. By loving, the Father has become woman (*Agapēsas ho patēr ethēlynthē*)."[20] Clement and other authors who dared to explore feminine imagery in God manifest a clear respect for biblical truth that has been neglected for far too long by far too many scholars and ecclesiastical leaders.

GYNOPHOBIC MISTRANSLATIONS OF SCRIPTURE

Translations of the texts of Scripture have often been inadequate and, in some cases, downright deceptive. As a result of the determination of some to solidify their belief that God is somehow masculine (and by all means *not* feminine), they have misrepresented—if not outright mistranslated—various biblical texts that speak of God in feminine terms. Gynophobic translators have sought to obfuscate the clear intent of statements made either by God or by prophets who spoke about God so as to conceal the fact that the God of the Hebrews was

---

[17] Firestone, p. 217.
[18] See Rosemary Radford Ruether, "Sexism and God-Language," in *Weaving the Visions: New Patterns in Feminine Spirituality,* ed. Judith Plaskow and Carol Christ (San Francisco: Harper & Row, 1989), p. 154.
[19] Clement of Alexandria, *"Quis Dives Salvetur,"* quoted from J. P. Migne, *Patrologia Graeca*, vol. 9, col. 641, in Leonard Swidler, *Biblical Affirmations of Women* (Louisville, KY: Westminster John Knox Press, 1979), p. 66.
[20] Clement, quoted from Migne in Swidler, p. 66.

not afraid to manifest feminine as well as masculine qualities and to speak of himself or be spoken of by others in feminine terms and with feminine imagery.

A particularly egregious example of outright mistranslation of Hebrew texts in order to obscure or remove feminine imagery from the masculine image that has been ecclesiastically imposed on God is found in the New King James Version rendering of Deuteronomy 32:18: "Of the Rock who begot you, you are unmindful, and have forgotten the God who *fathered* you" (emphasis added).[21] In this text, two modes of parenting are noted in the same verse. In most versions, the first clause of this sentence, "You neglected the Rock that begot you," is rendered accurately though in varied forms. In this clause, the Hebrew word that is translated "begot" in the New King James Version nd "fathered" in NIV is יְלָדְךָ (*yeladcha*), from the root יָלַד (*yalad*), which means "to beget" but also means to "bear" or "bring forth." The word יָלַד (*yalad*), with a minor difference in pronunciation, is the same as the word יֶלֶד (*yalad*), which means "child." In יְלָדְךָ (*yeladcha*), both the idea of fatherhood and motherhood can rightly be applied because both father and mother are necessary for the birth of a child. In this case, the use of יְלָדְךָ (*yeladcha*) likely confirms the premise in the context of this passage where Moses emphasized that Yahweh was the "father who bought [acquired, created] you . . . made you, and established you."[22] God is, indeed, the creator, the father of Israel.

The serious problem of mistranslation in the NKJV that totally occludes the comprehensive meaning of this text is found in the rendering of the second clause of this sentence: "You have forgotten the God who *fathered* you."[23] The Hebrew word that is rendered "fathered" in this version of the text is חֹלְלֶךָ (*cholelecha*). When literally translated, *cholelecha* means "writhed in labor [with] you." *Cholelecha*, therefore, could never mean "fathered you" even in the greatest stretch of the imagination. "Writhing in labor" is neither physically nor metaphorically possible for a father. Men simply do not "writhe in labor" when they "father" a child! The New King James Version, then, is clearly inaccurate in its translation. The King James Version equally mistranslates this clause as "[thou] hast forgotten the God

[21] The New International Version renders this text far more accurately: "You deserted the Rock, who fathered you; you forgot the God who gave you birth" (emphasis added). This translation is more faithful to the intent of the Hebrew text in that it speaks of fatherhood and motherhood.
[22] Deuteronomy 32:6.
[23] Emphasis addeed.

that *formed* you." The word *formed* is also not even remotely possible as a translation of חֹלֶלֶךָ (*cholelecha*). In reality, this Hebrew passage would be more accurately translated thus: "Of the Rock who created you, you are unmindful, and you have forgotten the God who writhed in labor with you," or even thus: "Of the Rock who *fathered* you, you are unmindful, and you have forgotten the God who *mothered* you."[24]

Both the King James Version and New King James Version renderings of *cholelecha* were likely influenced by the inadequate translation of the Septuagint, which rendered the Hebrew word חֹלֶלֶךָ (*cholelecha*) with the Greek phrase τρέφοντός σε (*tréphontós se*), which literally means "to curdle you" but figuratively means "to breed you" or "to rear you." In this Greek rendering, there is no hint of the Hebrew meaning, "to writhe in labor with you." This inaccuracy in the Septuagint was the foundation of the further mistranslation of the text in the Latin Vulgate: *"Deum qui te genuit dereliquisti et oblitus es Domini creatoris tui"* ("You have forsaken the God who begot you and have forgotten the Lord that created you"). Could it be that the gynophobia and misogyny of the Greco-Roman world that filtered down into the church prompted the rendering of the graphic Hebrew term for "writhe in labor" with the Greek word for "breed" and subsequently with the Latin word for "create"? It appears that the Greek and Latin translators took the liberty of rendering the word *cholelecha* as "breed" or "create" because they could not possibly imagine God as having feminine attributes and certainly not as having done anything associated with gynecology or feminine physiology. The Hellenized and Latinized God could "breed" or "create," but he would never lower himself to "writhe in labor"!

It is obvious from the Hebrew text that as Moses was concluding the writing of the Torah, God chose to emphasize through his prophet that the Israelites were, indeed, his children and that he had "created" (יְלָדְךָ) this corporate people and had "writhed in labor" (חֹלֶלֶךָ) with them. The predominant image in this complete text is that of God as Father, as is expressly demonstrated in verse 6 of the context. Still God makes it clear through Moses that the God of Scripture is neither a

---

24 To their credit, NASB, NIV, NRS, NAB, ESV, CJB, and NET (among other modern language versions) translate *cholelecha* as "gave you birth," which maintains the essence of the text even though it does not maintain the graphic imagery that leaves no doubt about the feminine image. The TNK renders *cholelecha* "brought you forth," and the JPS translates it "bore thee." It is the outright mistranslation of *cholelecha* in masculine terms that is totally unacceptable.

male god nor a female goddess. The one God manifests attrributes of both genders, for he both fathers and mothers his children. He makes this clear by employing the graphic imagery that is commonly associated with the Hebrew Scriptures, which are not hesitant to describe what God was not ashamed to create. This approach was consistently employed in Scripture primarily because the Hebrews understood that God had made everything, including both the female anatomy and the male anatomy, and that he had declared everything he had made to be "good" and "very good" from the moment of creation. For the biblical authors, therefore, nothing material, particularly human beings, could be considered to be inherently evil.

Yet another example of inadequate translation that obscures the feminine imagery which Scripture ascribes to God is found in Isaiah 63:14-16: "[Lord], where are your zeal and your strength, the yearning of your heart and your mercies toward me? . . . You, O Lord, are our Father, our Redeemer from of old is your name" (NKJV). In this case, the phrase translated "yearning of your heart" is הֲמוֹן מֵעֶיךָ (*hamon me'ehcha*) which in Hebrew literally means "the murmur of your internal organs" or "the murmur of your intestines."[25] The word *me'eh* (in *me'ehcha*) even more commonly means "organs of procreation" or "womb."[26] Whether the Hebrew phrase הֲמוֹן מֵעֶיךָ (*hamon me'ehcha*) in Isaiah's prophecy means "the murmur of your intestines" or "the murmur of your womb," one thing is certain, it should never be translated "yearning of your heart."[27] Indeed, since the Hebrew word that is consistently used 202 times in the Hebrew Scriptures for "heart" is

---

[25] Figuratively, the word *me'eh* can also mean "the place of emotions."

[26] The correct translation of the word *me'eh* is dictated by the context in which it is used. In Genesis 15:4, it is clear that *me'eh* refers to testes as God affirms to Abraham, "One who will come forth from your own *me'eh* shall be your heir." When God declares in Isaiah 48:19, "Your seed would have been like the sand, and the offspring of your *me'eh* like its grains," it is obvious that *me'eh* means "testes" (because it is associated with "seed" or sperm in the context). In Genesis 25:23, however, it is certain that *me'eh* means "uterus" when God declares to Rebekah, "Two nations are in your womb, and two peoples will be separated from your me'eh." Similarly, when David says of God in Psalm 71:6, "You are he who took me from my mother's *me'eh*," it is obvious that he is speaking of the womb. On the other hand, it is clear in 2 Samuel 20:10 that *me'eh* means "intestines" since it speaks of a wound in battle in which "*me'eh* spilled out on the ground." When 2 Chronicles 21:15 says, "You will suffer severe sickness by disease of your *me'eh* until the disease causes your *me'eh* to come out," it is clear that it is referring to some intestinal malady. Though *me'eh* occasionally does mean "intestines," more generally it refers to organs of procreation, both male and female. Clearly, when *me'eh* is connected with divine mercy—which is directly associated etymologically with the womb—it is understood to mean "womb." In no way, however, could *me'eh* be construed to mean "heart" in any of these references, and it certainly does not mean "heart" in Isaiah 63:14-16.

[27] Of the 39 uses of the word *me'eh* in Scripture, only one (Jeremiah 4:19) could be said to refer to the heart: "My *me'eh*, my *me'eh*! I am pained at my very heart [*lev*]."

לֵב—*lev*, clear contextual evidence must be present in the text for *me'eh* to be translated "heart." The fact that "murmur of your womb" is the correct translation is established by the immediate context wherein the prophet seeks God's "mercies." The Hebrew word translated "your mercies" is רַחֲמֶיךָ—*rachamecha*, which is derived from the root רחם—*rchm* from which also comes רָחַם—*racham* ("mercy") and רֶחֶם—*rechem* ("womb"). The connection between "womb" and "mercy" is apropos to this text because the safest place in the universe for an unborn fetus, where it is not only protected but also nurtured and brought to term, is in its mother's womb. The spiritual lesson of this metaphor confirms the fact that the safest place on earth for any human being is in the mercy of God. The abstract concept of divine mercy, then, is based in the concrete image of the female uterus. Once again, the prophet's prayer to Yahweh is that might, ardor, and strength (traditional masculine images) should be enlisted to the community's need, along with the murmuring or trembling of God's womb or mercy (traditional feminine images). Yahweh, who is clearly genderless, chose to manifest himself in theomorphisms that contain imagery of both male and female—and at the same time! This, no doubt, was intentional so that both male and female hearers would not ascribe either divine masculinity or divine femininity to God but would still be able to relate fully to the Divine from their own experience.

In Jeremiah 31:20-21, the same language and imagery are employed as God refers to Ephraim as his "dear son," and declares, "My heart [*me'eh*] yearns for him; I will have mercy [*racham*] on him." Just as is the case with Isaiah 63:14-15, the meaning of this text has also been obscured in translation, for the word מֵעֶה (*me'eh*) is again translated "heart" when it should have been translated as "womb." The fact that the author intended *me'eh* to mean "womb" and not "intestines" in this instance is clear from the context where the word *me'eh* is used in connection with the word *racham*, which is correctly translated here as "mercy" and is clearly related to *rechem*, meaning "womb." Yahweh's yearning and mercy for his "dear son" Ephraim comes from God's womb, not from his heart. The strong feminine imagery of this text is further confirmed by the fact that God's promise continues with this statement: "The Lord has created a new thing in the earth—A woman will encompass a man."[28] This appears to be a graphic device

---

[28] Jeremiah 31:22, NASB.

that is intended to emphasize that God will do a new thing in that he will embrace Ephraim, his "dear son," in an intimate, motherly way that will return him to the degree of safety that is imaged only by the security of an unborn child in its mother's womb. God will encompass Ephraim in his womb as a mother encompasses a fetus in her womb. Graphic? Yes! Confusing? No.

In Isaiah 42:13, the prophet again used both masculine and feminine imagery to describe God's actions. He first predicted that "The Lord will go forth like a warrior . . . he will prevail against his enemies." Immediately, however, this masculine imagery was expanded by expressly feminine language: "Now, like a woman in labor I will groan, I will both gasp and pant." The King James Version—as is often the case—apparently had problems with graphic imagery of the Hebrew "gasping and panting," for it translated these words as "I will destroy and devour at once." Once again, the androcentric theologians and the translators of the King James Version[29] manifest their gynophobia at best and their misogyny at worst. Apparently for them, the image of God as a "mighty man of war" required that he "cry, yea, roar . . . like a travailing woman" and "destroy and devour," but he could not possibly "gasp and pant" as a "woman in labor."[30]

Other biblical passages also contain clear feminine images of God. In Isaiah 49:15, God compared his concern for Israel with that of a woman toward her child: "Can a woman forget her nursing child and have no compassion on the son of her womb? Even these may forget, but I will not forget you." Again, in Isaiah 66:10-13, God spoke reassuring words to Israel, using very graphic mother-child language to describe his blessing: "Be joyful with Jerusalem . . . that you may nurse and be satisfied with her comforting breasts. . . . You will nurse and be carried on the hip and fondled on the knees." Then God declared that this comfort actually would come from the Divine: "As one whom his mother comforts, so I will comfort you; and you will be comforted in Jerusalem." In this extended metaphor, both Jerusalem and God are imaged in feminine terms as Israel's mother so that being

---

[29] There is little doubt about the King James Version translators' prejudice against women; however, they were only reflecting the views of their sovereign, King James I, of whom it was said, "The moment [he] had the crown placed securely on his head, he gave notice that . . . he would take every opportunity to trample women into permanent invisibility."—King James I, quoted in Selma Williams, *Divine Rebel: The Life of Anne Marbury Hutchinson* (New York: Holt, Rinehart and Winston, 1982), p. 35.

[30] To their credit, virtually all modern versions of Scripture translate the passage more accurately as the NKJV's: "Now I will cry like a woman in labor, I will both pant and gasp at once."

nursed, carried on the hip, and fondled on the knees of Jerusalem actually described the consoling activity that God as mother directed to the children of Israel.

FEMININE AND MASCULINE IMAGES

God created both male and female in his own image and likeness; therefore, both the female and the male are theomorphic. Since both reflect God's image, God must, of necessity, have both female and male qualities even though he is clearly genderless. Both men and women, therefore, may rejoice because God has made it clear that feminine as well as masculine traits and roles are active in the divine being. Neither women nor men have any reason to view themselves or to view one another as less than perfect and equal reflections of the image and likeness of God, for God unequivocally said, "Let me make humanity in our image, after our likeness," and when he fulfilled his intentions, he "created humanity in his image, in the image of God created he him, male and female created he them . . . and [he] blessed them, and called their name Adam, in the day when they were created."[31]

SPRINGBOARD FOR DISCUSSION

1. Analyze examples of Scripture that have been either mistranslated or inadequately translated in order to mask the attribution of feminine imagery to God. What impact has traditional androcentric interpretations of Scripture had on our understanding of God?

2. Discuss how Scripture sometimes depicts God in both masculine and feminine terms at the same time. How can God be genderless while manifesting qualities usually associated with both men and women? How does this aid in your understanding of God? How does such understanding contribute to your own self-evaluation as being in the image and likeness of God?

3. Evaluate the use of feminine anatomical features to construct an image of God as full of mercy (the womb) and an all-sufficient provider (the breasts)? How do these images confirm God's positive evaluation of women as bearing his image and likeness?

4. Discuss the difference between the Hebraic tradition that con-

---

[31] Genesis 1:27; 5:2.

sidered women and their attributes good and positive and those of other pagan traditions that considered women to be evil and negative forces. Cite examples of positive images for women in Scripture. How does the biblical treatment of women reinforce a positive anthropology? What impact does this truth have on your thinking?

CHAPTER 9

FEMININE IMAGES AND THE HOLY SPIRIT

It has often been asserted that the Holy Spirit bears a feminine image of God. It is certainly interesting that of the 84 scriptural uses of the Hebrew word רוּחַ—*ruach* ("spirit"), 75 are either clearly feminine (because a verb or modifier associated with them is also feminine in gender) or indeterminable (because they have no verb or modifier). Only nine times is the word *ruach* used in conjunction with masculine verbs or modifiers. The preponderance of textual evidence, then, supports the belief of many that the Holy Spirit somehow demonstrates feminine imagery as a reflection of the overall revelation and manifestation of God.

In early Christian history, some church fathers, particularly those in Eastern tradition, identified the Holy Spirit as representative of a feminine aspect of God. Early Semitic and Syrian Christians unhesitatingly described the Holy Spirit in female terms, ascribing motherly characteristics that had already been manifest in reference to God in the Hebrew Scriptures themselves.[1] The Jewish sects of the Ebionites and the Nazoraeans believed that the Holy Spirit was actually feminine. They supported their contention by appealing to the statement in the pseudepigraphic *Gospel According to the Hebrews* that the Holy Spirit was the mother of Jesus.[2] Because of their efforts to impose legalism on the entire church (much in the spirit of the Galatianism that

---

[1] Robert Murray, "The Holy Spirit as Mother," in *Symbols of Church and Kingdom* (London: Cambridge University Press, 1975), pp. 312-320. See also P. A. De Boer, *Fatherhood and Motherhood in Israelite and Judean Piety* (Leiden: Brill, 1974).
[2] Keith Akers, *The Lost Religion of Jesus* (New York: Lantern Books, 2000), p. 52.

Paul condemned), the constituents of these sects were considered to be heretics by the larger church. There is no evidence, however, that their depictions of the Holy Spirit in feminine terms were at that time attacked as heretical.

Until 400 A.D., Syriac Christians imaged the Spirit in feminine terms as a brooding mother bird.[3] They pointed out that the Spirit hovered over Mary empowering her to form Jesus as the only human being "made [entirely] of woman."[4] Likewise, they noted that the Spirit in the bodily form of a dove empowered and commissioned the ministry of Jesus at his baptism.[5] They also taught that the Spirit is the believers' mother,[6] bringing them "to birth out of the watery womb of the baptismal font."[7] On the basis of Isaiah's comparison of Yahweh to a mother comforting her child[8] and Jesus' reference to the Holy Spirit as the "Comforter,"[9] Makarios, an early Syrian father, concluded that "the Spirit is our mother."[10] By the third century, the Syriac-language *Didascalia Apostolorum* spoke of deaconesses "as a type of the Holy Spirit,"[11] extending the feminine metaphor of the Holy Spirit to women who served in a ministry that was at that time ecclesiastically limited and was eventually abandoned altogether.

In ways somewhat similar to their Syrian counterparts, many Greek theologians of early Christian centuries believed that the Holy Spirit, while not actually being feminine, still manifested feminine qualities of God. As a matter of fact, some Orthodox thinkers even gave precedence to the Spirit as the *second* person of the Trinity, while viewing Jesus (the *Logos*) as the *third* person, perhaps because the Spirit was present and hovering before the Word was manifest in the Genesis narrative[12] and because the Spirit overshadowed Mary at the conception

---

[3] Dale T. Irvin and Scott Sunquist, eds., *History of the World Christian Movement* (Maryknoll, NY: Orbis Books, 2001), vol. 1, p. 63

[4] Galatians 4:4 implies that Jesus was, indeed, made of woman.

[5] Luke 3:22.

[6] James Hastings, John Selbie, and Louis H. Gray, eds., *Encyclopedia of Religion and Ethics* (New York: Charles Scribners' Sons, 1922), vol. 12, p. 171.

[7] Elizabeth A. Johnson, *She Who Is: The Mystery of God in Feminist Theological Discourse* (New York: The Crossroad Publishing Co., 1992), p. 86. Also, Beverly Jane Phillips, *Learning a New Language: Speech about Women and God* (Lincoln, NE: iUniverse Publishing, 2005), p. 54.

[8] Isaiah 66:13.

[9] John 14:16.

[10] Makarios, quoted in Elisabeth Moltmann-Wendel and Jürgen Moltmann, *Humanity of God* (New York: Pilgrim Press, 1983), p. 103.

[11] *Didascalia* II.26.4.

[12] The Spirit of God first appears in Genesis 1:2 while the Word of God is first mentioned in Genesis 1:3 in terms of "God said." This fact may have influenced some church fathers' thinking about the Holy Spirit's perspective in the Trinity.

of Jesus. According to a fragment of the lost Gospel of the Hebrews which was referenced by Origen, Jesus was even said to have referred to the Holy Spirit as "my mother."[13]

With more recent influences from feminism and from postmodern multiculturalism, some scholars have taken the reflections of these Syriac fathers to greater, even radical extremes. They identify the *Logos* as the masculine aspect of God, ascribing to him "order, novelty, demand, agency, and transformation" while identifying the Spirit as the feminine aspect of God, relating to her "receptivity, empathy, suffering, and preservation."[14] Thomas Hopko has suggested correspondence on some level between male humanity and Christ on the one hand and between female humanity and the Holy Spirit on the other.[15] Some scholars have even suggested a parallel between Christ as male and the Spirit as female on an ontological level, arguing that the male gender is an image of Christ and the female gender is an image of the Holy Spirit.[16] Paul Evdokimov has opined that "in accordance with the distinction of persons . . . there is an ontic affinity between the masculine and the Word, as there is an ontic affinity between the feminine and the Holy Spirit."[17] Valerie Karras is right, however, in pointing out that these notions have "dangerously heretical" implications with possibly "serious theological and soteriological repercussions."[18] Yves Congar has been more cautious and judicious in observing that while some historical precedence refers to the Spirit as the feminine person in God or as God's femininity, these concepts should focus on the Spirit's active motherly attributes rather than forcing women into a "harem" of prescribed roles and traits like passivity, empathy, receptivity, and the like.[19]

In the Hebrew Scriptures, virtually every term that describes divine input into the universe is feminine in gender, including *torah* (di-

[13] Origen, *Commentary on John* 2.12, quoted in Phipps, *Genesis*, p. 69. See also Albertus Frederik Klijn, *Jewish-Christian Gospel Tradition* (Leiden, The Netherlands: E. J. Brill, 1992), p. 7.

[14] John B. Cobb, *Christ in a Pluralistic Age* (Philadelphia: Westminster Press, 1975), p. 264. Also, Johnson, p. 51.

[15] Thomas Hopko, "On the Male Character of the Christian Priesthood," *St. Vladimir's Theological Quarterly* 19:3 (1975), pp. 147-173.

[16] Valerie A. Karras, "Patristic Views on the Ontology of Gender," in *Personhood: Orthodox Christianity and the Connection between Body, Mind, and Soul*, ed. John T. Chirban (Westport, CT: Bergin & Garvey, 1996), p. 114.

[17] Paul Evdokimov, *Woman and the Salvation of the World*, tr. Anthony P. Gythiel (Crestwood, NY: St. Vladimir's Seminary Press, 1994), p. 27.

[18] Karras, p. 114.

[19] Yves Congar, "The Motherhood in God and the Femininity of the Holy Spirit," in his *I Believe in the Holy Spirit*, tr. David Smith (New York: Seabury Press, 1983) vol. 3, pp. 155-164.

vine instruction), *emet* (truth), *hokmah* (wisdom), *dat* (faith, custom), *chesed* (grace, tender mercy), *shekhinah* (divine presence), *ruach* (spirit), and others.[20] While the grammatical gender of these terms does not in itself prove that the things they represent are also feminine, it does present evidence that the Hebrews had no problem ascribing feminine imagery either to God or to divine activities in God's relationship with humanity. It should be noted also that these and other aspects of the divine nature and divine impartations to humanity do not fit into neat stereotypes that some have attempted to establish as norms for what is "feminine" or what are "feminine" qualities.

Of the many Hebrew terms for divine impartation, the words *ruach* and *hokmah* have been the focus of much controversy in Christianity for centuries, particularly because they have been virtually personalized both in Scripture and in tradition. Both *ruach* (spirit) and *hokmah* (wisdom) have feminine imagery attached to their manifestation in Scripture itself. Indeed, *ruach* (more precisely *Ruach haKodesh*—the Holy Spirit) is hypostatized and *hokmah* is virtually hypostatized in Scripture and is specifically personified as feminine. Despite controversy over the feminine implications or interpretations of both *ruach* and *hokmah*, a study of these terms is important and can be fruitful for understanding the feminine imagery in the Divine that God confirms. At the same time, however, care must be exercised in such study, for profoundly heretical ideas have been advanced from this imagery that represent little more than pagan goddess worship covered in a thin veneer of Christian religious jargon.

In Scripture, the Holy Spirit is seen, not merely as an agent of God, but as God himself.[21] The Spirit is not an emanation from God, nor is the Spirit merely the motive force of God. The Spirit is God. This is one of the reasons why the Spirit must be recognized as one of three equal persons in the triunity of the one God. Tragically, however, as Heribert Mühlen has observed, when most Christians in history and even in the present have discussed theology, the Holy Spirit seems almost like an appendage, the forgotten God, little more than an ac-

---

[20] Interestingly enough, the Hebrew word for nature, *tevah*, is masculine. (So, it actually should be "Father Nature," not Mother Nature and "Father Earth," not Mother Earth!)
[21] Acts 5:3-4; Psalm 139:7-8; 1 Corinthians 2:10-11; See Millard J. Erickson, *Introducing Christian Doctrine* (Grand Rapids, MI: Baker Book House, 1992), p. 103; T.C. Hammond, *In Understanding Be Men: A Handbook of Christian Doctrine* (Downers Grove, IL: InterVarsity Press, 1968), pp. 54-56, 128-131; Charles Ryrie, *The Holy Spirit* (Chicago: Moody Press, 1965); J. Oswald Sanders, *The Holy Spirit and His Gifts: Contemporary Evangelical Perspectives* (Grand Rapids, MI: Zondervan Publishing House, 1976).

cessory to the Father and the Son.[22] Many scholars, therefore, believe that much more attention should be given to pneumatology, the study of the Spirit, for the benefit of both men and women in the Christian community and for the benefit of the church itself. Elizabeth Johnson has rightly maintained that "forgetting the Spirit is not ignoring a faceless, shadowy third hypostasis but the mystery of God closer to us than we are to ourselves, drawing near and passing by in quickening, liberating compassion."[23]

There is clear feminine imagery in the very first mention of the Spirit in Scripture: "The Spirit of God was hovering over the waters."[24] A literal translation of Genesis 1:2 says, "The Spirit of God, she was hovering over the waters," for the word *she* is contained in the verb רַחֶפֶת (*rachemet*) in its suffixed ending, ת (*tav*). The word translated "hovering" or "moving" is רָחַף (*rachaph*) which can also mean "flutter," as is the case in Deuteronomy 32:11 where it speaks of an eagle that "flutters [*rachaph*] over its young." Even in the creation of humanity, the language of Scripture indicates the Spirit's involvement. "The Lord God formed humanity of dust from the ground, and breathed into his nostrils the breath of life."[25] Job 33:4 reiterates and parallels the language of the creation narrative: "The *Spirit* of God has made me, and the breath of the Almighty gives me life."[26] The "Lord God" and the "Spirit of God" are, therefore, one and the same.

The symbolism for the Spirit as a hovering mother bird is also repeated in the account of Jesus' baptism: "The Holy Spirit descended upon him in bodily form like a dove."[27] It is certain that the Spirit who descended upon Jesus "like a dove" is the same Spirit who brooded over the expanses of the primordial waters in preparation for the creative Word that brought order out of chaos.[28] Indeed, this "dove" was no ephemeral image: it was a bodily manifestation demonstrating the presence of the Holy Spirit in person at the point in time at which Jesus assumed his ministry. It should have come as no surprise, then, that Jesus also saw his relationship to his nation and his fellow countrymen in similarly maternal terms which he described in this manner:

---

[22] Heribert Mühlen, "The Person of the Holy Spirit," in *The Holy Spirit and Power,* ed. Kilian McConnell (Garden City, NY: Doubleday, 1975), p. 12.
[23] Johnson, p. 131.
[24] Genesis 1:2, NIV.
[25] Genesis 2:7.
[26] Emphasis added.
[27] Luke 3:22.
[28] Genesis 1:2.

"How often I wanted to gather your children together, the way a hen gathers her chicks under her wings."[29]

FEMININE IMAGERY IN THE SPIRITUAL BIRTH

Jesus was no more apprehensive of female metaphor than the eternal Father was. As a matter of fact, he chose feminine imagery for the very foundation for the experiential impartation of divine grace that secured human acceptance before God. He also employed feminine imagery to describe entrance into the kingdom of heaven, likening the spiritual experience to a woman's giving birth. Speaking to Nicodemus, a significant leader in the Jewish community, Jesus observed that humans who had been born through the natural process of human generation would be required to be "born from above" by the Spirit in order to be a part of God's kingdom.[30] Nicodemus expressed shock and dismay at this declaration and asked Jesus incredulously, "How can a man be born when he is old? He cannot enter a second time into his mother's womb and be born, can he?"[31] Jesus responded by saying that one must be born of "water" and "the Spirit," for "flesh gives birth to flesh, but the Spirit gives birth to spirit."[32] The parallel could not have been more apparent: just as all humans are born from the female womb, so all believers are reborn from the womb of the Spirit.

Then, Jesus asked Nicodemus a question of his own, "Are you the teacher of Israel and do not understand these things?"[33] Indeed, the rabbi should have understood the metaphor, for Judaism had long applied the same rebirth imagery to its *mikveh* tradition in which ritual immersion was used to mark rites of passage from one state to another.[34] By that time the sages had extended to all the Israelites the ceremonial ablutions that had always been required of the priests before their service in the temple.[35] This was especially true when God's commands for dealing with certain ceremonial "uncleanness" included

---

[29] Matthew 23:37.
[30] John 3:3, 7.
[31] John 3:4, NASB.
[32] John 3:6, NIV.
[33] John 3:10, NASB.
[34] Examples of the use of the *mikveh* include the culmination of proselyte baptism, appointment of rulers, consecration of priests, and achievement of ritual purity in the case of utensils used for food, women after menses or childbirth, men after emissions of semen, both men and women after abnormal discharges of bodily fluids, after healing of skin conditions (including leprosy), and after contact with a corpse or grave. The *mikveh*, therefore, came to be an outward demonstration of a change in status.
[35] Numbers 19:7.

instructions that the people "wash" themselves.[36]

In that day, the Jewish people routinely immersed themselves in *mikvot* (ritual immersion pools) in order to achieve ceremonial purity or to demonstrate a transition or change in status. The ocean or sea was considered to be the first and best *mikveh*; therefore, the Israelite *mikveh* tradition was solidly grounded in the second verse of the Genesis narrative itself.[37] Eventually, in diverse places the Jewish people constructed *mikvot*, pools that were filled with "living water" from rainfall or from a spring or a flowing stream. Kings and leaders immersed themselves in a *mikveh* upon their inauguration to indicate their change of status. Priests were consecrated by immersion in the *mikveh*, and they again immersed themselves before every service in the temple. The High Priest also immersed himself after making the sin offering on *Yom Kippur* (the Day of Atonement). Women who had been "forbidden" to their husbands during menses, immersed in the *mikveh* to indicate a new or renewed state of ceremonial purity,[38] as did men after emissions of semen.

Shortly before the time of Jesus, the *mikveh* tradition had been expanded to include the final initiation rites for proselytes who had embraced the Jewish faith. Converts from Gentile cultures were required to immerse themselves in the waters of the *mikveh* as the consummation of the process of conversion that had included physical circumcision, offering a sacrifice in the temple, and learning the Torah. Since immersion in water was a symbol of death, emergence from water was a symbol of resurrection or new life; therefore, when proselytes broke the plane of the water after immersing themselves, a forensic change occurred in their lives. At that moment persons who had been Gentiles instantly became Jews. Second-temple Jewish leaders had come to view immersion in the *mikveh* as a death, burial, and resurrection

---

[36] Exodus 30:20. These were the ceremonial ablutions (baptisms) to which the writer of Hebrews referred (9:10).

[37] The Hebrew word מִקְוֶה (*mikveh*) literally means "gathering" as a collection of water. This is the word that is used in Genesis 1:10: "The gathering [*mikveh*] of the waters he called seas." The ocean is the largest and best "gathering" of waters, and, indeed, the dry land emerged from the "waters" as a result of the divine word of creation, an image of the emergence of new life and status from the waters of the *mikveh*. After the world had been corrupted by the sin of its people (Genesis 6), the Lord immersed the whole world in the flood to cleanse it, leaving the occupants of the ark to begin life anew.

[38] See Rivkah Slonim, *Total Immersion: A Mikvah Anthology* (Rowman & Littlefield Publishing, 1997) and Hayim Halevy Donin, *To Be a Jew: A Guide to Jewish Observance in Contemporary Life* (New York: Basic Books, 1972), pp. 121-126. In biblical times, women were considered *tameh* during menses. While the word *tameh* meant "unclean," the emphasis was on the fact that women were "forbidden" to their husbands for intercourse during menses.

experience. They had also come to understand ritual immersion as a rebirth, with the waters of the *mikveh* symbolizing the waters of the womb and emergence from the water viewed as being reborn or "born again."[39] Gentile proselytes were considered to be reborn as Jews when they were immersed.

The ancient schools of rabbinic thought represented by Hillel and Shammai debated whether both circumcision and immersion were required for males in the conversion rite.[40] In the Essene community and in other Jewish communities in the Diaspora, immersion in the *mikveh* came to be viewed as a substitute for physical circumcision, making circumcision optional or rendering it nonessential for proselytes or converts to Judaism.[41] This was the concept that the leaders of the earliest Christian church appropriated for application to the Gentiles who had become or would become Christians. Their immersion in baptism was considered to be a spiritual circumcision that made it unnecessary for them to be physically circumcised.[42] Perhaps following the more liberal Hillelian positions that his teacher Gamliel maintained, Paul taught specifically that all Christians were understood to have been circumcised "without hands," experiencing the circumcision of Christ by being "buried with him in baptism."[43]

Since the parallel between the *mikveh* immersion experience and the idea of spiritual rebirth was so commonly understood in Jesus' day, it was, indeed, remarkable for a leading rabbi in Israel to claim not to have recognized the imagery that Jesus was using when he declared that one must be "born from above" (or "born again") in order to enter the Kingdom of God. Nicodemus apparently had problems connecting the *mikveh's* womb-like experience of rebirth with his understanding of the relationship of Jews to the kingdom of God in which it was believed that Jews were physically born into God's kingdom and, therefore, had no need of being born again.[44]

Since Jesus was in no way gynophobic, he did not hesitate to im-

---

[39] Talmud: *Yebamot* 22a; 48b; 97b.
[40] Walter Jacob, *Contemporary American Reform Responsa* (Mars, PA: Publishers Choice Book for Central Conference of American Rabbis, 1987), p. 73.
[41] *The Origin and Significance of the New Testament Baptism* (London: Butler and Tanner, Ltd.), p. 12.
[42] See Acts 15:5-9.
[43] Colossians 2:11-12.
[44] Jews understood that their natural birth included them in the kingdom of God because the covenant that constituted them as a kingdom of priests was a perpetual covenant contracted by God with with their ancestors and their ancestors' progeny; therefore, they had no thought of a need to be reborn, born again, or born from above in order to enter the kingdom.

age the most foundational event of experiential faith in terms that were clearly feminine. And, to say the least, the extended metaphor cast feminine imagery upon the Holy Spirit. It could be said that just as being born from the womb of a woman produces human existence in the flesh, so being born from the womb of the Holy Spirit ("born from above") constitutes rebirth into the life of the Spirit, initiation into the family of God, and inclusion in the body of the Messiah. Both natural birth and spiritual rebirth clearly reflect feminine images in relationship to the kingdom of God and initiation into the covenant of grace.

Christianity appropriated the immersion tradition from Judaism and transformed John's baptism of repentance[45] into the rite for confirming entrance into the Christian faith. According to Paul, baptism into Christ constituted a putting on of Christ (the "new man")[46] which rendered external distinctions such as ethnicity, social status, and gender of no consequence: "There is neither Jew nor Greek, there is neither slave nor free, there is neither male nor female; for you are all one in Christ Jesus."[47] This status constituted what the apostle described as a "new creation"[48] (καινον κτίσις—*kainon ktīsis* in Greek), employing precisely the same term that the rabbis used to describe persons who had converted from idolatry to Judaism.[49] Emerging from the womb waters of baptism established a "new creation" in the same way in which proselyte baptism in Judaism had forensically transformed Gentiles into Jews. The idea of the "new creation," then, was more than pious talk for the earliest Christians. It conceptualized and dramatized "the Christians' awareness of their peculiar relationship to the larger societies around them" in which they thought of themselves as a "new genus of mankind, or as the restored original mankind."[50] Tey were a "new creation" in Christ Jesus. As Wayne Meeks observes, "Where the image of God is restored, there, it seems, man is no longer

---

[45] Interestingly, John's baptism featured the repentant worshiper's leaving the land of promise at the same place where their ancestors entered Canaan, then turning around (the meaning of the Hebrew word for repentance, *teshuvah*), immersing themselves in the waters of the Jordan through which their ancestors had passed, and then reentering the land. This, too, was a kind of rebirth ritual. John's baptism was at the ford of the River Jordan just north of the Dead Sea.

[46] Colossians 3:10.

[47] Galatians 3:27-28, NASB.

[48] 2 Corinthians 5:17.

[49] See Babylonian Talmud, *Yebamoth*, 22a: "One who has become a proselyte is like a child newly born."

[50] Wayne Meeks, *In Search of the Early Christians*, ed. Allen R. Hilton, H. Gregory Snyder (New Haven, CT: Yale University Press, 2002), p. 4.

divided—not even by the most fundamental division of all, male and female."[51] All believers are one in the Messiah without any distinction or division.

DEFEMINIZING THE HOLY SPIRIT

How did virtually all vestiges of the feminine attributes ascribed to the Holy Spirit disappear from Christian teaching? The demise of such imagery became a virtually foregone conclusion when the Hebrew word *ruach* was translated into Greek and Latin. First, the Septuagint translated *ruach* with the Greek word *pneuma*, which is neuter in gender. This effectively neutered subsequent references to the Spirit. Then, when the Scriptures were translated into Latin, the masculine word *spiritus* was chosen to translate the feminine Hebrew word *ruach* and the neuter Greek word *pneuma*. Because the word *spiritus* is masculine, it was merely a short step of logic for Latin church fathers like Augustine to reject as "absurd" the "gynomorphic imagery for the Holy Spirit which he found in Greek Christianity."[52] Because he was conflicted over human sexuality in general, and over his own personal incontinence in particular, Augustine insisted that even if believers of "most chastely thought," could conceive of a maternal Holy Spirit, non-Christians would think in crudely physical terms; therefore, any such thought had to be abandoned.[53]

So it was that "in time the custom of speaking about the Spirit in female terms waned in the West along with the habit of speaking very extensively about the Spirit at all."[54] Rosemary Ruether is correct in her contention that though the use of female imagery for the Spirit was manifest in earliest Christianity, it was gradually "marginalized by a victorious Greco-Roman Christianity that repressed it,"[55] using its rightful aversion to the heresies of Gnosticism as an excuse for obliterating all such references. In this case, the reaction to Gnostic abuses resulted in misinterpretation and misapplication of Scripture at best and in downright perversion of biblical thought at worst. The use of polemics against heresy can—and often does—create still other

---

[51] Wayne Meeks, *The Image of the Androgyne: Some Uses of a Symbol in Earliest Christianity* (Chicago: The University of Chicago Press, 1974), p. 185.
[52] Phipps, *Genesis*, p. 70.
[53] Augustine, *On the Trinity*, XII, 5. See Augustine, *Basic Writings of Saint Augustine* (New York: Random House, 1948), p. 811.
[54] Johnson, p. 50.
[55] Rosemary Radford Ruether, *Sexism and God-talk* (Boston: Beacon Press, 1983), p. 59.

heresies, sometimes greater than the ones which they replace. In this case, attacks against perceived evils of theologies that project masculinity on God have resulted in the propounding of theologies that are equally evil in the projecting femininity on God.

ABUSING THE FEMININE AND THE SPIRIT

Without a doubt, one of the greatest problems with early Christian references to the Holy Spirit in feminine terms was that they were easily taken to extreme so that they became foundational to such Gnostic heresies. The Mandaean Gnostics, descendants of the Babylonians, represented the Spirit in a female figure called *Ruha d-Qudsa* (Holy Spirit) and made her the mistress of "the detested Jewish god Adonai."[56] The Ophites, another Gnostic sect, believed in a trinity of Universal God, Second Man, and female Holy Spirit, and they went so far as to term the Spirit "the first woman" and the "mother of all living."[57] They even posited a convoluted theology and Christology in which the "Father of All" (called "First Man") produced a "Thought," the "Son of Man" (called "Second Man"), then generated through union with the "Spirit" (called "First Woman") the "Third Male" (called "Christ"). The "Father" and the "Son" then united with the "Spirit" so that she became "Mother of the Living."[58]

One need only consider these two instances to see how ancient Babylonian myths, added to Greek philosophy, produced horrendous heresies that attacked the very foundations of the Hebrew Scriptures themselves as well as the Hebraic-based Christian faith. In making the Holy Spirit a female being rather than in seeing feminine qualities in the Holy Spirit, they perpetuated and "Christianized" pagan religions based in sexual imagery and emphases—the very ideas that God had commanded Israel never to entertain. Lacking the Jews' two-millennia history of exposure to God's explicit laws against idolatry and sexual perversion and to the unrelenting denunciation of such practices by Israelite prophets and sages,[59] Gentile Christians easily lapsed into old and perverse manners of thinking about God and humanity in a recidivism that continues to the present day. Perversion of truth by whatever

---

[56] Jorunn Jacobsen Buckley, *A Rehabilitation of Spirit Ruha in Mandaean Religion* (Chicago: University of Chicago Press, 1982), p. 22. Also Buckley, *The Mandaeans* (New York: Oxford University Press, 2002), p. 40.
[57] Robert McQueen Grant, *Irenaeus of Lyons* (London: Routledge Publishing, 1997), p. 104.
[58] Grant, p. 99.
[59] Jeremiah 44:19.

source does not, however, negate truth. It can and often does require a greater measure of caution in order to avoid the pitfalls that have entrapped others; however, truth cannot be jettisoned simply because in some way it has been polluted.[60] Indeed, heresy is often nothing more than a truth that has been thrown out of balance one way or the other.[61]

This same principle should be applied to the issue of historical feminine imagery for the Holy Spirit. There are inherent dangers—indeed, grave dangers—when such images are taken to extreme, for they have the potential for being extrapolated into idolatrous practices. A careful, balanced position, however, can provide solid scriptural insight that will tend toward healthy views and practices. If nothing else, this understanding can provide for a more accurate imaging of the Divine by underscoring the genderless nature of God while at the same time confirming that both masculine and feminine imagery are employed in theomorphic metaphor and anthropomorphism that guard against the sins of andromorphic or gynomorphic idolatry.

RESTORING THE BALANCE

Lack of balanced emphases regarding the Spirit has resulted in the Holy Spirit's becoming the virtually "forgotten God" and in the general neglect that has made pneumatology a virtual "Cinderella" of theology, as Kilian McConnell has observed.[62] Whether the church has simply neglected the Spirit or has attempted to control it within an exclusively androcentric hierarchical bureaucracy and *clerus*, the end result has been the same: the church has muzzled and marginalized the Spirit and, at the same time, it has bound and gagged women. When biblically Hebraic emphases on the gifts and operations of the Spirit were replaced by Greek rationalism, the church made a determined move away from the more existential and emotional aspects of faith, which were seen as being deficiently feminine in nature, toward the

---

[60] A clear example of this truth is seen in the fact that the most sacred and (for Jews) ineffable name of God, YHWH, has been used for centuries in the magical incantations of the occult world. Surely no one would suggest that the name should be jettisoned because of its misuse.
[61] Consider, for example, the issue of "the law." On the one hand the heresy of legalism has been advanced; on the other hand, the heresy of antinomianism has been promoted. Neither is truth; however, there is ample scriptural evidence for the value of the law of God that establishes a middle ground between the two heresies, a foundation on which believers can successfully build solid lives of faith so that "through faith" they "establish the law." See Romans 3:31.
[62] Kilian McConnell, "A Trinitarian Theology of the Holy Spirit?" *Theological Studies* 46 (1985), pp. 191-193. See also Kilian McConnell, *The Other Hand of God* (Collegeville, MN: Liturgical Press, 2003), p. 4.

more controlled and respectable masculine traits of rationality. Rationalism, however, is declared scripturally to be the enemy of the Spirit, for the "carnal mind" cannot understand the things of the Spirit[63] and, indeed, "hates God."[64]

When the church in history elevated rationalism over Spirit, it violated the heart of God's relationship with humanity. The consequent devaluation and limitation of women consigned the church into a man's world—cold and clinical, devoid of beauty and freedom and, indeed, often lacking life itself. It is time to renew both the Holy Spirit and the feminine imagery associated with it. It is also time to release all the *charismata* of the Spirit, including the charism of femininity and all that pertains to it.

SPRINGBOARD FOR DISCUSSION

1. Evaluate the emphases placed on feminine imagery in the Holy Spirit by ancient Syriac and Greek teachers. Were these thinkers marginal in the broader scope of early Christianity, or were their ideas mainstream beliefs?

2. Discuss how the lack of emphasis on pneumatology in previous centuries may have resulted from the fear that androcentric church leaders had of feminine metaphors for God and especially for the Holy Spirit. Why should scholars give more attention to the study of the Holy Spirit?

3. Consider the text of Genesis 1 and its references to the Holy Spirit. How does the Hebrew word translated *fluttering* lend credence to feminine imagery in God? How does this compare with the sign of the dove at Jesus' baptism and with his use of the metaphor of a mother bird in relationship to his prayers for Jerusalem?

4. Evaluate the discussion Jesus had with Nicodemus regarding being "born from above" (or "born again"). How are images of the Spirit connected with rebirth and initiation into God's new covenant? How did the *mikveh* tradition in contemporary Judaism impact the teaching of Jesus and the apostles regarding baptism and the new birth?

[63] 1 Corinthians 2:14.
[64] Romans 8:7.

5. Discuss the translation of the Hebrew word *ruach* (feminine) to *pneuma* (neuter) in Greek and finally to *spiritus* (masculine) in Latin. How did this translation affect later theological discussion of possible feminine imagery in the Holy Spirit? How did the church's negative view of women (sometimes as inherently evil) eventuate in even masculine images for the Holy Spirit?

6. Do Christians today need to be careful of the influences of Babylonian myths and other neo-pagan influences on their theology? Does the need to guard against heresies make it necessary to avoid all consideration of biblical texts relating to God and the Holy Spirit that underscore feminine qualities?

7. Discuss the emphasis on masculine images of God and avoidance of feminine ones in the early centuries of Christianity. How did this lead toward rationalism and bureaucratic control in later centuries?

8. Evaluate the feminine images applied to the Holy Spirit. How important is it that you seek a renewed emphasis on the Holy Spirit and the qualities of Christian conduct that have been suppressed because they have been viewed as less than masculine traits? Does consideration of the Holy Spirit as bearing feminine images of God encourage you to appreciate and develop such qualities in your life?

CHAPTER 10

FEMININE IMAGES
AND DIVINE WISDOM

The fact that the Holy Spirit has been biblically imaged in feminine terms provides a foundation for understanding what is meant when divine wisdom (*hokmah*) is also described in Scripture with unmistakably feminine designations. Indeed, *Hokmah* is one of the clearest examples of feminine imagery connected with the Divine in all of Scripture. The words for *wisdom* in Hebrew (*hokmah*), Greek, (*sophia*), and Latin (*sapientia*) are all feminine in gender. Interestingly enough, however, Scripture does not just introduce wisdom as a concept or as an attribute of God. Instead, it presents wisdom as a feminine personification, with the word *hokmah* appearing more than three hundred times in the Hebrew Scriptures. Indeed, Wisdom "is the most developed personification of God's presence and activity in the Hebrew Scriptures, much more acutely limned than Spirit, torah, or word."[1]

A wide range of possible interpretations of *hokmah* is offered in the academic community.[2] Some scholars view *hokmah* as cosmic order,[3] while others believe *hokmah* to be God's intellect.[4] Many con-

---

[1] Elizabeth A. Johnson, *She Who Is: The Mystery of God in Feminist Theological Discourse* (New York: Crossroad Publishing Company, 1998), p. 87.
[2] See Aidan O'Boyle, *Towards a Contemporary Wisdom Christology* (Rome: Gregorian University Press, 2001), pp. 51-54.
[3] Silvia Schroer, *Wisdom Has Built Her House: Studies on the Figure of Sophia in the Bible,* tr. Linda M. Maloney, William McDonough (Collegeville, MN: The Liturgical Press, 2000), pp. 3-7. See also Gerhard von Rad, *Wisdom in Israel* (Nashville, TN: Abingdon Press, 1972).
[4] Colin E. Gunton, *Act and Being: Towards a Theology of the Divine Attributes* (Grand Rapids, MI: Wm. B. Eerdmans Publishing Co., 2002), p. 40. See also R. N. Whybray, *Wisdom in Proverbs: The Concept of Wisdom in Proverbs 1-9* (Naperville, IL: A. R. Allenson, 1965).

sider *Hokmah*, wisdom personified, to be a revealing and acting agent for God, a hypostasis, prefigured by the Egyptian goddess *Ma'at*, or similar to that of the *Logos* that was manifest in the incarnation of Jesus.[5] Some scholars mistakenly consider *Hokmah* to be a Hebrew appropriation of *Ma'at*. Because the various *Hokmah* texts in the Hebrew Scriptures, like those of the Logos in Apostolic Scripture, were developed within the context of Jewish monotheism that makes not the slightest allowance for the existence of more than one God, it is reasonable to acknowledge that *Hokmah* is actually Israel's God unequivocally imaged in female descriptives.[6] Tirzah Firestone maintains that *Hokmah* is, in fact, "the most highly developed feminine personification of God's presence and activity in Hebrew scriptures."[7] Rather than projecting *Hokmah* as a divine being, however, the sages of Israel spoke of her as a "personification . . . of a *function* of Yahweh" so that, as James D. G. Dunn notes, they were able to speak "about God himself . . . expressing [in *Hokmah*] God's active involvement with his world and his people without compromising his transcendence."[8] In Jewish thought, therefore, *Hokmah* is the transcendent God in the immanence of self-disclosure, and when this divine immanence is manifest, it is clearly expressed in feminine imagery.

This gynomorphic motif can be clearly seen in Hebraic conceptualizations of creation. The Book of Proverbs portrays *Hokmah* as pregnant with the potential to create,[9] even identifying her as one of the agents—if not the agent—of creation itself: "By wisdom the Lord laid the earth's foundations."[10] The wisdom author continues, quoting *Hokmah* as making this startling declaration of he preexistence of divine wisdom: "From everlasting I was established, from the beginning,[11] at the origin of the earth. . . . Then I was beside [God], as a master workman; and I was daily his delight, rejoicing always

[5] Ralph Marcus, "On Biblical Hypostases of Wisdom," *Hebrew Union College Annual* 23 (1953), p. 43. Also Gail Ramshaw, *Liturgical Language* (Collegeville, MN: The Liturgical Press, 1996), p. 14; Helmer Ringgren, *Word and Wisdom: Studies in the Hypostatization of Divine Qualities and Functions in the Ancient Near East* (Lund: H. Ohlssons, 1947), p. 147; and Oliver S. Rankin, *Israel's Wisdom Literature* (New York: Schocken Books, 1969), p. 224.

[6] Johnson, p. 91. Also James D. G. Dunn, "Was Christianity a Monotheistic Faith from the Beginning?" *Scottish Journal of Theology* 35 (1982), pp. 319-320.

[7] Tirzah Firestone, *The Receiving: Reclaiming Jewish Women's Wisdom* (San Francisco: HarperCollins Publishers, 2003), p. 132.

[8] James D. G. Dunn, *Christology in the Making* (Cambridge: Cambridge University Press, 1993), p. 176.

[9] Firestone, p. 129.

[10] Proverbs 3:19.

[11] Proverbs 8:23, NASB.

before him."[12] In Firestone's words, "God looked into the Torah, the cosmic blueprint of creation, to see how to create the world."[13] Wisdom, therefore, was not only "involved in the creation of the world but served as the matrix from which all creation emerges."[14] The scriptural tradition of creation theology here receives another dimension with the idea that creation was not simply "the act of a solitary male deity,"[15] but was rather undertaken in concert with masculine and feminine principles manifest by the one genderless God. Clearly, then, Wisdom's activities and involvement in creation were not that of a divine vicar or plenipotentiary but that of God himself. *Hokmah* is the feminine personification of God in divine immanence.

Continuing with his personification of *Hokmah*, Solomon urged his disciples: "Say to *Hokmah*, You are my sister[16] . . . exalt her, and she will promote you."[17] Then, he declared that *Hokmah* is "better than jewels, and nothing you desire can compare with her."[18] He even argued that because of *Hokmah* "kings reign and rulers make laws that are just."[19] A divine feminine principle, then, creates and maintains order and justice in human society. Jesus himself continued to use and confirm the feminine imagery of the *Hokmah* tradition in the Hebrew Scriptures when he declared, "Wisdom is vindicated by all her children."[20]

There is one thing that is certain about divine Wisdom: the biblical depictions of *Hokmah* are consistently female, revealing her "as sister, mother, female beloved, chef and hostess, preacher, judge, liberator, establisher of justice, and a myriad of other female roles wherein she symbolizes transcendent power ordering and delighting the world."[21] The very introduction of *Hokmah* into the scriptural record defies most of the restrictions placed on women throughout Christian history and in much of Jewish history under the influence of Rabbinic Judaism. While images of traditional feminine roles, such as receptivity and openness, have been ascribed to women and traditional male symbols of power

---

[12] Proverbs 8:30, NASB.
[13] Firestone, p. 129, noting Genesis *Rabbah* 1.1.
[14] Firestone, p. 133.
[15] Johnson, p. 88.
[16] Proverbs 7:4.
[17] Proverbs 4:8-9.
[18] Proverbs 8:11, NIV.
[19] Proverbs 8:15-16, NIV.
[20] Luke 7:35.
[21] Johnson, p. 87.

and aggression have been ascribed to men, *Hokmah* breaks out of the mold, having omnipotence and creative energy ascribed to her.[22]

In Scripture, Lady Wisdom first "makes a brief debut as a hidden treasure whose whereabouts are known only to God."[23] Then, she "strides onto the stage with unabashed bravado in the book of Proverbs,"[24] making "a noisy public appearance" as "a street preacher" with "a message of reproach, punishment, and promise."[25] She cries out "at the heights along the way, where the paths meet; she cries beside the gates leading into the city; at the entryways, she shouts."[26] Interestingly, all of the locations described as venues of Lady Wisdom's proclamations were sites for the exercise of legislative, judicial, and executive functions of the civil governments of the ancient world. These were venues in which Hebraic women in biblical times clearly had a voice but in which women of other cultures would not even dare to be seen, much less heard! In the Hebraic imagery of this passage, the feminine voice of Lady Wisdom was not only heard: she was *the* chief counselor. She even dared to declare that anyone who would not listen to her commands would suffer drastic judgments. Amazingly, this woman assumed authority and made declarations that no self-respecting woman in most of Christian history would have ventured to undertake without immediate recrimination, excoriation, and even excommunication, or worse yet, corporal punishment or martyrdom! She acted in ways that Jewish women in times contemporary with early Christianity found off-limits because of their virtual domestication. This biblical wisdom woman had a divine calling, and she had the *chutzpah* to match!

Hokmah is said to have been responsible for building her house and for hewing out seven pillars as a rock-solid foundation for that structure.[27] The metaphorical feminine imagery involved in constructing the house is very powerful. It certainly parallels the feminine and household imagery that was used throughout Scripture to describe both the congregation of Israel and the church of Jesus Christ. Israel and the church are considered to be "God's Wife"[28] and the "Bride

---

[22] Proverbs 1:20-23; 4:13; 8:35; 9:1-6.
[23] Firestone, p. 131.
[24] Firestone, p. 131.
[25] Johnson, p. 87.
[26] Proverbs 1:21.
[27] Proverbs 9:1.
[28] Isaiah 62:5.

of Christ"[29] respectively, and both are considered to be the house of God.[30] Israel and the church, however, are always portrayed in feminine terms. Both are constructed by Lady Wisdom.[31] When both Israel and the church are built up, divine wisdom is at work, the mysterious wisdom "which God ordained before the world."[32] The very foundation of the Christian church is divine wisdom personified in the chief cornerstone of its faith, Jesus, the divine *Logos,* and in the wisdom of God, *Hokmah.*[33]

It should come as no surprise that many of these characteristics that Scripture ascribes to *Hokmah* were also attributed to Scripture's composite woman, Solomon's "Woman of Valor."[34] This woman does not represent, as some have mistakenly supposed, a biblical demand for every woman to be a superwoman. She serves rather as a demonstration of the diverse opportunities that women may freely choose to fulfill their lives. By her own actions, *Hokmah* made it clear that feminine imagery is diverse and all-inclusive. It is never limited to house, kitchen, or bedroom! While each of these images—including healthy and expressive sexuality—is biblically ascribed to godly women, Wisdom affords all women the opportunity to realize the fulfillment of their God-given talents not only in domestic life but also in all aspects of societal and religious life. Interestingly enough, motherhood, which has been "the primary and universally recognized assigned status of women" in both Judaism and Christianity is virtually unmentioned "in the female imagery applied to the Wisdom-Woman."[35] Indeed, she is chef, an importer, a real estate developer, a vintner, a merchant, a fabric maker, a philanthropist, a clothing designer, and a woman of wisdom.

HOKMAH AND *LOGOS*

The language of Solomon's declarations about *Hokmah* is also strikingly similar to those ascribed to the Divine *Logos,* the person of Jesus in the Apostolic Scriptures.[36] And, indeed, Jesus is described

---

[29] Revelation 21:2, 9.
[30] 1 Timothy 3:15; Isaiah 54:5.
[31] Proverbs 9:1.
[32] 1 Corinthians 2:7.
[33] 1 Corinthians 1:24; 1 Peter 2:6-7.
[34] Proverbs 31:10-31.
[35] Jane Sally Kiasiong-Andriamiarisoa, "A Woman's Voice," *Shabbat Shalom* (April, 1988), vol. 45, no. 1, p. 25.
[36] Colossians 1:15-16; Hebrews 2:10.

by Paul as *Hokmah*, the "Wisdom of God."[37] Samuel Sandmel[38] suggested that the *Logos* concept likely represents a blending of terms and ideas from the encounter of Jewish thought with Greek concepts before and during the time of Philo of Alexandria.[39] Philo was likely the first Jewish scholar to make systematic efforts to expunge female imagery from *Hokmah*. With a typical Hellenistic mindset, he argued in direct contradiction to Scripture that "pre-eminence always pertains to the masculine, and the feminine always comes short of it and is lesser than it is. Let us, then . . . say that . . . Sophia is not only masculine but father."[40]

Leonard Swidler maintains that "the feminine divine Wisdom of the Hebraic-Judaic tradition bifurcated in the Christian tradition," retaining the usual Hebraic association of the feminine with the Holy Spirit (*Ruach*) while adapting the Hebraic association of *Hokmah* with the feminine to a rare Judaic association of Wisdom with the masculine *Logos*, the Word of God.[41] As a result, one person of the triune God, the Holy Spirit, came to be identified with the feminine divine Wisdom and at times was described in feminine imagery, while a second person of the Trinity, the Logos, was also identified with the feminine divine Wisdom but was only rarely described in feminine imagery.[42] Ultimately, John's Gospel condensed and coalesced Jewish concepts of both the eternally preexistent *Torah* and the *Hokmah* tradition in order to formulate the ultimate *Logos* declaration: "The *Logos* was God. . . . and the *Logos* became flesh . . . the Son of God."[43]

It seems, however, that John's identification of Jesus as the *Logos* was the apostle's use of the Greek term *logos* to translate the Hebrew word *d'var* ("word") or the Aramaic word *memra* ("spoken word") that had been substituted for the word *God* (both *Elohim* and *YHWH*) in the *Targumim* (Aramaic translations of the Hebrew Scriptures that

---

[37] 1 Corinthians 1:24.
[38] Samuel Sandmel, *Judaism and Christian Beginnings* (New York: Oxford University Press, 1978), p. 298.
[39] Rather than letting Scripture speak for itself, the Hellenized Philo felt it necessary to repress *Hokmah* "as preexistent to creation into the Greek idea of masculine *logos* or by spiritualizing Wisdom as a divine figure in human flesh as a female personification of evil."—Joan Chamberlain Engelsman, *The Feminine Dimension of the Divine* (Philadelphia: The Westminster Press, 1979), pp. 74-75. See also Robert L. Wilken, ed., *Aspects of Wisdom in Judaism and Early Christianity* (South Bend, IN: University of Notre Dame Press, 1975).
[40] Philo, *Fuga*, pp. 41-52.
[41] Leonard Swidler and Arlene Swidler, *Women Priests: A Catholic Commentary on the Vatican Declaration* (New York: Paulist Press, 1977), pp. 63-66.
[42] Swidler, pp. 63-66.
[43] John 1:1, 14-15.

were used extensively in the time of Jesus, particularly in synagogue worship). It is true, then, as Martin Hengel has noted, that the earliest church concretized Jesus' saving work in a Christology that identified Jesus with both with *Torah* and *Hokmah*.[44] Raymond Brown maintains that in the Gospel of John, "Jesus is personified Wisdom,"[45] while James Dunn concludes that "Jesus is the exhaustive embodiment of divine wisdom."[46] It is clear that the disciples of Jesus came to understand that both the *Memra* and the *Hokmah* traditions of the Judaisms of their time were personified in Jesus of Nazareth, the eternally preexistent Son of God, both the Word and the Wisdom of creation.

DANGERS OF *HOKMAH* ABUSE

It is clear that both *ruach* and *hokmah* present clear images of feminine qualities in the nature of the Divine; however, *hokmah*, like *ruach*, is vulnerable to exploitation and extrapolation into images that God never intended—and, indeed, specifically and strongly forbade. Too much emphasis on *Hokmah* tends toward creating a feminine God, which is just as improper as attributing masculine gender to God. This is the problem with much of religious feminism which, having rejected the authority of Scripture, turns to "*Sophia*" as its "goddess." It is very interesting that most Christian feminists prefer the Greek *Sophia* over the Hebrew *Hokmah*! Perhaps it is because they can apply their preconceived notions about goddess worship to *Sophia*, the Hellenized representation and perversion of *Hokmah*, more readily than they can to the Hebrew *Hokmah*. *Sophia* was so prominent in the heretical Gnostic sects in early Christianity because *Sophia* could be manipulated by amalgamating the psychosexual images of goddess worship prevalent in both Greek religion and in Eastern cults, covering them with a thin veneer of Christian terminology, and then packaging them as the "true" faith of Jesus and the apostles.

Some scholars have even attempted to expropriate the biblical *Hokmah* tradition as confirmation for their erroneous contention that goddess worship was an integral part of the Hebraic faith of antiquity. They argue that *Hokmah* was actually Israel's God expressed in lan-

---

[44] Martin Hengel, *Judaism and Hellenism* (London: SCM Press, 1973), vol. 1, pp. 157-162.
[45] Raymond Edward Brown, *The Gospel According to John* (Garden City, NY: Doubleday, 1966), p. 125.
[46] Dunn, p. 195.

guage and imagery of pre-Canaanite goddess worship. Carl Jung even called Wisdom "God's self-reflection."[47] These projections, however, are based on the myth that goddess worship preceded the worship of male deities not only in the ancient near East, including in the Hebrew culture, but also around the world. These are the purported "goddess-worshipping, earth-centered cultures of prehistory"[48] which are said by some to have been overwhelmed by patriarchy and the worship of male gods sometime between the third and the twelfth millennia B.C.[49] Unfortunately for rabid feminist devotees of goddess worship, Merlin Stone's dictum, "At the very dawn of religion, God was a woman,"[50] is nothing but pure myth, as Lynn LiDonnici's research clearly reveals.[51]

Catherine Kroeger attributes the development of *Sophia* cults in Christianity to a "Judaized paganism" that carried over into the church from the goddess worship that had often made incursions into the Israelite community,[52] bringing with them attempts to syncretize Yahwist faith with pagan goddess worship in the *Asherahs* that are mentioned in the Scriptures.[53] While goddess cults in the cultures that surrounded the Hebrew people often seduced members of that community into their fertility rites, a clear and constant defense against such practices was consistently mounted by Israelite prophets, priests, and kings. Kroeger's assertion fails to account for this strong prophetic element in Israel that consistently and unequivocally stood against all forms of idolatry—especially that of goddess worship—and finally prevailed during the time of King Josiah, after which idolatrous practices were rarely manifest among the Israelites. And, indeed, one of the greatest voices that were raised against goddess idolatry in that time was that of Hulda, who was a prophetess and spiritual leader in

[47] C. G. Jung, *Answer to Job* (Princeton: Princeton University Press, 1969), p. 86.
[48] See Marja Gimbutas, *The Goddesses and Gods of Old Europe* (Berkeley: University of California Press, 1982).
[49] Salvatore Cucchiari, "The Gender Revolution and the Transition from Bisexual Horde to Patrilocal Band: The Origins of Gender Hierarchy," in Sherry B. Ortner and Harriet Whitehead, eds., *Sexual Meanings: The Cultural Construction of Gender and Sexuality* (New York: Cambridge University Press, 1981), pp. 31-80.
[50] Merlin Stone, *When God Was a Woman* (San Diego: Harcourt, Brace, and Javonovich, 1976), p. 1.
[51] Lynn LiDonnici, "Women's Religions and Religious Lives in the Greco-Roman City," in *Women and Christian Origins*, ed. Ross Kraemer and Mary Rose D'Angelo (Oxford: Oxford University Press, 1999), p. 83.
[52] See Deuteronomy 12:3-4; Judges 3:7; 1 Kings 14:15, 23; 18:4; 21:7.
[53] Catherine Clark Kroeger, "The Challenge of the Re-Imaging God Conference," *Priscilla Papers* 8:2 (Spring 1994), pp. 7-8.

Israel, a woman of great spiritual valor and insight.

All idolatry, including goddess worship, was certainly rejected by the various Judaisms of the second-temple period, all of which made no room for such practices. Any effort to identify "Judaized paganism" as the source of Christian idolatry is not supported by the Scriptures or by history. Christians who adopted *Sophia* worship were influenced not by Jewish thought or practice but by Gnosticism and mystery religions in open defiance of the Hebraic foundations of original Christianity. By the time of Jesus, such perversion was virtually unknown in the larger Jewish community, as evidenced by the fact that Jesus never mentioned it. There is, therefore, no linear connection between the practices of idolatry—particularly goddess worship—that infiltrated the church after the time of Jesus and the worship of pagan feminine deities in ancient Israel.

It was astonishing, however, that early Christianity, birthed in the matrix of second-temple Judaism, came to be influenced so quickly and so easily by the same cults over which Judaism had been victorious centuries before the time of Jesus. Tragically, when the door of Christian faith was opened to the Greco-Roman world, that same door swung both ways, exposing the church to the corrosive influences of pagan religion, which made *Sophia* worship a focal point of its faith and experience. The proof that paganism challenged the earliest Gentile missions of the church is confirmed by the first apostolic council's specific instructions to the Gentiles which focused exclusively on prohibitions against idolatry—namely, abstinence from "pollutions of idols, from blood, from things strangled, and from fornication,"[54] all of which were practices central to the worship of the pagan gods and goddesses.

What actually did occur in early Christianity was the introduction into the church of eclectic Egyptian, Persian, Indian, and Syrian mysticism amalgamated with Hellenism to form Gnosticism, the first heresy to attack the nascent church. This "Christianized Gnosticism" drew on the goddess images of the pagans—particularly Cybele,[55] the Phrygian mother of the gods—and connected them with *Sophia*. Some Gnostics even went so far as to engage in various perverse sexual practices and to employ semen and menstrual blood as offerings to their

[54] Acts 15:20.
[55] Cybele was also connected with Diana (Greek: Artemis), the goddess of the Ephesians whose cult Paul confronted in Acts 19:23-31.

goddess.[56] Despite current popular efforts to revive Gnostic practices and make them fashionable and acceptable in today's postmodern world, they are still what they were two millennia ago, nothing more than deviant heretical concepts and practices that are inimical to all the tenets of biblical faith. Kroeger is right on target when she warns that the same syncretism that challenged the earliest church through Gnosticism now threatens the church in efforts to blend anient ideas of *Sophia* worship with Christian teaching and practice and to establish the worship of a female version of God.[57]

A major problem that has compounded the current incursion of Sophia worship into Christian circles has been the recovery of various Gnostic texts and scholarly attempts to authenticate these texts as expressions of normative early Christianity. For centuries, scholars in the science of Biblical Introduction have made every effort to date the texts of the Pseudepigrapha, particularly those from Gnostic backgrounds, to times that were much earlier than their actual composition while at the same time dating the texts of the New Testament canon much later than their actual composition. In a perverted sense of what is right, wrong, and "fair," they have considered all of these writings to have come from essentially the same time period and, as such, to retroject anachronistically the diversity and pluralism of politically correct postmodernity into the earliest church. The notions on both sides of that dating controversy are equally preposterous. First, the apostolic writings were composed much earlier than has generally been projected, actually dating back to the middle of the first century, as the preponderance of Hebraicisms in the texts clearly suggests.[58] Second, the pseudepigraphical writings, particularly those of Gnostic thought (including and especially the Nag Hammadi texts), were composed much later than projected, dating well into the third and fourth centuries. These texts did not represent what has been purported to be a profound diversity or pluralism in original Christianity: they were perversions of the Hebraic foundations of earliest Christian faith designed to accommodate and exploit the beliefs and practices of the Greco-Roman and pagan worlds.

---

[56] Kroeger, pp. 7-8.
[57] Kroeger, pp. 7-8.
[58] For detailed discussion of the multiplicity of Hebraicisms in the Gospels and for arguments for much earlier dating of the Gospels, see Claude Tresmontant, *The Hebrew Christ: Language in the Age of the Gospels* (Chicago: Franciscan Herald Press, 1989) and Jean Carmignac, *The Birth of the Synoptics* (Chicago: Franciscan Herald Press, 1987).

This is reflective of the problem with many scholars who move from what is in vogue one day to what is considered *avant-garde* the next day. With many liberal theologians the important thing is to appear to be "in the know" so that one achieves virtual guru status. Likewise, the more preposterous the phantasmagoria that one can present, the more likely it is to sell books and to garner for the author the tweedy appearance of intellectual superiority.[59] These pretenders to scholarship and to mystical and esoteric insight could well profit from Paul's advice: "Do not go beyond what is written."[60] Doubtless, they will be judged by biblical principle that curses those who either add to or take from the written Word of God.[61]

In the final analysis, Christian faith can be established only on the written and canonical Word of God. Jesus clearly established this truth when he answered the question, "What shall I do to inherit eternal life?" by asking, "What is written in the Law? . . . How do you read it?"[62] Paul was faithful to this methodology: "This I admit to you, that according to the Way which they call a sect I do serve the God of our fathers, believing everything that is in accordance with the Law and that is written in the Prophets."[63] Answers for faith and practice are found, not in the latest musings of academic gurus, but in the rightly divided words of Scripture.

GYNOMORPHIC IMAGERY IN DIVINE DESIGN

Despite all the perversions and extremisms that are in vogue in an increasingly cynical postmodern world, ample images of feminine qualities have been applied to God throughout the texts of Holy Scripture. This gynomorphic imagery clearly confirms that the Eternal is not merely a masculine deity who created a man in his image and then, in a divine afterthought, added woman as an inferior and subservient being. God is neither male nor female; however, because both males and females are theomorphic, both the feminine and the masculine have been used in Scripture to bring understanding of the Divine to

---

[59] Such books as Dan Brown's *The Da Vinci Code* (New York: Doubleday, 2003) demonstrate how gullible the general public and some elenets of Christianity are to such preposterous ideas.

[60] 1 Corinthians 4:6, NIV. The Complete Jewish Bible may well capture the meaning Paul intended in this statement with this translation: "I have used myself and Apollos as examples to teach you not to go beyond what the *Tanakh* says."

[61] Revelation 22:19 speaks specifically of the prophecy of John; however, the declaration can be projected to all of Scripture as well.

[62] Luke 10:26.

[63] Acts 24:14.

humanity. These facts make it possible to engage in a fair analysis of what God meant when he declared that he would make humanity "in our image and likeness." By understanding what the Scriptures truly say about God, a basis emerges for understanding what they also say about humanity—male and female. By providing a clear theological context for the first and most basic declaration of anthropology, "Let us make humanity in our image and likeness," a foundation can be laid for discovering God's design for humanity and thereby for confirming God's design for woman.

Springboard for Discussion

1. Discuss the instances in the Bible where divine wisdom (*hokmah* in the Hebrew Scriptures) is described in terms that virtually make it a personification of God's activity in relationship to the creation. Why do you think that Wisdom is personified in feminine terms? Is *Hokmah* an agent of God or is she God manifested in creation?

2. Consider how the sages of Israel attempted to reconcile the statements in Scripture that personify Wisdom as feminine and contain language that overlaps between Wisdom and God. How does the personification of Wisdom in feminine imagery conflict with absolute monotheism? Is *Hokmah* God or a means of manifesting qualities of God's transcendence in immanence?

3. How does *Hokmah* participate in the very creation itself? In what way does this involvement parallel or interact with the statements of Scripture that all things were created by the Word of God (John 1:14; Colossians 1:16)?

4. Discuss the ways in which Solomon personified Wisdom. How did this device underscore the importance of embracing divine wisdom?

5. Analyze the description of *Hokmah* in feminine terms. How do these descriptions defy the norms in which women were considered in most of the world throughout history? How do they offer insight into God's own valuation of womanhood and the roles and opportunities available to women in family, society, and religious community?

6. Evaluate the connection between divine Wisdom and the Woman of Valor whom Solomon describes in Proverbs 31. Does this

connection indicate that women are limited in some ways, or does it indicate that opportunities for women are limitless? Why is wisdom connected with the feminine? How might this be connected with what has been called "women's intuition"?

7. Consider the connection between divine Wisdom and the divine *Logos*, the Word of God. Is it possible that Jesus, though masculine in gender in the incarnation, also manifested feminine qualities and attributes ascribed to *Hokmah* in the Hebrew Scriptures? Do you think that the subsuming of Wisdom language into *Logos* statements resulted from some gynophobia or from a determination to protect the Christian community from the dangers of Gnosticism or goddess worship?

8. Evaluate the emphasis on *Sophia* images among feminists and particularly among those who are proponents of goddess worship. Why has it always been important in biblical tradition to guard against such activities?

9. Discuss the dangers of neo-Gnosticism, the attempts to revive the ancient Greek teaching that both the apostles and later leaders of the church defended so strongly against. Is it possible to recover feminine imagery for God in Scripture without becoming vulnerable to the influences of Gnostic and neo-pagan thought? How can balance be maintained?

10. Consider reasons why everything in Christian experience must be built upon the foundation of the Scriptures themselves. Can the Scriptures be interpreted in the light of philosophy or human reasoning? Can ideas that are not confirmed in Scripture be considered?

11. Establish ways in which Scripture confirms the truth that God created humanity in his own image and likeness as both male and female. How does feminine imagery of divine Wisdom help you to understand that both women and men bear and reflect the image of God?

CHAPTER 11

THE IMAGE AND LIKENESS OF GOD

After God had completed the creation of the inanimate universe and had filled the earth with a profound diversity of animate creatures, his final creative declaration was this: "Let us make humanity." To this statement, however, were appended words that would forever set apart the final terrestrial creation, for God declared his intention to form this special creature *"in our image, after our likeness."*[1] Then, just as he had planned in careful deliberation, God "created humanity in his own image," and when he did, "male and female created he them."[2] The divine focus on the creation of humanity could not have been more apparent: this, the final animate being, was to image God himself in the earth! In fact, this single verse of Scripture twice repeats the statement, "God created humanity in his own image," employing a common Hebraism that adds emphasis through repetition,[3] thereby highlighting and underscoring precisely what God did. The fact that the same statement is also repeated in reverse order in this text serves further to confirm and make the stated truth undeniable: humankind

---

[1] Genesis 1:26, NIV.
[2] Genesis 1:27, NASB.
[3] The Hebrew language uses the device of repetition to give emphasis and to create comparatives and superlatives. This can be the repetition of words or phrases, or it can be the repetition of entire sentences or passages, as is the case where the Psalms use the word *selah* to instruct the reader to reflect on or repeat the previous statement. (During the singing of the psalm, the word *selah* was used to indicate an interlude or a pause, serving essentially the same purpose as the word *amen* in that it stressed the importance of what had come before. Some scholars have also suggested that *selah* comes from the Hebrew word *calah*, meaning "to hang" or "to weigh," which could imply the same meaning of pausing to consider and weigh what had just been sung. Yet others suggest that *selah* can mean "forever.") The linguistic and syntactical device of repetition is also an important factor as a mnemonic device in Hebrew.

is the very image and likeness of God in the earth.[4]

Humanity, therefore, did not eventuate upon planet earth through a process of evolution, either evolving or devolving through a chain of successive mutations initiated by chance electro-chemical reactions upon or within some primordial ooze. It was God—not blind fate or evolution—who created humanity with all its distinctives, and his creation was by intricate and superintelligent design so that every aspect of human existence has a contribution to make to the overall integrity and welfare of the human race. Humanity was created in a moment of time when the God of the universe breathed the breath of life into the being that he had formed from the very dust of the planet. At that instant, the human entity became "a living being," a vivified creature that was different from everything else that God had created. No other being in the terrestrial creation was ever said to have been made a "living being [soul]," and no other being was formed with the intention of bearing the "image and likeness of God."

For the first time in the creation narratives, God identified himself in "the self-referential first person" and thereby invested his own personal "identity in this human creature."[5] Until the time came for the creation of humanity, God had simply spoken everything into existence. When he generated human life, however, God said, "Let us make humanity in our image, after our likeness," and he proceeded with his own fingers to form the human entity, exercising ingenious dexterity and delicate loving care. Then he proceeded to vivify the structure that he had formed with a mouth-to-mouth infusion of his own breath. Of all of God's creative profundity, therefore, "only humanity is envisioned as comparable to divinity."[6]

As David Clines has noted, "man is not a mere cipher, chosen at random by God to be His representative, but to some extent also expresses, as the image, the character of God."[7] It is for this reason that when Talmudic sage, Ben Azai, was asked, "What is the most impor-

---

[4] In the first biblical instance where the phrase *image and likeness* is used, the Hebrew text reads: וַיִּבְרָא אֱלֹהִים אֶת־הָאָדָם בְּצַלְמוֹ ("Created he [God] the-human in likeness his"). This is normal syntax for this statement in Hebrew. When the statement is repeated, however, it reads, בְּצֶלֶם אֱלֹהִים בָּרָא אֹתוֹ ("In image of God created he him"). The fact that this instance is in reverse syntax adds even greater emphasis to the declaration. See Joseph E. Coleson, *Ezer Cenegdo: A Power Like Him, Facing Him as Equal* (Grantham, PA: Wesleyan/Holiness Women Clergy, 1996).

[5] W. Randall Garr, *In His Own Image and Likeness: Humanity, Divinity, and Monotheism* (Leiden, The Netherlands: Koninkijke Brill, 2003), p. 4.

[6] Hans Walter Wolff, *Anthropology of the Old Testament,* tr. Margaret Kohl (Philadelphia: Fortress Press, 1974), p. 159.

[7] David J. A. Clines, "The Image of God in Man," *Tyndale Bulletin* 19 (1968), p. 92.

tant verse in the whole Bible?" he responded immediately, "The verse from the Book of Genesis that says: 'Man was created in the Divine image.'"[8] Claus Westermann agrees, observing that "the most striking statement" of the biblical creation narratives "over and above God being the creator, preserver and sustainer of creation, is that God created human beings in his image."[9] Bruce Demarest is correct in asserting that "the implications of human persons created in the image of God are immense for theology, psychology, ministry, and Christian living," embracing issues of "human dignity and value, personal and social ethics, relations between the sexes, [and] the solidarity of the human family."[10] Abraham Joshua Heschel said, "The symbol of God is . . . not a temple or a tree . . . a statue or a star . . . [but] *man, every man.* God created man in His image, in His likeness."[11]

The image of God refers to God's own self-expression through humanity, even to God's own "becoming-in-self-expression."[12] Humanity may not be a photocopy of God, but "in some way [it is] a representation of him."[13] As Karl Barth observed, "In God's own being and sphere there is a counterpart: a genuine but harmonious self-encounter and self-discovery; a free co-existence and co-operation; an open confrontation and reciprocity. Man is the repetition of this divine form of life; its copy and reflection."[14] Phyllis Bird has rightly noted that "the concept of God-likeness" is, therefore, "fundamental to theological anthropology."[15]

As J. Philip Newell has observed, "The image of God [is] woven into the mystery of our being" so that God's image "is not simply

---

[8] Ben Azai, *Genesis Rabba* 24, quoted in Irwin Cotler, "Jewish NGOs, Human Rights, and Public Advocacy: A Comparative Inquiry," Jewish Political Studies Review 11:3-4 (Fall, 1999), p. 3. Also *Religious Conscience, the State, and the Law: Historical Contexts and Contemporary Significance,* ed. John McLaren and Harold G. Coward (New York: State University of New York Press, 1999), p. 78. Ben Azai considered this verse more important than the commandment to "love your neighbor as yourself."

[9] Claus Westermann, *Genesis: An Introduction,* tr. John J. Scullion (Minneapolis: Fortress Press, 1992), p. 111.

[10] Bruce A. Demarest, *The Human Person in Theology and Psychology: A Biblical Anthropology for the Twenty-first Century* (Grand Rapids, MI: Kregel Publications, 2005), p. 141.

[11] Abraham Joshua Heschel, in Samuel H. Dresner, ed., *I Asked for Wonder: A Spiritual Anthology—Abraham Joshua Heschel* (New York: Schocken Books, 1991), p. 49, Heschel's emphasis.

[12] Karl Rahner, *Foundations of Christian Faith: An Introduction to the Idea of Christianity,* tr. William V. Dych (New York: Seabury Press, 1978), p. 223.

[13] P. J. Harland, *The Value of Human Life: A Study of the Story of the Flood (Genesis 6-9)* (Leiden: The Netherlands: E. J. Brill, 1996), p. 180.

[14] Karl Barth, *Church Dogmatics: The Doctrine of Creation,* III/2, ed. G. W. Bromiley and T. F. Torrance, tr. G. W. Bromiley (London: T & T. Clark, 2004), p. 182.

[15] Phyllis Bird, "Bone of My Bone and Flesh of My Flesh," in *Theology Today,* 50:4 (Jan, 1993), p. 530.

a characteristic of our humanity" but "the essence of our being."[16] Describing humanity in its "essential, undifferentiated nature," is the "primary determinant that must find expression"[17] in all of the various forms of human distinctives, including gender differentiation. The divine image in humanity, consequently, "cannot be quantified or qualified," an eternal truth that Bird succinctly encapsulated when she concluded that "to be human is to be created in the image of God, irrespective of age, condition, or character."[18] Indeed, for both Jews and Christians, humanity's existence in God's image without qualification or distinction assigns both dignity and sacredness to all human life. This is why the sages of Israel have taught that the image of God in humanity "obligates us to honor man" because the image and likeness of God in humanity give "value and meaning to human existence."[19]

Vladimir Lossky has suggested the possibility that when the Scriptures declared that God made humanity in his image and likeness, they may have been targeting "the Egyptian cult of theriomorphic gods" so that the expression *in the image* "has a negative meaning," implying that "animals have nothing of the divine, for only man is made 'in the image of God.'"[20] Lossky also argues that the phrase *after our likeness* "still further limits the positive force of 'in our image,' perhaps to avoid at the same time the Iranian myth of the 'heavenly man': man is *only* in the image of God [not a god-man]."[21] The distinction that humanity is the only creation made "in the image and likeness" of God has been and continues to be of vital importance because of various pagan attempts to assert godhood or divine image in virtually all of creation or to posit the existence of demigods or of superhuman creatures. It is essential to both theology and anthropology that God's account of creation in which only humanity was made "in our image, after our likeness" be understood and accepted without reservation. The most important aspect about the human creation, then, was that humanity was intentionally formed for the express purpose of imaging of the God of heaven in the earthly creation. Indeed, no other

[16] J. Philip Newell, *Echo of the Soul: The Sacredness of the Human Body* (Norwich, UK: Canterbury Press Norwich, 2000), p. xi.
[17] Bird, p. 530.
[18] Bird, p. 530.
[19] Chaim Navon, David Straus, *Genesis and Jewish Thought* (New York: KTAV Publishing House, 2008), p. 43.
[20] Vladimir Lossky, *In the Image and Likeness of God* (Crestwood, NY: St. Vladimir's Seminary Press, 1964), p. 128.
[21] Lossky, p. 128.

beings in the universe were ever said by God to have been designed to bear his image and likeness. Humanity was truly *sui generis*, for "there is one way in which God is imaged in the world and only one: humanness!"[22] Humanity is the only part of the entire creation that "discloses to us something about the reality of God."[23]

While God had noted that each phase of his creation was "good" (טוֹב — *tov*),[24] when he created humanity, his observation became a virtual sigh of complete satisfaction when he described everything that he had made—climaxed by his creation of humanity—as being "very good" (טוֹב מְאֹד — *tov me'od*).[25] The term *tov me'od* means "exceedingly, abundantly good"; therefore, God's observation about his final creation underscored the abundance of the excellence manifest in his precise development of a creature that reflected his divine image. Evdokimov also maintains that *tov* implies that something is in "precise conformity with its destination."[26] God's exclamation that humanity was "very good" resulted from the fact that "the faithful image conveys the perfect likeness. God views Himself in His icon, notices the pure water of the likeness, and says, good. He rejoices on seeing Himself in His living mirror."[27]

The divine image in the human creation should be carefully considered in the light of Paul's declaration that all of God's creation provides understanding of truths about the Eternal.[28] Doubtless the entire creation—especially the creation that was purposefully formed to reflect the divine image—must produce some insight by which God is "clearly seen ... [and] understood." Perhaps the theomorphic nature of humanity as God's prime revelatory image was what the apostle had in mind when he observed that "even [God's] eternal power and divinity" are "clearly seen" and "understood" through the creation.

DEFINING "IMAGE" AND "LIKENESS"

What is meant by the phrase *image and likeness of God*? Doubtless, massive amounts of theological and philosophical reflection have

---

[22] Walter Brueggemann, *Genesis* (Louisville, KY: John Knox Press, 1982), p. 232.
[23] Brueggemann, p. 232.
[24] Genesis 1:4, 10, 12, 18, 21, 25.
[25] Genesis 1:31.
[26] Paul Evdokimov, *Woman and the Salvation of the World: A Christian Anthropology of the Charisms of Women*, tr. Anthony Gythiel (Crestwood, NY: St. Vladimir's Seminary Press, 1994), p. 140.
[27] Evdokimov, p. 140.
[28] Romans 1:20.

been expended upon analyzing the human creation in an effort to discover precisely what God meant when he said, "Let us make humanity in our image, after our likeness." The answer to this question is important for all humans because it reveals the true self-identity of each human being and because it holds the key to human understanding of relationship to and interaction with the Creator himself as well as interaction with other human beings. The declaration of humankind's bearing the *imago Dei* is so intentional and profound in the Genesis narrative that it is emphasized in the Hebrew text with two similar, yet different words and with two similar yet different syntactical devices. The Hebrew words for "image" and "likeness" are צֶלֶם (*tzelem*) and דְּמוּת (*demut*) respectively.[29] *Tzelem* is derived from the Hebrew verbal root that means "to carve" or "to cut,"[30] connecting the imagery of sculpture with the idea that humanity images God "as a representation of God."[31] God literally sculpted an image of himself when he created the earthling. *Demut* comes from the Hebrew verbal root that means "to be like,"[32] indicating that in some manner and to some degree humanity is like God. In the text, the nouns *tzelem* and *demut* are introduced and governed by the prepositions ב (*be*) and כ (*ke*) respectively. It is interesting that the two words used to describe humanity's direct relation to the creator can even be said to demonstrate the fact that the basis for gendered existence was present from the beginning in the first earthling, for in Hebrew the word *tzelem* is masculine in gender while the word *demut* is feminine in gender.[33] Image and likeness can never be limited to a single gender. Both male and female are required for the complete manifestation of God's image and likeness in humanity.

Because of the use of two similar terms in describing the relationship of humanity to the Divine, much speculation about the meaning of the terms *tzelem* and *demut* has resulted in a wide variety of inter-

[29] For an expansive discussion of *tzelem* and *demut*, see P. J. Harland, *The Value of Human Life* (Leiden, The Netherlands: E. J. Brill, 1996), pp. 177-210.
[30] Francis Brown, S. R. Driver, and Charles Briggs eds., *Hebrew and English Lexicon of the Old Testament* (New York: Houghton Mifflin, 1907), p. 853.
[31] Anthony A. Hoekema, *Created in God's Image* (Grand Rapids, MI: Wm. B. Eerdmans Publishing Co., 1986), p. 14.
[32] Brown, Driver, Briggs, pp. 197-198.
[33] Too much attention should not be given to this fact of Hebrew grammar, for Hebrew has no neuter with which to describe such things. This is not an indication that the male had God's image while the female had God's likeness: they shared equally in both the divine image and the divine likeness. The fact that both genders are represented in the words is, however, an interesting aside.

pretations.[34] W. Randall Garr has observed that the terms *image* and *likeness* "are strangely suitable characterizations of the divine-human relationship . . . they are semantically alike; the nouns are each representational terms that express simulative content," with *tzelem* and *demut* implying "two foci of comparison between the divine and human spheres."[35] Some scholars have suggested that the term *tzelem* (image) generally refers to something concrete, whereas *demut* (likeness) is more abstract.[36] Arguing with the majority of scholarship,[37] J. Andrew Dearman asserts that the inversion of "likeness" and "image" in Genesis 5:1 and 9:6 "implies that the two words are used synonymously with reference to the divine image.[38] Other scholars, however, have argued that the two terms are more than synonymous, with each either expanding the implications of the other or dealing with a different aspect of the human correspondence to God. Walther Eichrodt has asserted that בְּצֶלֶם (*b'tzelem*) is both limited and weakened by כִּדְמוּת (*k'demut*) so that it excludes the idea of the human's being merely a copy of God and limits image to similarity instead.[39] Garr also argues against the contention that the two words are used interchangeably and indiscriminately,[40] and he concludes that it is also incorrect to assert that these terms describe only one relationship instead of two, that *demut* merely defines and reinforces *tzelem* or that *demut* mitigates, weakens, limits, or attenuates the force of *tzelem*.[41]

Karl Barth maintained that the preposition ב in בְּצֶלֶם (*b'tzelem*) indicated the origin of the mould so that humankind was "created in

---

[34] See Gunnlaugur A. Jónsson, *The Image of God: Genesis 1:26–28 in a Century of Old Testament Research*, tr. Lorraine Svendsen (Lund, Sweden: Almqvist and Wiksell, 1988) for a survey of historical interpretation of *tzelem* and *demut*.

[35] Randall Garr, p. 128.

[36] Marcia J. Bunge, Terence E. Fretheim, Beverly Roberts Gaventa, eds., *The Child in the Bible* (Grand Rapids, MI: Wm. B. Eerdmans Publishing Co., 2008), p. 314.

[37] Cf. Claus Westermann, "Missing Persons and Mistaken Identities" in *Harvard Theological Review*, 74 (1981), p. 140. Also *Image of God and Gender Models in Judaeo-Christian Tradition*, ed. Kari Elisabeth Børresen (Oslo: Solum, 1991), p. 27. See also Westermann, *Genesis*.

[38] J. Andrew Dearman, "Theophany, Anthropomorphism, and the *Imago Dei*," in *The Incarnation*, Stephen T. Davis, Daniel Kendall, Gerald O'Collins, eds. (Oxford: Oxford University Press, 2002), p. 40.

[39] Walther Eichrodt, *Theology of the Old Testament*, tr. J. A. Baker (Philadelphia, PA: Westminster Press, 1961), vol. 2, pp. 78ff.

[40] Randall Garr, p. 165.

[41] Randall Garr, p. 165. See also Willem A. M. Beuken, *Louvain Studies 24* (1999), Ivan Engnell, "'Knowledge' and 'Life' in the Creation Story," in *Wisdom in Israel and in the Ancient Near East Presented to Professor Harold Henry Rowley*, ed. M. Noth and D. Winton Thomas; *Vetus Testamentum* Supplements 3 (Leiden: E. J. Brill, 1955), p. 112, and Julian Morgenstern, "The Sources of the Creation Story—Genesis 1:1–2:4," *The American Journal of Semitic Languages and Literatures*, 36 (1920), p. 192.

correspondence with the image of God," such that "God created a being to correspond to his own self."[42] Gerhard von Rad concluded that the "basic word *selem* (image) is more closely explained and made precise by *demut* (similarity) with the simple meaning that this image is to correspond to the original . . . that is to resemble it."[43] Von Rad argued that the Hebrew בְּצֶלֶם אֱלֹהִים (*b'tzelem Elohim*) should be translated "as the image of God" rather than "in the image of God" by suggesting that the *beth* (בּ) is a *beth essentiae* (*beth* of essence) rather than a *beth* of norm, "thus implying that the whole person, rather than some quality of the person, is God's image."[44] Using the example of Exodus 6:3: וָאֵרָא בְּאֵל שַׁדָּי (*v'ra b'El Shaddai*—"I appeared *as* El Shaddai") in which the preposition *beth* before *El Shaddai* must be translated "as," not "in," P. J. Harland has suggested that if *beth essentiae* is understood in this text, "man is created not as an *imitation* of the divine image but *as* the image of God."[45] Barth also agreed, saying flatly, "Man *is* the image of God."[46] The complete human being—not merely a part or an attribute thereof—is, therefore, God's image in the earth. Humanity is the connection between the heavenly and the earthly. "Ostensibly, humanity is envisioned to be, and created as, a token of divine presence and participation in the world," for *tzelem* and *demut* suggest that "humanity will resemble, replicate, or mimic God and his divine community" so that "humanity is (like) a theophany."[47] As Karl Rahner has observed, human beings represent "the event of God's absolute self-communication."[48]

THEOMORPHIC HUMANITY

The God of Scripture is not an anthropomorphic imagination concocted by human beings in a human attempt to create a god in their own image. Instead, human beings are theomorphic: they were created by God to be his representatives who would fully manifest his own

[42] Barth, p. 197.

[43] Gerhard von Rad, *Genesis* (London: SCM, 1970), p. 58.

[44] For more detailed study of these concepts, see Gerhard von Rad, *Genesis: A Commentary*, rev. ed., tr. John H. Marks (Philadelphia: Westminster Press, 1972), p. 56. Also David J. A. Clines, *On the Way to the Postmodern* (Sheffield, England: Sheffield Academic Press, Ltd., 1998), pp. 468-473, Noreen L. Herzfeld, *In Our Image: Artificial Intelligence and the Human Spirit* (Minneapolis, MN: Augsburg Fortress, 2002), p. 22.

[45] P. J. Harland, pp. 184-185, emphasis added.

[46] Barth, p. 323.

[47] Randall Garr, p. 128.

[48] Karl Rahner, *Foundations of Christian Faith: An Introduction to the Idea of Christianity*, tr. William V. Dych (New York: Seabury Press, 1978), p. 126.

image and likeness in the earth.[49] Carl Henry pointed out, however, that because biblical theology is based in divine self-disclosure, it is a "colossal projection" for human beings to conceive that "the one God [is] a human personality inflated to infinity."[50] David Blumenthal offers a nuanced view of this truth by suggesting that an anthropopathic view of God is to be preferred over the anthropomorphic perspective because "it is not we [humans] who project ourselves onto God, but God Who projects Godself onto humanity."[51]

David Clines has observed that declaring humankind to be God's image means that humanity is "the visible corporeal representative of the invisible, bodiless God: he is representative rather than representation, since the idea of portrayal is secondary in the significance of the image."[52] This is in keeping with the Hebraic understanding inherent in Holy Scripture that values function over form. Kallistos Ware maintains that "the human person is the crown and fulfillment of the divine creation-microcosm and mediator, priest of the cosmos, God's royal image."[53] In this context, Ware reasoned that "by virtue of the divine icon placed in our hearts, we are capable of mutual love, open to unending growth, endowed with self-awareness, entrusted with free will, and each of us distinctive and unique."[54]

Augustine observed that the image of God was not intended to make humanity equal with God, for humanity was created by God, not born of him; therefore, humanity is "not made equal by parity, but approaches Him by a sort of likeness."[55] In order to conceptualize humanity's constitution as a task toward imaging the Divine; therefore, many early Greek and Latin church fathers distinguished between "image" and "likeness" in the biblical creation narrative. They asserted that "image" is human nature that cannot be lost, while "likeness" is the human relationship with God that can be lost. Their argument

---

[49] David R. Blumenthal, "Tselem: Toward an Anthropopathic Theology of Image," in Frymer-Kensky, Novak, Ochs, Singer, and Fox Sandmel, *Christianity in Jewish Terms* (Boulder CO: Westview Press, 2002), pp. 337-339.

[50] Carl F. H. Henry, *God, Revelation, and Authority* (Wheaton, IL: Crossway Books, 1999), vol. 5, pp. 166-167.

[51] Blumenthal, p. 338.

[52] Clines, p. 75.

[53] Kallistos Ware, "'In the Image and Likeness': The Uniqueness of the Human Person," in *Personhood: Orthodox Christianity and the Connection between Body, Mind, and Soul,* ed. John T. Chirban (Westport, CT: Bergin & Garvey, 1996), p. 11.

[54] Ware, p. 11.

[55] Augustine, *On the Trinity* 6:12. See Augustine, *The Trinity,* tr. Stephen McKenna (Washington, DC: Catholic University of America Press, 1963), p. 240.

rested in part on the greater differentiation of the Greek terms for image (*eikon*) and likeness (*homoiosis*) which are more clearly distinct than the Hebrew terms *tzelem* and *demut*.[56]

Maximos the Confessor succinctly summed up the teaching of those church fathers who differentiated between the terms *image* and *likeness* in this way: "Every intelligent nature is in the image of God, but only the good and the wise are in His likeness."[57] Origen sought to prove the differentiation by noting that whereas both terms are mentioned in Genesis 1:26, only "image" is mentioned in Genesis 1:27. He argued that God's final intention for humanity was sketched out in Genesis 1:26, requiring both image and likeness to be mentioned there. The lack of mention of likeness in Genesis 1:27 indicated that humanity "received the honor of God's image in his first creation, whereas the perfection of God's likeness was reserved for him at the consummation."[58] Thus, for Origen, likeness could be acquired by human beings only through imitation of God.[59]

Adolf von Harnack explained that the Greek fathers saw *image* as "the inalienable spiritual plan of man," while they viewed *likeness* as "moral similarity to God."[60] He noted that the church fathers "were unwilling . . . to rest content with the thought that the inalienable spiritual natural endowment of man constituted the divine image, but they found no means of getting beyond it."[61] Harnack concluded that "their conception of moral goodness as a product of human freedom hindered them."[62] This line of thought is foundational to the Orthodox concept that human divinization (*theosis*) is attained through self-abnegation and through contemplation and imitation of God;[63] however, this separation of image from likeness represents an interpolation rather than an interpretation of the biblical text, for God's Word simply does not bifurcate image and likeness. All humans have both

---

[56] For a more detailed discussion of text-based distinctions between the Greek terms for image and likeness, see Lars Thunberg, "The Human Person as Image of God," in *Christian Spirituality: Origins to the Twelfth Century*, ed. Bernard McGuinn and John Meyendorff (New York: Crossroad Publishing Co., 1985), p. 298.

[57] Maximos the Confessor, *On Love*, III, 25.

[58] Origen, *On First Principles* 3.6.1.

[59] Henri Crouzel, referenced by Anneli Lahtala, "Grammar and Dialectic," in McGinn, Meyendorff, and Ledercq, p. 297.

[60] Adolph Von Harnack, *History of Dogma, Vol. III,* tr. James Millar (London: Williams & Norgate, 1896), p. 261.

[61] Von Harnack, p. 261.

[62] Von Harnack, p. 261.

[63] Vladimir Lossky, "The Theological Notion of the Human Person," in Lossky, pp. 111-123.

the image and the likeness of God.

It is important to underscore the fact that each aspect of humanness, both female and male, reflects something of the divine image. This is true for ordering right relationships between human beings, and it is also important for understanding how the perfection of deity could be manifest in the perfection of humanity in the person of Jesus. As von Rad claimed, the implications of "image and likeness" help establish the connection between the anthropomorphisms, theophanies, and *imago Dei* in the Hebrew Scriptures and the apostolic claim that Jesus was uniquely "in the form"[64] of God, the very "image and glory" of God,[65] and the "exact stamp/imprint" of God.[66] It is a simple truth that "what remained linked but mysteriously unexplored in the [Hebrew Scriptures]—that is the correspondence between the divine and human form—emerges in the early church as a way to understand the claim that 'God was in Christ.'"[67]

David Blumenthal has observed that the doctrine of the incarnation of Jesus is "not beyond the Jewish theological imagination. It can be seen as an extension of the anthropopathic understanding of God." While Blumenthal believes that "thinking about it could help Jews, and Christians, understand the theology of the image of God in which we are created," he categorically states that "Jews cannot accept the doctrine of the incarnation" because "it is too anthropomorphic."[68] It is one thing to say that "God has anthropopathic qualities, characteristics that we think of as human," but it is "quite another to say that God has (or had) an actual body."[69] Thus, the "the prohibition against imaging God extends" in "biblical, rabbinic, and mystical traditions," to "giving God a real body, though not to giving God a mind-bound body."[70]

WHAT CONSTITUTES IMAGE AND LIKENESS?

Seeking to define the image of God in humanity is difficult because of the profound differences between divine being and human being. As George Shillington has observed, "humans are mortal; God

---

[64] Philippians 2:6, NASB.
[65] 1 Corinthians 11:7; 2 Corinthians 4:4; Colossians 1:15; Hebrews 1:3.
[66] Hebrews 1:3, NRS.
[67] Dearman, p. 2.
[68] Blumenthal, p. 338.
[69] Blumenthal, p. 338.
[70] Blumenthal, p. 338.

is not; humans are finite; God is infinite. Humans are bound by time and space. God is eternal."[71] At the same time, however, "within the mortal, finite, temporal, spatial existence of human beings there exists a consciousness of the Other, of God."[72] And, there is an innate sense in humans that their existence is more than mere chemical or biological fact, for inherent in every human being is an awareness of something beyond, of a higher power (whether acknowledged or not).

The understanding of "image and likeness" is important for establishing the divine imprint upon all of humanity—both male and female—without reservation or differentiation. If one is even to begin to understand the image and likeness of God, it is first essential to recognize that the image and likeness are universal—that they are manifest in every human being. Each individual human is made in the image and likeness of God and shares that image by living among and interacting with other human beings. As Abraham Joshua Heschel observed, each human being is "an original, not a copy."[73] Each human person, therefore, "has the right to be treated as a stand-in for God in all circumstances."[74] Regardless as to one's saintly or depraved nature, "nobody can be more of the image of God than anyone else."[75] As Desmond Tutu has observed, "the Bible claims for all human beings this exalted status that we are all, each one of us, created in the divine image"[76] so that particular extraneous divine attributes cannot be claimed only for certain people while being denied for others. Even John Calvin, who strongly emphasized the depraved and deformed nature of fallen humanity, admonished people to "look at the image of God in all men," for, in his opinion, though one might declare another human being to be "contemptible and worthless," the Lord "shows him to be one to whom he has deigned to give the beauty of his image."[77] Without exception, every human being in every aspect of his humanity bears the image and likeness of God in the earth. Calvin even concluded that there is no part of humans, "not even the body

---

[71] V. George Shillington, *Reading the Sacred Text: An Introduction to Biblical Studies* (London: T & T Clark, 2002), p. 13.
[72] Shillington, p. 13.
[73] Abraham Joshua Heschel, *Who Is Man?* (Palo Alto, CA: Stanford University Press, 1965), p. 37.
[74] Blumenthal, pp. 337-339.
[75] Blumenthal, pp. 337-339.
[76] Desmond Tutu in *Religious Human Rights in Global Perspective: Religious Perspectives*, ed. John Witte and J. D. Van der Vyver (The Hague, The Netherlands: Kluwer Law International, 1996), p. x.
[77] John Calvin, *Institutes of the Christian Religion*, III.7.6.

itself, in which some sparks [of the Divine] did not glow."[78]

Just as the ultimate worth of human beings as the image and likeness of God cannot be established or distinguished on the basis of personal merit, they can never be judged according to race, ethnicity, social class, age, or gender. God's image is "a universal quality of human beings" and not something that is "limited to a few just or wise people."[79] Consequently, "all people, without fail, are equally to be treated as one would treat God."[80] The fact that all humans equally bear the image of God predicates human dignity on God's gift, not on human or societal recognition. In Hebraic understanding, the value of each human being does not depend upon societal utility or function, as in the philosophies of Plato and Aristotle. Human value is solely dependent upon existence, since all human beings manifest the image and likeness of the Creator equally. "The self does not have an automatic dignity; it is a conferred dignity" granted by God such that "the weak, the fragile, the foolish, the faulty also are to be treated with dignity"[81] and "may not be violated."[82] Indeed, those who, for all intents and purposes, appear to be the smallest and the weakest in church and society can be the very ones who best demonstrate what being human in the image and likeness of the Divine truly means. Those who are often ignored or despised can be used by God to instruct those who are powerful and self-absorbed that the greatest quality of God's image in humanity is the openness to relationship with God and with others.

Likewise, the universality of the image of God in humanity cannot be taken from any human. God's image in humanity "is not lost or effaced by sin, and it cannot be increased or diminished."[83] Though many theologians in history have suggested that the image "had been obscured, deprived, or depraved," even that discussion maintained a belief that despite the fall into sin, "humanity was God-like" so that what humans once had, they could regain."[84] The truth is, however, that the image of God in humanity was never lost. Emil Brunner observed correctly that "in the thought of the Old Testament the fact that

---

[78] Calvin, I.15.3.
[79] Blumenthal, pp. 337-339.
[80] Blumenthal, pp. 337-339.
[81] Mamta Rajawat, *Burning Issues of Human Rights* (Delhi: Kalpaz Publications, 2001), p. 156.
[82] Max L. Stackhouse and Stephen E. Healey, "Religion and Human Rights: A Theological Apologetic" in Witte and Van der Vyver, p. 499.
[83] Bird, p. 530.
[84] Frymer-Kensky, pp. 330-331.

man has been 'made in the Image of God' means something which man can never lose; even when he sins, he cannot lose it."[85] Randall Garr agrees: "Inherent in the human race from its very inception, the early history of the 'image' demonstrates that it is perdurable as well."[86]

In the recapitulation of the human creation in Genesis 5, it is clear that the image of God in which Adam and Eve were created was continued in Seth: "Adam . . . had a son in his own likeness, in his own image."[87] The continuing chronicles of the generations of the children of Adam confirm the fact that "the divine image in man holds equally in all generations."[88] Jürgen Moltmann succinctly observed that "human sin may certainly pervert human beings' relationship with God, but not God's relationship to human beings," a relationship that was "created by him, and can therefore never be abrogated or withdrawn except by God himself."[89] Regardless as to what else may be concluded about humanity's first or continuing sins, they "by no means infringe directly upon the divine image" in all human beings.[90] As a matter of fact, Genesis 9:6 is incontrovertible evidence that God's image is fully and continually manifest in all humans, for God himself in his post-diluvian prohibition against murder declared to Noah that "whoever sheds the blood of a human, by a human shall his blood be shed; for in the image of God has God made humankind."[91] The thrice-repeated word *adam* in the Hebrew text deliberately and emphatically confirms that God's image continued to be manifest in all humanity, for the word *adam* is properly translated "human," not "man." Genesis 5:3 confirms that the image of God that was intrinsic to the creation of the first man and woman continued unabated and unrestricted in Seth, and Genesis 9:6 concludes that that same image was still present in all human beings without exception after the flood. The prohibition against murder is directly connected with the fact that anyone who sheds the blood of another human being is answerable to God because every human is created in the image of God.

In seeking to understand image and likeness, it is first important,

---

[85] Emil Brunner, *The Christian Doctrine of Creation and Redemption*, tr. Olive Wyon (Philadelphia: Westminster Press, 1953), p. 57.
[86] Randall Garr, p. 153.
[87] Genesis 5:3.
[88] Randall Garr, p. 153.
[89] Jürgen Moltmann, *God in Creation: A New Theology of Creation and the Spirit of God* (London: SCM Press, 1985), p. 233.
[90] Randall Garr, p. 153.
[91] Genesis 9:6, NRSV.

as Blumenthal has suggested, to "examine Scripture to see how God describes Godself." In so doing, "we admit that Scripture represents the way God wishes to communicate with us and, hence, we induce from scriptural language what it is that God says God is."[92] On the other hand, it is also possible to observe characteristics of humanity, examine human nature, and reason backward by analogy to God, recognizing that "God must possess these characteristics since we are in God's image."[93] Both of these methods are "theologically acceptable, the one recognizing God's communication to us and the other following the inner logic" in the phrase *in the image of God* so that ultimately, "the results will be much the same."[94]

Historically, assertions about what entails the image and likeness of God in humanity have been developed in three general categories: the *substantive*, the *functional*, and the *relational*.[95] The substantive interpretation has maintained that the human race shares a physical or spiritual commonality with God in a substantive manner, with some even suggesting that humanity "is an exact physical replica of God . . . a mirror image of his physical makeup."[96] The functional view argues that humanity's primary manifestation of the image of God is seen in the function of ruling over the earth as God's delegated representative. The relational view argues that the image of God is reflected in relationship with God, which is expanded such that the human characteristic of interpersonal relationship further reflects the divine image. It is likely, however, that a combination of the three views represents a more accurate, comprehensive manifestation of the *imago Dei* in humanity, for human beings are in some ways substantially similar to God, whether physically or spiritually, they imitate God in the power that they have been delegated to exercise dominion over the terrestrial creation, and they image God in that they have the capacity for relationship both with God and with one another, thereby mirroring the essence of divine love.

Perhaps understanding the phrase *image and likeness* is as simple as John Calvin's declaration: "[The] image of God extends to everything in which the nature of man surpasses that of all other species

---

[92] Blumenthal, p. 338.
[93] Blumenthal, p. 338.
[94] Blumenthal, p. 338.
[95] Millard Erickson, Christian Theology (Grand Rapids, MI: Baker Book House, 1994), pp. 498-510.
[96] Erickson, pp. 498-510.

of animals."[97] Many, like Calvin, recognize the *imago Dei* as human-ity's qualities and abilities that the animals do not share.[98] This line of thought may well offer a means of incorporating all the various views on the image and likeness of God in humanity into a comprehensive understanding—a "both . . . and" approach of inclusion rather than an "either . . . or" determination of exclusion. A wide range of options exists, each of which is dependent upon its proponents' perspective on the nature of God and the nature of humanity. These include the image of God that is reflected in human rationality, personhood and personality, conscience, gender differentiation, and free will, as well as in the human capacity for dominion, for co-creation (reproduction), for morality, for love, for relationship both with God and with other humans, and even in a host of other possibilities.

Tikva Frymer-Kensky noted the complexity of attempting to es-tablish definitively what is meant by the image and likeness of God: "We can no more pin down the exact nature of this God-like quality than we can pin down the nature of God. . . . Whatever God is, as God's image, humans share in the divine."[99] As von Rad observed, the image of God "is not limited to any part of man. Man is like God in the way in which he is called into existence, in the totality of his being."[100] Evdokimov agreed and urged that "above all, we should eliminate any substantialist concept of the image," for "the image is not placed in us as one component of our being, but the *totality* of the human being was created, fashioned, 'in the image.'"[101] Every aspect of the human creation, therefore, was designed by the Creator to mirror his own image and likeness and to demonstrate what true relationship with the Divine means. Nothing about human existence is superfluous: every-thing is designed by God to reflect his image. As Emil Brunner said, "Actually, man in his psycho-physical totality is an image of God."[102] Edward Curtis argues that "the way in which a son resembles his fa-ther is in some sense analogous to the way in which the human is like God."[103] This assertion makes sense in the light of the unequivocal

---

[97] Calvin, I. xv, 3.
[98] Franklin Sherman, "God as Creative Artist," *Dialog* 3 (1964), p. 284.
[99] Frymer-Kensky, p. 331.
[100] von Rad, *Genesis: A Commentary*, p. 59.
[101] Evdokimov, p. 61.
[102] Emil Brunner, *Man in Revolt: A Christian Anthropology*, tr. Olive Wyon (Cambridge: The Lut-terworth Press, 1957), p. 338.
[103] Edward M. Curtis, "Image of God, Old Testament" in the *Anchor Bible Dictionary*, ed. David Noel Freedman, et. al., 6 volumes (New York: Doubleday, 1992), p. 398.

statement in Scripture that "Adam was the son of God."[104]

Despite the profound challenges of analysis and description, however, there is perhaps one quality in humanity that manifests the *imago Dei* to such a degree that it stands out as a preeminent overarching way of mirroring the essence of the Divine in humanity. It is clear that the nature of God as pure love was manifest in absolute relationality—a relationality that first was present within Deity before all time, that second was the agent of universal creation, that third was the impetus for limiting divine sovereignty in order to permit the exercise of human free will, that fourth was the source of divine kenosis necessary for establishing the means of human redemption, and that fifth remains the foundation of all divine-human and human-human interrelationality. With this fundamental understanding, it is possible to conclude that the image of God is mirrored in humanity in the form of pure relationality that is manifest in absolute equality and mutuality. On this foundation, a host of other aspects of the *imago Dei* can be examined and established as the various qualities of the Divine that humanity mirrors, for such an understanding would not render all the other possibilities irrelevant but rather would make them subsets of such an overarching reflection of God's image and likeness in humanity.

INDISPENSABILITY OF FEMALE AND MALE

Whatever projections may be made about the image and likeness of God, it is categorically true that God's image is fully manifest in both female and male. Despite the fact that some Christian church fathers argued that "woman herself alone is not the image of God" and that "man alone is the image of God,"[105] females fully and equally image the Divine in the earth. Indeed, without the presence of the female, God's image could never be fully manifest as God himself intended it, for God's design was specific: "God created humanity in his own image, in the image of God he created him, male and female he created them."[106] All the androcentric and misogynist musings of both theologians and philosophers are meaningless in the face of God's clear and unequivocal declaration: both female and male are created in God's image. As individuals, both are indispensable for demonstrating God's likeness by mirroring divine qualities. Together, however, they

[104] Luke 3:38.
[105] Augustine, *On the Trinity* 7.7.10.
[106] Genesis 1:27.

produce the fullest possible imaging of the divine essence, the mutual interpersonal indwelling of three persons within the very being of the one God. By replicating the unity of the first human couple, female and male are no longer two but one,[107] and their mutuality as equal powers conjoined into one superentity mirrors the interrelationality of the triune God in a dimension that could not be achieved by either male or female separately. The female, therefore, is just as indispensible to the manifestation of God's image in the earth as the male.

SPRINGBOARD FOR DISCUSSION

1. Discuss God's determination from the moment he announced his intention to create humanity to make human beings in his own image and likeness. How does this declaration impact every human being? How important is it to the concept of the inherent equality of all humans? Why do scholars assert that the most important verse in the Bible says that "God created humanity in his own image, male and female"?

2. Consider the importance of proper anthropology. Is it fair to say that the sole purpose for humanity's creation is to reflect the image and likeness of God? Can any human being bear the image of God more than another human being? Do males bear God's image more completely than females? Is the full manifestation of God's image restricted by race, ethnicity, or religion? How does Scripture prove your premise?

3. Consider the implications of both image and likeness as they relate to human mirroring of the divine. What is the difference between "image" and "likeness"? Do you agree with church fathers who argued that somehow humanity lost either the image or the likeness or both because of sin? How can human beings still manifest God's image even in a sinful state?

4. Evaluate the idea that the entire human being—not just a part of or some quality of humanity—is made in God's image and reflects something about God's image in the creation. How does God's declaration that the creation of humanity, both male and female, was

---

[107] Mark 10:8.

"very good" imply that every part of every human being (spiritual and corporeal) somehow reflects the image of God? How can visible, corporeal human beings reflect the image of the invisible, incorporeal God?

5. Discuss the transmission of the image of God from generation to generation. Is the continuing image of God in humanity more foundational to biblical faith than concepts of "original sin"? How does God's "original blessing" impact God's perspective in relationship to human beings? What impact does God's view of humans as being in his image have on his relationship with all mankind?

6. Consider an overview of the image of God in humanity in terms of the substantive, the functional, and the relational. Do you think that any one of these manifestations of God's image is more important than the others? Can all of the different viewpoints be developed as subsets of one dimension? Since God's essence is love, how does the image of God in humanity facilitate the manifestation of God's love for his creation in general and humanity in particular? How does the human capacity for love of God and love of fellow human beings mirror the very essence of God?

7. Analyze the ways in which both female and male fully and equally manifest every aspect of the image and likeness of God. Are both male and female required for God's image to be manifest fully and perfectly in humanity?

CHAPTER 12

GOD'S IMAGE IN HUMANITY

SPIRITUAL DIMENSIONS

When God said, "Let us make humanity . . . in our image and after our likeness," he made what is perhaps the most important declaration that has ever been made regarding human beings. This statement of intention confirms unequivocally and irrevocably the fact that all of humanity, irrespective of gender, race, ethnicity, intellect, or erudition equally possesses the very likeness of God himself, the quality that sets humans apart from the rest of creation and endows them with the very reason for their existence. God has bestowed upon all human beings a dignity and honor that is utterly profound: he considers them to be a reflection of his own image and likeness. And, it is not merely some small aspect or quality of human being that mirrors the Divine, it is the totality of humanness that reflects what it means to be an image-bearer for God himself.

Profound amounts of philosophical and theological energy have been expended in attempts to determine precisely what constitutes the image and likeness of God and how God implanted his image in humanity. Varied discourse has been developed that has attempted to confine the understanding of that image to specific aspects of human life. Because they have so focused on mere qualities of human existence, some of these have erroneously and tragically argued that God's image is applicable only to certain genders, certain races, and certain intellectual levels. The truth is that every aspect of human existence reveals something about the One who created humanity as a manifestation of his image and likeness. God is not a reflection of human image and likeness: humanity is, by divine proclamation, a reflection of God's image and likeness. As such, everything about the way God made humanity contains a part of God's self-disclosure, his divine revelation encoded in the very existence of human beings.

RATIONALITY AND GOD'S IMAGE

Throughout history, the preponderance of Christian and Jewish scholarship has concluded that God's image in humanity is almost exclusively manifest in human rationality. To a great degree, this focus—even fixation—on the power of reason as evidence for the image of God has resulted from the influence of Greek philosophy on both Judaism and Christianity. Hermann Häring observes that "in a platonically shaped culture," the power of reason "has long been considered humankind's most important faculty."[1] The Greek fascination with—and even worship of—the human mind filtered into Judaism and Christianity when both adopted and adapted religious and philosophical elements from Hellenism. What Paul excoriated in the Greco-Roman world, his later rabbinic and Christian counterparts came to revere.[2] Rabbinic Judaism, as well as most of primitive, medieval, and post-Reformation Christianity, came to believe that the image of God was properly identified with the power of reason, to the virtual exclusion of every other option.

Christianity extended this argument much further than Judaism because of its preference for exalting the human mind while deprecating the human body.[3] This emphasis emerged as the church was further influenced by Greek dualism, which posited a created order far different from what is described in Scripture and in rabbinic Judaism. In this nonbiblical worldview, everything material, including the human body, was considered to be inherently evil while everything spiritual, including the human mind, was considered to be good. The body, therefore, came to be viewed as evil while the rational mind was seen

---

[1] Hermann Häring, "From Divine Human to Human God" in *The Human Image of God*, ed. Hans-Georg Ziebertz, Friedrich Schweitzer, Hermann Häring, Don Browning (Boston: Brill, 2001), p. 9.

[2] See Romans 1 for Paul's perspective on Greek rationalism.

[3] Mainstream Judaism never fell prey to the concepts of Platonism and Gnosticism that viewed the human body as inherently evil.

as good. The mind (or the soul) was in the image of God while the body was little more than a Christianized version of Plato's idea that bodies were evil physical entrapments for souls. As time progressed, "the clash between what we may call (with all due caution) the Hebraic and the Hellenic, or the biblical and the philosophical, dimensions of the Jewish heritage became acute."[4] This was especially true for Maimonides, who argued that only the soul—which he believed to be the intellect—was connected with God.[5] Maimonides also advanced the idea that the soul that "survives death is the acquired intellect."[6]

With the revival of Greek philosophy in the Age of Reason, human rationality came to be viewed as the sole reason for human existence, an idea that came to be encapsulated in René Descartes' dictum: "*Cogito ergo sum*" ("I think; therefore, I am").[7] For the philosophers of that time, God was Reason personified; therefore, humans were considered to be in God's image solely because they were the only rational beings in the terrestrial creation. Very often—and very tragically—many Enlightenment rationalist philosophers extended their arguments to exclude certain human beings (e.g., slaves and women) from being viewed as fully human because these philosophers, like their Greek forbears, did not consider women or slaves capable of rational thought. Sadly, so many of the ancient and modern philosophers connected human self-worth and even their creation in the image of God with the level of intelligence and rationality that they possessed. Of course, the philosophers established their own standards for what could be considered rational thought. Because women have greater capacities for intuitive thought and are more connected with their emotions, they were considered to be lacking God's image altogether or at least to being deficient in the divine image and likeness.

Despite the exaggerated emphasis on the power of reason in Hellenized Christianity, it remains a certitude that humanity does possess the divine endowment of thought, reason, and logic. The capacity for reason was imparted to humankind when God breathed into the earthling's nostrils the breath of life. Much more than mere oxygenation of mortal lungs occurred with this divine action, however: the inhaling of

[4] Jon Douglas Levenson, *Resurrection and the Restoration of Israel: The Ultimate Victory of the God of Life* (New Haven, CT: Yale University Press, 2006), pp. 17-18.
[5] Maimonides, *Guide for the Perplexed*, I, 1, ed. and tr. Shlomo Pines (Chicago: University of Chicago Press, 1963), p. 23.
[6] Maimonides, *Hikkot Yesode Hattora* 4:8-9. Also Levenson, *Resurrection*, p. 18.
[7] René Descartes, *Principles of Philosophy* (1644), Part 1, article 7.

divine breath brought more to humanity than physical vivification. A spark of the divine was deposited into the core of humanity to form what Scripture termed נֶפֶשׁ חַיָּה—*nephesh chayah* (literally "[a] living being").[8] Implanted in the human spirit were the very words of God himself.[9] Jewish Talmudist Nachmanides argued that "when God breathed the breath of life into man, he transferred to him of his divine essence. . . . Man contains a divine spark, an element of the divine spirit."[10]

This is the way Paul the apostle later described the residual benefit for humanity of what occurred in Genesis with the first human couple, a blessing that has been transferred generationally to all human beings through procreation: "The nations that have not the Torah [law] are a Torah unto themselves: The Torah is written on their hearts so that their consciences either condemn or excuse them."[11] This profound statement declares, quite simply, that somehow and to some degree God's instructions[12] have been engraved on the heart of every human being who has ever lived on this planet. In essence, God made a deposit the divine *Logos* in man, "so that man in his very structure would have access to the riddle of theology."[13] To one degree or another, the Word of God is a present reality in the lives of all humans.

This deposit of God's Word in the human heart is God's gift that separates human from animal. It is not only the power of reason but also the ability to reason from the premises of divine truth that have been established since eternity past in the Word of God. The divine *Logos* (*D'var* or *Memra*), who was the agent of all creation,[14] breathed a part of himself into the nostrils of the first human being and by doing so conveyed to the human creation the power to reason under the

---

[8] The Hebrew word *nephesh* is rendered "soul" in KJV; however, in most other versions it is translated more correctly as "being." The translation of *nephesh* as "soul" reflects the influence of the Greek idea that each human soul is, in effect, the incorporeal essence of a human person. Plato believed the soul to be a fragment of the gods (stars) that became entrapped in the human body and that awaited escape into the heavenlies to be rejoined with the gods. Greek thought considered human beings to be composed of body, soul, and spirit (mind). Hebraic thought maintained that the "living being" or "living soul" was the composite of the body and the spirit based on Scripture's declaration that when God breathed "spirit" into *ha-adam's* body, he became, at that moment, a "living being" or "living soul."

[9] Paul taught that all of Holy Scripture is God-breathed (2 Timothy 3:16). Since God breathed into *ha-adam* the breath of life, it is reasonable to assume that the same action also imbued the human creation with the very Word of God.

[10] Chaim Navon, David Straus, *Genesis and Jewish Thought* (New York: KTAV Publishing House, 2008), p. 56.

[11] Romans 2:15.

[12] The Hebrew word *Torah* means "instruction."

[13] Photius of Constantinople, quoted in Paul Evdokimov, *Woman and the Salvation of the World*, tr. Anthony P. Gythiel (Crestwood, NY: St. Vladimir's Seminary Press, 1994), p. 32.

[14] John 1:3.

influence of the implanted God-breathed Word of truth.[15] God's Word is in man's heart and is passed along from generation to generation in concert with the breath of life.

Instead of being lost in endless contemplation of exalted reason, human beings will find it more productive to rejoice in the fact that God has imparted to them the power of cognitive thought through which they have an awareness of their existence and the capacity for the relationality that truly images the Divine. They then learn the wisdom reflected in Helen Oppenheimer's observation: "Instead of lone thinkers trying to discover whether there are any other minds, we are human beings learning from each other about the world and how to live in it."[16] The fullness of the divine image in humanity is much deeper than the ability to think or determine. It is not merely a cerebral function. Indeed, it is a visceral gift, resident in the heart and manifest in the ability to engage in those interpersonal relationships of love manifest in the self-giving of God. This is the human imitation of the mutual encircling and interpenetration within God, the coinherence that creates, nurtures, and sustains relationships of divine love.

Humans must have "a willingness to embody a spirit of equality and mutuality, true interdependence grounded in the equal dignity of each one."[17] Whenever this mindset becomes the standard, "even those who seem vastly unequal in terms of intelligence, productivity, or physical beauty have equal dignity as persons."[18] Each person is of infinite value, and each one's self-worth is predicated upon God's gift of life, not on utility to the state or on other artificial societal criterion. Issues of the "quality of life" disappear as well, for God, as the giver of life, can be the judge of what is a quality life, and only he has the power and right to give and take away life.

The gifts of life and freedom are endowments from the creator, not from any social structure. Every human being manifests equally and without exception the totality of God's image and likeness as the

---

[15] 2 Timothy 3:16.

[16] Helen Oppenheimer, "Ethics and the Personal Life," in *Companion Encyclopedia of Theology,* ed. Peter Byrne and James Leslie Houlden (London: Routledge, 1995), p. 744. Also J. V. Taylor, *The Primal Vision* (London: SCM Publications, 1963), pp. 49-50; J. S. Pobee, *Toward an African Theology* (Nashville: Abingdon Press, 1979), p. 49; Helen Oppenheimer, *Incarnation and Immanence* (London: Hodder & Stoughton, 1973), pp. 118-124; 131-139; and Helen Oppenheimer, *Looking Before and After: The Archbishop of Canterbury's Lent Book* (London: Collins, 1983), pp. 30-60.

[17] Michael Downey, *Altogether Gift: A Trinitarian Spirituality* (Maryknoll, NY: Orbis Books, 2000), p. 73.

[18] Downey, p. 73.

creator originally designed it. And, like the creator himself, this image is demonstrated in pure relationality of mutuality and respect. Adopting this manner of viewing God's image in humanity might result in replacing the Cartesian dictum, *Cogito, ergo sum* ("I think, therefore I am") with Vladimir Berzonsky's summation, *"Amo, ergo sum"* ("I love, therefore I am")[19]—or perhaps even Helen Oppenheimer's, "I participate, therefore I am"—as the proof of human existence.[20] These statements encapsulate the concept that is manifest in relationality, first in intimate relationship with God and, as a consequence of that relationship, in proper interaction with other humans on whatever level that life offers or dictates, all with the dignity and mutuality that mirrors the divine being. They also facilitate the conclusion that rationality, though a significant part of the image of God in humanity, serves more importantly to facilitate the interrelationality of God and humans and of humans with one another.

Both women and men are rational beings, fully imaging God's rationality and supra-rationality[21] in the varying degrees of interaction between the two hemispheres of the brain. The cognitive abilities of male and female are equal and complementary despite differences in brain size and hemisphere interconnectivity. The rationality of one is neither inferior nor superior to the other. Both are absolute reflections of God's image in this aspect of human existence. Any attempt to diminish the rationality of one gender also deprecates the rationality of the other gender for both were formed equally to reflect the divine likeness and to complement and supplement each other.

Personhood and God's Image

Greek philosophy and the rationalism that it spawned was revived in the sixteenth-century Age of Reason and more particularly in the eighteenth-century Enlightenment, and it continues to this day. In

---

[19] Vladimir Berzonsky, *The Gift of Love* (Crestwood, NY: St. Vladimir's Seminary Press, 1985), p. 53. Also Evdokimov, *Woman and the Salvation of the World*, tr. Anthony P. Gythiel (Crestwood, NY: St. Vladimir's Seminary Press, 1994), pp. 42-43. See also Otto Weininger, *Gedanken über die Geschlechtsprobleme* (Berlin: Concordia Duetchse, 1922), p. 53, quoted in *An Anthology of Russian Women's Writing, 1777-1972*, ed. Catriona Kelly (Oxford: Oxford University Press, 1998), p. 172. See also Nicholas V. Sacharov, *I Love, Therefore I Am: The Theology of the Archimandrite Society* (Crestwood, NY: St. Vladimir's Seminary Press, 2002).

[20] Oppenheimer, "Ethics and the Personal Life," p. 744. Also Taylor, pp. 49-50; Pobee, p. 9; Oppenheimer, *Incarnation and Immanence*, pp. 118-124, 131-139; Oppenheimer, *Looking Before and After*, pp. 30-60.

[21] God's wisdom is beyond human understanding or rationality (Isaiah 55:8; 1 Corinthians 3:19); however, it is not irrational: it is simply supra-rational.

this system of thought, God is viewed as perfect reason; however, he cannot possibly be considered to have personhood any more than he could possibly be thought to have physical being. Many theologians have adopted this Greek system of thought and have ruled out physicality, personhood, and relationality in God, concluding, therefore, that human physicality and personhood do not reflect God's image and likeness. Others have have had difficulty believing that human physicality can in any way mirror God's image because of the Greek philosophical insistence on the incorporeality of God; however, they have also believed that God is more than detached reason. Some of these have suggested, therefore, that it is proper to claim that personhood and personality reflect the *imago Dei* in humanity.[22] This is particularly true among Jewish scholars and theologians because one of the cardinal rules of faith in the Jewish community declares that God is completely incorporeal.[23] David Blumenthal, therefore, has suggested that in describing the image of God in humanity, *anthropopathic* comparisons should be made rather than *anthropomorphic* ones because God has "characteristics of the human personality," rather than of human physicality.[24] He maintains that "since personhood is the core of our being and since we are created in God's image, God must also have personhood."[25] In anthropopathic theology, therefore, "God has a Face and a real Personal Presence or Personality,"[26] and human personhood, with "its expression as face, presence, and personality," exists "because God has created us in God's image."[27]

The God of Scripture, unlike the God of Greek philosophy, is pure personhood, for he is a personal being, not an abstraction or force. John Sanders says it well: "God is not an 'in-itself,' apart from others, but the epitome of love in relation."[28] While God's personhood

---

[22] LeRoy S. Capper, "The Imago Dei and Its Implications for Order in the Church," *Presbyterion* 2 (1985), p. 24.

[23] Insistence upon incorporeality was a major premise of Maimonides' Thirteen Principles that were adopted by most of Judaism several centuries after the great Talmudist projected them. His insistence on divine incorporeality was, however, grounded in Greek philosophy, not in Scripture and was strongly influenced by his efforts to counter the Christian argument that Jesus was God incarnate.

[24] David Blumenthal, "Tselem: Toward an Anthropopathic Theology of Image," in *Christianity in Jewish Terms*, ed. Tikva Frymer-Kensky, David Novak, Peter Ochs, David Fox Sandmel, and Michael A. Singer (Boulder CO: Westview Press, 2000), p. 338.

[25] Blumenthal, p. 338.

[26] Blumenthal, p. 338.

[27] Blumenthal, p. 338.

[28] John E. Sanders, *The God Who Risks: A Theology of Divine Providence* (Downers Grove, IL: InterVarsity Press, 2007), p. 148.

is not specifically mentioned or described in the biblical record,[29] it is evident from his interactions with the people of Scripture that he exists as person. The concept of God's personhood "naturally flows out of the biblical witness and incapsulates an important aspect of the God who has disclosed himself to us."[30] God's personal disclosure was made in appearances to various patriarchs, prophets, and apostles during which he communicated with human beings on very personal levels, even "face to face"[31] and "mouth to mouth."[32] Holy Scripture presents God's self-revelation "not as a category but as a person who has entered into relation with [humanity] in history."[33] Indeed, the Gospel of Jesus is "not about a God abstracted from historical particularity ... [but] about the God who becomes human [and] experiences the vicissitudes of earthly existence."[34]

The Hebraic understanding of God as person is underscored in one of the earliest prayers that were developed by the Jewish people, the *Avinu, Malkenu* ("Our Father, Our King"). In this prayer, the emphasis is first on God as Father and then on God as Sovereign. This is also true in the case of the more than 100 *berachot* (blessings) that can be recited daily by the Jewish people. All of these begin with the formula: "Blessed are you, O Lord, our God, Sovereign of the universe," in which God is recognized first as "our God," a relational being, before he is acclaimed as "Sovereign of the universe." Recognizing God's personhood and relationality before any other divine quality affirms the fact that self-giving, mutuality, and interdependence are at the very heart of God's being God. Human beings exist in relationship from and toward others because they mirror the divine being whose very existence is focused in the interrelationship of interpersonal love.

Because the God of Scripture has personhood, he can and does exist in the relationship of the divine community in which three persons dwell in perfect oneness through total mutuality. God also relates to humans as persons in his image in an ongoing, person-to-person dynamic. This unbroken and unbreakable commitment of relationality of the divine Person to human persons is in stark contrast to

[29] John 4:24 says, "God is spirit"; however, there is no confession in Scripture that "God is person."
[30] Stanley J. Grenz, *Theology for the Community of God* (Grand Rapids, MI: Wm. B. Eerdmans Publishing Co., 1994), p. 83.
[31] Exodus 33:11.
[32] Numbers 12:8.
[33] Sanders, p. 167.
[34] Sanders, p. 167.

those religions that view God as being a force of nature or some other impersonal entity. Such views project the idea that the ideal conclusion is either complete loss of being and personhood by escaping into nothingness[35] or total absorption into an all-encompassing Absolute.[36] Biblical faith, however, champions the expectation of eternal personal relationship between God and humans, a relationship that will become even more personal and intimate in eternity future following the resurrection of the entire human person—body and spirit and, therefore, soul.

Stating that God is a person is not, however, a suggestion that God is somehow human. To declare that God is a person is to say that he is infinite personhood and to "affirm the divine ability and willingness to relate to others."[37] Indeed, as J. R. Illingworth has affirmed, God should be thought of "as social being or society,"[38] such that "the divine being is constituted by the communion of the three trinitarian persons."[39] Sanders is right to conclude that "personhood, relationality, and community—not power, independence, and control—become the center for understanding the nature of God."[40] Understanding the personhood of God is merely an affirmation of what is obvious in Scripture: God's personhood is the basis of his relationality, both the interrelationality of Father, Son, and Spirit within the one divine Being and the interrelationality of God with humanity as creator and father intimately related to his creation and his children.

The same philosophies that insist that God could not possibly have personhood also contend that God could never have sentience, for sensitivity, feelings, and emotions are beneath the dignity that a God who is Infinite Reason should exhibit. Despite philosophical contentions to the contrary, it is important from a biblical perspective to recognize that God is a sentient being as well as a rational being. Indeed, says Milton Terry, God "is an infinitely sentient Being, capable of emotion, affection, and the uttermost sensitiveness to all that is right and wrong, pure and impure."[41] Divine sentience does

---

[35] This is the ideal and profound hope of Eastern Monism.
[36] This was the ideal of most of Greek philosophy, including neo-Platonism.
[37] Alistair Iain McGrath, *Christian Theology* (Malden MA: Blackwell Publishing, 2001), p. 205.
[38] J. R. Illingworth, *The Doctrine of the Trinity* (London: Macmillan, 1907), pp. 142-143.
[39] John D. Zizioulas, *Being as Communion: Studies in Personhood and the Church* (Crestwood, NY: St. Vladimir's Seminary Press, 1985), p. 101.
[40] Sanders, pp. 175-176. Also Schweitzer, Häring, Browning, p. 168.
[41] Milton S. Terry, *Biblical Dogmatics: An Exposition of the Principal Doctrines of the Holy Scriptures* (Eugene, OR: Wipf & Stock Publishers, 2002), pp. 552-553.

not deprecate or depreciate divine intellect. It merely interrelates with divine will to make the personhood and personality of God complete and perfect. Without sentience, God could be the emotional iceberg of Greek thought, totally detached from any other reality except himself, the perfect narcissist. With sentience, however, God is the God of Scripture, "full of compassion," such that the justice (*tzedekah*) of his omniscience is a factor of his tender mercy (*chesed*) or of his omnisentience.

The idea that God is sentient in experiencing the emotions that Scripture ascribe to him has also been deprecated by philosophers and theologians alike. The purely rational God of their imaginations could not possibly have had any experience of emotion or any sensory perceptions that might somehow have altered his immutability or impacted his impassibility. Nicholas Wolterstorff observed that the God of many such theologians "turns out to be remarkably like the Stoic sage: devoid of passions, unfamiliar with longing, foreign to suffering, dwelling in steady bliss, exhibiting to others only benevolence."[42] Such thinkers could profit from the pithy retort of second-century Christian writer Lucius Caelius Lactantius, who answered his teacher Arnobius' assertion that God is completely "at rest" to such a degree that human prayers make no difference to God by declaring that "to be perfectly at rest is to be dead."[43]

Personality as the image of God is an essential ingredient in the overarching manifestation of the divine image and likeness in relationality. The pure relationality of God that is confirmed by his personhood and personality, by his rationality, his sentience, and his will is mirrored in human personhood and personality that demands relationship and achieves its highest manifestation of relationality in the "one flesh" superentity of marriage. It is for this reason that the sanctity of marriage must be respected as the ultimate relationality of human personhood and personality. The personhood of God, quite simply, is imaged equally in the personhood of masculine *and* feminine humanity—physically, mentally, and emotionally. Despite the fact that female and male dispositions and emotions manifest great degrees of diversity, each human being, whether masculine or feminine, equally

---

[42] Nicholas Wolterstorff, "Suffering Love," in *Philosophy and the Christian Faith,* ed. Thomas Morris (Notre Dame, IN: University of Notre Dame Press, 1988), pp. 210-254.
[43] Lactantius *On Divine Anger* 4. Also H. Wayne House and Matt Power, *Charts on Open Theism and Orthodoxy* (Grand Rapids, MI: Kregel Publications, 2003), p. 47, and Sanders, p. 147.

images God's personhood, the quality that not only makes possible, but also demands, interrelationality.

HUMAN CONSCIENCE AND GOD'S IMAGE

Significant numbers of scholars have considered the conscience to be the manifestation of God's image in humanity. The human ability to "make moral decisions which involve self-awareness and social awareness," has been a "widely accepted interpretation" of the image of God in human beings.[44] In this school of thought, the divine image is seen as the capacity for morality.[45] Justin Martyr was one of the first Christian theologians to make the suggestion that both reason and the faculty of moral judgment were demonstrations of the image of God.[46] Dale Moody maintains that "conscience is the human capacity by which the principles of moral responsibility are grasped. It forms a threshold between the animal and the human."[47] This is why Robert Jamieson argued that God's image in humanity does not consist of "the erect form or features of man; not in his intellect . . . not in his immortality . . . but in the moral dispositions of his soul, commonly called original righteousness."[48]

Richard Gabriel has argued that "civilization requires evidence of moral thinking if it is to be distinguished from a collection of archaeological artifacts, for civilization is no more the sum of its architecture, art, and technology than a warehouse full of spare parts is equivalent to a functioning machine."[49] Moral sensitivity and right thinking are, therefore, central to intellectual life and to the life of humans in community. Gabriel is absolutely correct when he says that "without the dawn of conscience, the history of man would be nothing but a long, dark night,"[50] for before God's sovereign act of creating humans in his own image by infusing them with a moral compass—the human

---

[44] G.W. Bromiley, "Image of God," in *International Standard Bible Encyclopedia*, ed. G.W. Bromiley (Grand Rapids, MI: William B. Eerdmans, 1988), vol. 2, p. 804.

[45] James D. Tyms, "Moral and Religious Education for the Second Reconstruction Era," *Journal of Religious Thought* 31:1 (1974), p. 28.

[46] Justin Martyr, *Apology*, 1.28.

[47] Dale Moody, *The Word of Truth: A Summary of Christian Doctrine Based on Biblical Revelation* (Grand Rapids, MI: William B. Eerdmans Publishing, 1981), pp. 238-239.

[48] Robert Jamieson, *Genesis–Deuteronomy* in *A Commentary, Critical, Experimental, and Practical on the Old and New Testaments,* ed. Robert Jamieson, A. R. Fausset, and David Brown (Grand Rapids, MI: Zondervan Publishing House, 1983), vol. 1, p. 8.

[49] Richard A. Gabriel, *Gods of Our Fathers: The Memory of Egypt in Judaism and Christianity* (Westport, CT: Greenwood Publishing Group, 2002), p. 1.

[50] Gabriel, p. 1.

conscience—there was nothing but darkness "upon the surface of the deep."[51] Indeed, utter chaos might even be described as the absence or obliteration of conscience.

"The conscience . . . [is] the place where it is decided what man truly is,"[52] says Gerhard Eberling. It is obvious that the conscience is a divine impartation to human beings, a spark of the Eternal implanted in the first human person and in all subsequent human progeny. Many rabbis have maintained that the image of God in man is his moral inclination, what they term the *yetzer tov* or the inclination toward good.[53] Eliezer Berkovits is correct when he argues that the image of God is "the secret of [a human's] humanity," and that "to guard that image, to live in a manner worthy of it, is [humankind's] responsibility on earth."[54]

The conscience and its moral compass are essential to human inter-relationality in equality and mutuality. Without the guidance of God's Word manifest through the divine teaching that is engraved upon the human heart through the conscience, humanity is hopelessly caught up in a vortex of sin's domination through the irrepressible, vicious, and violent "I," the tyranny of the one, the unbridled narcissistic drive for self-gratification and self-actualization. Egotism inevitably breeds egocentricity, and egocentricity can easily expand into megalomania. The despots of history were not born: they were made in progressive steps as their God-given conscience was systematically overridden and finally obliterated and replaced by the purely evil vain imaginations of the reprobate mind.[55] When the inclination toward good does not suppress the inclination toward evil, humans devolve into animal-istic behavior, indulging in unimaginable atrocities from murder, rape, and pillage to genocide.

The truth of this statement is clearly seen in the virtual absence of moral or ethical conduct on the part of those who stand in open defiance of the God of Scripture and champion militant humanism, the occult, and neo-paganism. These are the same as those whom the apostle described as having their "consciences seared with a hot

[51] Genesis 1:2, TNK.
[52] Gerhard Eberling, "Existence between God and God: A Contribution to the Question of the Existence of God," tr. James P. Carse, *Journal for Theology and the Church*, 5 (1968), p. 384.
[53] Navon, Straus, p. 54.
[54] Eliezer Berkovits, *With God in Hell, Judaism in the Ghettos and Death Camps* (New York: Sanhedrin Press, 1979), p. 33. See also Eliezer Berkovits, *Faith After the Holocaust* (New York: KTAV Publishing, 1973).
[55] Romans 1:28.

iron."[56] The prime example, of course, was Adolf Hitler, who openly ranted and raved against the idea of the conscience. He argued that the conscience was a "Jewish invention" that "like circumcision . . . mutilates man." He insisted that "there is no such thing as truth," that "one must distrust mind and conscience" and that "one must place one's trust in one's instincts."[57] The implementation of such vile, perverted, and vicious attacks against God and his Word dragged humanity into the abyss of barbaric, virtually subhuman atrocities in the systematic murder of six million Jews, including more than one million children. The Holocaust was truly *sui generis*, unequaled in human history in its ferocious effort at genocide of a people solely because of their covenant relationship with the God of Scripture. It was, indeed, based on Hitler's denial of the power of the conscience as part of God's image in humanity, and it resulted, therefore, in inhuman actions.

Recent history is also replete with other tyrants like Stalin, Mao Tse-Tung, and Pol Pot whose secular amorality escalated into utter immorality that led to the slaughter of millions of their own countrymen in the name of political or ideological expediency.[58] These horrible facts of history have demonstrated indisputably the truth that the conscience of humanity is a God-designed and God-given blessing that elevates humans above mere animalistic behavior.

By yielding to the prodding of the God-given conscience, however, humans can rise above the mere animal instinct for survival and stature to mirror the altruistic likeness of God by developing and strengthening relationship with God and with fellow humans. The conscience, then, is a divinely imparted quality that is shared equally from birth by all human beings, male and female. It is a means of reinforcing the divine demand for moral and ethical human conduct that is manifest in social justice and relational mutuality. Pure human interrelationality, which is nothing more than true love in action, demands human self-sacrifice—serving one another[59] and submitting one to another out of respect for God.[60] The conscience constantly prods every

---

[56] 1 Timothy 4:2.
[57] Adolph Hitler, quoted in John M. Oesterreicher, *Auschwitz: The Christian, and the Council* (Montreal: Palm Books, 1965), p. 19.
[58] Of all the massive slaughters of human beings in history, the Holocaust is *sui generis*, for only it was not focused on war with other nations or political domination of a nation over its own people. The Holocaust was designed and implemented as a vehicle for the genocide of an entire nation of people solely because of their genetic, ethnic, and religious heritage.
[59] Galatians 5:13.
[60] Ephesians 5:21.

human being toward God's design for humanness: a life that focuses on the other as well as on self and that sacrifices self in the best interest of the community of others while worshipping and serving God in obedience to his imperatives and instructions.

There is absolutely no theological or historical truth to the assertion of philosophers from virtually all of the cultures of the world—including theologians in ecclesiastical history—that women are of weaker conscience than men or that women are more susceptible to evil than men. The propensity to sin, along with the inclination toward good, is universal. The inclination toward evil is resident in every human being from birth. All humans have sinned and come short of the glory of God.[61] At the same time, the conscience that God breathed into the original human being is equally active in both male and female in the present world just as it was in the beginning. Women mirror the divine image in the inner workings of the conscience just as effectively as men do. Indeed, many scholars have argued that women are inherently more sensitive to the spiritual than men. Both genders are equal in the impact of the God-designed and God-implanted conscience of humanity that images the Eternal in every human being.

FREEDOM AND GOD'S IMAGE

Many theologians have suggested that God's image is manifest in humanity in the freedom that God has given to humans to make choices for themselves. While much of the world functions under worldviews that feature fatalism and the imposition of absolute divine sovereignty, both Judaism and much of Christianity recognize God's gift of free will to human beings. Søren Kierkegaard observed that the "most tremendous thing granted to humans is choice, freedom."[62] Desmond Tutu has opined that "an unfree human being is a contradiction in terms. To be human is to be free. God gives us space to be free and so to be human."[63] Without such space, humans would not be free and in effect would not be human in God's image. Nicolas Berdyaev went a step further and argued that "freedom alone should be recog-

---

[61] Romans 3:23.
[62] Søren Kierkegaard, *The Journals of Søren Kierkegaard,* tr. A. Dru (London: Oxford University Press, 1938), p. 372. Also Kallistos Ware, *The Inner Kingdom* (Crestwood, NJ: St. Vladimir's Seminary Press, 2000), p. 187.
[63] Desmond Tutu, in *Religious Human Rights in Global Perspective* (The Hague, The Netherlands: Kluwer Law International, 1996), p. xii.

nized as possessing a sacred quality," for "God is truly present and operative only in freedom."[64]

The question that has puzzled theologians for centuries is how God who is immutable and omnipotent—and, therefore, sovereign over all—can permit human freedom. Debates have raged for centuries over whether God can permit human freedom and at the same time remain sovereign over all things. Alistair McFadyen maintains that the creation began "with a primal letting-be,"[65] of creating space for material existence. This is in context with the Lurianic concept of *tzimtzum*[66] in mystical Judaism which maintains that God contracted hmself or withdrew from a part of infinity so that the universe could be created "out of nothing." If he had not done so, his omnipresence would have necessitated that he create the universe out of himself, in which case the universe would be divine. The creation of humanity, then, was simply another step—and the logical conclusion—of God's self-limitation and self-emptying to make possible the existence of beings who would truly have the capacity to love. This is why God permitted humanity existence beyond himself "the autonomy in which it can now stand over against God as an independent order of being."[67]

To make genuine human freedom possible, God limited "Godself in creation" through a "voluntary relinquishment of absolute power" so that God exercises his dominion "indirectly, through a creature, one who shares with all creatures their ephemeral and vulnerable nature and destiny."[68] God's self-limitation in order to provide true human freedom arose from the greatest exercise of his omnipotence. As Kierkegaard noted, the omnipotence of self-constraint is the "marvelous omnipotence of love"[69] in which the God "who almightily takes from nothing and says, 'Be,' lovingly adjoins, 'Be something even in opposition to me.'"[70] John Sanders has rightly suggested, therefore,

---

[64] Nicolas Berdyaev, *Dream and Reality: An Essay in Autobiography* (London: Geoffrey Bles, 1950), p. 46.

[65] Alistair I. McFadyen, *The Call to Personhood: A Christian Theory of the Individual in Social Relationships* (Cambridge: Cambridge University Press, 1990), p. 20.

[66] Joseph P. Schultz, *Judaism and Gentile Faiths: Comparative Studies in Religion* (East Brunswick, NJ: Farleigh Dickinson University Press, 1981), pp. 89-92. The concept of *tzimtzum* was introduced by Rabbi Isaac Luria in the sixteenth century and has been further refined by mystical Judaism since that time.

[67] McFadyen, p. 20.

[68] Douglas John Hall, *Professing the Faith: Christian Theology in a North American Context* (Minneapolis: Augsburg Fortress Press, 1996), p. 350.

[69] Søren Kierkegaard, *Christian Discourses*, tr. Walter Lowrie (New York: Oxford University Press, 1939), p. 132.

[70] Kierkegaard, p. 132.

that "the power of the triune God is not raw omnipotence, but the power of suffering, liberating, and reconciling love."[71] This is what Abraham Joshua Heschel described as the God of pathos, the God who suffers with the universe and, in particular, with his people,[72] a God who, in the language of the apostles can be touched with the feeling of human infirmities and can comprehend with them in all things. As Dietrich Bonhoeffer observed, it is in Jesus that "God lets himself be pushed out of the world on to the cross. . . . Only the suffering God can help . . . the God of the Bible, who wins power and space in the world by his weakness."[73]

The Jewish community has also emphasized human freedom and the power of choice as a reflection of God's image in humanity. Meir Simcha ha-Kohen has argued that "the image of God refers to man's ability to choose freely without his nature coercing him, to act out of free will and intellect."[74] He maintains that when God said to himself, "Let us make man in our image," he said, in effect, "Let us leave room for man to choose . . . that he have the free will to do good or evil as he desires."[75] God was willing to risk the rejection of his love for creation in the hope that humanity would be delivered from the bondage of corruption and volunteer love for him, thereby reciprocating and completing the perfect love that he had extended without qualification or limitation to his human creation.[76]

Kallistos Ware has argued that it is in "human freedom according to God's image that we find the explanation for the uniqueness of each human being."[77] It is through "personal decisions" made through the freedom of choice that each human being "expresses the divine image in his or her characteristic and distinctive way," making possible an "inexhaustible variety" of human expressions.[78] "Our vocation," Ware argues, "is not to become copies of each other, repetitive and unoriginal, but through the use of our freedom to become each authenti-

---

[71] Daniel Migliori, *Faith Seeking Understanding: An Introduction to Christian Theology* (Grand Rapids, MI: Wm. B. Eerdmans Publishing Co., 1991), pp. 114-116.

[72] Abraham Joshua Heschel, *The Prophets* (San Francisco: HarperCollins Publishers, 1962), pp. 393-413.

[73] Dietrich Bonhoeffer, *Letters and Papers from Prison* (New York: Macmillan, 1972), pp. 360-361.

[74] Meir Simcha ha-Kohen, *Meshekh Chokhma,* quoted in Navon, Straus, pp. 47-48.

[75] ha-Kohen, in Navon, Straus, pp. 47-48.

[76] Romans 8:20-21.

[77] Kallistos Ware, "In the Image and Likeness: An Interview with Bishop Kallistos Ware," J. Morgan, *Parabola* 10.1 (1985), p. 11.

[78] Ware, p. 11.

cally our own unique self precisely because everyone is made in the image of the God of freedom."[79] Chasidic Rabbi Zusya encapsulated this concept in his observation: "In the coming world, they will not ask me: 'Why were you not Moses?' They will ask me: 'Why were you not Zusya?'"[80]

All human beings, female or male, must be completely and equally free in order for the image of God's freedom to be fully manifest in them and in their interaction with one another. If one human being by nature is given control over another human being, then neither human being is free. The whole idea of domination—whether of male over female as a presumed ontological prerogative of the male creation, or of sovereign over subjects as if by an imagined divine right, or of one race, class, or ethnicity of humans over others as an demonstration of their supposed innate superiority—is a product of human failure to maintain the original state of equality in which humanity was created by divine design. All domination is, in essence, a form of idolatry in that it either makes some humans superhuman or other humans subhuman. The absence of freedom, then, is the essence of sin, and its continuing manifestation on planet earth is evidence of the domination of sin over the human race. A course toward the end of sinful domination is charted when the inherent ontological freedom and equality of all human beings, male and female, are acknowledged, established, and maintained.

Neither gender can be ontologically submitted or placed under the authority of the other and at the same time exercise the free will with which God endowed all of humanity as a part of his image and likeness. Both women and men must be completely at liberty to follow the dictates of their own consciences and to make decisions for themselves without any demands that they surrender their liberty to the control of the other. When it comes to free will in the image of God, both female and male are completely equal. Both stand before God with the power to choose and to bear responsibility for their choices without a requirement for submission to the will of the other. Women have precisely the same level of freedom that men possess, and the integrity of their consciences must be respected at every level, in family, in society, and in religious community.

---

[79] Ware, p. 11.
[80] Zusya, quoted in Martin Buber, *Tales of the Hasidim,* The Early Masters (New York: Schocken Books, 1968), vol. 1, p. 251.

Without freedom, humans would be automatons, and they would be virtual carbon copies of one another. The freedom of choice is God's gift to humanity that images his own freedom to act as he wills. As such, it is the dynamic that makes possible the endless variety of human choices that produce the profound diversity of human actions and accomplishments. God's determination to impart this single aspect of the divine image and likeness to his human creation is more responsible for human achievement than any other divine action. It also has made possible the free expression of human love for God, the reciprocation of the love that God lavishes on humanity.

While the freedom of choice makes it possible for humans to choose evil rather than good (as was demonstrated by Adam and Eve in Eden), freedom was not designed by God to be a libertine license for human indulgence. It should not be viewed, therefore, as merely the right to be "free from," but the right to be "free for."[81] It is "freedom for" voluntary self-submission both in relationship with God and in relationship with others. It is "freedom for" reciprocal exchanges of love between the creator and the creation. It is also "freedom for" interrelationality between humans who dwell together in the unity of mutuality. It is freedom to do God's will of one's own volition, not out of constraint. Indeed, God's instructions become a "law of liberty"[82] to those who choose to walk therein, not for the purpose of puntilious performance but for the purpose of demonstrating a love for the creator that parallels the love that Jesus had for his Father.[83] Likewise, freedom is not designed for the establishment of isolated individuality, in "freedom from" relationship with God or with humanity. Free will is based in and is foundational to relationality, the pure love that is essential to the very being of God and is the heart of God's image in humanity. Humans were not created with freedom merely for freedom's sake. Instead, "God gives freedom as a necessary requirement for love to develop."[84]

Without free will, relationality is impossible, for all beings, including God, must be able to choose whether or not to relate in order for relationship to be truly relational. If relationship is forced or contrived so that it is not the product of free choice, it is not true relationship.

---

[81] Evdokimov, p. 36.
[82] James 1:25.
[83] John 14:15; 15:10.
[84] Sanders, p. 207.

Giving freedom to another is an act of self-limitation. God's gift of free choice to humanity was in essence a limitation of his own omnipotence and as such an exercise and demonstration of self-sacrifice or self-limitation which is foundational to relationality. The image of God manifest in human freedom is a "freedom of association" because humans are "created for family, for togetherness, for community" to such a degree that "the solitary human being is an aberration" and "a totally self-sufficient human being would be subhuman."[85] Human beings reflect the image of God in that they are relational beings, and they do so because they, like God, have the freedom to choose. Humans were intended for relationality, for they image the perfect relationality inherent in the very being of God.

CREATIVITY AND GOD'S IMAGE

Both Jewish and Christian theologians have speculated that humans reflect the image and likeness of God in that they share God's creativity and, in effect, become co-creative beings alongside God. Indeed, humans were intended "to be creative, to resemble God in His creativity,"[86] mirroring the God who has ever created and who continues to speak the word of creation. Though humans utterly lack God's ability to create something out of nothing, they have been given the ability to create by reforming and restructuring what God himself has created.

The inventiveness of humanity is beyond question. As a matter of fact, even God himself observed that, given the right circumstances, "nothing that [humans] purpose to do will be impossible for them."[87] The creative genius of humanity is a gift of God that enables human beings to reflect the creator's image both in the activity of the human mind and in the implementation of that activity by the human hand. The power of reason and creative intuition produce an unending and amazing array of human discoveries, inventions, and insights. Like their Creator, humans are inventive first in their thoughts and then in their ability to gather materials to form whatever their minds have imagined. God said, "Let us make," and then proceeded to form humanity. Likewise, humans resolve to create and then give form to what they have blueprinted in their minds.

[85] Tutu, p. xii.
[86] Tutu, p. xiii.
[87] Genesis 11:6.

Rabbi Joseph Soloveitchik recognized in humanity's creative activity a reflection of the divine image: "There is no doubt that the term 'image of God' . . . refers to man's inner charismatic endowment as a creative being. Man's likeness to God expresses itself in man's striving and ability to become a creator."[88] Soloveitchik concluded that, "the Torah describes the creation at length in order to teach us a very important lesson—'to walk in all His ways'—and to instruct man to imitate his Creator and be himself a creator."[89]

Because God worked for the first six days of creation, the first way in which humans manifest the divine image of co-creativity is in work. David Hubbard has observed that "wholesome work is something humans need to be truly human."[90] This is why God puts such high value on human work. Though the labor of work was greatly expanded as a part of the penalty for sin, work itself was intrinsic to the roles of creativity and dominion that God assigned to humanity. David Hubbard has rightly concluded that "there is an intimate connection between work and worship, for to work is to give glory to God."[91] This truth is demonstrated in biblical Hebrew, where one of the words for work (עֲבֹדָה–*abodah*)[92] is the same as one of the words for worship[93] (עֲבֹדָה–*abodah*).[94] The word *abodah* derives from the verb עָבַד (*abad*), which simply means "to work," "to labor," or "to serve." It is the root and basis of the word עֶבֶד (*eved*), which means "servant" or "slave."[95] In similar manner, the word *abad*, like the word *abodah*, is also frequently translated "to worship."[96]

The connection between work and worship in Hebrew accords greater dignity to all human labor that is done in fulfillment of God's command. Unlike the non-Hebrew world, where work was consid-

---

[88] Joseph B. Soloveitchik, *The Lonely Man of Faith* (New York: Doubleday/Random House, 2006), p. 11, first published in *Tradition*, Summer, 1965.

[89] Joseph B. Soloveitchik, *Yemei Zikaron,* tr. Moshe Kroneh (Jerusalem: World Zionist Organization, 1986), p. 86.

[81] Tutu, p. xiii.

[91] David A. Hubbard, "The Wisdom of the Old Testament," in *Messiah College Occasional Papers* (Grantham, PA: Messiah College, August, 1982), no. 3, p. 23, quoted in Marvin R. Wilson, *Our Father Abraham: Jewish Roots of the Christian Faith* (Grand Rapids, MI: Wm. B. Eerdmans Publishing Co., 1989), p. 310.

[92] Exodus 5:9 is the first use of עֲבֹדָה translated "work." The other primary Hebrew word for work is מַעֲשֶׂה (*ma'aseh*).

[93] The most common Hebrew word for "worship" is שָׁחָה (*shachah*).

[94] Exodus 12:25 is the first use of עֲבֹדָה (*abodah*) in relationship to worship, where it is translated "service."

[95] The word *eved* is used to describe the Israelites who were "slaves" in Egypt, as well as those who were "servants" in a household or "servants" of God.

[96] Isaiah 19:21.

ered a demeaning exercise reserved for slaves and people of lesser stature (including women), the Hebrew people viewed work as an element of human dignity and a reflection of God's image. The fourth of the Ten Commandments that focuses primarily on God's instruction to humans that they "remember the Sabbath" also says, "Six days you shall labor and do all your work."[97]Indeed, Scripture declares that on the seventh day God completed his work.[98] The question is, what did God create on the seventh day? The answer is that on that day God created *menuach* (rest in the sense of cessation).

Because God's creative work in the beginning is mirrored in the co-creativity of human work in daily life, the Scriptures elevate all human work to a "spiritual" or "theological" status. This is why the "ancient Hebrews made no dichotomy between sacred and nonsacred occupations."[99] As Marvin Wilson has suggested, the Western world today "would do well to remind ourselves of the sanctity of hard physical work."[100] Jesus was a carpenter or stonemason,[101] Paul was a leather-worker or tentmaker,[102] and most of the earliest rabbis "had secular occupations in addition to their duties as scholar-teachers."[103] As a matter of fact, one of the earliest rabbinic texts observes, "An excellent thing is the study of the Torah combined with some secular occupation, for the labor demanded by them both puts sin out of one's mind."[104] In Hebraic thinking, therefore, no greater value or dignity is accorded to intellectual labor than to manual labor. Additionally, the work that men do is in no way superior to the work that women do. Indeed, there is no such thing as work that is categorically "woman's work" or "man's work." All work is holy in that it is the fulfillment of God's purpose and instructions to humanity.

Interestingly enough, in Hebraic thought, work and study are both considered to be worship. George Foot Moore observed that study "as well as prayer, is worship," and like worship, is "called by the name of the service of the altar (*'abodah*)."[105] In fact, the Talmud

---

[97] Exodus 20:9.
[98] Genesis 2:2.
[99] Wilson, p. 223.
[100] Wilson, p. 223.
[101] Mark 6:3; cf. Matthew 13:55.
[102] Acts 18:3.
[103] Wilson, pp. 222-223.
[104] Talmud, *Pirke Avot* 2.2.
[105] George Foot Moore, *Judaism in the First Centuries of the Christian Era* (Cambridge, MA: Harvard University Press, 1927), 2:240; cf. 217ff., referenced in Wilson, pp. 310, n. 63.

uses the word *education* as a synonym for "heavenly work."[106] This is why Scripture condemns those who do not fulfill God's commandments both to study and to work, branding their inactivity as "disorderly conduct"[107] and giving instructions that "if anyone is not willing to work, neither is he to eat"![108] Apparently, God values the labor of humanity, the work of human creativity that images the God who "finished his work in six days."

Randall Garr argues that humanity's reflection of the image and likeness of God by sharing in the power of creation is also manifest in human procreation, noting that human offspring participate in likeness (דְּמוּת — *demut*]) "of their (pro-)creator"[109] because the word *demut* "points to the likeness children have to their parents through birth."[110] The "likeness that humans have to God through creation" is manifest in the fact that "God and Adam each create אדם תולדת [*toldot adam*] in a manner that is appropriate to their nature," for "God 'creates' the human race" while "Adam 'fathers' a son."[111] Thereafter, likeness is "a mechanical, genealogical, and self-perpetuating inheritance."[112] Continuing with Walter Volgel's argument that *demut* "suggests a likeness between the role of God as creator and the human role as procreator,"[113] Garr appealed to Phyllis Bird's assertion that after God had created humanity, likeness was "transmitted not through repeated acts of God but through . . . procreation."[114] Then, he concluded for himself that the likeness that is shared "by divine creator and human procreator is homological"[115] so that Adam and Eve imitated God when they successfully replicated God's first act of human creation by birthing a child.[116] For Garr, then, likeness is a "genealogical trait that

---

[106] Abraham J. Feldman, *Contributions of Judaism to Modern Society* (New York: The Union of American Hebrew Congregations), p. 18, referenced in Wilson, p. 310, n. 64.
[107] 2 Thessalonians 3:6.
[108] 2 Thessalonians 3:10, NASB.
[109] Randall Garr, *In His Own Image and Likeness: Humanity, Divinity, and Monotheism: Culture and History of the Ancient Near East* (Boston: Brill Academic Publishers, 2003), p. 127.
[110] Walter Vogels, "The Human Person in the Image of God (Gn 1:26)," *Science et Esprit* 46 (1994), p. 193, quoted in Randall Garr, p. 127.
[111] Randall Garr, p. 127.
[112] Randall Garr, p. 127.
[113] Vogels, p. 193, quoted in Randall Garr, p. 127.
[114] Phyllis A. Bird, "'Male and Female He Created Them': Gen. 1:27b in the Context of the Priestly Account of Creation," *Harvard Theological Review* 74 (1981), p. 174.
[115] Randall Garr, pp. 127-128.
[116] Bird, p. 174; Jeffrey H. Tigay, "'He Begot a Son in His Likeness after His Image' (Genesis 5:3)," in *Tehillah le-Moshe, Biblical and Judaic Studies in Honor of Moshe Greenberg*, ed. Mordechai Cogan, Barry L. Eichler, and Jeffrey H. Tigay (Winona Lake, IN: Eisenbrauns, 1997), p. 140, noted in Randall Garr, p. 128.

connects humankind and divinity . . . in a homological function" in which humans "imitate God in perpetuity," registering "his everlasting presence in the world." In so doing, humans become a "theophany," or "God-like" in that they "engender, produce, and sustain human life,"[117] the life that God created in his image. Humans continue to participate in creation by means of procreation, thereby reflecting the image of God as creator. They do so as male and female in absolute equality, for the co-creative activity of procreation is impossible without both female and male.

It should come as no surprise that the Hebrew Scriptures emphasize a continuous chain of human reproduction. "This is implicit in the genealogical *leitmotif* of Genesis: a *toledoth* of God's sons."[118] Indeed, from a biblical perspective, history itself is procreation, for the only Hebrew word that connotes "history" is תּוֹלְדוֹת (*toledot*),[119] which means "generations" or the birth of children. This biblical emphasis on the transmission of the divine image through procreation continues unabated into the apostolic portion of the Hebrew Scriptures, where both Matthew and Luke devote extensive ink to delineating the "generations" of Jesus the Messiah.[120] In order to establish the absolute humanity of the man Jesus, the apostles maintained the Hebraic emphasis on *toledot* as a means of securing a "historical" connection between Jesus and the patriarchs of his people. As the divine *Logos*, Jesus was the Son of God from before all time; however, as the Son of Man, he was also the Son of God by his unbroken lineage from "Adam, the son of God."[121] Jesus lived as a human being among fellow humans who were also children of God by being descendants of Adam. Just as the *Logos* enfleshed was the Son of God through procreation, so all human beings, male and female, are children of God through linear descent from Adam.

God's directive to humanity that they "be fruitful and multiply," then, was more an encouragement to image the creator than it was a command to populate the world.[122] The image of God in humanity is most creative in the capacity to generate and maintain relationships.

---

[117] Randall Garr, p. 132.
[118] Thomas L. Thompson, *The Mythic Past: Biblical Archaeology and the Myth of Israel* (New York: Basic Books, 1999), pp. 360-361.
[119] Genesis 10:1; 11:10.
[120] Matthew 1:1-17, Luke 3:23-38.
[121] Luke 3:38.
[122] Oppenheimer, "Ethics and the Personal Life," p. 749.

The manifestation of relationality was God's ultimate purpose in creating humanity: relationality is the goal of human reason and creativity, and it is the purpose of human creativity. Consequently, as Helen Oppenheimer notes, "God's blessing on procreation belongs with the announcement that human beings are made in God's image and likeness: they are fit to be granted a share in God's creativeness."[123] Unlike animal reproduction, human procreation manifests God's creativity through co-creativity in which human beings transmit God's image and likeness to their progeny, an act in which both male and female participate equally.

In effect, therefore, humans have a duty to continue to create, to image God in creation by doing so in procreation. Michael Fishbane argues that "human beings must re-create a residence for God on earth."[124] Indeed, the ongoing manifestation of humanity's relationship with the Divine is contingent upon human reproduction. In order to provide vessels for the indwelling of the Spirit of God in the earth, humans must continue to manifest the divine image in creativity through procreation. Even in this process, however, God is not limited entirely to human reproductive capabilities, for on those occasions when it has become necessary, he has asserted himself supernaturally to fulfill his promises by giving children to infertile couples.[125] In doing so, God confirmed that the power "to populate the world with human beings, in imitation of God's creation, remains a gift of God."[126] God created, and he continues to create, even interrupting the natural order of generation and the malfunctioning of human anatomical systems to ensure the fulfillment of his promises when necessary.

Interaction and interrelationship with God inspires human beings with the insight and the drive to be creative themselves, whether in what they create with their minds and their hands or in what they create with their reproductive systems. Such creativity is the manifestation of God's image in his human creation. This is why Carl Braaten observes that "God's creating is the norm for human co-creating, not in the sense that *Homo sapiens* is to equate its activity with God's, but rather in the sense that human activity is perverse if it does not finally qualify as participation in and extension of God's primordial will of

[123] Oppenheimer, p. 749.
[124] Michael A. Fishbane, *Biblical Text and Texture* (New York: Schocken Books, 1979), p. 13. Also Randall Garr, p. 233.
[125] Genesis 21:1-3; 30:1-2, 22-23; 1 Samuel 1:1-20.
[126] Randall Garr, p. 233.

creation."[127] Human co-creation is a divine gift from the creator and serves to reflect the image and likeness of God in the earth. When male and female share equally in procreation, they together mirror God's creativity in a way that transcends all other human creativity.

In truth, it is woman who extends the co-creative imagery of God beyond conception by also imaging God's creativity in the very process by which the new human body is formed in the womb: woman provides the nourishment that fuels the multiplication of cells that eventuates in a viable human life. In a very real way, then, the woman's body delicately and faithfully labors to empower the ongoing formation of the fetus in a manner that is clearly parallel with God's careful and deliberate formation of the first human from the dust of the earth.[128] David even described fetal development as an activity of God taking place within the female body: "You formed my inward parts; you knit me together in my mother's womb . . . when I was being made in secret, intricately woven in the depths of the earth." When he considered God's work in his mother's womb, Israel's king exclaimed, "I am awesomely and wonderfully made."[129] Human co-creativity is clearly manifest in the work of procreation which replicates God's act in creating the first human being by passing along that creative spark in the generation of new human life that is made in God's image.

It is self-evident that female and male share equally in manifesting the divine image in human co-creativity, especially in reproduction. Human generation would be utterly impossible without the joint involvement of both man and woman. There is no such thing as natural abiogenesis or parthenogenesis in human beings, as can be the case in lesser organisms. Human reproduction requires the joining together of the two halves of humanity in order to parallel and image the creativity of God in human generation and to replicate the first human entity that God created in his own image and likeness. At the moment of conception both genders contribute equally to the biological material necessary for human generation.[130] The miracle of conception, which instantly produces new human life, requires both ovum and

---

[127] Carl E. Braaten and Robert W. Jenson, eds., *Christian Dogmatics* (Philadelphia: Fortress Press, 1984), p. 326.
[128] Psalm 139:13-19, NRS.
[129] Psalm 139:14, TNK.
[130] This despite the fact that until a mere two centuries ago men were thought to contribute all the material necessary for new human life (with women merely serving as an incubator or as a place for the nurture of new life, much like the relationship of the earth to a planted seed).

sperm.[131] In the final analysis, the joint participation of male and female in the creativity of human generation confirms the equality that male and female share in every aspect of human creativity. Both male and female equally mirror the creative image of the divine creator.

DOMINION AND GOD'S IMAGE

Significant numbers of scholars have also maintained that God's image and likeness in humanity is manifest in the divine commission for—and the human capability of—ruling over the earth. Hans Walter Wolff states the viewpoint of these scholars unequivocally, "It is precisely in his function as ruler that [man] is God's image."[132] This contention is based on the fact that, as God announced his intention to make humanity "in our image, according to our likeness," he immediately continued, "and let them have dominion."[133] Jon Levenson has suggested, therefore, that the "essence of the idea of creation in the Hebrew Bible" can be captured in one word: "mastery."[134] This Hebraic idea contrasts profoundly with the Babylonian creation narrative that makes humans little more than "scavengers of the gods."[135] Levenson maintains further that God "has appointed humanity to be his viceroy, the highest ranking commoner as it were, ruling with the authority of the king. The human race is YHWH's plenipotentiary, his stand-in."[136] This understanding, says Desmond Tutu, "embues [humans] with profound dignity and worth."[137] As Joseph Coleson has observed, God's original blessing for humankind was "not merely the bestowing of material goods or provisions" but a much higher bless-

---

[131] From the ancient Greeks to the scientists of the nineteenth century, the commonly held belief was that human procreation resulted only from the implantation of spermatozoa in the female uterus. A sperm cell was considered to be a tiny complete human (*homunculus*) that needed only to be nurtured by the woman in much the same way that seed is planted in the earth to reproduce plants. For this reason, it was believed that woman contributed nothing of substance to the formation of a new human life. Even when the microscope was invented by Anthony Leeuwenhoeck, he insisted that he saw complete humans in human sperm (as well as complete animals in the sperm of other species). In this case, instead of "seeing is believing," believing led to seeing! It was not until 1827 that Karl von Baer discovered the human ovum, and it was not until the twentieth century that scientists came to understand that both male and female contribute equally 23 chromosomes for the development of a fetus, but even then controversy still remained based on the centuries-old tradition of the *homunculus*.

[132] Hans Walter Wolff, *Anthropology of the Old Testament*, tr. Margaret Kohl (Philadelphia: Fortress Press, 1974), p. 160.

[133] Genesis 1:26.

[134] Jon Douglas Levenson, *Creation and the Persistence of Evil: The Jewish Drama of Divine Omnipotence* (Princeton, NJ: Princeton University Press, 1988), p. 3.

[135] Tutu, p. xi.

[136] Levenson, pp. 113-114. Also Randall Garr, p. 170.

[137] Tutu, p. xi.

ing, "the delegation of oversight and responsibility."[138]

The creation of humanity in the image of God "confers on human beings a dominion over the animals analogous to that which God enjoys over the whole of his creation."[139] It is clear that "Adam was created in God's image in the capacity to exercise responsible and benevolent stewardship over the earth and its non-human inhabitants."[140] In his translation of the texts of Genesis 1-3, Sa'adya Gaon even rendered the Hebrew word *betzalmo* ("in his image") as, "He created him as a ruler," thereby directly associating the "image of God" with dominion.[141] Likewise, Chayyim Volozhiner said, "God created mankind in His own image . . . for just as He, blessed be His name, is Elohim, possessor of the powers that exist in all the worlds, He who arranges and leads them at every moment to His will, so, too, He, blessed be He, gave man dominion."[142]

Dominion is "part of human nature and purpose, for as the representative . . . of God on earth, humanity cannot *not* be in charge," says David Blumenthal.[143] Whether the word *dominion* is defined as "the right of conquest" or as "the demand of stewardship," it is clear that human beings have "power over and in the world," regardless as to whether they accept that power or demur from it.[144] Genesis 1, therefore, is confirmation of humanity's divinely granted right to rule over the created order that should be embraced not as an act of hubris but as the acceptance of responsibility and accountability for this facet of the created order as God designed it.[145]

Dominion is essential to humanity's opportunity to image the divine character. God's power and the way in which he exercises that power are the models for humanity's ruling role: humans can rule on earth only as God's stewards and with God's delegated authority, and they can rule rightly only within the dynamics of dominion that God himself designed and employs. Because of God's self-emptying

---

[138] Joseph E. Coleson, *Ezer Cenegdo: A Power Like Him, Facing Him as Equal* (Grantham, PA: Messiah College, 1996), p. 7.

[139] Vladimir Lossky, *In the Image and Likeness of God* (Crestwood, NY: St. Vladimir's Seminary Press, 1974), p. 128.

[140] Coleson, p. 4.

[141] Chayyim Volozhiner, *Nefesh ha-Chayyim, sha'ar* 1, chap. 3., quoted in Navon, Straus, pp. 51-52.

[142] Volozhiner, p. 52. Volozhiner's idea of human dominion, however, was that humans would gain dominion over "the upper worlds rather than dominion in this world."

[143] Blumenthal, p. 338, emphasis in the original.

[144] Blumenthal, p. 338.

[145] Blumenthal, p. 338.

and self-limitation in relationship to the creation, his rule "is mediated through a creature that is itself part of creation, subject to all of creation's laws, rather than imposed directly, heteronomously, upon the creation."[146] This, says Douglas Hall, is "an integral aspect of the divine respect for creation's otherness."[147] In order to image God's dominion, humans must exercise authority over the earth, but only in the context of the self-limiting stewardship that God himself has always manifest toward the entire creation. Anything less is exploitative and thereby perverts God's image as he intended it to be manifest in humanity. Whatever is not of love is sin,[148] and the unbridled quest for and worship of unrighteous gain is the root of all evil.[149]

This truth is clearly established in the recorded discussion of the purpose for which God created humanity and the role of dominion to which he assigned them. God gave Adam and Eve dominion (רָדָה— *radah*) over the earth to subdue (כָּבַשׁ—*kabash*) it. On casual reading, this text appears to indicate that God gave them authority to subjugate and forcefully abuse the earth; however, their responsibility was not to abuse but to serve the ground from which the divine fingers had extracted them. Before the earthling (*ha-adam*) was created, the earth (*ha-adamah*) had already existed; however, "there was no *adam* ["human"] to till the *adamah* ["ground"]."[150] The Hebrew word translated "till" or "cultivate" is עָבַד (*abad*), the verbal form of עֶבֶד (*eved*), the word for "servant." The word *abad* connotes service, respect, and even reverence or worship. To "till" the earth, then, is to "serve" the earth; to "subdue" the earth is to "guard" it, not to exploit or abuse it.

In order to create a servant for the earth, therefore, God took a part of the same earth, formed it into a human, and gave dominion to that entity—both male and female.[151] This is further expanded and clarified in Genesis 2:15: "Then the Lord God took the human and put him into the garden of Eden to cultivate [עָבַד—*abad*] it and keep [שָׁמַר—*shamar*] it." In order to subdue the earth and have dominion over it, Adam and Eve had to serve (עָבַד—*abad*) the earth by caring for it with honor and respect. Likewise, they were instructed to keep

---

[146] Hall, p. 350.
[147] Hall, p. 350.
[148] Romans 14:23 notes that "whatever is not of faith is sin," while Galatians 5:6 confirms that "faith operates through love."
[149] 1 Timothy 6:10; Matthew 6:24.
[150] Genesis 2:5.
[151] Ironically, it is to that same earth that every human body returns as even in death the human continues to serve the earth from which it was created.

(שָׁמַר—*shamar*) the earth by observing and guarding it in an act of protection rather than exploitation. Both *abad* and *shamar* connote attention and care, not domination and plunder. As Elgin Tupper has noted, worshipping and imaging the God of Scripture "includes the renunciation of dominating power and overwhelming force as the way to accomplish the will of God."[152]

The human authority and capacity for rulership is based in and governed by the human imaging of divine relationality which is the manifestation of pure love. This was the way in which humans functioned as God's plenipotentiaries before sin entered the human scene: they exercised loving care for the earth. Only the influence of sin changed the equation and introduced unrestrained lust for power and control, domination over other human beings, and exploitation of the earth itself. Human obsession with dominance began only when sin came to dominate the first human couple, but it quickly spread and multiplied itself in their progeny. Consequently, as Ray Anderson observed, "the image of God as social, spiritual and moral health was corrupted and became the source of pride, jealousy, hatred, and violence against others."[153]

It is also important to underscore the limits of human dominion: it was over "all the earth . . . the fish . . . the birds . . . the cattle . . . all terrestrial creatures."[154] Tikva Frymer-Kensky argues that humanity's bearing the image of God "means that human beings can have dominion only over the earth and over animals" and that "no person can have full dominion over another human being."[155] She asserts that "there can be no distinctions between 'lesser' or 'greater' images of God, autonomous or subordinate," for when such distinctions are made, the concept of the image and likeness of God becomes nothing more than a "meaningless bit of self-congratulation."[156] Indeed, the idea of humanity as the image of God "makes no sense if it does not limit the ability of one human or one group of humans to exert their will over another."[157] Frymer-Kensky is entirely correct in asserting that this understanding is (or should be) "a bedrock concept in Juda-

---

[152] Elgin Frank Tupper, *Scandalous Providence: The Jesus Story of the Compassion of God* (Macon, GA: Mercer University Press, 1995), p. 133.

[153] Ray S. Anderson, "Theological Anthropology" in *The Blackwell Companion to Modern Theology*, ed. S. Gareth J. Jones (Oxford: Blackwell Publishing Ltd., 2004), p. 88.

[154] Genesis 1:26.

[155] Tikva Frymer-Kensky, "Image of God," in Frymer-Kensky, Novak, Ochs, Singer, and Fox Sandmel, *Christianity in Jewish Terms,* p. 333.

[156] Frymer-Kensky, p. 333.

[157] Frymer-Kensky, pp. 334-235.

ism and Christianity"[158] because it is foundational to all Scripture.

It should be made clear, therefore, that the right and the commission to rule over the earth were specifically conveyed to "them," not to "him." God's announcement of intent in creating humanity was "Let *them* have dominion." God blessed the newly formed and vivified human entity that he had created "male and female" and said to *them*, "Be fruitful, and multiply, and fill the earth, and subdue it, and *rule.*"[159] The Hebrew text clearly establishes the fact that the blessing and the commission were made to both male and female in that each of the five imperative verbs in God's declaration regarding humanity are plural and refer to the antecedent *them*. The order of these plural commands could not be clearer: After humanity was created male and female, God blessed *them*, and he commanded *them* to 1) *be fruitful*, 2) *multiply*, 3) *fill* the earth, 4) *subdue* the earth, and 5) *have dominion*. Human dominion, therefore, is the coequal coregency of male and female, not the rule of the male over the entire creation, including the female, or the rule of the male over creation with some degree of authority delegated by the male to the female. The female neither was nor is part of the "all the earth" that God consigned to *ha-adam's* oversight. As Gilbert Bilezikian has observed, "Only God was in authority over Adam and Eve. Neither of them had the right to usurp divine prerogatives by assuming authority over each other."[160] Joseph Coleson concluded that "for one half of humanity to subjugate the other half robs both of God's intended blessing upon all humans."[161]

It is safe to say, then, that the dominion for which humanity was designed was and should remain a product of the divine concern with care and protection, not with an egocentric drive for domination. Only when humans exercise the level of self-sacrifice that God has manifest in his relationship with the universe in general and with humanity in particular can they truly mirror the exercise of divine dominion by doing what is in the best interest of both the earth and their fellow human beings rather than what their own perverted sense of glorified self-interest demands. Exercising dominion over the earth and its nonhuman occupants is a reflection of the image of God only when it mirrors the divine condescension by the emptying of self in

---

[158] Frymer-Kensky, p. 334.
[159] Genesis 1:28.
[160] Gilbert Bilezikian, *Beyond Sex Roles: What the Bible Says About a Woman's Place in Church and Family* (Grand Rapids, MI: Baker Book House, 1986), pp. 40-41.
[161] Coleson, p. 4.

order to accomplish the greater good and by manifesting the pure love of divine superrelationality by promoting and facilitating "peace on earth, good will toward men."[162]

Humanity's reflection of God's image and likeness by exercising compassionate dominion can only be accomplished when that dominion is shared equally by male and female. Anything less than complete equality between women and men is a perversion of the nature of divine sovereignty that is to be imaged in humanity, and it is clearly a form of aberrant behavior that is a perversion of God's design for human life and activity. When either male or female attempts to rule over the other, clear evidence is present that sin is the force that has dominion, and sin's dominion is never benevolent or compassionate. Dominion through domination is a perversion of the image of God, especially when one human being demeans and deprecates another. Truly imaging the divine in dominion demands equality, mutuality, and self-emptying—an acknowledgement of and submission to the divine intention: "Let us create humanity in our image . . . and let *them* have dominion."

SPRINGBOARD FOR DISCUSSION

1. Analyze personhood and its implications about the nature of God. Would it have been possible for God to have created human beings in his image and likeness as persons if God were not a person? What impact does attributing personhood to God have upon anthropology and the demand for respect for all human beings regardless of gender, race, ethnicity, or religion?

2. Consider how personhood in God is manifest in relationship, first within the very being of God, then in God's interaction with creation and humanity. How important is it to understand God as a family or community and humanity as the image of family and community in the earth? Could God have true relationship with human beings if he were not a person? How important is it to you to be able to relate to God as a person?

3. Evaluate the cognitive ability and capacity for rational thought that God gave to human beings. How does the operation of the human mind reflect the image of God? Is it possible to place too much

---

[162] Luke 2:14.

importance on rationality as *the* image of God? What negative consequences can result from such overemphasis?

4. Consider the core of human existence. Which of these better
sums up your understanding of human existence: *Cogito, ergo sum* ("I
think, therefore I am"), *"Amo, ergo sum"* ("I love, therefore I am"), or
"I participate, therefore I am"? Why?

5. Why is God's Word foundational to the conscience? How it
is possible that all human beings have a conscience, even those who
have never heard of the Bible? Why do all humans have an inclination
toward good and an inclination toward evil?

6. Evaluate the concept of human freedom as essential to the image and likeness of God in humanity. How important is the foundational understanding of human freedom to establishing understanding
of equality and mutuality between human beings regardless of gender,
race, ethnicity, or religion?

7. Consider the concept of divine self-limitation. How was this
manifest in creation? How was it manifest in the life of Jesus? How
can God can be sovereign over all things while at the same time grant-
ing the sovereignty of free will to human beings? Why is freedom
important to genuine interrelationship between God and humanity
and between humans and other humans?

8. Discuss the continuing replication of human beings through
procreation as an aspect of God's image in humanity. How do humans
mirror God's creative powers when they participate in procreation
and bring forth new beings in God's image and likeness?

9. Consider the nature of God's dominion as that of loving care,
protection, and blessing rather than impersonal domination. What is
true leadership: dominance or service? How has God demonstrated
servant leadership? How did Jesus manifest this kind of leadership? In
what ways does benevolent stewardship mirror divine leadership in
family, society, and community?

10. Establish the fact that the right to dominion over the earth was
given to *them*, not to *him*. How important is this to your own evaluation of your role in your family, in your society, in your church? How
does the capacity for dominion in humans mirror the image of God?

CHAPTER 13

GOD'S IMAGE IN HUMANITY

PHYSICAL DIMENSIONS

Foundational to all biblical faith is the proscription against idols of any sort. Immediately after the first of God's Ten Words, "I am the Lord your God," came the first divine prohibition, the second commandment of the Decalogue: "You shall have no other gods before me. You shall not make for yourself an idol or any likeness. . . . You shall not bow down to worship them."[1] God specifically and irrevocably forbade the construction of any physical image, whether human or animal, male or female, to stand as a representation of the Divine in the earth. At the same time, however, God did not limit himself in any way from creating humanity for the specific purpose of demonstrating theomorphically the image and likeness of divine being in the material creation.

For all of human existence, therefore, men and women have had significant problems in maintaining balance in their thinking about God and about the relationship between God and humanity. They have had great difficulty in maintaining dynamic tension between God's stated purpose for human creation and the divine prohibition

---

[1] Exodus 20:3-5. This entire prohibition is the second commandment in the Jewish enumeration of the Ten Commandments in which "I am the Lord your God" is understood to be the first commandment. The Christian enumeration of the commandments makes "You shall have no other gods before me" as the first commandment, followed by "You shall not make for yourself an idol" as the second commandment.

against constructing images to represent the Divine. On the one hand, men of all cultures and times have constructed idol images—both physical and mental—to represent deity, and they have prostrated themselves before such images. On the other hand, some have taken the divine prohibition out of context and have made it a proscription against all images, even the human imagery of deity that God himself outlined in his own self-disclosure, the revelation of Holy Scripture.[2] It was God, not man, who announced his intention to create humanity in his own image and likeness; therefore, everything about human existence somehow manifests something about God. In some misguided attempt to protect the dignity of the Eternal, human beings should not, therefore, attempt to prohibit God from saying and doing what he himself determined: to make human beings in his image and likeness. They should instead accept what God in his own sovereignty did: create humanity in such a way that the entire human person— male and female, physical and spiritual—is a reflection of the divine image and likeness.

In more than two millennia of thought about the manifestation of God's image and likeness in human beings, the focus has been almost exclusively on the spiritual dimensions of the human person. Little consideration has been given to the possibility that human beings somehow reflect the image and likeness of God in their physiology, their corporeality. Much of this propensity toward exclusive focus solely on the spiritual aspects of humanity has been a product of the Christian tendency to view the human body as somehow inherently evil. Most of the anthropology of the Christian church has been derived from and has rested on neo-Platonic and other Greek philosophies that viewed existence in dualistic terms: a good spiritual realm and an evil material realm. The human body, therefore, has been considered little more than an evil entrapment of the sparks of divinity, from which the human spirit struggles to experience release and absorption into the heavenlies. The perspectives of the Hebrew Scriptures, however, present an entirely different story when they are ex-

---

[2] The commandment does not say, "You shall not make for yourself any image." It says, "You shall not make . . . an idol (פֶּסֶל—*pesel*)," and it continues "You shall not bow down to worship them." The intent was not to prohibit the construction of images but to proscribe the construction and worship of idol images. Both two-dimensional and three-dimensional images are not evil; worshipping them is. If the directive had been against all images, then God himself violated his own proscription by commanding Moses to construct of cherubim to overshadow the mercy seat of the ark of the covenant in Israel's tabernacle. The intent of the commandment is clear: humans are not to construct idol images or worship any image.

amined in their purest and clearest sense and not filtered through the lens of Greek philosophical musings. The human body was formed and vivified by God with his own breath and was fully intended by God to be a manifestation of the divine image and likeness in the material creation.

CORPOREALITY AND GOD'S IMAGE

For centuries, the vast majority of both Jewish and Christian scholarship has concluded that the human body cannot possibly reflect the image and likeness of God. Because they have been—either knowingly or unwittingly—influenced by Greek philosophical ideas about God, past and present interpreters have been reluctant to take literally God's statement of purpose in human creation: "Let us make humanity in our image and likeness." Corporeal images of God in the Hebrew Scriptures have, therefore, been deprecated or dismissed in favor of concepts of utter divine transcendence demanded in Greek philosophy. Anthropomorphic images of the Divine, even in Scripture, have been discounted as naïve imaginations of primitive peoples or as God's communicating with humans in "baby talk" since they could not possibly understand what he actually did.[3] The truth is that God had quite enough intellect himself to design humans with intelligence adequate to the task of understanding anything about God that he wanted to communicate to them and he was honest enough to use language that conveyed accurately the information about himself that he desired to communicate.

Despite centuries-old traditions discounting or disqualifying the human body as a part of the image of God, an objective study of God's image must also consider what the Scriptures have to say about the human body and its portrayal of that image. Does human corporeality, then, play any part in the declaration that humanity was made "in the image and likeness" of God? Are human anatomical features in any way theomorphic? For centuries, most Jewish and Christian theologians have registered a resounding "No!" to these questions. Even though much of the rationale for such contentions was based in

---

[3] When confronted with scriptural statements about God that did not fit the Augustinian theology of utter divine immutability and his own concept of total predestination, John Calvin argued that biblical representations of God that imply divine change (whether in response to human intercession or to other stimuli) are nothing more than the baby talk of a mother or nursemaid to an infant or young child ("lisping," as Calvin described it). See John Calvin, *Institutes of the Christian Religion* 1.13.1

the understanding that the human body was somhow evil, such negative responses have not been without good reason, for many texts in the Hebrew Scriptures clearly assert that God is neither fleshly nor human.[4] Indeed, God specifically and unequivocally reminded Israel when they were confronted with the divine presence at Sinai, "you heard the sound of words, but you saw no form; there was only a voice."[5]

What may have had even greater impact on both Jewish and Christian theology, however, are those texts that specifically prohibit the creation of images of God in any form,[6] whether of humans, male or female,[7] or of any other creature.[8] The impact of these prohibitions upon Judaism and Christianity cannot be overstated, for "aniconism set Israel and second-temple Judaism apart as decisively in cultural and theological terms"[9] as did its understanding of monotheism, and the same has been true for Christianity which was birthed from the matrix of second-temple Judaism. Daniel Boyarin is correct, however, when he observes that "*only* under Hellenic influence do Jewish cultures exhibit any anxiety about the corporeality or visibility of God; the biblical and Rabbinic religions were quite free of such influences and anxieties."[10]

From fifth-century B.C. Xenophanes to the time of Plato and Aristotle, the major Greek philosophers argued that the true God had no body at all but was an incorporeal principle or force.[11] Robert Renehan has pointed out that the idea of divine immateriality was actually Plato's brainchild.[12] Indeed, Plato actually coined the Greek word *asomatos* ("incorporeal").[13] Aristotle was the first person who actually used the term *asomatos* to describe his idea of the Deity (his "Un-

---

[4] Cf. Numbers 23:19; Hosea 11:9.
[5] Deuteronomy 4:12, 16 NRS.
[6] For example, see Exodus 20:4-6 and Deuteronomy 4:12-18, 5:8-9.
[7] Deuteronomy 4:16.
[8] Deuteronomy 4:17-18.
[9] J. Andrew Dearman, "Theophany, Anthropomorphism, and the *Imago Dei*," in *The Incarnation*, ed. Stephen T. Davis, Daniel Kendall and Gerald O'Collins (Oxford: Oxford University Press, 2002) p. 43.
[10] Daniel Boyarin, "The Eye in the Torah: Ocular Desire in Midrashic Hermeneutic," *Critical Inquiry* 16 (2009), p. 553, emphasis in original.
[11] See Jean-Pierre Vernant, "Dim Body, Dazzling Body," in *Fragments for a History of the Human Body*, ed. Michal Feher, Ramona Naddaff, and Nadia Tazi (New York: Zone Publishing, 1989), p. 21. Because of the dualism of Greek philosophy which dichotomized the spiritual and the material, it was inconceivable to the philosophers that God could have any kind of body.
[12] Robert F. Renehan, "On the Greek Origins of the Concepts of Incorporeality and Immateriality," in *Greek, Roman, and Byzantine Studies* 21 (190), pp. 105, 138.
[13] Renehan, pp. 127-130.

moved Mover").[14] This understanding was summed up and codified for Judaism in the third of Maimonides' Thirteen Articles of Faith, which affirms the belief in the incorporeality of God.[15]

Under the influence of Greek philosophy, Maimonides considered the image of God in humanity to be limited solely to the intellect, and he even restricted the application of the divine image to a few select people, declaring that "only those people whose intellect is in its most perfect state are really the image of God."[16] While Maimonides attempted to adduce support for his idea from Scripture and from prior rabbinic comentary, his efforts were clearly ventures into scriptural eisegesis and to anachronistic retrojection of his own philosophy into original talmudic texts. Perhaps this was one of the reasons why the teaching of Maimonides was rejected by the majority of the Jewish community for at least a century after his death. Herbert Davidson is clearly correct when he concludes that the idea of divine incorporeality is a "philosophic doctrine [that] entered Jewish thought in the train of philosophy."[17] Tragically the same Greek philosophical perspective infiltrated Christian theology and gained an even greater ascendancy there than it did in Judaism.

The obvious problem with the doctrine of absolute divine incorporeality is that there are numerous references in Scripture where God appeared to humans and was seen and touched by them. The ancient Israelites had no trouble recognizing God as either having a humanlike body or at least as manifesting himself in a humanlike body when he so desired. They were quite certain that one could not see God in his transcendent glory and live to tell about it;[18] however, they were able to balance this clear-cut understanding with the record of actual experiences, holding both in dynamic tension (in typical Hebraic fash-

---

[14] Aristotle, Cael. 279.a.17; Metaph. 1073.a.5, noted in Renehan, pp. 134-135.

[15] Maimonides, *Perush ha-Mishnah (Commentary on the Mishnah)*, in *Tractate Sanhedrin*, chapter *Perek Helek* (chapter 10). Maimonides' third principle states: "This is to accept that this Oneness that we have mentioned above is not a body and has no strength in the body, and has no shape or image or relationship to a body or parts thereof. . . . This is all to say that He does not partake of any physical actions or qualities. And if He were to be a body then He would be like any other body and would not be God. And all that is written in the holy books regarding descriptions of God, they are all anthropomorphic." Maimonides' observations clearly were based more in Greek philosophical perspectives than in Scripture itself.

[16] Tikva Frymer-Kensky, "Image of God," in *Christianity in Jewish Terms*, ed. Tikva Frymer-Kensky, David Novak, Peter Ochs, Michael A. Singer, and David Fox Sandmel (Bolder, CO: Westview Press, 2002), p. 329.

[17] Herbert Davidson, *Moses Maimonides, The Man and His Works* (New York: Oxford University Press, 2004), p. 238.

[18] Exodus 33:20; Genesis 32:30.

ion). This allows for the literal interpretation of the many texts that speak of God's having chosen to reveal himself to humans while manifesting humanlike attributes and appearances. These were the biblical accounts of theophany,[19] in which neither reluctance nor equivocation was used in describing God's interactions with humans in terms of divine embodiment. These were not experiences of human imagination or emotion. They were visual self-manifestations of God in appearances to humans that were undertaken by divine initiative, not by human fantasizing, hallucination, or phantasmagoria. The biblical record is clear: God appeared to humans in a visible, material form that approximated human physiology.[20]

A lucid, sraight-forward account of theophany is recorded in Abraham's experience when "the LORD appeared to him by the oaks of Mamre, while he was sitting in the entrance to his tent in the heat of the day."[21] This was neither a "night vision" (as with Daniel and Paul[22]), nor a dream (as with Abimelech, Laban, or Solomon[23]), nor a case of one's hearing a voice (as with Adam and Eve, Cain, Noah, and Samuel[24]). This event occurred in the "heat of the day" or mid-afternoon.[25] The LORD—identified unambiguously by name as YHWH—came to Abraham's tent with two other "men" who were later identified as "angels."[26] Apparently Abraham recognized God[27] from his prior encounter with the Lord at Shechem;[28] therefore, he needed no introduction. The fact that God identified Abraham as his "friend" in subsequent Scripture[29] bespeaks an ongoing relationship of continuing contact and communication between God and the patriarch.

Abraham welcomed all three celestial visitors to the tent he had pitched in the oak grove at Mamre. Together, Yahweh, his two companions, and Abraham's family ate bread and meat and drank milk.

---

[19] The word *theophany* is from the Greek words *theōs* (god) and *phainō* (to appear).

[20] See J. Maxwell Miller, "In the 'Image' and 'Likeness' of God," *Journal of Biblical Literature*, 91 (1972), p. 292.

[21] Genesis 18:1, NAS, NRS.

[22] Daniel 2:19; Acts 16:9; 18:9.

[23] Genesis 20:6; 31:24; 1 Kings 3:5.

[24] Genesis 3:9-19; 4:9-15; 6:13.

[25] See 1 Samuel 11:11.

[26] Genesis 19:1.

[27] Johannes Lindblom, "Theophanies in Holy Places in the Hebrew Religion," *Hebrew Union College Annual Suplement* 32 (1961), p. 116.

[28] Genesis 12:1-4, 6-8.

[29] Isaiah 41:8 quotes God as saying Abraham was his friend. In 2 Chronicles 20:7, Jehoshaphat notes that Abraham was God's friend forever. James 2:23 declares two millennia after the fact that Abraham was called "The Friend of God."

Following this meal, God confirmed his promise to Abraham and Sarah that their long-desired son would be born. Finally, the Lord shared the purpose of his mission with his friend Abraham: he had come to destroy the evil cities of Sodom and Gomorrah. Then the story continued with the account of Abraham's unsuccessful negotiation with God on behalf of the doomed cities, an action that was necessary for Abraham because he had been designated by God as a prophetic intercessor for blessing to "all the families of the earth."[30] Finally, the Lord departed from Abraham's presence and proceeded to rain down fire and brimstone upon Sodom and Gomorrah "from the LORD out of heaven."[31]

This account is too literal to be taken metaphorically. None of this language is Calvin's "lisping" or baby talk. The text is simply stated: God appeared to Abraham, and he ate, blessed, and communicated with him in a bodily form that not only Abraham but also Sarah and the family servants discerned. Robert Letellier observes, "YHWH appears here as a man. . . . This is not to be confused with mere anthropomorphism. . . . God wills to appear and does so in human shape."[32] Charles Aalders reluctantly confessed the consternation of most Christian interpreters over this perplexing story: "It is totally beyond our understanding that God Himself should appear with two of His holy angels in such realistic human form that they actually ate human food. But this is precisely what God tells us in His word. . . ."[33]

Besides Abraham's encounters with the Divine, Scripture chronicles similar accounts of theophany in the lives of Jacob,[34] Moses,[35] Samuel,[36] Isaiah,[37] and Ezekiel.[38] The most straightforward of these is Moses' relationship with God in which Scripture declares that God conversed with Moses "face to face as a man speaks to his friend."[39] When Moses and a small contingent of his leaders saw "the God of Israel" enthroned atop Sinai, they all observed that God's feet were

---

[30] Genesis 12:3, NASB.
[31] Genesis 19:24.
[32] Robert Ignatius Letellier, *Day in Mamre, Night in Sodom: Abraham & Lot in Genesis 18 & 19* (Leiden: E. J. Brill, 1995), p. 39.
[33] G. Charles Aalders, *Bible Student's Commentary* (Grand Rapids, MI: Zondervan Publishing, 1981), p. 5.
[34] Genesis 32:24-30.
[35] Exodus 3:3, 6; 33:21-23.
[36] 1 Samuel 3:21.
[37] Isaiah 6.
[38] Ezekiel 1:26-27.
[39] Exodus 33:11.

on a pavement of sapphire.[40] Ezekiel saw the same sapphire throne that Moses and the elders viewed and described God as having an "appearance of a human" sitting on that throne with a gleam above his loins and a fire beneath them. Jacob's experience of God was that of wrestling with a "man" who chose to remain unnamed so that when Jacob eventually came to recognize him as God, he did so in retrospect and then only through faith, not empirical knowledge.[41] Jacob named the location of his encounter "Peniel," for "I have seen God face to face, yet my life has been preserved."[42] Isaiah saw Yahweh sitting on a throne but was overwhelmed with divine glory as the skirt of God's robe filled the temple.[43] God revealed himself to Samuel by his Word—the voice that spoke to the prophet from his youth the divine words that never failed."[44] None of these experiences is to be confused with God's appearance to all of Israel at Sinai when he concluded, "You saw no form . . . you heard only a voice."[45] Moses, Aaron, Nadab, Abihu, and seventy of Israel's elders at least saw God's feet, and they were, indeed, "feet."[46] The intimate personal appearances of the Divine to the prophets were shockingly real and profoundly discernable by every aspect of human sensory perception.

Michael Fishbane has argued that it is "tendentious" to dismiss the "unabashed and pervasive depictions of God in anthropomorphic and anthropopathic terms" that "occur in the monotheistic canon of Scripture" by blaming them on "inadequacy of human language" or "limitation of human thought."[47] He wondered, "On what basis should one assume that the plain sense of Scripture is some (quasi-allegorical) approximation of a more spiritual or purely metaphorical content?" Further, he asked, "Is it even possible to get past the thick immediacy of biblical language and its concrete and sensible accounts of God?"[48] As Heschel said, the prophets' encounters with God were "overwhelmingly real" because God was "shatteringly present" with them.[49]

---

[40] Exodus 24:10.
[41] Genesis 32:30.
[42] Genesis 32:30, NASB.
[43] Isaiah 6:1.
[44] 1 Samuel 3:19-21.
[45] Deuteronomy 4:12.
[46] Exodus 24:10-11.
[47] Michael A. Fishbane, *Biblical Myth and Rabbinic Mythmaking* (Oxford: Oxford University Press, 2003), pp. 6-7.
[48] Fishbane, pp. 6-7.
[49] Heschel, *The Prophets*, p. 285.

James Barr has suggested that the most important question about the biblical reports of theophany is better phrased not as "Is God conceived of as essentially in human form?" but as "When [God] does appear in a form at all, is it thought that the human form is the natural or characteristic one for him to assume?" Barr concludes that Scripture is clear: when God chooses to appear to human beings, the normative form of his appearance takes on the likeness of human physiology.[50] The real issue, then, is whether "Israel's effort to depict God anthropomorphically is also a way that the invisible God has chosen to reveal himself, and if so, to what end?"[51]

This is why even the earliest of Jesus' Jewish disciples began to understand that the theophanies of the Hebrew Scriptures were actually Christophanies, instances in which the Word of God who became incarnate in the person of Jesus had previously manifest himself to human beings either in angelic or in human form. Paul identified Jesus as "the Rock who accompanied" the Israelite community in the wilderness.[52] John declared that Jesus was actually the theophany that Isaiah had seen. The apostle affirmed that Jesus had fulfilled the prophecies that Isaiah had made at the time at which the prophet had seen "Jesus' glory [as Isaiah's LORD high and lifted up] and spoke about him."[53]

Accepting and understanding the simple biblical truth that God really appeared to human beings with form and substance corresponding to human physicality restores the dignity of human corporeality to the perspective in which God created humankind in the beginning. It also liberates human beings from the opprobrium and deprecation that Greek philosophical musings and similar anthropological traditions have heaped upon the human body and its functions, and it restores the healthy, balanced, and all-inclusive perspectives of Scripture that underestand human corporeality to be a reflection of God's image and likeness.

Such insight avoids the ideologies of pagan polytheism and philosophy as well as the erroneous dehumanizing concepts of some historical Christian theology based in those ideas. It eliminates historical androcentric deprecation of the female anatomy while also mitigating against the extremes of radical feminism's mischaracterization of male

---

[50] James Barr, "Theophany and Anthropomorphism in the Old Testament," *Congress Volume, Oxford* (Leiden: E. J. Brill, 1960), p. 33.
[51] Barr, p. 33.
[52] 1 Corinthians 10:4.
[53] John 12:37-41, NIV.

physiology and body chemistry. It restores the human body—and all of its attendant parts—to the dignity in which God created it. Such insight represents a restoration of truth that has long been obscured and polluted by Hellenistic and monistic philosophies. It returns the evaluation of the human body to the perspective in which God viewed it in the beginning and in which he still views it: a reflection of his own image and likeness.

One simple truth remains: God himself declared that he created humanity in his image, and he continued in the same breath to say, "Male and female created he them."[54] David Clines concluded that "it is . . . the corporeal animated man that is the image of God. The body cannot be left out of the meaning of the image. . . . Man is the flesh-and-blood image of the invisible God."[55] Physicality is indubitably associated with the "image and likeness" of God in both the texts of Scripture and in practical manifestations, for human physicality is designed by the Creator to be the means that makes it possible for humans to reflect the relationality that exists within the Eternal as the essence of his being.

The reason for gender-specific human creation was first and foremost to provide a means of intimate relationship that would be capable of mirroring the mutual encircling and interpenetration, the coinherence of the three persons in the one God.[56] Humanity images God in the earth through emotional, psychological, and somatic relationality which facilitates a level of corporeal expression that incorporeality could never produce in the material creation. Since humans were designed from the beginning to be physical beings, both female and male genders are necessary for the full manifestation of God's image of pure interrelationality. Without the fullness of humanity, both in the female spirit and body and in the male spirit and body, therefore, God's image and likeness could not be fully manifest in humankind. This is specifically what God himself declared when he announced his

---

[54] Genesis 1:27; 5:1.

[55] David Clines, "The Image of God in Man," *Tyndale Bulletin 19* (1978), p. 86.

[56] Gender differentiation was only secondarily designed for human reproduction. It was first designed for intimate relationship. Before *ha-adam* was sexually differentiated, God observed, "It is not good for *ha-adam* to be alone." The woman was fashioned in order to provide companionship and interrelationality. This was before the human couple sinned and the finality of the penalty for sin, death, made reproduction necessary for the survival of the species. Though God commanded them to "be fruitful and multiply and fill the earth," there is no scriptural evidence to indicate that any reproduction occurred until after they sinned and had been expelled from the Garden of Eden. Prior to that time, their conjugation must have served the primary purpose of relationship.

intention to create human beings in the first place: "In the image of God he created him, male and female he created them."[57]

GENDER AND GOD'S IMAGE

Neither Jewish nor Christian scholars in history have given much regard to the possibility that the gendered nature of human beings could in any way reflect the image and likeness of God. The biblical declaration regarding human creation, however, was profoundly straightforward and transparent: "God created humanity in his image; male and female created he them." Emil Bruner maintained that "in the whole long history of man's understanding of himself this statement has only been made *once* and at this point. . . . On account of this statement alone the Bible shines out among all other books in the world as the Word of God."[58] This account unequivocally established the truth that God's image in humanity is inextricably connected with the fact God created more than one human and that he created male and female. Brunner further argued that this declaration has "a lapidary significance, so simple indeed that we hardly realize that with it a vast world of myth and Gnostic speculation, of cynicism, and asceticism, of the deification of sexuality and the fear of sex completely disappears."[59] Brunner was correct to lament the fact that "in a hundred different ways, man has always said something that contradicts this statement; sometimes he says too little and sometimes too much."[60] The history of humanity has been littered with the carnage of psychological, spiritual, and physical suffering that has been the consequence of adding to or taking away from the definitive words that God spoke in his account of human genesis.

God's image is connected with male and female and their interrelationship on all levels because the declaration of God's Word is clear and unmistakable. Thomas Hopko has suggested that gender differentiation in humans is "an essential element in their ability to reflect and participate in God's divine being and life whose content is love" and that human sexuality "is an essential part of their humanity."[61] It

---

[57] Genesis 1:27, NRS.
[58] Emil Brunner, *Man in Revolt: A Christian Anthropology* (Philadelphia: Westminster Press, 1947), p. 346.
[59] Brunner, p. 346.
[60] Brunner, p. 346.
[61] Thomas Hopko, "God and Gender: Articulating the Orthodox View," in *St. Vladimir's Theological* Quarterly, 37: 2-3 (1993), p. 160.

is precisely as men and women and in the intercommunion between them, "that human beings find and fulfill themselves as creatures made in God's image and likeness."[62] It is a simple truth: without gender and sex, humans are not human, and they do not bear the image and likeness of God. Everyone on earth has God's Word on it! "God is neither male nor female, yet is present in and through all relatedness, including that of gender."[63]

In the very first biblical reference to gender, where the text says, "God created humanity in his image and likeness, male and female he created them," the Hebrew words for male and female could not be more graphic as to God's intention.[64] God did not—as some Greek and Latin fathers mistakenly supposed—create humanity as male and female without fully functional male and female genitalia or sexuality, which they believed came into existence either in the act of, in divine preparation for, or as a consequence of "original sin." In this text, gender is specified by graphic references to genitalia, not by psychological or spiritual masculine or feminine characteristics. The Hebrew word translated "male" is זָכָר (*zakar*) which means "piercer"[65] (from its core meaning "sharp") invoking the image of an erect penis. The Hebrew word translated "female" is נְקֵבָה (*nekebah*), which means "the pierced" or "a hole," coming from the word נֶקֶב (*nekeb*),[66] which means "a hole or cavity" and hence "vagina." Gender in Scripture was more than psychological predispositions or mere "masculinity" and "femininity." Male and female were differentiated and identified by God specifically and exclusively by their genitalia.

It is entirely likely, therefore, that the biblical prohibition against sculpting male or female images pertained not merely to statues of human beings but to the phallic or vaginal stone images that were worshipped by much of the non-Israelite world of antiquity and are still

---

[62] Hopko, p. 160.

[63] Rosemary Radford Ruether, "Christian Understandings of Human Nature and Gender," in *Religion, Feminism, and the Family*, ed. Anne Carr and Mary Steward Van Leeuwen (Louisville, KY: Westminster John Knox Press, 1996), p. 107.

[64] The statement, "male and female created he them," was completed when what pertained to the feminine was surgically removed from undifferentiated humanity so that both male and female were constructed. The first human being was not a hermaphrodite, possessing both male and female genitalia; however, explicit genitalia were manifest when the surgical process was completed and male and female were distinct, individual creations. See John D. Garr, *Feminine by Design: God-Fashioned Woman* (Atlanta: Golden Key Press, 2010).

[65] *Tyndale Bible Dictionary*, ed. Walter A. Elwell, Philip W. Comfort (Carol Stream, IL: Tyndale House Publishers, 2001), p. 850.

[66] *Nekeb* comes from the verbal form נָקַב (*nakab*) which means "to bore through" or to "perforate."

openly worshipped in some cultures today.[67] Amazingly, pagan cultures believed that they were to worship the phallic and the vaginal images and to engage in indiscriminate acts of sexual intercourse in order to incite erotic passions in the gods (the stars and planets) so that the gods themselves would engage in intercourse and thereby cause the earth to be fruitful and produce vegetation for food. This worldview and mindset took views of human gender and sexuality to the opposite extreme from the platonically and Gnostically influenced Christian view. The prohibitions of Scripture against idolatry certainly included commands designed to keep God's people from such perverse excesses as these.

Paul Evdokimov maintained that the phrase *male and female he created them* implies that "these two aspects of man are inseparable, to such a degree that a male or female human being taken separately and viewed *in se* is not a perfect human being."[68] The differentiated natures of men and women are, therefore, "indispensable to one another because they share in human nature only as they share in one another."[69] This position parallels traditional Jewish understanding that places emphasis on the importance of marriage as the act of bringing two incomplete parts of humanity together into one complete superentity. Rabbi Eliezer declared, "An unmarried man is not a complete man,"[70] and he said, "A woman is an unfinished vessel until she marries,"[71] while the *Zohar* affirms that "he who has not married a woman . . . remains but half a person."[72] Reuven Bulka, therefore, concludes that in Judaism "anyone who is unmarried is a deficient person, an incomplete being."[73] Michael Kaufman suggests that "in the single, defective state, a person possesses only the potential for attaining completion and for giving completion to another."[74] These positions illustrate an important truth that is underscored by the fact that humanity was cre-

[67] See Ellen Quejada, *Phallic Worship in Japan* (Toronto: University of Toronto, 1998) and Karen A. Smyers, *The Fox and the Jewel" Shared and Private Meanings in Contemporary Japanese Inari Worship* (Hololulu: University of Hawaii Press, 1999), pp. 134, 146.
[68] Paul Evdokimov, *Women and the Salvation of the World,* tr. Anthony P. Gythiel (New York: St. Vladimir's Seminary Press, 1994), p. 139.
[69] Alistair Iain McFadyen, *The Call to Personhood: A Christian Theory of the Individual in Social Relationships* (Cambridge: Cambridge University Press, 1990), p. 34.
[70] Talmud, *Yebam.* 63a; *Genesis Rabbah* 68:4.
[71] Talmud, *Sanhedrin* 22b.
[72] *Zohar, Kedoshim* 24.
[73] Reuven P. Bulka, *Jewish Marriage: A Halakhic Ethic* (New York: KTAV Publishing House, 1986), p. 3.
[74] Michael Kaufman, *Love, Marriage, and Family in Jewish Law and Tradition* (Northvale, NJ: Jason Aronson, Inc., 1992), p. 7.

ated in the beginning as male and female and that both male and female are, therefore, necessary for the image and likeness of God to be fully manifest.

This understanding should not suggest, however, that an individual, unmarried human being is not wholly and fully human or that he or she individually does not reflect God's image. The divine image is manifest in every human being without regard to gender, ethnicity, nationality, race, or marital status. Both male and female genders, therefore, equally reflect God's image. At the same time, however, both men and women should be perceived "as essential, even indispensable to one another."[75] Individuals should seek the fellowship of both male and female in community, and the highest expression of the image of God should be recognized in the marriage of one man and one woman. God himself designed humanity to be dual gendered so that they would seek the companionship and complementarity of the other half of humanity, join together, and thereby reflect the image of God's supra-relationality. The conjoining of female and male into "one flesh" produced the high level of relationality that was manifest in a oneness and unity that paralleled and mirrored the oneness of God himself. Human two-in-oneness mirrored divine three-in-oneness, thereby fulfilling God's original intention in the creation of humanity: that male and female together might be the image and likeness of God in his creation.

The dualistic thinking of the Greek and Latin church fathers projected the female body in such a light that some had difficulty believing that women were even made in God's image.[76] Almost all of them believed that feminine anatomy projected weakness, seduction, susceptibility to temptation, and even sin itself. In this theology, man was a higher, spiritual form while woman was a lower, sensual form. Harking back to the Greek philosophers, church leaders viewed men

---

[75] Kaufman, p. 8.

[76] Church canon law even said: "Woman was not created in God's image. . . . Therefore it is proper that the man be lord and master over the woman. . . . The law commands that the woman be subject to the man and be his servant." See Lily Braun and Alfred G. Meyer, *Selected Writings on Feminism and Socialism* (Bloomington, IN: Indiana University Press, 1987), p. 143. The argument of the patristics seemed to be that woman as woman was not created in God's image but woman as human being did bear God's image. Fourth-century writer Ambrosiaster perhaps summed up this idea when he maintained that women were not created in God's image because the *imago Dei* in the male's being was the source of all other human beings. See Robert Austin Markus, William E. Klingshirn, Mark Vessey, *The Limits of Ancient Christianity: Easays on Late Antique Thought and Culture* (Ann Arbor, MI: University of Michigan Press, 1999), p. 145. Others took this argument to extreme, even wondering if women actually had souls.

as rational creatures who were in control of their mental processes and emotions[77] while they considered women to be emotional creatures who were more often than not out of control and irrational.[78] Unfortunately, such thinking as this continued even into the modern era, with theologians like Søren Kierkegaard arguing that the female anatomical structure proves that "woman is more sensuous than man."[79] Kierkegaard even maintained that "the female body before the Fall was already precariously tilted, by its aesthetic and ethical functions, toward the Fall that will make her sensuousness sinful."[80]

The real problem with a virtually unending parade of ecclesiastical recriminations against women was not the libidinous, lubricious, or seductive nature of women: it was, and remains, the incontinence and lack of self-control in men! It also represents the continuing male propensity that originated in the Garden of Eden to blame the woman for his own failures: "The woman whom you gave to be with me—she gave me fruit from the tree, and I ate it."[81] From that moment forward, the same blame game has continued with men in various societies and religions blaming women for their own incontinence and to this day demanding that women dress in such a way as to obliterate or obscure the visual image of their self-identity as a creation in the image and likeness of God. The female body is not "tilted precariously toward sin,"[82] nor is woman "the devil's gateway."[83] The female anatomy was designed by God and was delicately fashioned, not to be an instrument of temptation or sin, but to reflect the divine image and likeness and to make possible the highest and most intimate reflection of the oneness of divine being.

The writers of Scripture had none of the later Christian misgivings

---

[77] This was the reason for Augustine's view that the erotic nature of sexual intercourse was "original sin." His realization that the tumescence of the penis could not be controlled by the rational male mind when a man was in the presence of exposed parts of the female anatomy (or was seized upon with thoughts about eroticism or intercourse) caused Augustine to conclude that the inability of the rational male mind to exercise control over the erection of the penis was evidence of sin and must have been either the cause of or the result of what he termed "original sin."

[78] This is confirmed in the Greek language where the word for womb is *hystera*, the root of the word *hysteria*. The womb, therefore, is the reason for perceived female irrationality! Until the middle of the twentieth century, hysteria was believed by medical professionals to be an exclusively female malady.

[79] Søren Kierkegaard, *The Concept of Anxiety*, ed. and tr. Reidar Thompte with Albert B. Anderson (Princeton: Princeton University Press, 1980), p. 66.

[80] Kierkegaard, p. 66.

[81] Genesis 3:12.

[82] Kierkegaard, p. 66.

[83] Tertullian, *On the Apparel of Women*, I.1.1.

and embarrassment about human sexuality. Indeed, one entire book in the canon of Hebrew Scripture, the Song of Songs,[84] is devoted to human love depicted with vividly erotic and sexual imagery. Many sages of Israel and virtually all Christian church fathers were embarrassed by this fact and saw only allegorical value in the Song of Songs. Some of the sages questioned whether the Song of Songs should be included in the canon of Scripture, with Rabbi Judah arguing that even handling the book rendered one's hands unclean. In response to this charge, Rabbi Akiva was prompted to call this book the "Holy of Holies" of Holy Scripture.[85]

Richard Davidson argues that just as in the account of Genesis, so in the Song of Songs, "the sexual experience within marriage is not linked with the utilitarian intent to propagate children. Lovemaking for the sake of (married) love . . . is the message of the Song." On the basis of the Hebrew text of Song of Songs 8:6, Davidson rightly calls human sexuality the "flame of Yahweh,"[86] underscoring the fact that it was a divine creation. The truth is that the Song of Songs celebrates unashamedly the erotic relationship of a married couple—probably Solomon and the Shulamite—as a paradigm for face-to-face, full and free expression of human sexuality within the context of marriage wherein husband and wife should rightly be as Adam and Eve in the beginning: naked and unashamed. Every expression of human emotion and erotic impulse and every act of physical intimacy are "good and very good," a fulfillment of the divine design for the entire human being, spirit and body, female and male, to reflect the image and likeness of God. Nothing about the human experience of physical or emotional pleasure is evil—or even tends toward evil—when it is enjoyed within the parameters of God's instructions.

Alistair McFadyen is correct in declaring that "whilst the status of sexuality ought not to be overemphasized, it also ought not to be

---

[84] Song of Songs is the literal title for the book from the Hebrew *Shir ha-Shirim*. It has been called Song of Solomon, Solomon's Song of Songs, and Canticles in various translations of Scripture.

[85] Rabbi Akiva, *Mishnah, Yadayim* 3:5. Akiva said, "For all the Scriptures are holy, but the Song of Songs is the holy of holies." Akiva and other sages considered the Song of Songs the "holy of holies" because they interpreted it allegorically as a demonstration of the relationship between God and Israel. As a matter of fact, Akiva said, "He who trills his voice in the chanting of the Song of Songs in the banquet-halls and makes it a secular song has no share in the world to come." Most church fathers followed in this same perspective because of their aversion to sexuality.

[86] Richard M. Davidson, *The Flame of Yahweh: Sexuality in the Old Testament* (Peabody, MA: Hendrickson Publishers, 2007), p. 605.

isolated out from male-female (and, indeed, all human) relation."[87] Indeed, "male and female community is not a mystical union of disembodied subjectivities but a shared bodiliness"[88] that is "the cement of the highest of human relationship, marriage between man and woman."[89] The truth is that God himself very carefully designed the human anatomy, including genitalia, as a means of imaging something about the Divine—in this case, the profoundly intimate interrelationality that exists within God: Father, Son, and Spirit. Helen Oppenheimer rightly observes that "the human 'one-flesh' union, therefore, has far transcended its mere biological function."[90] As Davidson notes, the narratives of human creation concluded with "the divine approbation upon uninhibited sensuous—yes, erotic—sexuality," noting that "Adam and Eve stand before each other, naked and unashamed."[91] It is the unity of two humans, male and female, into one superentity that most fully images the oneness of God. As long as husband and wife remain faithful in covenant, neither their shared private nudity nor the erotic nature of their sexuality is either shameful to them or offensive to God. Indeed, both are holy, designed by God to be a means by which they celebrate the image and likeness of God.

McFadyen has also zeroed in on the real reason for God's creation of gender and sexuality in humanity to reflect his own image: "Using sexual differentiation as a paradigm for humanity points to the fact that what is intended by existence in God's image is not only distinction (individual or communal discreteness) but [also] relation."[92] It is for this very reason that God created humans *male* and *female* "in sexual encounter rather than simple opposition."[93] Adam and Eve were not solely polar opposites confronting or complementing one another; they were "one flesh," a union that paralleled and mirrored the *echad* (oneness) of God. Indeed, the creation narratives "affirm that it is only through this encounter, through the *and* which unites the different, that life may be called human, an image of God."[94] As Sherwin Bailey notes, "The 'adam' is not a single human individual,

---

[87] McFadyen, p. 36.
[88] McFadyen, p. 36.
[89] Helen Oppenheimer, *Marriage (Ethics: Our Choices)* (London: Continuum International Publishing, 1990), p. 13.
[90] Oppenheimer, "Ethics and the Personal Life," p. 749.
[91] Davidson, p. 51.
[92] McFadyen, p. 32.
[93] McFadyen, p. 32.
[94] McFadyen, p. 32.

but a mysterious sexual duality of which man and woman are the relational poles" wherein is manifest "the clue to the meaning of human sexuality."[95] McFadyen concludes that "Adam and Eve's mutual acceptance, as the conjoining of distance and relation, symbolizes the basis for all human life in God's image."[96]

It is also important to establish the fact that God's creation of gendered and sexually differentiated humanity was not solely for the purpose of reproduction. This is confirmed by the fact that the second of the human creation narratives, while explicating the first, has no reference to or connection with the divine imperative to "be fruitful and multiply." David Carr argues that the separating of one humanity into two gendered beings was focused on "an intimacy grounded in the bodily joining of two embodied creatures whom God has so carefully made for shared work as equals."[97] It is because of the primordial need for relational intimacy that "men and women are forever drawn toward each other by their sense of incompleteness and the primal magnetic power of their original bodily connection to each other."[98] This includes the spiritual as well as biological connection of human intimacy. Male and female are drawn to one another not just by simple hormonal attractions but also by the spiritual need to return to the wholeness and oneness of original humanity.

Phyllis Trible has concluded, therefore, that "humans were created for erotic connection with one another, a connection without any focus on having children."[99] It is clear that "this convergence of opposites is a consummation of union" in which "no procreative purpose characterizes this sexual union, [for] children are not mentioned."[100] The truth of this statement is confirmed by the fact that not every part of the female reproductive anatomy is purely utilitarian, designed solely for reproduction. The clitoris has no reproductive function whatsoever and serves the sole purpose of providing pleasure for the woman, heightening the intensity of the physical and spiritual unity that the biological pair experiences in intercourse. And, it is equally true of female and male: erotic sexual pleasure is just as powerful and

---

[95] D. Sherwin Bailey, *Sexual Relations in Christian Thought* (New York: Harper & Row, 1959), p. 267.
[96] McFadyen, p. 34.
[97] David Carr, *The Erotic Word* (New York: Oxford University Press, 2005), p. 32.
[98] Carr, p. 32.
[99] Carr, p. 33.
[100] Phillis Trible, *God and the Rhetoric of Sexuality: Overtures to Biblical Theology* (Philadelphia: Fortress Press, 1978), p. 104.

proper for women as it is for men.[101] Indeed, the woman's glans clitoris has twice the number of sensory nerve endings as the man's glans penis; therefore, the female orgasm may be even more intense than that of the male. Likewise, the clitoris is equal in size, sensitivity, and function with the penis. Because the vast majority of the clitoris is internal to the female anatomy with only its tip visible to external observation, women have been considered anatomically deficient by physicians and psychologists of the past and—worst of all—by themselves.[102]

Both clitoris and penis develop from the same tissue in the human embryo, depending upon the presence or absence of a Y (male) chromosome in the blastocyst, the fertilized ovum,[103] that divides into the multicelled zygote which then becomes an embryo and finally a fetus.[104] This anatomical understanding alone utterly debunks the myth that women are somehow deformed males, and it frees women from any religious or societal implications that they should somehow be

[101] While orgasm may differ in intensity from individual to individual, on the whole it produces equal pleasure in both female and male.

[102] Modern anatomical studies have eliminated all factual basis for the fixation of Freudian psychologists on "penis envy" as a major psychological problem for prepubescent, pubescent, adolescent, and adult females. Freud himself considered the realization of a young female that she has no penis to be a defining moment in her psychosexual development. Likewise males have no reason to fear Freudian "castration anxiety," thinking that females are somehow castrated males. Amazingly, God has made male and female equal even in their sexual organs—and perhaps especially so.

[103] From the moment of conception, every human embryo is both male and female, with both the Wolffian (male) and Muellarian (female) ducts that contain the germ cells for the reproductive systems. Soon after conception, the blastocyst of both sexes deactivates one X chromosome, leaving either an X (if the embryo is to be female) or a Y (if the embryo is to be male). Until the sixth week of gestation, the embryo continues to follow an ambiguous pattern for sexual organ development, including the gonadal tissues that will become either ovaries or testes, the connective tissues that will become either fallopian tubes or vas deferens, and the external tissue that will become either the labia majora and minora of the vagina or the scrotum, depending on whether the embryo is genetically female or male. (The uterus is the only anatomical part in the female that has no correspondence in the male.) During the embryo's sixth week, if a Y chromosome is present, the synthesis of testosterone begins, initiating the process of male sexual differentiation with the formation of testes, vas deferens, scrotum, penis, and glans penis, while disabling the female sexual features. If an X chromosome is present, the pattern of female development continues with the formation of ovaries, fallopian tubes, uterus, vagina, and clitoris, including the glans clitoris and the disabling of male sexual features. Nonetheless, the external genitalia remain identical for both sexes until the eighth week of gestation. For details see Jean Bertrand and Raphael Rappaport, *Pediatric Endocrinology: Physiology, Pathophysiology, and Clinical Aspects*, ed. Pierre C. Sizonenko (Baltimore, MD: Williams & Wilkins, 1993), pp. 88-99. Also Anne Moir and David Jessel, *Brain Sex: The Real Difference Between Men & Women* (New York: Random House, 1989), pp. 21-29. Also John D. Garr, *Feminine by Design: God's Plan for Women* (Atlanta: Golden Key Press, 2011).

[104] The blastocyst is the fertilized ovum that contains half of the DNA from each of the two parents. When it divides by mitosis to produce a multicellular organism, it becomes a zygote, which, in turn, develops into an embryo, a recognizable, though rudimentarily functioning body. The embryo becomes a fetus around the eighth week of gestation with final gender differentiation.

totally incapable of experiencing sexual pleasure or at least that they should be unwilling to engage in intercourse "with concupiscence."[105] Though many Christian theologians in history have argued that godly women should be essentially asexual, the truth is that God designed all women with the functionality and the capacity for complete sexual satisfaction and fulfillment. As Gary Thomas has noted, "Sex feels good because God designed it so."[106] This conforms to the biblical perspective that God created nothing that was evil in itself but made everything in creation inherently "good." God expects humans to enjoy what he has created for their pleasure within the parameters which he established for its enjoyment. As one of Israel's sages declared, "He who sees a legitimate pleasure and does not avail himself of it is an ingrate against God who made it possible."[107]

James Phillips has pointed out that the apostle Paul[108] strongly and unequivocally "depicts a completely *co-equal* and *complementary* pattern of sexual relationship as *given by God.*"[109] Indeed, it is clear that Paul "feels constrained to remind his readers that . . . there is co-equality and *fully reciprocal interdependence* between male and female."[110] As a matter of fact, Paul strongly advocated male and female equality even in the most intimate of human experience, sexual intercourse: "The husband should give his wife her conjugal rights, and likewise the wife to her husband, for the wife does not have authority over her own body, but the husband does; likewise the husband does not have authority over his own body, but the wife does." He then issued this command: "Stop depriving one another [of sexual intercourse]."[111] Because God himself noted that humans were created

---

[105] This was the term for the erotic nature of sexual intercourse that Augustine, Thomas Aquinas, and other Christian theologians used because they believed erotic pleasure to be sinful *in se*. Even looking upon the body of a marital partner with "concupiscence" was considered sin because it was equated with idolatry, worshipping something beside God. For Augustine, "concupiscence" in intercourse was the means of the transmission of "original sin" from generation to generation. See Raymond J. Devettere, *Practical Decision Making in Health Care Ethics: Cases and Concepts* (Washington, DC: Georgetown University Press, 2010), p. 235.

[106] Gary Thomas, *Sacred Marriage: What if God Designed Marriage to Make Us Holy More than to Make Us Happy?* (Grand Rapids, MI: Zondervan Publishing House, 2000), p. 207.

[107] *Gemara Nazir* 19A. See Milton Steinberg's translation in *Basic Judaism* (New York: Harcourt, Brace, and World, Inc., 1947), p. 62.

[108] 1 Corinthians 7:3-4.

[109] James H. Phillips, "The Future of Monogamous Marriage from a Christian Perspective," *The Duke Divinity School Review,* 43:1, (Winter, 1978), p. 82, emphasis in original.

[110] Phillips, p. 82, emphasis in original.

[111] 1 Corinthians 7:3-5. Various translations have attempted to euphemize Paul's clear intent by rendering "The husband should give his wife her conjugal rights" as "Let the husband render unto his wife due benevolence" and "Stop depriving one another" as "Defraud ye not one another" (KJV).

in his image and likeness "male and female," it is essential that gender and sexuality be recognized as significant aspects of God's image in humans and that they not be deprecated, condemned, or limited by misguided unctuous prudery.

In declaring that "man is joined to [literally, "glued to"] his wife" so that they "become one flesh,"[112] the Genesis narrative implies sexual eroticism; however, the "climactic outcome of the text is the embodied relationship between these humans."[113] In Carr's view, this is the "superlative example of human interconnectedness" in which "erotic intimacy is the ultimate solution" to God's observation that "it is not good that the human be alone."[114] This is why the very first expression of joy in the biblical account was that of the first man when he recognized the consubstantiality and coequality of the partner whom God had created for him and exclaimed, "This, at last, is bone of my bone and flesh of my flesh!"[115]

Since God is genderless, humanity's gender can reflect the divine image only by confirming the essence of God as the perfect love that God shared with humanity and is manifest in human interpersonal relationality and intimacy. God designed humans to reflect the relationality that exists within his own being to manifest the image of the One who himself is a community of diversity. He designed two equal and complementary genders for humanity as the means by which the highest demonstration of love in relationship could and should be manifest. As God observed in his statement of intention for creating humanity, the divine image and likeness are fully manifest only when male and female are equally present and when ultimately they share the divine *echad* in the intimacy of biblically defined marriage.

SPRINGBOARD FOR DISCUSSION

1. Discuss God's commandment to Israel: "You shall have no other gods before me. You shall not make for yourself an idol or any likeness. . . . You shall not bow down to worship them." How is the prohibition against material images essential to the command to wor-

---

[112] Genesis 2:24. Various English translations render this statement, "cleave," "be joined to," "be united to," "cling to," "hold fast to," "unite with." The Hebrew word *dabak*, however, means to "cling" in the sense of being "glued to."

[113] Carr, p. 33.

[114] Carr, p. 33.

[115] All other options from the animal kingdom were not bone of his bone and flesh of his flesh and, therefore, were not coequal and suitable as a partner for the human being.

ship God only? How did this impact the understanding of the Hebrew peoples about God? What was the difference between the Hebrew perspective and that of surrounding cultures?

2. Consider Greek philosophy's emphasis on the utter incorporeality of God. How did the concept of divine incorporeality impact Greek thinking about the transcendence and impassibility of God? What impact did this thinking have on the theology and anthropology of both Christianity and Judaism?

3. Evaluate the way in which the people of Scripture envisioned God. Can their corporeal imagery be discounted as superstition or lack of sophistication in their evaluation of God? Were these myths or the uncontrolled vivid imaginations of men and women? Why do you think that God appeared in the form of a man (or an angel)?

4. Discuss the implications of the scriptural descriptions of God's manifestation in human imagery. Do these events give the impression that God has some kind of form? Does the fact that God is Spirit mean that God has no substance?

5. Analyze the immediate connection in Scripture of the "image and likeness" of God and "male and female." How does the gendered nature of human beings reflect truth about God's image and likeness?

6. Evaluate the language of Scripture in identifying femininity and masculinity with genitalia. Why is Scripture not ashamed to discuss in specific terms what God was not ashamed to create? Do you think that sexuality is a part of God's creation that was "very good"?

7. Consider the importance of physical gendered relationship as the perfect reflection of the image and likeness of God who is a being of utter relationality in love. How does physical intimacy reflect the spiritual intimacy of marriage?

8. Confirm the physical, emotional, and spiritual unity of male and female as a reflection of the image of the oneness of God. How do equality and mutuality contribute to unity in marriage?

9. Discuss the importance of maintaining the integrity of God's creation of human beings as both physical and spiritual creatures. What are the dangers of Greek dualism and the benefits of Hebraic holism in relation to a balanced view of human existence?

CHAPTER 14

THE FULLNESS OF GOD'S IMAGE IN HUMANITY

RELATIONAL DIMENSIONS

The ultimate expression of the *imago Dei* in humanity is manifest in the human relationality that mirrors the core and essence of divine being. Relationship was the fundamental reason for the creation of humanity in the first place. God did not decide to create the universe and human beings because he had nothing better to do with his time. Human creation was by divine design. From the very first inclination of divine thought expended upon the idea of human creation, God purposed to make humans "in his own image and likeness." It should come as no surprise, therefore, that the beings who image God should reflect the essence of his being in their personal interaction with the Divine and in their personal interaction with one another.

RELATIONSHIP WITH GOD

Understanding God's image in humanity begins with recognizing the relationality that exists within the very being of God. The three persons—Father, Son, and Holy Spirit—dwell together in one being of substance in the supreme manifestation of interrelatedness. They are "a tripersonal community in which each member of the triune being gives and receives love from the others."[1] Love, along with the relationality that it demands, is not merely an attribute of God. The

---

[1] John E. Sanders, *The God Who Risks: A Theology of Divine Providence* (Downers Grove, IL: InterVarsity Press, 2007), p. 175.

Apostle John unequivocally declared that "God is love." Love, therefore, is the essence or at the very core of God's being.[2] Relationality is essential to God in the mutuality expressed among the three divine persons in the one divine being. The unity of God demonstrates the fact that "personhood, relationality, and community—not power, independence and control—become the center for understanding the nature of God."[3] Since the purest love was manifest fully in eternity past within the Godhead, creation was a free act of God, not out of any necessity, but as an expression of the self-contained love of the Divine. John Sanders succinctly observes that it was in loving freedom that the "triune God decide[d] to create creatures with whom to share this agape love."[4] God, as three-in-one, "is a family, and thus man in God's image must be made a family as well,"[5] a social construct in which each human being shares love and relationship with God and with others, thereby manifesting the likeness of God in the earth.

From a slightly different perspective, Jürgen Moltmann argued that when Scripture describes God as love, it "is not concerned with defining the nature of God; rather, it tells of God's actions," making a "summation of the countless stories and experiences of God's loving action."[6] The God who is perfect love, therefore, created beings on whom he could lavish his love—beings who, at the same time, could reciprocate that love in freely given relationship, thereby completing the love continuum. It is for this reason that "the ability to know and love God must stand forth prominently in any attempt to ascertain precisely what the image of God is."[7] It is clear from Scripture that a significant part of God's image in humanity is the human capacity—yea, longing and even passion—for relationship with the Divine.

This is why "the biblical theme of creation is not ultimately concerned with cosmogony or cosmology but with the relationship between God and God's creatures."[8] This truth becomes clear when one

---

[2] 1 John 4:8.
[3] Sanders, p. 168.
[4] Sanders, p. 176.
[5] See David Kyle Foster, *The Divine Marriage: God's Purpose and Design for Human Sexuality* (Franklin, TN: Mastering Life Publications).
[6] Hermann Häring, "From Divine Human to Human God," in *The Human Image of God*, ed. Hans-Georg Ziebertz, Friedrich Schweitzer, Hermann Häring, and Don Browning (Boston: Brill, 2001), p. 9.
[7] Roy B. Zuck, *Vital Theological Issues: Examining Enduring Issues of Theology* (Grand Rapids, MI: Kregel Publications, 1994), p. 60.
[8] Alistair I. McFadyen, *Personhood: A Christian Theory of the Individual in Social Relationships* (Cambridge: Cambridge University Press, 1990), p. 18.

considers that of the 79,976 words in the Torah, less than 1,000 deal with creation.[9] It is safe to say, then, that God has focused much more attention on revealing himself as the God who is in relationship with his people than on being viewed as the God who is the creator of the universe. God is understood in biblical terms more as the "covenant God" than as the "creator God." All humans—including philosophers and theologians—would do well to imitate divine priorities by focusing on relationship with God and, by extension, with fellow human beings instead of being fixated on cosmogony and cosmology and vain attempts to define God in metaphysical and non-relational terms.

Personal interaction with God is, therefore, the core of Hebraic thought. The God of Scripture simply is the God of relationship. As Kierkegaard said, "God is not an idea that one proves, but a being in relation to whom one lives."[10] God created human beings for the purpose of relating to them. "Whereas the main motif of the Neoplatonic God concept is that of distance and unrelatedness," the biblical understanding is that "to be God is to be related in love."[11] Having learned from God's own self-disclosure that he desired people who would "worship him in spiritual truth,"[12] the Hebrews intuitively sought relationship with God by walking with him[13] and by communicating with him in prayer.[14] God reciprocated by engaging in conversation,[15] disclosing his Word,[16] thereby revealing himself so that humans could understand God. He also filled humans with his Spirit so that they could experience God.[17] In his "pre-eternal counsel," God decided "to deposit the *logos* in man, so that man in his very structure would

---

[9] Of the 187 chapters in the Torah (Pentateuch), only the first three deal specifically with creation.

[10] Søren Kierkegaard, *Kierkegaard's Concluding Unscientific Postscript,* tr. David F. Swenson (Princeton: Princeton University Press, 1941), p. 485.

[11] Sanders, p. 177.

[12] John 4:23. The phrase *Spirit and truth* is a hendiadys in Greek, in which the words stand in apposition to one another so that they can rightly be translated "the Spirit which is truth," or simply, "spiritual truth."

[13] Before there was any exercise of religion, including Judaism and Christianity, patriarchs and prophets simply "walked with God." See Genesis 5:22; 6:9. While later generations walked in God's ways (*halakhah*), Adam, Eve, Enoch, and Noah simply "walked with God," indicative of the interpersonal relationship that they had with their creator, one of immediacy, intensity, and intimacy.

[14] The Hebrew word for prayer is תְּפִלָּה (*tephillah*), which comes from the word פָּלַל (*pallal*), which in the *piel* means to judge. From this fact, the Jewish understanding of prayer is that of standing in God's presence and willingly receiving his judgment.

[15] Genesis 18:23-32.

[16] 1 Samuel 3:21; 1 Kings 6:11; Isaiah 38:4; Jeremiah 24:4; Ezekiel 1:3; Hosea 1:1; Joel 1:1; Haggai 2:20; Zechariah 4:8.

[17] Exodus 31:3; Micah 3:8; Luke 1:15.

have access to the riddle of theology,"[18] a means of understanding and experiencing God in genuine interrelationship. The God of Scripture is, quite simply, a God of relationship, and his relationality is mirrored in the human creation as the focus of the God image and likeness.

God specifically chose to image his own relationality in the human creation, and he said so very clearly: "In the image of God created he him, male and female created he them." Divine relatedness that was first manifest within God—in which Father, Son, and Holy Spirit interrelate in total equality and mutuality and in utter mutual interpenetration—was imaged by this relational God in the human creation. Hendrikus Berkhof was correct when he noted that "the structure of the Trinity describes precisely the fellowship with man, for which God emerges out of himself."[19] He warned that "we may not let ourselves be held back from [that intention] by a tradition, imposing though it may be, which is artificial in its abstractness [and] dangerous to faith."[20] Recognizing the interpersonal relationship within God makes it possible to understand how God's relational nature is mirrored in the human capacity for relationship, first with God and then with other human beings. It also confirms that the community of faith, as designed by God, must reflect to the greatest degree possible the very unity of God.[21] No wonder David exclaimed, "How good and pleasant it is for brothers to dwell together in unity."[22] The pleasant unity of community is the oneness of the *echad* that mirrors the *echad* of the Divine.

In God's design for women and men, the tyranny of the one is ruled out in favor of the blessing of the two and, beyond the two, the blessing of the community. The "not good" of the one[23] is replaced by the "very good" of the two[24] and the many. Absolute singularity is "not good" either for God or for human beings. The God who is three-in-one created humanity as two-in-one. God's observation that his creation was "very good" was not made until after both male and

---

[18] Paul Evdokimov, *Woman and the Salvation of the World,* tr. Anthony P. Gythiel (Crestwood, NY: St. Vladimir's Seminary Press, 1994), p. 32.
[19] Hendrikus Berkhof, *Christian Faith: An Introduction to the Study of Faith* (Grand Rapids, MI: Wm. B. Eerdmans Publishing, 1979), p. 337.
[20] Berkhof, p. 337.
[21] John 17:11.
[22] Psalm 133:1.
[23] Genesis 2:18. The first thing that God observed about his creation that was "not good" was the fact that the human he had created was alone.
[24] Genesis 1:31.

female had been manifest.[25] All of the blessings of relationality are the direct result of humanity's creation in the image and likeness of God. Humans were designed for fellowship and relationship so that they will be complete first by strong relationship with God and then by healthy relationships with one another which parallel the eternal relationality of the Divine. Both male and female equally manifest the image of God in that they share equal access to and relationship with the God who created them, and they share the mutuality of true relationship with one another in marriage and in community.

RELATIONSHIP WITH HUMANS

The image and likeness of God is most fully manifest in human beings by their natural compulsion to participate in relationships, to be interconnected with other human beings. By design, humanity is a gregarious creation. This human drive for interconnective relationship mirrors the interrelational nature of the creator. In the limitless expanses of timeless eternity, God was ever a community of perfect love and infinite relationality; however, he was not content to dwell in isolation but created the angelic hosts of heaven. When this purely relational God determined to create beings in his image and likeness, then, it was unavoidable that he would produce another community of love. God knew from his own essence that it would not be good for humanity to be alone, so when he created humanity, he created community. Human relationality, therefore, is entirely dependent upon and derived from divine relationality.

It should come as no surprise that the smallest recognized social unit in biblical times was not the individual, but the "family, which was set in the context of community."[26] For the Hebraic peoples, self-identity was relational, for "corporate existence was the fundamental grounding of life."[27] Their personal identity was irreducibly tied to their families, then to their extended families, their clans, and their kindred people. Ultimately, the "family" in biblical times was understood to include the entire nation of Israel. Through history into the present, the Jewish idea of "family" ultimately includes all the Jewish

---

[25] The term *very good* was used for the first and only time in creation when undifferentiated humanity was surgically separated into male and female who were then brought together again in "one flesh." This was the final act of the last of the six days of creation.

[26] Carol Meyers, *Discovering Eve: Ancient Israelite Women in Context* (Oxford: Oxford University Press, 1991), p. 123.

[27] Meyers, p. 123.

people. This fact, says Carol Meyers, "is one crucial area of distinction between the biblical mind set and our own."[28] The modern perspective focuses on "the individual, on autonomous development and self-fulfillment,"[29] but as Johannes Pederson notes, "life is not something individual, to be shaped according to the needs of each individual. Man is only what he is as a link in the family."[30] It is for this reason that "when we look at the soul, we always see a community rising behind it. . . . The family forms the narrowest community in which [the soul] lives."[31] Each soul, therefore, "must live in community, because it is its nature to communicate itself to others, to share blessing with them."[32]

When God said, "Let us make," he made a clear declaration about community—the divine community. When Scripture said, "Male and female created he them," it announced the existence of community—the human community. It is clear, therefore, that the foundation for understanding the image of God as a social construct "lies in the creation narratives. . . . God creates the first human pair in order that humans might enjoy fellowship with each other."[33] Noreen Herzfeld states the truth: "Human beings were not alone but were created male and female, in fellowship with one another and with God."[34] About this divine action, Sherwin Bailey has made this judicious summary: "On the finite plane, the image or reflection of God is found to be essentially a 'being-in-relation'—just as true human existence is essentially 'existence-in-community.'"[35] Helen Oppenheimer has also observed that even though "the meaning of 'relationship' is elusive, sliding from geometry to sociology, its slipperiness can be put to use, with caution, to illuminate what persons are."[36] In the final analysis, "the image of God is a community concept. It refers to human beings

---

[28] Meyers, p. 124.
[29] Meyers, p. 124.
[30] Johannes Pederson, *Israel: Its Life and Culture* (Oxford: Oxford University Press, 1926), p. 259.
[31] Pederson, p. 263.
[32] Pederson, p. 263.
[33] Stanley J. Grenz, John R. Franke, *Beyond Foundationalism: Shaping Theology in a Postmodern Context* (Louisville, KY: Westminster John Knox Press, 2001), p. 200.
[34] Noreen L. Herzfeld, *In Our Image: Artificial Intelligence and the Human Spirit* (Minneapolis: Augsburg Fortress Press, 2004), pp. 26-27.
[35] D. Sherwin Bailey, *Sexual Relations in Christian Thought* (New York: Harper & Row, 1959), p. 267.
[36] Oppenheimer, *Incarnation and Immanence* (London: Hodder & Stoughton, 1973), pp. 71-73. Also Oppenheimer, "Ethics and The Personal Life" in *Companion Encyclopedia of Theology*, ed. Peter Byrne and James Leslie Houlden (London: Routledge, 1995), p. 750.

as beings-in-fellowship."[37] As human beings live in love—that is, as they give expression to true community—they reflect "the love which characterizes the divine essence."[38]

In God's act of creation, relationality was manifest both in God and in humanity. By God's design, "social relationship is an indispensable part of both human nature and human purpose, and there can be no utterly single human being."[39] The fundamental human need for relationship is well expressed in the German saying, *"ein Mensch ist kein Mensch"* ("one human is no human"), a formulation that "moves beyond the notion of sexual complementarity to the fundamental communal nature of human existence,"[40] as Phyllis Bird observed when she cited this German expression. In this same context, John Wesley said, "The gospel of Christ knows of no religion, but social; no holiness but social holiness."[41]

In the words of John Zizioulas, even God "has no ontological content, no true being, apart from communion."[42] It is communion, therefore, that "makes being 'be': nothing exists without it, not even God."[43] As beings-in-relation, humans can fully manifest the divine image and likeness and truly demonstrate "what God is like, for God is the community of love, the eternal relational dynamic enjoyed by the three persons of the Trinity"[44] who interrelate in perfect mutuality. While each human being individually reflects the image of God, the divine image in humanity reaches its zenith, its fullest expression—in relationships.

Human beings are not designed, nor were they ever intended, to "be alone." Like their creator, they function around a core of love that is the essence of their being. Just as God, within himself, is pure relationship, the perfect oneness of mutuality, the encircling and interpenetration of the three persons in the one divine Being, so human beings were designed by their creator to reflect the same divine nature

---

[37] Stanley J. Grenz, *The Social God and the Relational Self: A Trinitarian Theology in the Imago Dei Context* (Louisville, KY: Westminster John Knox Press, 2001), p. 180.

[38] Grenz, p. 180.

[39] Grenz, Franke, p. 200.

[40] Phyllis A. Bird, "Bone of My Bone and Flesh of My Flesh," in *Theology Today,* vol. 50, no. 4 (January, 1993), p. 524.

[41] John Wesley, *The Works of John Wesley,* Jackson Edition, "Preface to 1739 Hymns and Sacred Poems," 14:321.

[42] John D. Zizioulas, *Being as Communion: Studies in Personhood and the Church* (Crestwood, NY: St. Vladimir's Seminary Press, 1985), p. 16.

[43] Zizioulas, p. 17.

[44] Grenz, Franke, p. 200.

by participating in the fellowship of interactive interdependence and mutual submission that images the one who himself is Infinite Love.

Two-in-One: Perfecting God's Image in Humanity

The Genesis account of divine self-disclosure unequivocally confirms that humanity was created in God's image specifically as male and female; therefore, maleness and femaleness combined in community somehow must constitute the most complete manifestation of the divine image. The divine One, who exists eternally as three-in-one, created one undivided, sexually undifferentiated humanity with all the substance necessary for the formation of two individual human beings and, from the oneness of their union, all subsequent humankind. The two were essentially one superentity; therefore, humanity as two-in-one constituted the image of God. As Karl Barth observed, the relationship between the man and the woman has some correspondence to or was a copy of the interrelationship within the triune God that served as a prototype for human–human relations.

This is why the *Zohar*[45] declares, "Any image [of God] that does not embrace male and female is not the high and true image."[46] What God created in the Garden of Eden when he made the earthling that he called *ha-adam* as two-in-one, then separated them as male and female, and finally rejoined them together as "one flesh," constituted the divine institution of marriage. The conjoined male and female were designed to image their creator as a two-in-one superentity that mirrored the three-in-one divine being. The distinction and relationship of male and female, therefore, lies at the heart of the *imago Dei*.[47] Marriage is the most conspicuous and familiar example of unity-in-plurality that exists in human life; therefore, it is the best analogy to describe and understand the manifestation of divine immanence, the unity-in-plurality revealed as the three-in-one God.[48]

It was an utter impossibility that the God who is a community of three could have created a single male "in his image and likeness,"

---

[45] The *Zohar* was attributed to second-century rabbi Shimon bar Yochai; however, it was written and published in the thirteenth century in Spain by Moses de Leon. While it is a book of Jewish mysticism, it certainly draws from traditions of previous centuries of rabbinic thought.

[46] *Zohar: The Book of Enlightenment,* tr. Daniel Matt (New York: Paulist Press, 1983), p. 55.

[47] Barth, *Church Dogmatics* 3.1, p. 195.

[48] Peter Byrne and James Leslie Houlden, *Companion Encyclopedia of Theology* (London: Routledge, 1995), p. 751. Also Helen Oppenheimer, *Marriage, Divorce and the Church* (London: SPCK, 1971), pp. 165-180.

nor could he have created a lone female "in his image and likeness." Only humanity that was both male and female (two-in-one) could have reflected the image of divine being (three-in-one).[49] The image of God concept, then, supports this comparison "while allowing for unity, equality, and complementarity within the plurality of persons in the divine mode of existence as well as in human life."[50] In humanity's creation as male and female, relationship is also connected with both sameness and differentiation.[51]

The profound and mysterious degree of oneness in the marriage of the first man and the first woman was achieved because, in reality, even more than two persons were involved in the superentity of conjoined humanity: God himself was part of the equation. Two-in-one humanity was actually a three-in-one relationship. Maurice Lamm has outlined the Jewish perspective that a "newly married couple enters *kedushah*," a state of holiness that is "set above, elevated beyond their former status."[52] To this very day, Hebraic tradition, manifest in Jewish thought, understands that three persons—husband, wife, and God—are involved in every legitimate marriage, even in the act of coitus. As thirteenth-century Talmudist Nahmanides declared, "The union of man and woman, when it is right, is the secret of civilization. Through the act [of intercourse] they become partners with God in the act of creation."[53] This is the great mystery that prompted many of the sages to conclude that "when a man unites with his wife in holiness, the *Shekinah* is between them in the mystery of man and woman."[54] This *Shekinah* is the same presence experienced by Moses when God met with him face-to-face, and it was the same presence of God that dwelled on the mercy seat in the tabernacle's holy of holies.[55]

Because of this relationship, marriage is sacred in every aspect of its existence, including the spiritual, social, psychological, physical, and sexual dimensions of the relationship. This is why Nahmanides and other Jewish sages recommended that married couples should

---

[49] Aída Dina Spencer, *Beyond the Curse: Women Called to Ministry* (Nashville: Thomas Nelson, 1985), p. 21.

[50] Gilbert Bilezikian, *Beyond Sex Roles: What the Bible Says About a Woman's Place in Church and Family* (Grand Rapids, MI: Baker Book House, 1986), p. 253.

[51] Herzfeld, p. 26.

[52] Maurice Lamm, *The Jewish Way in Love and Marriage* (Middle Village, NY: Jonathan David Publishers, 1980), p. 37.

[53] Nahmanides, *Iggeret ha-Kodesh (The Holy Epistle)*.

[54] Nahmanides.

[55] Exodus 24.

regularly engage in sexual intercourse on the holiest day of the week, the Sabbath, in celebration of their faith and the holiness of their conjugal relationship.[56] The *Zohar* even declares that "where there is no union of male and female, people are not worthy to behold the Divine Presence."[57] The reason Moses de Leon could advocate this was his firm belief that everything God made—including the sexual organs, the pleasure of sexual touch, and the ecstasy of orgasm—is good because God created it and declared it to be good.[58] Philip Newell even suggests that "the holiness derives precisely from feeling the pleasure."[59] The conjunction of male and female and their being melded into one spiritual and physical superentity is an entrance into a state that elevates the couple to a higher status than they could ever have achieved as mere individuals.

In the Hebrew text, the term that describes the union of the first human couple was *echad* ("one"): "They shall be one [*echad*] flesh."[60] This is precisely the same word that expresses the oneness of God: "Hear, O Israel, the Lord our God, the Lord is one [*echad*]."[61] The use of the word *echad* to describe both the unity of God and of the first human couple is neither coincidental nor a textual anomaly, for God's Word is precise in its formulation and teaching.[62] The word *echad* is a clear indication from the mouth of God himself that his creation was, indeed, designed to manifest his own image. In this case, it mirrored the very oneness and utter uniqueness of God. Jesus emphatically declared that once the superentity is achieved by the covenant of marriage in which God is an active participant, "they are no longer two, but one flesh."[63] This is a mystery that reflects the supra-rationality of

---

[56] Gary Thomas, *Sacred Marriage: What if God Designed Marriage to Make Us Holy More than to Make Us Happy?* (Grand Rapids, MI: Zondervan Publishing House, 2000), pp. 205-206.

[57] *Zohar*, 3:59a.

[58] Genesis 1:21.

[59] J. Philip Newell, *Echo of the Soul: The Sacredness of the Human Body* (Harrisburg, PA: Morehouse Publishing, 2000), p. 88.

[60] Genesis 2:24. The Hebrew word *echad* means "compound unity," expressing the idea of unity in the midst of diversity.

[61] Deuteronomy 6:4.

[62] Much debate has sought to determine whether the inspiration of Scripture is verbal or plenary. While it is likely that both arguments have merit, it is clear that Jesus and the apostles considered the text to be inspired verbally. Jesus' argument that "God is a God of the living" (Matthew 22:32) was based on God's declaration that he was "the God of Abraham, and the God of Isaac, and the God of Jacob," not merely "the God of Abraham, Isaac, and Jacob" (Exodus 4:5). Consider also Paul's argument in Galatians 3:16 that God's promise to Abraham, "In Isaac shall thy seed be called" (Genesis 21:12), spoke of the Messiah and not just all of Abraham's progeny because, as the apostle noted, the word *seed (zera)* in the text is masculine singular absolute rather than plural.

[63] Matthew 19:6; Mark 10:8.

the divine mind and leaves human reason wondering, "How can two be one?" The answer is that husband and wife are one because of the creative power of the Word of God that declares them to be such. This answer is positioned on the same mystical level as the question, "How can three be one?" This question is answered in the classical Christian understanding of monotheism: the one God is three persons—Father, Son, and Holy Spirit.

Maurice Lamm has detailed the Jewish understanding of how the union of man and woman in marriage parallels and reveals classical Jewish monotheism.[64] "Since the close of the Bible, monogamy, the bond of one man and one woman, has come to reflect monotheism, the bond of one people and one God."[65] This oneness is clearly manifest in the Hebrew word *yichud*, which is used to describe the seclusion of a married couple in a private area in which their oneness is "based on *achdut ha-orie* (the oneness of the Creator)."[66] Lamm argues that "the theme of unity that is so prominent in Jewish mysticism and theology also underlies the structure of the Jewish family" for "*yichud* love assures that married life can continue to be imbued with a sense of the sacred."[67] Unlike *ahavah*, the common Hebrew word for love, "*yichud* connotes both complete, sustained love *and* the sex act within the framework of marriage."[68] For both Jews and Christians, then, the creation of *ha-adam* as one humanity, later separated by divine surgery, and finally made one again through the institution of marriage, images God in the earth as a significant, if not central, part of the *imago Dei*.

In the Christian understanding of the nature of Deity, three divine persons are incorporated into the one divine being of God by so mutually encircling and interpenetrating one another that they are virtually indistinguishable. What can be said of one person can be said equally of all three persons. Like soul and spirit in humanity, they can be discerned only by revelation from God's Word.[69] Similarly, in the eyes of God, Adam and Eve were "one flesh," one superentity that transcended the separateness of their material existence. Those who

---

[64] Jewish monotheism differs significantly from Christian monotheism in that it emphasizes the oneness of God to the exclusion of any plurality of person. Interestingly though, Jewish monotheism is seen as mirrored in the oneness of each married couple.

[65] Lamm, p. 21.

[66] Lamm, p. 21.

[67] Lamm, p. 21.

[68] Lamm, p. 19.

[69] Hebrews 4:12.

are mystically joined as husband and wife are virtually indistinguishable in the eyes of God, for they are one.[70] Humans view a married
couple and see two; God observes them and sees only one!

The highest qualities that pertain to God as three-in-one are imaged in humanity as two-in-one. Just as the three persons in God are
coequal, consubstantial, and coeternal, the two persons in the first human couple were coequal, consubstantial, and comortal. They shared
equally in every aspect of their existence. From the beginning, there
was nothing that could be said about the male that could not be said
about the female and vice versa. While they had distinguishing, yet
complementary characteristics, all of what both of them were was
necessary in order for one humanity to exist. If either had been absent,
the one humanity would not have been complete. The complementarity of the two, joined into one superentity, provided for equality and
mutuality that respected the individuality of both without demanding
that they be identical in every respect.

It would have been impossible for the human couple to have been
the "image and likeness of God" if they had not been absolutely coequal. The three persons in God have absolute, unqualified coequality.
If one were unequal or less than the other, he could not be God because God cannot be God and at the same time be inferior to God. If
one were subordinate to the other, the subordinated one could not be
God. Since all are God, they must of necessity be coequal. Likewise,
Adam and Eve were absolutely ontologically coequal. If Eve had been
ontologically inferior to Adam or had been divinely subordinated to
Adam, she would have been inherently less than human, like the animals that were subordinated to the human creation. Since both were
human, both were coequal.

Likewise, the coequality of the three persons in the one God is
contingent upon their consubstantiality, that they are of precisely the
same substance—in this case, the substance of spirit, not material being. Primordial humanity also imaged this quality of God by being
absolutely consubstantial. Both female and male participated in the
same essence and coexisted in the same substance. In effect, they were
one being. They were one in substance though different in aspect,[71]

---

[70] The absolute unity of man and woman in marriage does not obviate the fact that the individuality of both married partners is never violated and that they are individually judged by God for
their actions independent of one another.
[71] See *Collins English Dictionary* (Glasgow: HarperCollins Publishers, 2009).

which is the essence of consubstantiality whether of Deity or of humanity. This is why when God noted that it was not good for *ha-adam* to be alone and proposed to construct an equal power, a suitable companion, he did not again gather dust from the earth, form it, and vivify it as he had done with the original human creation. Instead, he extracted from the side of the human being that which pertained to the feminine and around that part of *ha-adam* built the perfect complement to the remaining male part of the original human being. This made it clear for all time that woman and man, female and male, are absolutely consubstantial. Even the first male was immediately able to discern the implications of this divine action: "At last, this is now bone of my bones and flesh of my flesh."[72] Since the first humans were consubstantial, they shared equally in the very essence of humanity.

The marriage of the first human couple—as well as that of all subsequent marital partners—also imaged the profound love that is the essence of the creator, a love that has forever been manifest and exchanged in the perfect harmony of the three persons in the one God. As Vigen Guroian has noted, "Husband and wife are joined together as *one* in holy matrimony. They are an ecclesial entity, one flesh, one body incorporate of two persons who in freedom and sexual love and through their relationship to Christ image the triune life of the Godhead."[73] In essence, the purest love that is manifest in human marriage is the closest approximation of the unfathomable love that is the very essence of God. The God who is love is imaged in humans who love.

The human creation was specifically envisioned and then brought to completion by God for the express purpose of manifesting his image and likeness in the earth. The ultimate formation of two beings who were declared by God to be one—two who were ontologically coequal and consubstantial—mirrored God in a mystical oneness that most perfectly expressed in marriage where spirit and body are joined in an ultra-relational superentity. The image of God in humanity, then, is most clearly manifest in the mystical unity of what appears to be two persons in human eyes but what has become one in God's eyes, two-in-one melded together in love that images the profound, inscrutable love that has existed and will exist eternally within the

[72] Genesis 2:23.
[73] Vigen Guroian, *Incarnate Love: Essays in Orthodox Ethics* (Notre Dame, IN: University of Notre Dame Press, 2002), p. 88.

very being of God—Father, Son, and Holy Spirit. "Man in the image of God is Man as male and female."[74] Two-in-one humanity is necessary to image the three-in-one God.

COMPLETING THE DIVINE IMAGE

God's declared intent when he contemplated the creation of humanity, "Let us make humanity in our image, after our likeness," is the most important anthropological statement in human history, equally important to female as well as to male, because creation in the image of God is what sets humanity apart from the rest of the created universe. All human beings, without any exception, bear the image of God in their very being. The image of God in humanity embraces a wide array of divinely imparted qualities and abilities. All aspects of the image of God that can be enumerated—including rationality, sentience, conscience, relationality, creativity, regency, physicality, gender, and any other aspect of human existence—are manifest to some degree in each human life.

The task that faces the believer is to embody the image in such a way that God is honored and humanity is served. Fully embracing the awesome potential of God's image by working in partnership with him in *Tikkun Olam* (the restoration of the world) is a profound opportunity for everyone. Only when the image of the Divine is fully demonstrated in the earth can humanity finally recover the dominion over all things for which God designed them in the beginning. This is the dominion that begins with the self-control of the Spirit-submitted life, extends to shared regency in the coequality and mutuality of marriage, expands into God-like communion and fellowship in community, and finally extends love, the very essence of God's being, to the world.

The one thing that was necessary for the completion of the image and likeness of God in humanity was the manifestation of divine relationality. Every single human being alone could fully manifest the qualities of rationality, sentience, conscience, creativity, regency, and physicality; however, no single human being in isolation could ever have imaged the divine essence of perfect love that is manifest in utter relationality. The human manifestation of love and relationality is,

---

[74] Karl Barth, quoted in Paul Jewett, *Man as Male and Female* (Grand Rapids, MI: Wm. B. Eerdmans Co., 1975), p. 14.

therefore, the highest and most complete reflection of the *imago Dei*. At some level, these qualities of the Divine can be manifest in all humans through expressed love and through relationship with God and with other humans; however, the highest manifestation is revealed in the mystical oneness of the "male-and-female" superentity that God specifically created to image himself in the universe.

This is the reason that God proceeded to make humanity "male and female" after he announced his intentions to make humanity in his "image and likeness."[75] The time that elapsed between the formation of *ha-adam* (Hebrew for "the earthling" or "humanity")[76] and the surgical separation that produced separate male and female entities made it possible for the earthling to recognize the need for an equal and comparable companion. The plurality of genders in humanity was not a divine afterthought. It was not God's alternate plan designed to make provision for what he knew would be the inevitable entrance of sin into the human equation. Likewise, it was not the cause or the product of the first human sin. God knew when he made the composite (and singular) human that it would not be "good for the human to be alone,"[77] so in order to complete the creation and bring it to its highest form, he created them "male and female" in the beginning. God knew what the earthling discovered after naming the animals: it was not good for the human to be alone. At the end of the sixth day of creation wherein humanity had been formed, separated, and rejoined, for the first time in the entire creative explosion of divine design, God observed that his work was "very good."[78] The fullness of divine satisfaction with his complete and perfect creation was clearly manifest in the exclamation.

The only way God could infuse humanity with the infinite love that is the essence of Deity and with the profound relationality of the coinherence of the three persons in the divine being was through the creation of humanity as "male and female." God simply did not create one human male to be his image and likeness and then create a female to be an assistant to him. In order to reflect the absolute one-

---

[75] Genesis 1:27.

[76] Contrary to much historical argument, God did not create one human male called Adam and then subsequently form a human female called Eve. The human creation was *ha-adam* (literally, "the adam" or "the earthling") because in that entity was contained all of humanity and the potentiality for both male and female. Indeed, from the beginning, God himself gave the name *Adam* to both male and female (Genesis 5:1-2).

[77] Genesis 2:18.

[78] Genesis 1:31.

ness of God, the three-in-one, he created two-in-one: a composite human whose design perfectly reflected the whole image of the Creator. Having put them in a physical world, the Creator separated their male and female parts into two bodies for the purpose of physical companionship. Both of these humans retained the image of God—one with a preponderance of masculine characteristics, the other with feminine qualities, both of which were divinely designed to complement each other in a delicately counterbalanced interrelationship.

The memory of their original form has always compelled humans to recreate physically the bond of two-in-one. When male and female leave their families and are joined together in marriage, they achieve the mystical oneness that the first human couple experienced before and after their separation into male and female. Then, as often as human beings in monogamous relationship come together in the most powerful—and pleasurable—relational act available to human beings, they reassemble, if only momentarily, the original God-designed "one flesh," and they glory in experiencing the oneness, the *echad*, of *ha-adam*.

In order to mirror the absolute coequality of the persons in his own divine being, God created male and female as coequal partners, both equal halves of the whole. In order to manifest the absolute oneness of the divine substance, he created them consubstantial, of precisely the same substance—from the same body—and he created a way for the two halves to be rejoined and thereby to recreate the original "one-flesh" state. In order to image the coeternity of the divine persons, he created them comortal with the equal opportunity of partaking of the Tree of Life and thereby becoming co-immortal. If they had chosen to eat of this tree rather than to experiment with the knowledge of good and evil, both of them then and there would have become co-immortal. Both in the terrestrial existence and in the realm of the age to come, male and female have always been and will always be designed to be absolutely coequal, consubstantial, and ultimately co-immortal.

In every respect, then, the utter equality of male and female in the one humanity images the absolute coequality of the persons in God. Only together did Adam and Eve manifest the *imago Dei* in their coequality, in their consubstantiality, in their being utterly *echad*, and in their perfect unity of being that they shared in the superentity first of sexually undifferentiated humanity and then of marriage. Without the woman, humanity was incomplete. Without the man, humanity was also incomplete. Together—female and male—they represented the complete and perfect image of God. "So God created humanity in his own image; male and female created he them, and blessed them and called their name Adam in the day in which they were created."[79] And so it is: female and male equally and without exception still bear the image and likeness of the one and only God, the God of Scripture. Women can take heart from the most ancient of anthropological statements, for in every aspect of their being, they are fully theomorphic and Christomorphic: they visibly bear the image and likeness of God in every respect and to every degree that their male counterparts share.

SPRINGBOARD FOR DISCUSSION

1. Consider that an understanding of God's image in humanity begins with recognizing the relationality that exists within the very being of God. How has infinite relationality always been manifest within the one divine being of God? How does God's relationality compare with the human capacity for relationship? How does this relate to God's observation that it was not good for *ha-adam* to be alone?

2. Discuss the fact that God is love. Can love really be love when it is not expressed in action? In what way was the creation of humanity somehow a manifestation of God's love and his desire for reciprocal relationship? How is the human capacity for love intrinsically involved in the highest expression of the image and likeness of God in humanity?

3. Evaluate the image that God presents in Scripture by characterizing himself as the God of Abraham, the God of Isaac, and the God of Jacob. Why does God not refer to himself as the God of creation? How does God's self-revelation confirm the fact that God is more concerned with relationship than with cosmology?

4. Discuss the interrelatedness of the persons of God—Father, Son, and Spirit—as being coequal. Is coequality absolutely essential

---

[79] Genesis 5:2.

to pure relationship that reflects the image and likeness of God? How does this relate to the family? How does it relate to the church? How does it relate to society at large? Is it possible for one to image God's relationality and at the same time seek to dominate other human beings because of differences in gender, race, ethnicity, or religion?

5. Consider the differences between Western emphases on individuality and the importance that the Scriptures attach to family and community. How does individuality negatively affect the family, society, and the church? How would you profit from greater emphasis on nurturing interpersonal relationships instead of fighting for individual personal rights?

6. Review the divine declaration concerning the creation of humanity. How does God's statement, "Let us make humanity in our image and likeness" convey the image of community both in the creator and in the creation? How does the statement, "Male and female created he them," speak to you about the importance of both female and male to the image and likeness of God? Do you agree with the Jewish understanding that the male is incomplete without the female and vice versa?

7. Evaluate the comparison between God, the three-in-one, and original humanity, the two-in-one. How is the three-in-one in God also imaged in three-in-one in marriage when God, man, and woman are joined in a holy covenant? How were the first man and the first woman one? In what ways did their oneness parallel the oneness of God? Based on Jesus' statement that in marriage there are no longer two but one, does each marriage mirror the oneness of God? Can it be rightly said that any image that does not embrace both female and male is not the highest image of God?

8. Consider the concept that God who is one yet a community of three is of one substance such that Father, Son, and Spirit are consubstantial. How does this truth relate to the oneness of humanity? Why is it important to underscore the fact that all human beings are of the same substance?

9. Discuss the importance of understanding that the creation of humanity included both male and female in one superentity that was later separated into two individuals and then rejoined in marriage. How does this view of the image and likeness affect your own self-

identity? How does it affect your evaluation of the worth of others, both male and female? Does this truth help you recognize the equality of all human beings regardless of gender, race, ethnicity, or intellectual capacity?

EPILOGUE

In this first volume of the *Feminine and Free* series, I have undertaken the task of initiating a discussion about the roles, responsibilities, and opportunities that are available to women in family, society, and church today. I began with the premise that the answers to today's questions and debates about women are to be found in the Holy Scriptures, indeed, in the most ancient of the documents of God's Word, the Genesis narratives. From those accounts, I have endeavored to demonstrate the truth that women in particular are integral to the reflection of God's image in the earth and, therefore, are called to manifest all the qualities of divine likeness that God chose to implant in humanity.

In order to comprehend God's image in humanity, however, I have attempted to outline and summarize as much understanding about the nature of God as can be discerned from Holy Scripture, the infallible vehicle of divine self-disclosure. Recognizing that it is impossible to establish correct anthropology without a proper understanding of theology, I endeavored to explicate fundamental truths about God as he revealed himself in the biblical texts; however, this exercise became far too extensive to be included in this volume, so I merely condensed and summarized that material in chapter six of this volume. (The entire discussion can be seen in my book, *Rediscovering the God of Scripture*.)

Having concluded that the very essence of God is love—a love that is not a static concept but a dynamic activity that demands expression through relationality—I endeavored to establish the understanding that humanity, male and female, fully manifests God's image when woman and man are interrelated in consubstantiality, coequality, mutuality, and unity that mirrors the total consubstantiality, coequality, mutuality, and unity of the three persons in the one God—Father, Son, and Spirit.

I then analyzed the feminine imagery that Holy Scripture applies anthropomorphically (gynomorphically) to God by demonstrating that God's self-initiated revelation in Scripture does not hesitate to portray God in feminine metaphor. This understanding dispels the myth that God is male by confirming from God's own words and from the words of the biblical authors that God has described himself and been described through both male and female imagery. It also establishes the truth that God is, indeed, genderless yet is very much a person and not just an abstract force of the universe.

Finally, I have considered a wide range of aspects of God's image and likeness in humanity and have established the fact that each of these qualities is manifest equally in both female and male humanity. My writing on the subject of the divine image also became so exhaustive that I was again forced to summarize the material in this volume and to publish it in its entirety as *Imaging the Divine: Mirroring God's Image and Likeness in the Earth.* Demonstrating the fact that the ultimate expression of the divine image and likeness is the pure relationality that was first manifest in God and then replicated in the first human couple, I have concluded that both male and female are indispensable to the manifestation of God's image that is achieved in the context of marriage and the family and then in the context of community.

Now you are ready to take the next step in this comprehensive and detailed study of biblical truth as you read *Feminine by Design: God's Plan for Women,* the second volume in my *Feminine and Free* series. *Feminine by Design* goes from the concept of humanity in God's image and likeness to the intricate details of God's creation of human beings, both male and female. In this volume, I thoroughly analyze each step of the process in human creation, including the way in which humanity was created out of nothing while being formed from the dust of the earth and also the manner in which gender-specific human beings were constructed. You will be both informed and inspired by the utter clarity of Holy Scripture as it chronicles and details the profound level of intricate design and loving care that God devoted to the creation of the first human being, to the formation of the first human body, and to the construction of the first woman from the substance of undifferentiated humanity.

Once again, you will be invigorated by the amazing truths that emerge from the Hebrew text of Scripture and from the Hebraic heritage and tradition of biblical faith in this most vital area of investigation. You will be equipped with understanding that confirms and explicates the outworking of God's image in humanity, both female and male. Then, you will be inspired to see the intricate detail that can be found in the Genesis narratives concerning the manner in which God fashioned woman, thereby completing gender-specific human existence. You will see that it was the construction of woman that finally made it possible for the image of God to be fully manifest in the earth by providing for the high level of interrelationship that the marriage of woman and man permits.

I continue in *Feminine by Design* to establish the reasons for God's creation of gendered human beings. You will be reassured from the actual texts of Scripture of the essential functions of both femininity and masculinity and the delicate counterbalance of complementarity that both bring to the human equation. You will understand that both female and male have clear distinctives that are based in divine design, not in evolution or social conditioning. You will also discover that limitless opportunities for being and for roles are available to—and proper for—both male and female within the templates of God's design for both. You will be able to establish clearly and safely on the firm foundation of biblical understanding the utter equality and mutuality of both female and male humanness. You will understand why men are men and why women are women, why neither is expendable, and why both can never be amalgamated into a unisex being of ancient or contemporary mythology or of today's political correctness.

When you have completed reading *Feminine by Design*, you will be amazed and refreshed all over again at the simplicity and clarity of Scripture and the details that it presents to those who have confidence in its inspiration at the hand of God himself. You will also see how important it is to return to the Hebraic foundations of the Christian faith by bypassing the centuries of Hellenization and Latinization that have so strongly impacted Christian theology and practice.

Then, you will be ready to launch into volume three of this *Feminine and Free* series which I have entitled *Free and Equal: Biblically Hebraic Women.* This book is my study of all the women in Scripture (many of them so obscure that you may never have heard of them) and the diverse roles and responsibilities to which God assigned them. I analyze the life of each woman in the context of the biblical community in which she lived, and I establish the God-given outworking of divine design for feminine relationships in the Hebraic culture as contrasted to the various cultures in the surrounding areas. This study includes a detailed analysis of the roles, responsibilities, and opportunities for women in the earliest Christian community. I give much detail to the life and ministry of Jesus, to his perspectives on women, and to the impact of his views upon women in his time. I also give an overview of the perspectives of Paul on women with care to use the grammatico-historical hermeneutic to give a balanced interpretation of the various texts from Paul that have been misunderstood, mistranslated, and misused in the history of the church.

Having established biblical paradigms for women in both the Hebrew Scriptures and the Apostolic Scriptures, you will be prepared for the fourth volume in the *Feminine and Free* series, the book I have entitled *Bound and Gagged: Secular and Ecclesiastical Misogyny and Its Impact on Women.* In this book, I analyze the perspectives on womanhood that characterized a wide range of ancient and contemporary cultures, focusing on the Greek worldview and mindset and the Hellenic view of women that so powerfully influenced the West in particular and much of the rest of the world as well. Then, I discuss in detail the impact of Hellenism upon both Judaism and Christianity and the ongoing view of womanhood in both communities. This volume is very important because it brings to light so many historical facts that have been occluded even to the present day. It also clarifies reasons for the prevailing and almost indelible mischaracterizations of women that have resulted in a virtual binding and gagging of women in nearly every culture in history and, to some degree, right to the present. *Bound and Gagged* is liberating to women because it helps them see the past and to resolve not to repeat it.

The final volume of the *Feminine and Free* series is entitled *Free Indeed: Releasing Women for Divine Destiny.* In this book, I evaluate the women in history who refused to be bound and gagged and who stepped forth in boldness on the promises and callings of God in their lives to accomplish astounding things even in androcentric political and ecclesiastical systems dominated by self-serving male bureaucracies. Then I discuss the liberating teachings of Jesus and the apostles relating to women in family, society, and church. Finally, I analyze the prophetic nature of God's clarion call to women to be communicators of the good news of salvation by grace through faith in Jesus. You will be amazed at the solid support that Scripture renders to roles and responsibilities for women in biblical faith. If you are a woman, you will be liberated to hear the release of God's call in your own life to advance in whatever role that God has assigned to you. If you are a man, you will be liberated to understand that you have an equal partner in faith and practice so that you can both affirm and be affirmed by the strength of true mutuality.

Finally, for those who do not have the time or inclination for such detailed studies, I offer *Feminine and Free: God's Design for Women* as a précis of this entire study, a *Readers' Digest* condensed version that contains the nuggets of truth. You will be able to cross reference simple statements in this text with details in the five volumes of the *Feminine and Free* series if you later decide to delve deeper after all.

I hope that you will avail yourself of all of these resources. I am confident that you will experience a life-changing paradigm shift in your own thinking that will be truly liberating. Whether you are male or female, you will agree that it is time for sin-induced domination-submission codependencies to be overcome by the faith-filled acceptance of biblical truth and by the empowerment of the Holy Spirit. It is time for believers to claim their heritage in the Hebraic faith of Jesus and the apostles and to begin to live the kind of lives in family, society, and worshipping community that God designed humanity to live in the beginning. Jesus provided relief from the dominance of sin for those who believe upon his Word, and he welcomes every believer to walk with him in kingdom living where mutual submission abounds.

To the end that you may be established in the Hebraic foundations of the most holy faith of Jesus and the apostles and grounded on the infallible Word of truth outlined in the Hebrew and Apostolic Scriptures, I encourage you to search the Scriptures diligently so that you may have the personal assurance of your calling in God and the gift that he has committed to your trust as a steward of his grace. Never accept anything simply because I or anyone else has said it. Make your calling and election sure in God by knowing for yourself what God has said. My prayer is that the care that I have exercised to be sure that every part of the text of this series of books conforms to the truth of Scripture as best I understand it will provide a foundation on which you can build your own life, free from the shackles of historical human tradition and fully liberated into the freedom of God's children. May both women and men experience the joy of being liberated by the Son of God to walk in truth and thereby to be "free indeed."

John D. Garr, Ph.D.

GLOSSARY

Abiogenesis: The theory that living organisms can arise spontaneously from inanimate material.

Androcentrism: The practice of centering on males and masculine interests; placing men (or masculine points of view) at the center of the world and its culture and history; *adj.* androcentric.

Androlatry: A neologism (newly coined word) that describes the practice of making an idol of men or the masculine.

Andromorphism: The attribution of masculine human characteristics to God; the image of men, the male, or the masculine; *adj.* andromorphic.

Aniconism: The practice of avoiding images of God even to the extent of shunning images of human beings and other living beings.

Ante-Nicene: Before the time of the Nicene Council in 325 A.D.

Anthropology: The study of human beings.

Anthropomorphism: The application of human characteristics to God; images of human beings; *adj.* anthropomorphic.

Anthropopathy: The attribution of human emotions to God; *adj.* anthropopathic.

Antinomianism: Literally "against the law." The belief that the law (Torah) has been terminated and replaced by grace.

Aphorism: An original thought or idea that is stated or written in a pithy, memorable manner.

Apocatastasis: Restoration, restitution, or reconstruction of anything to its original state or condition.

Apophatic: A theology that attempts to describe God by negation—that is, to speak only in terms of what God is not or in terms of what may not be said about the perfection or goodness of God.

Apperception: The process by which new experiences are perceived in relationship with past experience.

Aseity: The belief that God is the cause of his own existence; independence that applies to God alone in that he exists of and from himself.

Berachot: Hebrew word for "blessings." In Judaism, a system of bene- dictions that are spoken at various occasions and in private and public prayers in which God is praised for specific events, ideas, and things.

Blut und Boden: German phrase meaning, "Blood and ground"; the German ideology that focuses on ethnicity based on two factors: ancestry and homeland.

B'reshit: Hebrew phrase literally meaning "in beginnings"; the first word in the Bible usually translated, "In the beginning."

Charismata: Greek word for "gifts" (particularly of the Holy Spirit); the impartation of divine power and blessing.

Chauvinism: Originally, the belief in national superiority through exaggerated patriotism; by extension, partisanship of one people group against other people groups. More particularly the applica- tion of such attitudes toward men who consider masculinity to be superior to femininity as in "male chauvinism."

Chesed: Hebrew word for "tender mercy" or "loving kindness."

Christic: Pertaining to Christ.

Christology: The study of the nature, person, and work of Jesus Christ with a focus on both his deity and his humanity.

Christophany: Any appearance of Jesus Christ as the person of the Word of God before the time that the Word became flesh. "Old Testament" appearances of Jesus as either an angel or a man in which he was recognized as God.

Circumincession: Literally, encircling and interpenetrating; the theo- logical explanation of the mutual encircling and interpenetration of the three persons in the one God.

Coinherence: A spiritual fellowship involving human or divine per- sons that exists as a permanent and inseparable element, quality or attribute; originally referring to the dual human and divine nature of Jesus Christ.

Complementarian: Concept that male and female complement one another to one degree or another.

Corporeal: Having to do with the human body; pertaining to the physical body.

Cosmogony: Any theory as to why or how the universe came into existence or of how reality came to be.

Cosmology: Study of the universe in its totality.

Demiurge: Literally "craftsman," or "artisan"; the belief that the universe was fashioned and is maintained by a less-than-divine being; one of the features of Platonic, neo-Platonic, and Gnostic philosophies.

Deus absconditus: The God who is hidden; God who is unknowable to the human mind.

Deus otiosus: God who is idle or unemployed; used of God to indicate that the creator God essentially retired from the world following its creation and is no longer involved in its operation; the basic tenet of Deism.

Didascalia Apostolorum: A Christian treatise written in the early third century to describe church order which became the "manual" for Syriac Orthodox Christianity.

Dualism: The Greek concept that the universe is bifurcated into two realms, the spiritual (which is good) and the material (which is evil).

Ecclesiology: The study of the church.

Echad: Hebrew word for "one" denoting uniqueness and unity in the midst of plurality or diversity; a unit comprising more than one object.

Ecofeminism: The joining of the feminist movement with the ecology movements or ideas.

Egalitarianism: Favoring equality; the belief that all people should be considered equal in political, economic, and social life; *adj.* egalitarian.

Eisegesis: Literally "leading into"; the practice of introducing one's own ideas into a text rather than reading out of the text what is there.

Exegesis: Literally "drawing out"; the critical explanation or interpretation of a text, particularly of Scripture.

Filicide: A parent's killing his/her own son or daughter; *adj.* filicidal.

Gnosticism: A rather diverse belief system from antiquity which maintained that the universe was created by the demiurge (an imperfect god or the embodiment of evil), that matter is inherently evil, that salvation is gained by *gnosis*, esoteric self-knowledge in which humans come to know the superior god and in so doing are empowered to escape material existence.

Gynomorphism: The attribution of feminine human characteristics to

God; the image of women, the female, or the feminine; *adj.* gynomorphic.

Gynophobia: Morbid fear of women.

Hedonism: A school of Greek thought which maintains that pleasure is the only intrinsic good and which seeks to maximize pleasure and minimize pain.

Hellenism: Pertaining to ancient Greek culture or ideals, particularly those after the time of Alexander the Great.

Hermaphrodite: One who possesses the reproductive organs of both sexes.

Hermeneutics: The science of interpretation which makes laws governing exegesis of biblical texts.

Heteronomous: Subject to foreign laws; not autonomous.

Hillelian: Pertaining to the teaching of Hillel the Great, Jewish sage of the early first century A.D.

Hokmah: Hebrew word for "wisdom," particularly "divine wisdom."

Holism: In Greek philosophy, the theory that whole entities have existence other than the sum of their parts. In biblical perspective, the view of life in terms of all aspects of existence wherein there is no dualistic dichotomy.

Humanism: The idea that humanity's obligations are concerned wholly with the welfare of the human race; the concept that humanity can achieve perfection without divine assistance.

Hypostasis: Literally, "the existence" or "being" or "substantive reality" of something, particularly of the three persons of God—Father, Son, and Spirit.

Iconoclasm: Literally, "the breaking of images"; the destruction of a culture's own religious icons or other symbols, generally for religious or political purposes; the attacking of cherished beliefs and traditional institutions.

Imago Dei: Latin phrase for "the image of God."

Immanence: Refers to the manifestation of the divine presence in contrast with divine transcendence. Not to be confused with imminence, the quality of something about to occur.

Incorporeality: Not having material or physical existence; insubstantial; pertaining to nonmaterial beings.

Infanticide: The killing of infants.

In se: Latin for "in itself."

Machiavellian: Being or acting in accordance with Machiavelli's principles of government which place political expediency above morality and encourages the use of craft and deceit to maintain authority and carry out the policies of the state; characterized by subtle and unscrupulous deception and expediency.

Megalomania: A mental illness marked by delusions of greatness or even deity; *adj.* megalomaniacal.

Memra: Aramaic word for "spoken word"; parallel with the Hebrew word *d'var* and the Greek word *logos*, both of which mean "word."

Metaethics: A philosophy of ethics that deals with the meaning of ethical terms, the nature of moral discourse, and the foundations of moral principles.

Metanarrative: A story that is told to justify another story; a story that provides an overview of experiences.

Mikveh: Hebrew word meaning literally "collection"; refers to the collection of waters in a pool used for ritual immersion to achieve ceremonial purity; *pl. mikvot.*

Misogyny: Hatred of women.

Modernity: The post-medieval period characterized by capitalism, industrialization, secularization, rationalization; the belief that human society will continue to improve until utopia is reached.

Narcissism: Self-love; the personality trait of egotism; vanity; conceit; self-centeredness; name coined by Sigmund Freud after the Greek mythological character Narcissus who was pathologically self-absorbed with his own image reflected in a pool of water.

Neo-Gnosticism: Revival of Gnosticism.

Neo-paganism: The revival of paganism (the ancient religions of the pagan peoples) as an active religion; the new paganism.

Nicene: Pertaining to the Ecumenical Council of Nice at which the orthodox Christian doctrine of the Trinity was established.

Nihilism: The concept that supports the negation of one or more of the meaningful aspects of life; the total rejection of established laws and institutions; total and absolute destructiveness; the viewpoint that life is without objective meaning, purpose, or intrinsic value and that morality does not inherently exist.

Omnipotence: All powerful; having infinite power.

Omniscience: All knowing; having infinite knowledge.

Omnisentience: All feeling; having infinite feeling.

Ontic: Possessing the character of real rather than phenomenal (perceived) existence.

Ontology: The branch of metaphysics that studies the nature of existence and being; a systematic account of existence; *adj.* ontological.

Orthodoxy: Literally "straight belief"; the beliefs that are considered right and proper.

Orthopraxy: Literally "straight action" or "straight practice"; the actions that are considered right and proper.

Parthenogenesis: The development of an egg without fertilization; reproduction from an unfertilizaed, usually female, gamete.

Patriarchialism: Relating to a form of social organization in which the male is the family head and the title is traced through the male line; *adj.* patriarchal.

Patrician: Referring to the original senatorial aristocratic families of ancient Rome; a member of the hereditary ruling class in medieval societies; of high rank or noble family.

Pedagogy: The function or work of teaching; the science of education; instructional methods.

Pedophilia: The condition of being sexually attracted to children.

Perichoresis: The mutual encircling and interpenetrating of the three persons of the one God. See circumincession.

Peshat: In Jewish hermeneutics, the simple, obvious, literal meaning of a biblical text.

Phenomenology: The study of phenomena; literally "the study of what appears"; the systematic analysis of structures of consciousness and the phenomena that occur in consciousness.

Plebian: The common people (as contrasted with the patricians).

Plenipotentiary: From the Latin meaning "full power," this term designates a government representative who has the full power of the government.

Pleroma: A Greek word meaning literally, "a fullness"; the totality of divine powers.

Pneumatology: The study of the Holy Spirit.

Polyandry: Polygamy in which a woman has multiple husbands.

Polygyny: Polygamy in which a man has multiple wives.

Postmodernity: The economy or culture of society that exists after modernity; generally dated to the late twentieth century.

Proaction: Serving to prepare for, intervene in, prevent, or control an expected occurrence or situation; taking measures to solve a problem before it arises.

Pseudepigrapha: Literally "false writings"; writings that profess to be biblical in character but are not included in the cannon of Scripture or in the Apocrypha; *adj.* pseudepigraphical.

Rationality: The possession of reason; the exercise of reason; the state or quality of being rational or logical.

Relationality: Possessing the ability for relationship; the manner in which beings relate to and interact with one another.

Ruach: Hebrew word for "spirit."

Sefirot: Hebrew word for "enumerations"; in Jewish mysticism, the ten attributes or emanations through which God reveals himself.

Sentience: The ability to feel or perceive; sense perception not involving intelligence or mental perception.

Shekhinah: Hebrew word for "dwelling" or "settling"; the divine presence of God, especially in the Tabernacle or in the Temple.

Shema: Hebrew word for "hear [and obey]"; the first word of the section of the Torah that is the focus of Jewish liturgical prayers; the encapsulation of biblical monotheism.

Sociomorphism: Description of people who can change their personalities, behavior, emotions, habits, and beliefs to gain favor in society.

Sola fide: Latin ablative meaning literally, "by faith alone"; one of the slogans of the Reformation used to underscore the concept that individuals are justified before God only by faith (not by works or knowledge).

Sola scriptura: Latin ablative meaning literally, "by Scripture alone"; one of the slogans of the Reformation used to emphasize the fact that church tradition could not be equated with the written record of Holy Scripture.

Sophia: Greek word for wisdom.

Soteriology: Study of salvation; *adj.* soteriological.

Subordinationism: Any teaching that one or more persons of God is subordinate to another.

Sui generis: Literally, "of its own kind"; something that is totally unique; an idea that cannot be included in a wider concept.

Syncretism: Any effort to reconcile disparate beliefs by blending or amalgamating them; *v.* syncretize.

Tanakh: An acronym-based word for *Torah*, *Nevi'im*, and *Ketuvim*

(Law, Prophets, Writings, respectively); the Hebrew Scriptures.

Targum: Any Aramaic translation of the Hebrew Scriptures; *pl. Targumim.*

Tetragrammaton: Literally, "four letters"; the four-letter name of God in Hebrew, *Yud, Heh, Vav, Heh*, or YHWH (Yahweh).

Theodicy: Literally "God justice"; the effort to reconcile the fact that evil in the world does not conflict with the goodness of God.

Theomorphic: Bearing the image of God.

Theophany: An appearance of God to humans.

Theriomorphism: Applying animal qualities and images to God.

Tode ti: Literally "a thisness" or "this what," which Aristotle defined as "individual and numerically one," representing primary substance, such that all "what-ness" is either in the *tode ti* or is the *tode ti* itself.

Toledot: Hebrew word for "generations," literally "giving birth"; the Hebrew concept of history.

Tzimtzum: Literally "contraction," the withdrawal or limitation of God in order to have a space in which the universe could have been created "out of nothing." A concept of Lurianic mystical Judaism.

Übermensch: German word for "free spirit"; a person with great powers and abilities; a demigod or superman.

Yachid: Hebrew word for "absolute numerical oneness."

BIBLIOGRAPHY

Aalders, G. Charles. *Bible Student's Commentary*. Grand Rapids, MI: Zondervan Publishing, 1981.

Abelard, Peter. *Introductio ad Theologiam*.

Thomas Aquinas. *Summa Theologica*.

Akers, Keith. *The Lost Religion of Jesus*. New York: Lantern Books, 2000.

Aloi, Daniel. "Sudanese Scholar Finds Freedom to Write at Cornell." *Cornell University Chronicle*, April 14, 2009.

Ambrose of Milan. *The Consecration of a Virgin and the Perpetual Virginity of Mary* 8:52.

Anderson, Ray S. "Theological Anthropology." In *The Blackwell Companion to Modern Theology*. Edited by S. Gareth and J. Jones. Oxford: Blackwell Publishing Ltd., 2004.

Angus, Samuel. *The Mystery-Religions and Christianity: A Study in the Religious Background of Early Christianity*. New York: Dover Publications, 1966.

Aristotle. *Aristotle, Volume XIII: The Generation of Animals*. Translated by A. L. Peck. Cambridge: Harvard University Press, 1963.

Armstrong, Karen. *In the Beginning: A New Interpretation of Genesis*. New York: Alfred A. Knopf, 1996.

Augustine. *On the Good of Marriage*.

Augustine. *On the Trinity*, 6:12. In Augustine, *The Trinity*. Translated by Stephen McKenna. Washington, DC: Catholic University of America Press, 1963.

Augustine. *On the Trinity*, XII, 5. In Augustine, *Basic Writings of Saint Augustine*. New York: Random House, 1948.

Azai, Ben. *Genesis Rabba* 24. In Irwin Cotler, "Jewish NGOs, Human Rights, and Public Advocacy: A Comparative Inquiry." *Jewish Political Studies Review* 11:3-4 (Fall, 1999).

Bailey, D. Sherwin. *Sexual Relations in Christian Thought*. New York:

Harper & Row, 1959.

Barackman, Floyd H. *Practical Christian Theology: Examining the Great Doctrines of the Faith.* Grand Rapids, MI: Kregel Publications, 1981.

Baring, Anne and Andrew Harvey. *The Divine Feminine: Exploring the Feminine Face of God Throughout the World.* Berkeley, CA: Conari Press, 1996.

Barr, James. "Theophany and Anthropomorphism in the Old Testament." *Congress Volume, Oxford.* Leiden: E. J. Brill, 1960.

Barth, Karl. *Church Dogmatics I/1: The Word of God.* London: T & T Clark, 1936.

Barth, Karl. *Church Dogmatics III/2: The Doctrine of Creation.* Edited by G. W. Bromiley and T. F. Torrance, translated by. G. W. Bromiley. London: T & T. Clark, 2004.

Bavinck, Herman. *The Doctrine of God.* Grand Rapids, MI: Wm. B. Eerdmans Publishing Co., 1955.

BBC News. "The Child Slaves of Saudi Arabia." Documentary, broadcast March 2007.

Berdyaev, Nicolas. *Dream and Reality: An Essay in Autobiography.* London: Geoffrey Bles, 1950.

Berdyaev, Nicolas. *The Divine and the Human.* Translated by R. M. French. London: Geoffrey Bles, 1949.

Berkhof, Hendrikus. *Christian Faith: An Introduction to the Study of Faith.* Grand Rapids, MI: Wm. B. Eerdmans Publishing, 1979.

Berkovits, Eliezer. *Faith After the Holocaust.* New York: KTAV Publishing, 1973.

Berkovits, Eliezer. *With God in Hell: Judaism in the Ghettos and Death Camps.* New York: Sanhedrin Press, 1979.

Berzonsky, Vladimir. *The Gift of Love.* Crestwood, NY: St. Vladimir's Seminary Press, 1985.

Beuken, Willem A. M. "The Human Person in the Vision of Genesis 1-3: A Synthesis of Contemporary Insights." In *Louvain Studies* 24 (1999).

Biale, David. "The God with Breasts: El Shaddai in the Bible." In David Biale, *History of Religions*, 21:3.

Bilezikian, Gilbert. *Beyond Sex Roles: What the Bible Says About a Woman's Place in Church and Family.* Grand Rapids, MI: Baker Book House, 1985.

Bird, Phyllis A. "Bone of My Bone and Flesh of My Flesh." In

Theology Today, 50:4 (Jan. 1993).

Bird, Phyllis A. "'Male and Female He Created Them': Gen. 1:27b in the Context of the Priestly Account of Creation." In *Harvard Theological Review* 74 (1981).

Bloesch, Donald G. *Is the Bible Sexist? Beyond Feminism and Patriarchialism.* Westchester, IL: Crossway Publishing Co., 1982.

Bloesch, Donald G. *The Battle for the Trinity: The Debate over Inclusive God-Language.* Ann Arbor, MI: Servant Press, 1985.

Blumenthal, David R. "Tselem: Toward an Anthropopathic Theology of Image." In *Christianity in Jewish Terms.* Edited by Tikva Frymer-Kensky, David Novak, Peter Ochs, Michael Singer, and David Fox Sandmel. Boulder CO: Westview Press, 2002.

Bonhoeffer, Dietrich. *Letters and Papers from Prison.* New York: Macmillan, 1972.

Bonhoeffer, Dietrich. *The Cost of Discipleship.* Translated by R. H. Fuller. New York: SCM Press, 1959.

Børresen, Kari Elisabeth, ed. *Image of God and Gender Models in Judaeo-Christian Tradition.* Oslo: Solum, 1991.

Boyarin, Daniel. "The Eye in the Torah: Ocular Desire in Midrashic Hermeneutic." In *Critical Inquiry* 16 (2009).

Boyd, Gregory. *Trinity and Process: A Critical Evaluation and Reconstruction of Hartshorne's Dipolar Theism Toward a Trinitarian Metaphysics.* New York: Peter Land, 1992.

Braaten, Carl E. and Robert W. Jenson, eds. *Christian Dogmatics.* Philadelphia: Fortress Press, 1984.

Brayer, Menachem M. *The Jewish Woman in Rabbinic Literature: A Psychosocial Perspective.* Hoboken, NJ: KTAV Publishing House, 1986.

Bromiley, G. W. "Image of God." In *International Standard Bible Encyclopedia, Vol. 2.* Edited by G. W. Bromiley. Grand Rapids, MI: William B. Eerdmans, 1988.

Brown, Francis, S. R. Driver, and Charles Briggs. *Hebrew and English Lexicon of the Old Testament.* New York: Houghton Mifflin, 1907.

Brown, Harold O. J. *Heresies.* New York: Doubleday, 1984.

Brown, Raymond Edward. *The Gospel According to John.* Garden City, NY: Doubleday, 1966.

Brueggemann, Walter. *Genesis.* Louisville, KY: John Knox Press, 1982.

Brunner, Emil. *Man in Revolt: A Christian Anthropology*. Translated by Olive Wyon. Philadelphia: Westminster Press, 1947.

Brunner, Emil. *The Christian Doctrine of Creation and Redemption*. Translated by Olive Wyon. Philadelphia: Westminster Press, 1953.

Buber, Martin. *I and Thou*. Translated by Ronald Gregor Smith. New York: Charles Scribner's Sons, 1958.

Buber, Martin. *Tales of the Hasidim: The Early Masters, Vol. 1*. New York: Schocken Books, 1968.

Buckley, Jorunn Jacobsen. *A Rehabilitation of Spirit Ruha in Mandaean Religion*. Chicago: University of Chicago Press, 1982.

Buckley, Jorunn Jacobsen. *The Mandaeans: Ancient Texts and Modern People*. New York: Oxford University Press, 2002.

Bulka, Reuven P. *Jewish Marriage: A Halakhic Ethic*. New York: KTAV Publishing House, 1986.

Bunge, Marcia J., Terence E. Fretheim, and Beverly Roberts Gaventa, eds. *The Child in the Bible*. Grand Rapids, MI: Wm. B. Eerdmans Publishing Co., 2008.

Burrell, David. *Freedom and Creation in Three Traditions*. South Bend, IN: University of Notre Dame Press, 1993.

Burton, Keith Augustus. *The Blessing of Africa*. Downers Grove, IL: InterVarsity Press, 2007.

Buttrick, George, ed. *The Interpreter's Bible*. Nashville: Abingdon-Cokesbury, 1952.

Byrne, Peter and James Leslie Houlden. *Companion Encyclopedia of Theology*. London: Routledge, 1995.

Calvin, John. *The Institutes of the Christian Religion*. Edited by John McNeill. Philadelphia: Westminster Press, 1960.

Capper, LeRoy S. "The Imago Dei and Its Implications for Order in the Church." In *Presbyterion* 2 (1985).

Carmignac, Jean. *The Birth of the Synoptics*. Chicago: Franciscan Herald Press, 1987.

Carr, Anne E. *Transforming Grace: Christian Tradition and Women's Experience*. San Francisco: Harper & Row, 1988.

Carr, Anne E. and Mary Steward Van Leeuwen, eds. *Religion, Feminism, and the Family*. Louisville, KY: Westminster John Knox Press, 1996.

Carr, David. *The Erotic Word*. New York: Oxford University Press, 2005.

Chafer, Lewis Sperry. *Systematic Theology.* Grand Rapids, MI: Kregel Publications, 1948, 1976.

Clement of Alexandria. *"Quis Dives Salvetur."* Quoted from J. P. Migne, *Patrologia Graeca, Vol. 9*, in Leonard Swidler, *Biblical Affirmations of Women.* Westminster: John Knox Press, 1979.

Clines, David J. A. "The Image of God in Man." In *Tyndale Bulletin* 19 (1968).

Cobb, John B. *Christ in a Pluralistic Age.* Philadelphia: Westminster Press, 1975.

Cohen, Jeremy. *Sanctifying the Name of God: Jewish Martyrs and Jewish Memories of the First Crusade.* Philadelphia: University of Pennsylvania Press, 2004.

Coleson, Joseph E. *Ezer Cenegdo: A Power Like Him, Facing Him as Equal.* Grantham, PA: Messiah College, 1996.

Collins English Dictionary. Glasgow: HarperCollins Publishers, 2009.

Congar, Yves. "The Motherhood in God and the Femininity of the Holy Spirit." In *I Believe in the Holy Spirit, Vol. 3*. New York: Seabury Press, 1983.

Cottrell, Jack. *What the Bible Says About God the Redeemer.* Joplin, MO: College Press, 1987.

Crye, Susan. "Fallout Escalates Over 'Goddess' Sophia Worship." In *Christianity Today* (4 April 1994).

Cucchiari, Salvatore. "The Gender Revolution and the Transition from Bisexual Horde to Patrilocal Band: The Origins of Gender Hierarchy." In *Sexual Meanings: The Cultural Construction of Gender and Sexuality.* Edited by Sherry B. Ortner and Harriet Whitehead. New York: Cambridge University Press, 1981.

Curtis, Edward M. "Image of God, Old Testament." In the *Anchor Bible Dictionary*, edited by David Noel Freedman, et. al., 6 volumes. New York: Doubleday, 1992.

Dallmann, W. *The Battle of the Bible with the "Bibles."* St. Louis: Concordia Publishing House, 1926.

Daly, Mary. *Beyond God the Father: Toward a Philosophy of Women's Liberation.* Boston: Unitarian Universalist Association of Congregations in North America, 1973.

Daly, Mary. *Gyn/Ecology: The Metaethics of Radical Feminism.* Minneapolis: Winston, 1985.

Dart, John. "Balancing Out the Trinity: The Genders of the Godhead."

In *Christian Century* (February 16-23, 1983).

Davidson, Herbert. *Moses Maimonides: The Man and His Works.* New York: Oxford University Press, 2004.

Davidson, Richard M. *The Flame of Yahweh: Sexuality in the Old Testament.* Peabody, MA: Hendrickson Publishers, 2007.

Dawkins, Richard. *The God Delusion.* New York: Houghton Mifflin Co., 2006.

De Boer, P. A. *Fatherhood and Motherhood in Israelite and Judean Piety.* Leiden, The Netherlands: Brill, 1974.

de Caen, Roger. *Carmen de Mundi Contemptu.* In *Charming Cadavers: Horrific Figurations of the Feminine in Indian Buddhist Hagiographic Literature.* Liz Wilson. Chicago: University of Chicago Press, 1996.

de Secondat, Charles Baron de la Brede et de Montesquieu. *Spirit of the Laws.* New York: D. Appleton and Company, 1900.

Dearman, J. Andrew. "Theophany, Anthropomorphism, and the *Imago Dei.*" In *The Incarnation*, edited by Stephen T. Davis, Daniel Kendall and Gerald O'Collins. Oxford: Oxford University Press, 2002.

Demarest, Bruce A. *The Human Person in Theology and Psychology: A Biblical Anthropology for the Twenty-first Century.* Grand Rapids, MI: Kregel Publications, 2005.

Demos, John. *Past, Present, and Personal: The Family and the Life Course in American History.* New York: Oxford University Press, 1986.

Descartes, René. *Principles of Philosophy*, Part 1, article 7. 1644.

Devettere, Raymond J. *Practical Decision Making in Health Care Ethics: Cases and Concepts.* Washington, DC: Georgetown University Press, 2010.

Dockery, David S. *Biblical Interpretation Then and Now: Contemporary Hermeneutics in the Light of the Early Church.* Grand Rapids, MI: Baker Book House, 1992.

Donin, Hayim Halevy. *To Be a Jew: A Guide to Jewish Observance in Contemporary Life.* New York: Basic Books, 1972.

Donne, John. "To the Countesse of Huntingdon." In *Donne: Complete Poetical Works.* New York: Oxford University Press, 1971.

Doukhan, Jacques B. "Women Priests in Israel: A Case for Their Absence." In *Women in Ministry: Biblical & Historical Perspectives.* Edited by Nancy Vyhmeister. Berrien Springs, MI: Andrews

University Press, 1998.

Downey, Michael. *Altogether Gift: A Trinitarian Spirituality.* Maryknoll, NY: Orbis Books, 2000.

Dresner, Samuel H., ed. *I Asked for Wonder: A Spiritual Anthology— Abraham Joshua Heschel.* New York: Schocken Books, 1991.

Duck, Ruth C. *Gender and the Name of God.* New York: Pilgrim Press, 1991.

Dunn, James D. G. *Christology in the Making.* Cambridge: Cambridge University Press, 1993.

Dunn, James D. G. "Was Christianity a Monotheistic Faith from the Beginning?" In *Scottish Journal of Theology* 35 (1982).

Eberling, Gerhard. "Existence between God and God: A Contribution to the Question of the Existence of God." Translated by James P. Carse. In *Journal for Theology and the Church,* 5 (1968).

Edwards, Larry D. *The Twelve Generations of the Creation!* Longwood, FL: Xulon Press, 2006.

Eichrodt, Walther. *Theology of the Old Testament, Vol. II.* Translated by J. A. Baker. Philadelphia, PA: Westminster Press, 1961.

Elwell, Walter A. and Philip W. Comfort, eds. *Tyndale Bible Dictionary.* Carol Stream, IL: Tyndale House Publishers, 2001.

Engelsman, Joan Chamberlain. *The Feminine Dimension of the Divine.* Philadelphia: Westminster Press, 1979.

Engnell, Ivan. "'Knowledge' and 'Life' in the Creation Story." In *Wisdom in Israel and in the Ancient Near East Presented to Professor Harold Henry Rowley.* Edited by M. Noth and D. Winton Thomas. *Vetus Testamentum* Supplements 3. Leiden, The Netherlands: E. J. Brill, 1955.

Erickson, Millard. *Christian Theology.* Grand Rapids, MI: Baker Book House, 1994.

Erickson, Millard. *Introducing Christian Doctrine.* Grand Rapids, MI: Baker Book House, 1992.

Euripides. *Hippolytus.*

Euripides. *Iphigeneia at Aulis.*

Evans, Mary. *Woman in the Bible: An Overview of All the Crucial Passages on Women's Roles.* Downers Grove, IL: InterVarsity Press, 1983.

Evdokimov, Paul. *Woman and the Salvation of the World: A Christian Anthropology of the Charisms of Women.* Translated by Anthony P. Gythiel. Crestwood, NY: St. Vladimir's Seminary Press, 1994.

Feldman, Abraham J. *Contributions of Judaism to Modern Society.* New York: The Union of American Hebrew Congregations.

Feng, Jicai, David Wakefield and Howard Boldblatt. *The Three-Inch Golden Lotus.* Honolulu, HI: University of Hawaii Press, 1986.

Ferguson, Duncan Sheldon. *Biblical Hermeneutics: An Introduction.* Atlanta, GA: John Knox Press, 1986.

Ferrara, Jennifer and Sarah Hinlicky Wilson. "Ordaining Women: Two Views." In *First Things* (April 2003).

Fiorenza, Elisabeth Schüssler. *In Memory of Her: A Feminist Theological Reconstruction of Christian Origins.* New York: The Crossroad Publishing Company, 1983.

Firestone, Tirzah. *The Receiving: Reclaiming Jewish Women's Wisdom.* San Francisco: HarperCollins Publishers, 2003.

Fishbane, Michael A. *Biblical Myth and Rabbinic Mythmaking.* Oxford: Oxford University Press, 2003.

Fishbane, Michael A. *Biblical Text and Texture.* New York: Schocken Books, 1979.

Flannery, Edward. In *Restore!* 1:2.

Fleischer, Manfred P. "'Are Women Human?'—The Debate of 1595 between Valens Acidalius and Simon Gediccus." In *Sixteenth Century Journal* (1981).

Forell, Caroline A. and Donna M. Matthews. *A Law of Her Own: The Reasonable Woman as a Measure of Man* (New York: New York University Press, 2000.

Foster, David Kyle. *The Divine Marriage: God's Purpose and Design for Human Sexuality.* Franklin, TN: Mastering Life Publications.

Freedman, Noel, ed. *Anchor Bible Dictionary.* New Haven, CT: Yale University Press, 1992.

Fretheim, Terrence. *The Suffering of God: An Old Testament Perspective.* Philadelphia: Fortress Press, 1984.

Friedman, Paul. "On the Universality of Symbols." In *Religions in Antiquity.* Edited by Jacob Neusner. Leiden, The Netherlands: E. J. Brill, 1968.

Frymer-Kensky, Tikva. "Image of God: The Image: Religious Anthropology in Judaism and Christianity." In *Christianity in Jewish Terms.* Edited by Tikva Frymer-Kensky, David Novak, Peter Ochs, Michael Singer, and David Fox Sandmel. Boulder CO: Westview Press, 2002.

Fuchs, Esther. *Sexual Politics in the Biblical Narrative.* London:

Sheffield Academic Press, 2000.

Gabriel, Richard A. *Gods of Our Fathers: The Memory of Egypt in Judaism and Christianity*. Westport, CT: Greenwood Publishing Group, 2002.

Garr, W. Randall. *In His Own Image and Likeness: Humanity, Divinity, and Monotheism*. Leiden, The Netherlands: Koninkijke Brill, 2003.

Giles, Kevin. "The Subordination of Christ and the Subordination of Women." In *Discovering Biblical Equality: Complementarity without Hierarchy*. Edited by Ronald W. Pierce, Rebecca Merrill Groothuis, and Gordon D. Fee. Downers Grove, IL: InterVarsity Press, 2004.

Gimbutas, Marja. *The Goddesses and Gods of Old Europe*. Berkeley: University of California Press, 1982.

Glover, T. R. *The Conflict of Religions in the Early Roman Empire*. Boston: Beacon Press, 1960.

Gould, Stephen. *The Mismeasure of Man*. New York: Norton Publishing, 1981.

Grant, Robert McQueen. *Irenaeus of Lyons*. London: Routledge Publishing, 1997.

Grenz, Stanley J. and John R. Franke. *Beyond Foundationalism: Shaping Theology in a Postmodern Context*. Louisville, KY: Westminster John Knox Press, 2001.

Grenz, Stanley J. *Created for Community: Connecting Christian Belief with Christian Living*. Grand Rapids, MI: Baker Publishing Group, 1996.

Grenz, Stanley J. *Theology for the Community of God*. Grand Rapids, MI: Wm. B. Eerdmans Publishing Co., 1994.

Groothuis, Rebecca Merrill. *Good News for Women: A Biblical Picture of Gender Equality*. Grand Rapids, MI: Baker Books, 1997.

Gunton, Colin E. *Act and Being: Towards a Theology of the Divine Attributes*. Grand Rapids, MI: Wm. B. Eerdmans Publishing Co., 2002.

Gunton, Colin E. *Becoming and Being: The Doctrine of God in Charles Hartshorne and Karl Barth*. Oxford: Oxford University Press, 1978.

Guroian, Vigen. *Incarnate Love: Essays in Orthodox Ethics*. Notre Dame, IN: University of Notre Dame Press, 2002.

Gutiérrez, Gustavo. *The Power of the Poor in History: Selected*

Writings. Translated by Robert R. Barr. Maryknoll, NY: Orbis Books, 1983.

Haeri, Shahla. *Law of Desire: Temporary Marriage in Shi'I Iran.* Syracuse, NY: Syracuse University Press, 1989.

Hall, Douglas John. *Professing the Faith: Christian Theology in a North American Context.* Minneapolis: Augsburg Fortress, 1996.

Hallissy, Margaret. *A Companion to Chaucer's Canterbury Tales.* Westport, CT: Greenwood Press, 1995.

Hammond, T. C. *In Undersanding Be Men: A Handbook of Christian Doctrine.* Downers Grove, IL: InterVarsity Press, 1968.

Hampson, Daphne. *Theology and Feminism.* Oxford: Basil Blackwell, 1990.

Häring, Hermann. "From Divine Human to Human God." In *The Human Image of God.* Edited by Hans-Georg Ziebertz, Friedrich Schweitzer, Hermann Häring, and Don Browning. Boston: Brill, 2001.

Harland, P. J. *The Value of Human Life: A Study of the Story of the Flood (Genesis 6-9).* Leiden, The Netherlands: E. J. Brill, 1996.

Harris, Ellen Francis. *Guarding the Secrets: Palestinian Terrorism and a Father's Murder of His Too-American Daughter.* New York: Charles Scribner's Sons, 2005.

Hastings, James and John A. Selbie, eds. *Encyclopedia of Religion and Ethics.* Edinburgh: T. & T. Clark, 1927.

Hastings, James, John Selbie, and Louis H. Gray, eds.*Encyclopedia of Religion and Ethics.* Vol 12. New York: Charles Scribners' Sons, 1922.

Hayter, Mary. *The New Eve in Christ: The Use and Abuse of the Bible in the Debate about Women in the Church.* Grand Rapids, MI: William B. Eerdmans Publishing Co., 1987.

Healy, Emma T. *Women According to Saint Bonaventure.* New York: Georgian Press, 1956.

Hengel, Martin. *Judaism and Hellenism, Vol. 1.* London: SCM Press, 1973.

Henry, Carl F. H. *God, Revelation and Authority.* Wheaton, IL: Crossway Books, 1999.

Henry, Patrick. Speech at the Virginia Convention, March 1775.

Herzfeld, Noreen L. *In Our Image: Artificial Intelligence and the Human Spirit.* Minneapolis: Augsburg Fortress, 2004.

Heschel, Abraham Joshua. *God in Search of Man: A Philosophy of*

Judaism. New York: Farrar, Straus and Giroux, 1955.

Heschel, Abraham Joshua. *The Ineffable Name of God—Man: Poems.* Translated by Morton M. Leifman. New York: The Continuum International Publishing Group, Inc., 2004.

Heschel, Abraham Joshua. *The Prophets.* New York: Harper & Row, 1962; reprint New York: HarperCollins, 2001.

Heschel, Abraham Joshua. *Who Is Man?* Palo Alto, CA: Stanford University Press, 1965.

Hesiod. *The Theogony.* In *Hesiod, the Homeric Hymns and Homerica.* Translated by Hugh H. Evelyn-White. Cambridge: Harvard University Press, 1936.

Hick, John. *An Interpretation of Religion: Human Responses to the Transcendent.* New Haven, CT: Yale University Press, 1991.

Hill, William. *Knowing the Unknown God.* New York: Philosophical Library, 1971.

Hillel, Daniel. *The Natural History of the Bible.* New York: Columbia University Press, 2006.

Hodge, Charles. *Systematic Theology.* Grand Rapids, MI: Baker Book House, 1988.

Hoekema, Anthony A. *Created in God's Image.* Grand Rapids, MI: Wm. B. Eerdmans Publishing Co., 1986.

Hopko, Thomas. "God and Gender: Articulating the Orthodox View." In *St. Vladimir's Theological Quarterly,* 37:2-3 (1993).

Hopko, Thomas. "On the Male Character of the Christian Priesthood." In *St. Vladimir's Theological Quarterly* 19:3 (1975).

Horkheimer, Max and Theodor W. Adorno. *Dialectic of Enlightenment.* Translated by John Cumming. New York: Continuum Press, 1999.

House, H. Wayne and Matt Power. *Charts on Open Theism and Orthodoxy.* Grand Rapids, MI: Kregel Publications, 2003.

Howe, Thomas. *Objectivity in Biblical Interpretation.* Longwood, FL: Advantage Books, 2004.

Hubbard, David A. *"The Wisdom of the Old Testament."* In *Messiah College Occasional Papers,* 3. Grantham, PA: Messiah College, August, 1982.

Hughes, Thomas Patrick. *A Dictionary of Islam.* London: W. H. Allen & Co., 1896.

Illingworth, J. R. *The Doctrine of the Trinity.* London: Macmillan, 1907.

Irvin, Dale T. and Scott Sunquist, eds. *History of the World Christian Movement, Vol. 1.* Maryknoll, NY: Orbis Books, 2001.

Jacob, Walter. *Contemporary American Reform Responsa.* Mars, PA: Publishers Choice Book for Central Conference of American Rabbis, 1987.

Jamieson, Robert. *Genesis–Deuteronomy.* In *A Commentary, Critical, Experimental, and Practical on the Old and New Testaments.* Edited by Robert Jamieson, A. R. Fausset, and David Brown. Grand Rapids, MI: Zondervan Publishing House, 1983.

Jansen, Henry. *Relationality and the Concept of God.* Amsterdam-Atlanta, GA: Rodopi B.V., 1994.

Jedin, Hubert and John Patrick Dolan, eds. *Handbook of Church History.* New York: Herder and Herder, 1965.

Jewett, Paul K. *The Ordination of Women: An Essay on the Office of Christian Ministry.* Grand Rapids, MI: William B. Eerdmans Publishing Company, 1980.

Johnson, Elizabeth A. *She Who Is: The Mystery of God in Feminist Theological Discourse.* New York: Crossroad Publishing Company, 1998.

Johnson, Elizabeth A. "The Incomprehensibility of God and the Image of God Male and Female." In *Theological Studies*, 45:3 (1984).

Johnson, Luke Timothy. *The Real Jesus: The Misguided Quest for the Historical Jesus and the Truth of the Traditional Gospels.* San Francisco: HarperSanFrancisco, 1996.

Jónsson, Gunnlaugur A. *The Image of God: Genesis 1:26–28 in a Century of Old Testament Research.* Translated by Lorraine Svendsen. Lund, Sweden: Almqvist and Wiksell, 1988.

Jung, C. G. *Answer to Job.* Princeton: Princeton University Press, 1969.

Jung, Moses. "Religion in the Home." In *Marriage and the Jewish Tradition: Toward a Modern Philosophy of Family Living.* New York: Philosophical Library, 1951.

Jüngel, Eberhard. *God's Being in Becoming: The Trinitarian Being of God in the Theology of Karl Barth.* Edinburgh: T & T Clark, Ltd., 2001.

Jüngel, Eberhard. *The Doctrine of the Trinity: God's Being Is in Becoming.* Edinburgh: Scottish Academic Press, 1976.

Justin Martyr. *Apology*, 1.28.

Kaiser, Jr. Walter C. and Moses Silva. *An Introduction to Biblical*

Hermeneutics. Grand Rapids, MI: Zondervan Publishing House, 1994.

Kaiser, Jr., Walter C. "Correcting Caricatures: The Biblical Teaching on Women." In *Priscilla Papers*, 19:2 (Spring 2005).

Kant, Immanuel. "On the Distinction of the Beautiful and Sublime in the Interrelations of the Two Sexes." In *Philosophy of Woman: An Anthology of Classic to Current Concepts.* Edited by Mary Briody Mahowald. Indianapolis, IN: Hackett Publishers, 1983.

Karras, Valerie A. "Patristic Views on the Ontology of Gender." In *Personhood: Orthodox Christianity and the Connection between Body, Mind, and Soul.* Edited by John T. Chirban. Westport, CT: Bergin & Garvey, 1996.

Kasper, Walter. *The God of Jesus Christ.* Translated by Matthew O'Connell. New York: The Crossroad Publishing Co., 1984.

Kaufman, Gordon. *In the Face of Mystery: A Constructive Theology.* Cambridge, MA: Harvard University Press, 1993.

Kaufman, Michael. *Love, Marriage, and Family in Jewish Law and Tradition.* Northvale, NJ: Jason Aronson, Inc., 1992.

Kazantzakis, Nikos. *The Saviors of God: Spiritual Exercises.* New York: Simon & Schuster, 1960.

Keetley, Dawn. *Public Women, Public Words: A Documentary History of American Feminism.* Lanham, MD: Rowman & Littlefield Publishers, 2002.

Kelly, Catriona, ed. *An Anthology of Russian Women's Writing, 1777-1972.* Oxford: Oxford University Press, 1998.

Kelly, Christopher and Eve Grace, eds. *Rousseau on Women, Love, and Family.* Hannover, NH: Dartmouth College Press, 2009.

Kiasiong-Andriamiarisoa, Jane Sally. "A Woman's Voice." In *Shabbat Shalom, Vol. 45:1* (April 1998).

Kidd, Sue Monk. *The Dance of the Dissident Daughter: A Woman's Journey from Christian Tradition to the Sacred Feminine.* San Francisco: HarperCollins, 1996.

Kierkegaard, Søren. *Christian Discourses.* Translated by Walter Lowrie. New York: Oxford University Press, 1939.

Kierkegaard, Søren. *Kierkegaard's Concluding Unscientific Postscript.* Translated by David F. Swenson. Princeton: Princeton University Press, 1941.

Kierkegaard, Søren. *The Concept of Anxiety.* Edited and translated by Reidar Thompte with Albert B. Anderson. Princeton: Princeton

University Press, 1980.

Kierkegaard, Søren. *The Journals of Søren Kierkegaard.* Translated by A. Dru. London: Oxford University Press, 1938.

Klijn, Albertus Frederik. *Jewish-Christian Gospel Tradition.* Leiden, The Netherlands: E. J. Brill, 1992.

Kline, Meredith G. "Investiture with the Image of God." In *Westminster Theological Journal* 40.1 (Fall, 1977).

Ko, Dorothy. *Every Step a Lotus: Shoes for Bound Feet.* Berkeley, CA: University of California Press, 2001.

Kolakowski, Leszek. Speech given on November 5, 2003, upon being awarded the first Kluge Prize for lifetime achievement in the Humanities and Social Sciences.

Kroeger, Catherine Clark. "The Challenge of the Re-Imaging God Conference." In *Priscilla Papers* 8:2 (Spring, 1994).

Kvam, Kristen E., Linda S. Schearing, and Valarie H. Ziegler, eds. *Eve and Adam: Jewish, Christian, and Muslim Readings on Genesis and Gender.* Bloomington, IN: Indiana University Press, 1999.

Lactantius. *On Divine Anger* 4.

LaCugna, Catherine. "Problems with Trinitarian Reformulation." In *Louvain Studies* 10 (1985).

Lamm, Maurice. *The Jewish Way in Love and Marriage.* Middle Village, NY: Jonathan David Publishers, 1980.

Lange, Karl. *Apperception.* Boston: D. C. Heath & Co., 1903.

Langer, Suzanne. *Philosophy in a New Key.* Cambridge, MA: Harvard University Press, 1957.

Letellier, Robert Ignatius. *Day in Mamre, Night in Sodom: Abraham & Lot in Genesis 18 & 19.* Leiden, The Netherlands: E. J. Brill, 1995.

Levenson, Jon Douglas. *Creation and the Persistence of Evil: The Jewish Drama of Divine Omnipotence.* Princeton, NJ: Princeton University Press, 1988.

Levenson, Jon Douglas. *Resurrection and the Restoration of Israel: The Ultimate Victory of the God of Life.* New Haven, CT: Yale University Press, 2006.

Levy, Reuben. "The Social Structure of Islam." In *Orientalism: Early Sources*, Vol. XII. London: Routledge, 1957.

Lewis, Damien and Halima Bashir. *Tears of the Desert: A Memoir of Survival in Darfur.* New York: Random House, 2009.

LiDonnici, Lynn. "Women's Religions and Religious Lives in the

Greco-Roman City." In *Women and Christian Origins*. Edited by Ross Kraemer and Mary Rose D'Angelo. Oxford: Oxford University Press, 1999.

Lindblom, Johannes. "Theophanies in Holy Places in the Hebrew Religion." In *Hebrew Union College Annual Suplement* 32 (1961).

Lockyer, Herbert. *All the Divine Names and Titles in the Bible*. Grand Rapids, MI: Zondervan Publishing House, 1988.

Lossky, Vladimir. *In the Image and Likeness of God*. Crestwood, NY: St. Vladimir's Seminary Press, 1974.

Lowen, Alexander. *Love and Orgasm*. New York: Macmillan Publishing Company, 1975.

Luther, Martin. *D. Martin Luthers Werke, Kritische Gesamtausgabe Tischreden*. Weimar: Verlag Hermann Böhlaus Nachfolger, 1912.

Luther, Martin. "The Bondage of the Will" (1527). George Seldes. *The Great Thoughts*. Translated by George Seldes. New York: Random House, 1985.

Lyotard, Jean-François. *The Inhuman: Reflections on Time*. Translated by Geoffrey Bennington and Rachel Bowlby. Stanford, CA: Stanford University Press, 1991.

MacIver, R. M. "Signs and Symbols." In *Journal of Religious Thought*, X (1953).

Macquarie, John. *Principles of Christian Theology*. London: SCM, 1977.

Macy, Gary. "The Ordination of Women in the Early Middle Ages." In *Journal of Theological Studies* 61:3 (2000).

Mahowald, Mary Briody, ed. *Philosophy of Woman: An Anthology of Classic to Current Concepts*. Indianapolis, IN: Hackett Publishers, 1983.

Maimonides. *Guide for the Perplexed*, I, 1. Edited and translated by Shlomo Pines. Chicago: University of Chicago Press, 1963.

Maimonides. *Hikkot Yesode Hattora* 4:8-9.

Maimonides. *Perush ha-Mishnah*. In *Commentary on the Mishnah*, *Tractate Sanhedrin*, Chapter 10: *Perek Helek*.

Marcus, Ralph. "On Biblical Hypostases of Wisdom." In *Hebrew Union College Annual* 23 (1953).

Martin, Faith. *Call Me Blessed: The Emerging Christian Woman*. Grand Rapids, MI: Wm. B. Eerdmans Publishing Co., 1988.

Martos, Joseph and Pierre Hégy. *Equal at Creation: Sexism, Society, and Christian Thought*. Toronto: University of Toronto Press, 1998.

Maximos the Confessor. *On Love,* III, 25.

McConnell, Kilian. "A Trinitarian Theology of the Holy Spirit?" In *Theological Studies* 46 (1985).

McConnell, Kilian. *The Other Hand of God.* Collegeville, MN: Liturgical Press, 2003.

McFadyen, Alistair I. *The Call to Personhood: A Christian Theory of the Individual in Social Relationships.* Cambridge: Cambridge University Press, 1990.

McGinn, Bernard, John Meyendorff, and Jean Ledercq, eds. *Christian Spirituality: Origins to the Twelfth Century*. New York: Crossroad Publishing, 1985.

McGrath, Alistair I. *Christian Theology: An Introduction.* Malden, MA: Wiley-Blackwell Publishing, 1993.

McLaren, John and Harold Coward, eds. *Religious Conscience, the State, and the Law: Historical Contexts and Contemporary Significance.* New York: State University of New York Press, 1999.

Meeks, Wayne. *In Search of the Early Christians.* Edited by Allen R. Hilton and H. Gregory Snyder. New Haven, CT: Yale University Press, 2002.

Meeks, Wayne. "*The Image of the Androgyne: Some Uses of a Symbol in Earliest Christianity.* Chicago: The University of Chicago Press, 1974.

Mernissi, Fatima. *Beyond the Veil: Male-Female Dynamics in Modern Muslim Society.* Bloomington, IN: Indiana University Press, 1987.

Metz, Johannes B. "Theology Today: New Crises and New Visions." In *Catholic Theological Society of America Proceedings* 40 (1985).

Meyers, Carol. *Discovering Eve: Ancient Israelite Women in Context.* Oxford: Oxford University Press, 1991.

Migliori, Daniel. *Faith Seeking Understanding: An Introduction to Christian Theology.* Grand Rapids, MI: Wm. B. Eerdmans Publishing Co., 1991.

Miles, Jack. "Faith Is an Option; Religion Makes a Comeback. (Belief to Follow.)." In *New York Times Magazine* (December 7, 1997).

Miller, J. Maxwell. "In the 'Image' and 'Likeness' of God." In *Journal of Biblical Literature*, 91 (1972).

Moltmann, Jürgen. *Experiences in Theology.* Minneapolis, MN: Fortress Press, 2000.

Moltmann, Jürgen. *God in Creation: A New Theology of Creation and the Spirit of God.* London: SCM Press, 1985.

Moltmann, Jürgen. *The Crucified God.* Translated by. R. A. Wilson and John Bowden. New York: Harper & Row, 1974.

Moltmann, Jürgen. *The Spirit of Life: A Universal Affirmation.* Minneapolis: Fortress Press, 1992.

Moltmann-Wendel, Elisabeth and Jürgen Moltmann. *Humanity of God.* New York: Pilgrim Press, 1983.

Moody, Dale. *The Word of Truth: A Summary of Christian Doctrine Based on Biblical Revelation.* Grand Rapids, MI: William B. Eerdmans Publishing, 1981.

Moore, George Foot. *Judaism in the First Centuries of the Christian Era.* Cambridge, MA: Harvard University Press, 1927.

Morgan, J. "In the Image and Likeness: An Interview with Bishop Kallistos Ware." In *Parabola* 10.1 (1985).

Morgan, Robin, ed. *Sisterhood Is Powerful: An Anthology of Writings from the Women's Liberation Movement.* New York: Random House, 1970.

Morgenstern, Julian. "The Sources of the Creation Story—Genesis 1:1-2:4" In *The American Journal of Semitic Languages and Literatures,* 36 (1920).

Mühlen, Heribert. "The Person of the Holy Spirit." In *The Holy Spirit and Power.* Edited by Kilian McConnell. Garden City, NY: Doubleday, 1975.

Murray, Robert. "The Holy Spirit as Mother." In *Symbols of Church and Kingdom.* London: Cambridge University Press, 1975.

Nahmanides, *Iggeret ha-Kodesh (The Holy Epistle).*

Nassi, Rabbi Tzvi (Hirsch Prinz). *The Great Mystery or How Can Three Be One?* London: William Macintosh, 1863.

Navon, Chaim and David Straus. *Genesis and Jewish Thought.* New York: KTAV Publishing House, 2008.

Nazianzus, Gregory. "The Third Theological Oration." In *Nicene and Post-Nicene Fathers.* Translated by Philip Schaff and Henry Wace. Grand Rapids, MI: Wm. B. Eerdmans Publishing Co., 1974.

Neff, David. "Women in the Confidence Gap." In *Christianity Today* (22 July 1991).

Neville, Robert C. *A Theology Primer.* New York: State University of

New York Press, 1991.

Newell, J. Philip. *Echo of the Soul: The Sacredness of the Human Body.* Norwich, UK: Canterbury Press, 2000.

Newell, J. Philip. *The Book of Creation.* Norwich, UK: Canterbury Press, 1999.

Niebuhr, H. Richard. *The Meaning of Revelation.* Louisville, KY: Westminster John Knox Press, 1941.

Nietzsche, Friedrich. *Beyond Good and Evil: Prelude to a Philosophy of the Future.* Translated by Walter Kaufmann. New York: Random House, 1966.

Nietzsche, Friedrich. "On Truth and Lie in an Extra-Moral Sense." In *The Portable Nietzsche.* Edited and translated by Walter Kaufmann. New York: Penguin Books, 1954.

Nietzsche, Friedrich. *The Antichrist.* New York: Alfred A. Knopf, 1920.

Nietzsche, Friedrich. "The Genealogy of Morals: An Attack." In *The Birth of Tragedy and the Genealogy of Morals.* Translated by F. Golffing. New York: Doubleday, 1956.

Nietzsche, Friedrich. *Notebooks.* Summer, 1886–Fall, 1887.

Nunnally-Cox, Janice. *Foremothers: Women of the Bible.* New York: Seabury, 1981.

O'Boyle, Aidan. *Towards a Contemporary Wisdom Christology.* Rome: Gregorian University Press, 2001.

O'Collins, Gerald, ed. *The Incarnation: An Interdisciplinary Symposium on the Incarnation of the Son of God.* Oxford: Oxford University Press, 2002.

Oesterreicher, John M. *Auschwitz, the Christian, and the Council.* Montreal: Palm Books, 1965.

Oppenheimer, Helen. "Ethics and the Personal Life." In *Companion Encyclopedia of Theology.* Edited by Peter Byrne and James Leslie Houlden. London: Routledge, 1995.

Oppenheimer, Helen. *Incarnation and Immanence.* London: Hodder & Stoughton, 1973.

Oppenheimer, Helen. *Looking Before and After: The Archbishop of Canterbury's Lent Book.* London: Collins, 1983.

Oppenheimer, Helen. *Marriage (Ethics: Our Choices).* London: Continuum International Publishing, 1990.

Oppenheimer, Helen. *Marriage, Divorce and the Church.* London: SPCK, 1971.

Origen. *Commentary on John* 2.12.

Origen. *On First Principles* 3.6.1.

Origen. *Selecta in Exodus.*

Ovid. *Heroides*, Epistle XIII, 155.

Packer, James I. "The Gospel—Its Content and Communication: A Theological Perspective." In *Gospel and Culture.* Edited by John Stott and Robert T. Coote. Pasadena: William Care Library, 1979.

Pagels, Elaine. *The Gnostic Gospels.* New York: Vintage, 1981.

Pagels, Elaine. "What Became of God the Mother?" In *Womanspirit Rising: A Feminist Reader in Religion.* Edited by Carol P. Christ and Judith Plaskow. San Francisco: Harper & Row, 1979.

Palkovitz, Rob. "The 'Recovery' of Fatherhood?" In *Religion, Feminism, and the Family.* Edited by Anne E. Carr and Mary Steward Van Leeuwen. Louisville, KY: Westminster John Knox Press, 1996.

Pannenberg, Wolfhart. "Toward a Theology of the History of Religions." In *Basic Questions in Theology: Collected Essays.* Translated by George Kehm. Louisville, KY: Westminster John Knox Press, 1983.

Paul, Diana Y. and Frances Wilson. *Women in Buddhism: Images of the Feminine in Mahayana Tradition.* Berkeley, CA: University of California Press, 1985.

Pederson, Johannes. *Israel: Its Life and Culture.* Oxford: Oxford University Press, 1926.

Perot, Franceska. *The Re-Emergence of the Divine Feminine and its Significance for Spiritual, Psychological and Evolutionary Growth.* Boca Raton, FL: www.dissertation.com, 2008.

Peters, Ted. *God—The World's Future.* Minneapolis: Augsburg Fortress Press, 2000.

Phillips, Beverly Jane. *Learning a New Language: Speech about Women and God.* Lincoln, NE: iUniverse, 2005.

Phillips, James H. "The Future of Monogamous Marriage from a Christian Perspective." In *The Duke Divinity School Review*, 43:1 (Winter, 1978).

Philo. *Fuga.*

Phipps, William E. *Genesis and Gender: Biblical Myths of Sexuality and Their Cultural Impact.* New York: Praeger Publishers, 1989.

Ping, See Wang. *Aching for Beauty: Footbinding in China.* Minneapolis:

University of Minnesota Press, 2000.

Pinnock, Clark. "Biblical Authority and the Issues in Question." In *Women, Authority, and the Bible.* Alvera Mickelsen. Downers Grove, IL: InterVarsity Press, 1986.

Plato. *Timaeus.* Translated by H.D.P. Lee. Baltimore, MD: Penguin Press, 1965.

Pobee, J. S. *Toward an African Theology.* Nashville: Abingdon Press, 1979.

Pope, Richard M. *The Church and Its Culture: A History of the Church in Changing Cultures.* St. Louis: Bethany Press, 1965.

Quejada, Ellen. *Phallic Worship in Japan.* Toronto: University of Toronto, 1998.

Rahner, Karl. *Foundations of Christian Faith: An Introduction to the Idea of Christianity.* Translated by William V. Dych. New York: Seabury Press, 1978.

Rajawat, Mamta. *Burning Issues of Human Rights.* Delhi: Kalpaz Publications, 2001.

Ramshaw, Gail. *Liturgical Language.* Collegeville, MN: The Liturgical Press, 1996.

Rankin, Oliver S. *Israel's Wisdom Literature.* New York: Schocken Books, 1969.

Renehan, Robert F. "On the Greek Origins of the Concepts of Incorporeality and Immateriality." In *Greek, Roman, and Byzantine Studies* 21 (1980).

Ricoeur, Paul. *History and Truth.* Translated by Charles A. Kelbley. Evanston, IL: Northwestern University Press, 1965.

Ricoeur, Paul. "Naming God." In *Union Seminary Quarterly Review* 34 (1979).

Ricoeur, Paul. *Symbolism of Evil.* Translated by Emerson Buchanan. New York: Harper & Row, 1967.

Rieger, Joerg. *Christ and Empire: From Paul to Postcolonial Times.* Minneapolis, MN: Fortress, Press, 2007.

Ringgren, Helmer. *Word and Wisdom: Studies in the Hypostatization of Divine Qualities and Functions in the Ancient Near East.* Lund, Sweden: H. Ohlssons, 1947.

Rottenberg, Isaac C. *Judaism, Christianity, Paganism: A Judeo-Christian Worldview and Its Cultural Implications.* Atlanta: Hebraic Heritage Press, 2007.

Rottenberg, Isaac C. "The Reign of God." In *Restore!* Vol. 10:2.

Ruether, Rosemary Radford. "Christian Understandings of Human Nature and Gender." In *Religion, Feminism, and the Family.* Edited by Anne Carr and Mary Steward Van Leeuwen. Louisville, KY: Westminster John Knox Press, 1996.

Ruether, Rosemary Radford. *Gaia and God: An Ecofeminist Theology of Earth Healing.* London: HarperCollins, 2002.

Ruether, Rosemary Radford. *Goddesses and the Divine Feminine: A Western Religious History.* Berkeley, CA: University of California Press, 2005.

Ruether, Rosemary Radford. "Sexism and God-Language." In *Weaving the Visions: New Patterns in Feminine Spirituality.* Edited by Judith Plaskow and Carol Christ. San Francisco: Harper & Row, 1989.

Ruether, Rosemary Radford. *Sexism and God-talk.* Boston: Beacon Press, 1983.

Russell, Letty M., ed. *Feminist Interpretation of the Bible.* Philadelphia: Westminster Press, 1985.

Russell, Letty M. *Household of Freedom: Authority in Feminist Theology.* Philadelphia: Westminster Press, 1987.

Ryrie, Charles. *The Holy Spirit.* Chicago: Moody Press, 1965.

Sacharov, Nicholas V. *I Love, Therefore I Am: The Theology of the Archimandrite Society.* Crestwood, NY: St. Vladimir's Seminary Press, 2002.

Sanders, J. Oswald. *The Holy Spirit and His Gifts: Contemporary Evangelical Perspectives.* Grand Rapids, MI: Zondervan Publishing House, 1976.

Sanders, John E. *The God Who Risks: A Theology of Divine Providence.* Downers Grove, IL: InterVarsity Press, 2007.

Sandmel, Samuel. *Judaism and Christian Beginnings.* New York: Oxford University Press, 1978.

Santayana, George. "Reason in Common Sense." In *Life of Reason.* New York: Charles Scribner's Sons, 1905.

Schaef, Anne Wilson. *Women's Reality: An Emerging Female System in a White Male Society.* San Francisco: Harper & Row, 1981.

Schmidt, Alvin J. "Fundamentalism and Sexist Theology." In *Fundamentalism: What Makes It So Attractive?* Edited by Marla J. Selvidge. Elgin, IL: Brethren Press, 1984.

Schmidt, Alvin J. *Veiled and Silenced: How Culture Shaped Sexist Theology.* Macon, GA: Mercer University Press, 1989.

Scholar, David M. "1 Timothy 2:9-15 and the Place of Women in the Church's Ministry." In *Women, Authority and the Bible.* Edited by Alvera Mickelsen. Downers Grove, IL: InterVarsity Press, 1986.

Schroer, Silvia. *Wisdom Has Built Her House: Studies on the Figure of Sophia in the Bible.* Translated by Linda M. Maloney and William McDonough. Collegeville, MN: The Liturgical Press, 2000.

Schwartz, Howard. *Tree of Souls: The Mythology of Judaism.* Oxford: Oxford University Press, 2004.

Schweitzer, Friedrich. *The Human Image of God.* Edited by Friedrich Schweitzer, Hermann Häring and Don Browning. Boston: Brill, 2001.

Shelley, Louise. *Human Trafficking: A Global Perspective.* Cambridge: Cambridge University Press, 2010.

Sherman, Franklin. "God as Creative Artist." In *Dialog* 3 (1964).

Shillington, V. George. *Reading the Sacred Text: An Introduction to Biblical Studies.* London: T & T Clark, 2002.

Slonim, Rivkah. *Total Immersion: A Mikvah Anthology.* Lanham, MD: Rowman & Littlefield Publishing, 1997.

Smith, F. LaGard. *Crystal Lies.* Ann Arbor, MI: Servant Publications, 1998.

Smith, Huston. *Beyond the Post-Modern Mind: The Place of Meaning in a Global Civilization.* Wheaton, IL: Quest Books, 1989.

Smyers, Karen A. *The Fox and the Jewel: Shared and Private Meanings in Contemporary Japanese Inari Worship.* Hololulu: University of Hawaii Press, 1999.

Solanas, Valerie. *SCUM Manifesto.* San Francisco: AK Press, 1996.

Soloveitchik, Joseph B. *The Lonely Man of Faith.* New York: Doubleday/Random House, 2006.

Soloveitchik, Joseph B. *Yemei Zikaron.* Translated by Moshe Kroneh. Jerusalem: World Zionist Organization, 1986.

Sommers, Christina Hoff. *The War Against Boys: How Misguided Feminism Is Harming Our Young Men.* New York: Touchstone, 2000.

Sommers, Christina Hoff. *Who Stole Feminism? How Women Have Betrayed Women.* New York: Touchstone, 1994.

Spencer, Aída Dina. *Beyond the Curse: Women Called to Ministry.* Nashville: Thomas Nelson, 1985.

Stackhouse, Max L. and Stephen E. Healey. "Religion and Human

Rights: A Theological Apologetic." In *Religious Human Rights in Global Perspective: Religious Perspectives*. Edited by John Witte and J. D. Van der Vyver. The Hague: Kluwer Law International, 1996.

Stendahl, Krister. "God Worries About Every Ounce of Creation." In *Harvard Divinity Bulletin* 9 (5):5 (June/July 1979).

Steinberg, Milton. *Basic Judaism*. New York: Harcourt, Brace, and World, Inc., 1947.

Stendahl, Krister. *The Bible and the Role of Women; A Case Study in Hermeneutics*. Translated by Emilie T. Sander. Philadelphia: Fortress Press, 1966.

Stinson, Jerald M. "A Love Story." Sermon at First Congregational Church, Long Beach, CA.

Stoecker, Sally W. and Louise I. Shelley. *Human Traffic and Transnational Crime: Eurasian and American*. Oxford: Rowman & Littlefield Publishers, 2005.

Stone, Merlin. *When God Was a Woman*. San Diego: Harcourt, Brace, and Javonovich, 1976.

Stout, George Frederick. *Analytic Psychology*. New York: Macmillan & Co., 1896.

Stromberg, Roland. "The Philosophes and the French Revolution: Reflections on Some Recent Research." In *Eighteenth-Century Studies, Vol. 21*.

Sumner, Sarah. *Men and Women in the Church*. Downers Grove, IL: InterVarsity Press, 2003.

Swete, Henry Barclay. *The Ascended Christ*. London: Macmillan, 1916.

Swidler, Leonard and Arlene Swidler, eds. *Women Priests: A Catholic Commentary on the Vatican Declaration*. New York: Paulist Press, 1977.

Taban, Alfred. "Activist Says Child Slavery Exists in Sudan." News report by Reuters, July 19, 1997.

Taylor, J. V. *The Primal Vision*. London: SCM Publications, 1963.

Telushkin, Joseph. *The Code of Jewish Ethics: You Shall Be Holy*. New York: Random House, 2006.

Terry, Milton S. *Biblical Dogmatics: An Exposition of the Principal Doctrines of the Holy Scriptures*. Eugene, OR: Wipf & Stock Publishers, 2002.

Terry, Milton Spenser. *Biblical Hermeneutics: A Treatise on the*

Interpretation of the Old and New Testaments. New York: Phillips & Hunt, 1883.

Tertullian. *On the Apparel of Women.*

Thistlethwaite, Susan Brooks. "Every Two Minutes: Battered Women and Feminist Interpretation." In *Feminist Interpretation of the Bible.* Edited by Letty Russell. Philadelphia: Westminster Press, 1985.

Thomas, Gary. *Sacred Marriage: What if God Designed Marriage to Make Us Holy More than to Make Us Happy?* Grand Rapids, MI: Zondervan Publishing House, 2000.

Thompson, Phyllis. *A Transparent Woman: The Compelling Story of Gladys Aylward.* Grand Rapids, MI: Zondervan Publishing Company, 1971.

Thompson, Thomas L. *The Mythic Past: Biblical Archaeology and the Myth of Israel.* New York: Basic Books, 1999.

Thunberg, Lars. "The Human Person as Image of God." In *Christian Spirituality: Origins to the Twelfth Century.* Edited by Bernard McGuinn and John Meyendorff. New York: Crossroad Publishing Co., 1985.

Tigay, Jeffrey H. "'He Begot a Son in His Likeness after His Image' (Genesis 5:3)." In *Tehillah le-Moshe, Biblical and Judaic Studies in Honor of Moshe Greenberg.* Edited by Mordechai Cogan, Barry L. Eichler, and Jeffrey H. Tigay. Winona Lake, IN: Eisenbrauns, 1997.

Tillich, Paul. *Dynamics of Faith.* New York: Harper & Row, 1957.

Torjesen, Karen Jo. *When Women Were Priests: Women's Leadership in the Early Church and the Scandal of Their Subordination in the Rise of Christianity.* San Francisco: HarperCollins, 1995.

Tresmontant, Claude. *The Hebrew Christ: Language in the Age of the Gospels.* Chicago: Franciscan Herald Press, 1989.

Trible, Phillis. *God and the Rhetoric of Sexuality: Overtures to Biblical Theology.* Philadelphia: Fortress Press, 1978.

Tupper, Elgin Frank. *Scandalous Providence: The Jesus Story of the Compassion of God.* Macon, GA: Mercer University Press, 1995.

Tyms, James D. "Moral and Religious Education for the Second Reconstruction Era." In *Journal of Religious Thought* 31:1 (1974).

Verduin, Leonard. "A Dominion-Haver." In *Readings in Christian Theology Vol. 2: Man's Need and God's Gift.* Edited by Millard

Erickson. Grand Rapids, MI: Baker Book House, 1976.

Vernant, Jean-Pierre. "Dim Body, Dazzling Body." In *Fragments for a History of the Human Body*. Edited by Michal Feher, Ramona Naddaff, and Nadia Tazi. New York: Zone Publishing, 1989.

Verral, Arthur. *Euripides the Rationalist*. New York: Russell & Russell, 1967.

Vincle, Catherine. *Celebrating Divine Mystery: A Primer in Liturgical Theology*. Collegeville, MN: Liturgical Press, 2009.

Visser't Hooft, Willem Adolph. *The Fatherhood of God in an Age of Emancipation*. Geneva: World Council of Churches, 1982.

Vogels, Walter. "The Human Person in the Image of God (Gn 1:26)." In *Science et Esprit* 46 (1994).

Volozhiner, Chayyim. *Nefesh ha-Chayyim, sha'ar* 1, Chapter 3.

Voltaire. *Candide: Or Optimism*. Translated by John Butt. London: Penguin Books, 1947.

von Balthasar, Hans Urs. "The Unknown God." In *The Von Balthasar Reader*. Edited by Meard Kehl and Werner Löser. Translated by Robert Daly and Fred Lawrence. New York: Crossroad Publishers, 1982.

von Harnack, Adolph. *History of Dogma, Vol. III*. Translated by James Millar. London: Williams & Norgate, 1896.

von Rad, Gerhard. *Genesis: A Commentary*. London: SCM Press, 1972.

von Rad, Gerhard. *Old Testament Theology*. Edinburgh: Oliver & Boyd, 1962.

von Rad, Gerhard. *Old Testament Theology: The Theology of Israel's Prophetic Traditions, Vol. I*. Louisville, KY: Westminster John Knox Press, 1962.

von Rad, Gerhard. *Wisdom in Israel*. Nashville, TN: Abingdon Press, 1972.

Wall, John. *Moral Creativity*. New York: Oxford University Press, 2005.

Ware, Kallistos. "'In the Image and Likeness': The Uniqueness of the Human Person." In *Personhood: Orthodox Christianity and the Connection between Body, Mind, and Soul*. Edited by John T. Chirban. Westport, CT: Bergin & Garvey, 1996.

Ware, Kallistos. *The Inner Kingdom*. Crestwood, NJ: St. Vladimir's Seminary Press, 2000.

Weininger, Otto. *Gedanken über die Geschlechtsprobleme*. Berlin:

Concordia Duetchse, 1922.

Wesley, John. "Preface to 1739 Hymns and Sacred Poems." In *The Works of John Wesley*, Jackson Edition, 14:321.

Westermann, Claus. *Genesis 1-11: A Commentary.* Minneapolis: Augsburg Fortress Press, 1984.

Westermann, Claus. *Genesis: An Introduction.* Translated by John J. Scullion. Minneapolis: Augsburg Fortress Press, 1992.

Westermann, Claus. "Missing Persons and Mistaken Identities." In *Harvard Theological Review*, 74 (1981).

Whitman, John. *Interpretation and Allegory: Antiquity to the Modern Period.* Leiden: Brill, 2000.

Whybray, R. N. *Wisdom in Proverbs: The Concept of Wisdom in Proverbs 1-9.* Naperville, IL: A. R. Allenson, 1965.

Widener, Alice. *Gustav Le Bon: The Man and His Work.* Indianapolis, IN: Liberty Fund, Inc., 1979.

Wiesel, Elie. *Night.* Translated by François Mauriac. New York: Penguin Books, 1981.

Wilcox, John T. *Truth and Value in Nietzsche: A Study of His Metaethics and Epistemology.* Ann Arbor, MI: University of Michigan Press, 1974.

Wilken, Robert L., ed. *Aspects of Wisdom in Judaism and Early Christianity.* South Bend, IN: University of Notre Dame Press, 1975.

Williams, Selma. *Divine Rebel: The Life of Anne Marbury Hutchinson.* New York: Holt, Rinehart and Winston, 1982.

Wilson, Marvin R. *Our Father Abraham: Jewish Roots of the Christian Faith.* Grand Rapids, MI: Wm. B. Eerdmans Publishing Co., 1989.

Witte, John and J. D. Van der Vyver, eds. *Religious Human Rights in Global Perspective: Religious Perspectives.* The Hague: Kluwer Law International, 1996.

Wolf, Naomi. *Fire with Fire.* New York: Fawcett Columbine, 1993.

Wolff, Hans Walter. *Anthropology of the Old Testament.* Translated by Margaret Kohl. Philadelphia: Augsburg Fortress Press, 1974.

Wolterstorff, Nicholas. "Suffering Love." In *Philosophy and the Christian Faith.* Edited by Thomas Morris. Notre Dame, IN: University of Notre Dame Press, 1988.

Zikmund, Barbara Brown. "Feminist Consciousness in Historical Perspective." In *Feminist Interpretation of the Bible.* Edited by

Letty M. Russell. Philadelphia: Westminster Press, 1985.

Zizioulas, John D. *Being as Communion.* Crestwood, NY: St. Vladimir's Seminary Press, 1985.

Zohar: The Book of Enlightenment. Translated by Daniel Matt. New York: Paulist Press, 1983.

Zuck, Roy B. *Vital Theological Issues: Examining Enduring Issues of Theology.* Grand Rapids, MI: Kregel Publications, 1994.

INDEX

A

Abodah 188

Acidalius, Valens 4

Age of Reason 4, 170ff, 187

Akiva 216

Anderson, Ray S. 196

Androcentricity 10, 17, 45, 69, 107, 118, 132, 165, 209, 246

Anthropology 40, 63, 107, 152, 202, 236

Anthropomorphism 59, 80, 101, 156, 175, 203

Anthropopathic 157, 175, 208

Apperception 29, 36

Aquinas, Thomas 3

Aramaic 87, 93, 40

Aristotle 2, 64, 78, 161, 204

Armstrong, Karen 45, 78

Augustine 3, 52, 130, 157

Avinu, Malkenu 176

Aylward, Gladys 15

B

B'reshit 78

Bailey, D. Sherwin 228

Barth, Karl 55, 92, 151, 230

Bavinck, Herman 59

Berdyaev, Nicolas 44, 65, 182

Berkhof, Hendrikus 226

Berkovits, Eliezer 180

Berzonsky, Vladimir 174

Bilezikian, Gilbert 86, 198

Bird, Phyllis 151, 229

Bloesch, Donald 103

Blumenthal, David 101, 156, 159, 175

Blut und Boden 31

Bonaventure 3

Braaten, Carl E. 192

Breasted One 110ff

Broca, Paul 4

Brown, Harold O. J. 96

Brown, Raymond Edward 141

Brunner, Emil 12, 161

Buber, Martin 76

Buddhism 2, 53

Bulka, Reuven 213

C

Calvin, John 44, 160, 163, 203, 207

Cappadocian Fathers 91

Celtic tradition 55

Chafer, Lewis Sperry 110

Chaucer, Geoffrey 3

Chauvinism 1

Chesed 74, 111, 124, 178

Churchill, Winston 40

Chutzpah 138

Clement of Alexandria 2, 113

Clines, David 150, 157, 210

Clitoris 218, 219

Cobb, John B. 123

Codependency 5, 16, 24, 247

Coequality 87, 92ff, 220, 234

Coeternal 88, 93, 97, 234

Communion 46, 82, 91, 177, 229

Confucianism 2, 69

Congar, Yves 123

Conscience 164, 179

Consubstantial 75, 96, 234

Corporeality 202ff

Creativity 187, 192, 236

Cucchiar, Salvatore 142

Cybele 143

Cyril of Alexandria 3

D

D'var 54, 94, 140, 172

Daly, Mary 104

Darwinism 32

Davidson, Richard 216

Dawkins, Richard 45

Dearman, J. Andrew 155

de Caen, Roger 3

de Chardin, Pierre Teilhard 18

Demarest, Bruce 151

Demut 154, 190

Descartes, René 171

Deus absconditus 73

Deus otiosus 73

Diana 143

Didascalia Apostolorum 122

Divine Feminine 12, 46, 104, 111, 137

Dominion 96, 163, 194

Doukhan, Jacques B. 79

Downey, Michael 173

Duck, Ruth 104

Dunn, James D. G. 136

E

Eberling, Gerhard 179

Ebionites 121

Echad 84, 217ff

Edwards, Larry 110

Eichrodt, Walther 155

Elohim 87, 94, 140, 195

El Shaddai 109, 156

Embryo 219

Emet 124

Enlightenment 4, 30, 45, 171, 174

Erotic 217

Euripides 2, 65

Evans, Mary 18

Evdokimov, Paul 5, 40, 77, 123

Existentialist 30, 35, 60, 132

F

Fatalism 9

Feminism 6, 11, 14, 46, 123, 141, 209

Fiorenza, Elizabeth 14

Firestone, Tirzah 111, 136

Fishbane, Michael A. 192

Footbinding 69

Free will 157, 164, 184

Fretheim, Terrence 56

Frymer-Kensky, Tikva 164, 197

Fuchs, Esther 14

G

Gabriel, Richard 179

Galatianism 121

Gallagher, Joanne 32

Garr, W. Randall 150, 189

Gender development 210

Genitalia 212, 217, 219

Giles, Kevin 91

Gimbutas, Marja 142

Gnosticism 74, 106, 130, 143, 170

Goddess worship 12, 46, 80, 105, 141

Grammatico-historical 20

Gregory Nazianzus 80

Grenz, Stanley 226

Groothuis, Rebecca Merrill 12, 96

Gunton, Colin E. 135

Guroian, Vigen 235

Gutiérrez, Gustavo 32

Gynomorphic 104, 109, 130, 145, 244

Gynophobia 5, 9, 106, 109, 113, 128

H

Ha-adam 95, 98, 172, 196, 230

Ha-Kohen, Meir Simcha 183

Hall, Douglas John 183

Hampson, Daphne 14

Häring, Hermann 170

Hayter, Mary 105

Healy, Emma Thérèse 64

Hellenization 25, 48, 115, 140, 171, 245

Hengel, Martin 141

Henry, Carl F. H. 79, 102, 157

Henry, Patrick 35

Heresy 74, 95, 103, 130, 143

Hermeneutics 14, 19, 79, 246

Herzfeld, Noreen L. 228

Heschel, Abraham Joshua 47, 77, 101, 160

Hesiod 65

Hinduism 53, 66

Hodge, Charles 96

Hoekema, Anthony A. 154

Hokmah 124, 135ff

Homoousios 96

Homo sapiens 192

Hopko, Thomas 123, 211

I

Idolatry 44, 80, 93, 107, 131, 142, 201

Illingworth, J. R. 177

Imago Dei 154, 159, 164, 175, 223, 238

Incorporeality 175, 204

Infinite 53, 104, 159, 177, 230

Islam 53, 67

J

Jacob, Walter 128

Jansen, Henry 77

Jewett, Paul 9

Johnson, Elizabeth 8, 48, 78, 89

Johnson, Luke Timothy 32

Jukes, Andrew 110

Jung, Carl 141

Justin Martyr 179

K

Kant, Immanuel 4

Karras, Valerie A. 123

Kasper, Walter 89

Kiasiong-Andriamiarisoa, Jane Sally 139

Kidd, Sue Monk 12

Kierkegaard, Søren 182, 215, 225

Kolakowski, Leszek 31, 38

Kroeger, Catherine 142

L

Lactation 111

LaCugna, Catherine 80

Lamm, Maurice 233

Latinization 25, 48, 115, 245

Lazaroff, Allan 76

Le Bon, Gustave 5

Levenson, Jon Douglas 194

LiDonnici, Lynn 142

Liebnitz, Gottfried 36

Logos 54, 76, 79, 85, 122, 139, 172, 191

Lovemaking 216

Luther, Martin 3

M

MacLaine, Shirley 33

Macquarie, John 81

Macy, Gary 32

Maimonides 171, 205

Makarios 122

Mandaeans 131

Marcion 74

Marcus, Ralph 136

Matthews, Thomas 74

Maximos the Confessor 158

McConnell, Kilian 132

McFadyen, Alistair I. 183, 216

McGrath, Alister E. 76

Me'eh 116

Meeks, Wayne 129

Memra 54, 94, 140, 172

Mernissi, Fatima 67

Meyers, Carol 227

Misogyny 1, 5, 109, 115

Modernity 30

Mohammed 3

Moltmann, Jürgen 35, 104, 162, 224

Montesquieu 4

Moody, Dale 179

Moore, George Foot 189

Morgan, G. Campbell 110

Muellarian 219

Mühlen, Heribert 125

Muilenburg, James 105

Muslim 67
Mysticism 88, 143, 233
Mythology 65

N

Nag Hammadi 106, 144
Nahmanides 231
Napoleon 4
Nazoraeans 121
Nekebah 212
Neo-paganism 9, 31, 45, 180
Neo-platonic 117, 202, 225
Nephesh 172
New Age 9, 45
Newell, J. Philip 55, 80, 151
Niebuhr, H. Richard 75
Nietzsche, Friedrich 5, 30
Nihilism 7, 9

O

Olam 35
Ophites 131
Oppenheimer, Helen 173, 191
Origen 2, 20, 123, 158
Ousia 95
Ovaries 219
Ovid 57

P

Packer, James 22
Paganism 29, 80, 105, 131, 142, 213
Pagels, Elaine 106
Palkovitz, Rob 23
Pandora 65

Pannenberg, Wolfhart 47
Patriarchialists 5
Pederson, Johannes 228
Perichoresis 92
Personhood 73, 87, 95, 174
Phallus, penis 104, 212, 215, 218
Phelps, William 104
Philo of Alexandria 140
Phipps, William 44
Physicality 210
Physiology 206
Plato 2, 65, 161, 171, 204
Pneumatology 132
Polyandry 64
Polygamy 64, 67
Polygyny 64, 67
Postmodernism 7, 30, 45, 144
Procreation 172, 190
Pseudepigrapha 144
Pythagoras 2

Q

Queen of Heaven 9
Qur'an 67

R

Racham 112, 117
Rahner, Karl 151
Rechem 110, 112, 117
Relationality 76ff, 164, 174ff, 223ff
Renehan, Robert 204
Ricoeur, Paul 52
Rottenberg, Isaac 31

Rousseau 4

Ruach 55, 121, 124, 130, 140

Ruach haKodesh 124

Ruether, Rosemary Radford 14, 23, 130

Russell, Letty M. 14, 16, 48

S

Sander, John E. 223

Sanders, John 53

Sandmel, Samuel 139

Santayana, George 38

Sapientia 135

Schroer, Silvia 135

Sefirot 88

Sexual intercourse 220, 232

Sexuality 139, 211ff

Shaddim 110

Shekhinah 87, 124, 231

Shepherd, Cybill 33

Shillington, George 159

Socrates 2

Solanas, Valerie 6

Soloveitchik, Joseph B. 187

Sophia 46, 135, 141ff

Stendahl, Krister 48

Subordinationism 17, 91ff, 234

Sudan 69

Swidler, Leonard 140

Syncretism 43, 46, 75, 144

T

Talmud 128, 150, 172, 189, 204

TaNaKh 94, 107, 145

Targum 87, 94, 140

Tephillah 225

Tertullian 2, 8, 20

Theology 11, 48, 63ff, 73, 98

Theomorphism 47, 60, 101ff, 117, 156, 201

Theophany 85, 159, 191, 206

Theosis 158

Theriomorphism 59, 102, 152

Thistlethwaite, Susan 14

Thomas, Gary 219, 232

Three-in-one 88ff, 214, 224, 230ff

Tikkun Olam 236

Tillich, Paul 56

Toledot 79, 191

Torah 38, 107, 123, 137, 172, 188, 225

Torjesen, Karen Jo 10, 17, 23

Triuniverse 88

Tupper, Elgin Frank 196

Tutu, Desmond 160, 182, 194

Two-in-one 90, 214, 230ff

Tzedekah 178

Tzelem 154ff

U

Übermensch 31

Uterus 113, 219

V

Vagina 9, 212, 219

Verral, Arthur 65

Virgin Mary 9

visser't Hooft, Willem 103

Volozhiner, Chayyim 194

Voltaire 4

von Harnack, Adolph 158

von Hildebrand, Alice 7

von Rad, Gerhard 77, 155, 164

W

Ware, Kallistos 157, 184

Wesley, John 229

Westermann, Claus 5, 151

Wiesel, Elie 31

Wisdom of God 58, 87, 103, 124, 135ff

Wolffian 219

Wolterstorff, Nicholas 178

Womb 110, 112ff, 126, 193, 215

World Council of Churches 46

X

Xenophanes 59, 204

Y

Yachid 84

Yichud 233

Yom Kippur 127

Z

Zakar 212

Zeus 65

Zikmund, Barbara 14

Zizioulas, John D. 82, 88, 229

Zohar 213, 230

Zuck, Roy B. 224

Zusya 184

Zygote 219

HEBRAIC CHRISTIAN
GLOBAL COMMUNITY™
Sharing, Equipping, Serving

Understanding the Jewish roots of our faith is a golden key that unlocks the treasures of Holy Scripture and enriches Christian lives. This fundamental concept is the focus of Hebraic Christian Global Community, an international, transdenominational, multicultural publishing and educational resource for Christians. Hebraic Christian Global Community features individuals and congregations who share the vision for restoring Christianity's Hebraic foundations, for networking together in true community, and for returning the church to a biblical relationship of loving support for the international Jewish community and the nation of Israel.

We publish *Restore!* magazine, a high-quality journal featuring theological balance and scholarly documentation that helps Christians recover their Hebrew heritage while strengthening their faith in Jesus.

We also publish *Hebraic Insight,* a quarterly Bible-study journal that assists individuals, families, study groups, and congregations in inductive Hebraic study of the Scriptures that is accurate, balanced, and trustworthy.

We distribute *Golden Key* books in order to disseminate high-quality teaching about Christianity's Hebraic foundations that is non-threatening and non-judgmental and helps believers follow the leading of the Holy Spirit in their lives.

We also provide various media resources through *New Treasures* media productions. Many of these can be accessed on our website.

The ministry of Hebraic Christian Global Community is made possible by our many partners around the world who share in our *Golden Key Partnership* program. We invite you to join us in sharing the satisfaction of knowing that you are a partner in an organization that is making a difference in the world by restoring Christians to their biblically Hebraic heritage, by eradicating Judaeophobia and anti-Semitism, by supporting Israel and the international Jewish community, and by encouraging collaborative efforts among those who share this vision.

For information about Hebraic Christian Global Community and all our resources and services, contact us at:

Hebraic Christian Global Community
P. O. Box 421218
Atlanta, GA 30342
www.HebraicCommunity.org

HEBRAIC HERITAGE

CHRISTIAN CENTER

Hebraic Heritage Christian Center is an institution of higher education that is dedicated to the vision of restoring a Hebraic model for Christian education. A consortium of scholars, spiritual leaders, and business persons, the Center features a continually developing curriculum in which each course of study is firmly anchored in the Hebrew foundations of the Christian faith.

The Hebraic Heritage Christian Center vision combines both the ancient and the most modern in an educational program that conveys knowledge, understanding, and wisdom to a worldwide student population. The Center seeks to restore the foundations of original Christianity in order to equip its students with historically accurate, theologically sound understanding of the biblical faith that Jesus and the apostles instituted and practiced. At the same time the Center endeavors to implement the finest in innovative, cutting edge technology in a distance-learning program that delivers its user-friendly courses by the Internet.

Among the wide range of services and products that Hebraic Heritage Christian Center offers are the publications of Hebraic Heritage Press. These are delivered both in traditional print media as well as in electronic media to serve both the Center's student population and the general public with inspiring and challenging materials that have been developed by the Center's team of scholars.

Those who are interested in sharing in the development of Hebraic Heritage Christian Center and its commitment to restoring the Jewish roots of the Christian faith are invited to join the Founders' Club, people who support this team of scholars and leaders by becoming cofounders of this institution. Many opportunities for endowments are also available to those who wish to create a lasting memorial to the cause of Christian renewal and Christian-Jewish rapprochement.

Hebraic Heritage Christian Center
P. O. Box 450848
Atlanta, GA 31145
www.HebraicCenter.org

The
Feminine and Free
Series

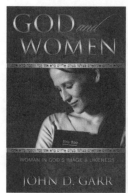  

Available 12/2010 **Available 3/2011** **Available 2012**

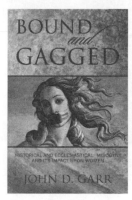 

Available 2012 **Available 2012**

www.HebraicCommunity.org

Other Books
by
Dr. John D. Garr

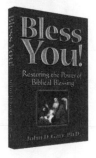

For complete listing, see
www.HebraicCommunity.org

Restore!

Hebraic Christian Global Community
P.O. Box 421218
Atlanta, GA 30342